AF538917

Wine Tourism around the World: Development, Management and Markets

Wine Tourism around the World: Development, Management and Markets

Saurabh Gupta

Wine Tourism around the World: Development, Management and Markets

---

ISBN 978-93-5111-551-9

Published in 2015 in India by

RANDOM PUBLICATIONS

4376-A/4B, Gali Murari Lal, Ansari Road
New Delhi-110 002
Phone : +9111-43580356, 011-23289044, 011-43142548
e-mail: sales@randompublications.com,
info@randompublications.com, randomexports@gmail.com

Reprinted 2018

Type Setting by : Friends Media, Delhi-110089
Digitally Printed at: Replika Press Pvt. Ltd.

Preface

Wine tourism refers to tourism whose purpose is or includes the tasting, consumption or purchase of wine, often at or near the source. Where other types of tourism are often passive in nature, wine tourism can consist of visits to wineries, tasting wines, vineyard walks, or even taking an active part in the harvest. Wine tourism is a relatively new form of tourism. Its history varies greatly from region to region, but in places such as the Napa Valley AVA, it saw heavy growth once a concerted marketing effort was implemented in 1975 that was given a further boost by the 1976 Judgment of Paris. Other regions, such as Catalonia, Spain have only started marketing wine tourism starting in the mid-2000s, primarily focusing on how it is an alternative form of tourism to the beach for which Spain is overall known. There was also a rise in the profile of wine tourism among English speakers with the 2004 release of the film, Sideways whose two central characters visit wineries and wine in the Santa Barbara region of Southern California. The industry around wine tourism has grown significantly throughout the first decade of the 21st century. In the United States 27 million travelers, or 17% of American leisure travelers, engaged in culinary or wine-related activities. In Italy the figure stands at approximately five million travelers, generating 2.5 billion euros in revenue. A private initiative by Recevin holds an annual "Wine Tourism Day" on the second Sunday of November each year to promote cellar visits in Germany, Austria, Slovenia, Spain, France, Greece, Hungary, Italy, and Portugal. In North America, the first Wine Tourism Day was established for May 11, 2013 with events scheduled throughout the continent.

I would like to thank my team for standing beside me throughout my career and writing this book. My special thanks go to "Random Publications" who have published the book.

– Saurabh Gupta

Contents

1

Wine Tourism

In Australia, New Zealand, but also in Europe, there are lots of articles and studies with theoretical and practical views in terms of wine tourism and factors of success that contribute to attract and motivate wine tourists, in comparison with Romania, where the research in this field is still at an early stage. Hall and Getz are well-known authors in this field who made the first studies in this area. This paper is to cover a field few developed in specialized Romanian literature - that one of wine tourism.

In the present days we think it will be very interesting and useful to do some research in this area because Romania is an important European wine producer country. The analysis of the current situation in Romanian wine tourism and the identification of the factors that may contribute to attract and motivate wine tourists is a step forward in the viticulture research and also of the possibilities to increase ecoefficiency of investments in this area. In this paper, in order to present the factors of success in attracting and motivating wine tourists, we strongly considered being appropriate to express some on the concepts regarding wine tourism and the ones of the road of wine. Also, we presented the facilities and the motivations of the wine tourists in order to visit the promotional activities; we mentioned the main classifications regarding wine tourist‘s profile and we briefly described the situation of the Romanian wine tourism.

WINE TOURISM

The specific activities of tourism must be applied in the wine industry. Wine tourism is an opportunity for the development of the wine industry. Wine is often associated with relaxation, communication with friends, hospitality. On vacation, tourists want hospitality, looking to relax with friends, learn new things, to explore, to discover. Wine tourism is a form of tourism. Visit to wineries, attending a wine route is a product of wine tourism. Wine tourism, development and marketing of wine tourism represents a relatively recent phenomenon. In Europe, wine tourism was often associated with the official wine routes and wine roads. Studies and research on wine tourism were performed for the first time in 1990; the first conference, which focused on the wine tourism was held in Australia in 1998. The works done in that period were comparative studies with descriptive character that were highlighting the need to study this new activity. This area has been studied by researchers around the world.

Because there are many wine regions with wine tourism activities, they perform aggressive marketing to attract more clients and getting competitive positions against competitors; this has become a strategic issue nationwide.. Australia, which is a pioneer in this field, has developed a national strategy for wine tourism and is currently implementing it to develop this area. There is no uniform approach for defining wine tourism. From a marketing perspective, wine tourism means identifying the needs of current and potential wine tourists. Most definitions of wine tourism are considering motivations to go on a vacation, to make a journey, to have new experiences, learn new things.

The number of definitions given to wine tourism grows once with the industry. Hall and Macionis define wine tourism as follows: "...visitation to vineyards, wineries, wine festivals and wine shows for which grape wine tasting and/or experiencing the attributes of the grape wine region are the prime motivating factors for visitors". Other authors say that wine tourism involves also developing a marketing and planning strategy. In the Western Australian Wine Tourism Strategy, Wine tourism is defined: "...travel for the purpose of experiencing wineries and wine regions and their links to lifestyle.

Wine tourism encompasses both service provision and destination marketing". Getz defined the wine tourism from three perspectives: a strategy for development of visitor attractions, a form of consumer behaviour visiting favorite destinations, an opportunity for wineries to educate their clients and directly sell their wine. Wine tourism, in our opinion, includes three main components:

- Visits of wine connoisseurs and buyers to specific vineyards for buying or scientific purposes – business tourism;
- Visits to vineyards in general, with the aim of understanding process of producing wine and/or wine tasting. This is considered an advertising activity by self-financing performed by vineyards to encourage the sale on the spot and long-term customer loyalty;
- Wine Routes - scenic routes through areas of vineyards linking different plantations.

WINE ROUTE

Wine route concept relates to a defined space that is vital to its existence and reflects for wine producers who are part of this space, their identity consisting of unique features specific to their wines and their cultural heritage. Wine producers whose vineyards are part of a wine route, in order to differentiate from competitors, emphasize characteristics that make them unique; these characteristics refer to the type of grape and wine they produce, the soils and climate that give wine distinctive attributes, and cultural heritage. Wine route is a tourist route that includes several vineyards and wineries in an area. This route may include: natural attractions such as mountains, sea, landscapes and more, industrial objectives such as wineries of the vineyards, roads and signs to help tourists reach the winery.

Most wine routes take the form of a wine region that is most often officially delimited by an appellation of controlled origin or an area with geographical indication (GI), such as for example Rioja, Napa Valley, Champagne. In short, the wine route is a route to the main tourist attractions of wine: wine and winery. Other authors define the route of wine as: "...usually a wine route consists of a designated itinerary through the wine region which is thematically signposted as well as being interpreted via a free leaflet and map, which notes the different vineyards and winemakers and provides information on sites of historical and other interest...". Tourism and wine industry are based on a branding of the area.

Identity geographic or regional origin of the wine was formalized through denomination of controlled origin. In Romania, there are wines with designation of controlled origin and wines with geographical indication. Each wine route tries to highlight a set of regional features, which gives a brand identity and a distinctive note or something that makes it unique. This combination of natural, cultural and social features is perceived by tourists as being distinctive.

Tourists make the difference of scenery, cultural framework when visiting vineyards that are included on a wine route in a region.. Wine route concept is the possibility of introducing the notions of exploration and discovery. Wine route involves a journey that can bring a range of new unexpected experiences.

Wine route allows tourists to explore the many natural and cultural features of the landscape. In the current global context, it is important to understand that the basis for a brand, a successful winery image is the promotion of wine region or of the country where the wine originates; this will contribute to further development of the wine industry. Wine is one of those goods that builds its brand on its geographical origin. Wine regions where wine tourism is practiced and where there is a wine route established, are the framework where the government, private companies and associations, the tourism industry, wineries and local governments can successfully collaborate. Their synergy contributes to cultural, regional and economic development by creating jobs.

WHY TO VISIT A WINERY?

The main reasons for visiting a vineyard, a winery, a wine region can be diverse, including: visiting wine factories, participation in festivals devoted to wine and traditional food, shows, sightseeing and other attractions, recreation, visiting relatives and friends. Ancillary activities, promotional activities and facilities offered to tourists have a big role in the conquest of new segments of tourists. Table shows some support activities that wineries are practicing to attract many tourists.

Table. Tourist and visitor facilities available at winery/wine estate

Wine tasting	Wine/other festivals	Firplace
Cellar-door sales	Historic building/Museum	4x4 Race track
Winery orgainzed tours	Educational tours	Petrol/filling station
Meet the winemaker	Cooking classes	Amphitheatre
Wheelchair facilities	Vineyard walking	Animal feeding and/or watching
Social function facilities	Craft/Gallery/Souvenir shop	Hiking/biker trails
Picnic facilities	Restaurant-arrangement only	Horse/pony rides
Conference facilities	Overmight accommodation	Swimming
Restaurant-all week	Children's playground facilities	Golf
Cellar lunches	Restaurant-all weekend	Beauty classes
Barbeque facilities	Fruit picking by visitors	Spa
Visitor centre	Fresh produce sold	Spectacular views

In understanding the phenomenon of wine tourism, an important role is played by understanding the real reasons behind the decision of a tourist to visit a winery. These are presented in Table. Identification of these reasons should underpin the achievement of promotion strategy in order to attract and retain more tourists.

Table. Specific visitor motivations to visit wine route estate

Wine purchasing	Meeting the winemaker
Wine tasting/sampling	Socializing with family/friends
Country setting/vineyards	Festivals or events
Winery tour	Eating at winery (restaurant/cafe)
Learning about wine and winemaking	Entertainment

THE PROFILE OF THE WINE TOURIST

To get a clear idea about wine tourism activity, we must first build a profile of wine tourists. Conducting professional studies in this field is necessary because there is little research and information at this time on wine tourism profile. There are researchers who are concerned about this issue and have developed some general views on wine tourism profile. So, the South Australian Tourism Commission characterizes the tourist as being "Couples with no children and those with higher education and incomes in professional occupations". Other authors, Dodd and Bigotte, argue that income is the factor that determines the consumption of wine, and therefore the tourist will not choose wine special offers.

These are tourists who have a higher level of financial and educational terms. Hall said that demographic data represent a simple segmentation tool for wine tourist profile, while psychographic data that refers to values, lifestyles, attitudes, interests, include more important information for researchers, wine having an important role in the life style of consumers. Analysis, evaluation, lifestyle, consuming style are often used in marketing to achieve advertising strategy, segmentation, product development. For the wine industry, we have developed a research tool called wine related lifestyle (the role of wine in lifestyle and wine related lifestyle) which refers to the monitoring of wine products market.

The reason this tool was developed concerns that customer segmentation according to how they see the value of the wine can improve consumer understanding of any market. Charters and Ali-Knight are classifying the wine tourists in five segments:: "Wine Lovers", "Connoisseurs" which are a sub-segment of "Wine Lover", "Wine Interested", "Wine Novices", and "Hangers-on" which are visiting a winery as part of a group that decided to go there, having no interest in wine. Each of these five categories has specific reasons to visit attractions wineries. A "Wine Lover" is visiting a vineyard, a winery primarily to taste wine, buy wine, learn about wine, how to pick grapes, how wine is produced. Reasons for a visit by a "Wine Novice" wineries are less defined: the attractions of ancillary activities offered by winery such as excursions in the grapery or to eat in the wine cellar restaurant. Hall and Macionis are setting three segments of wine tourists: "wine lovers", "wine interested" and "curious tourist". In Table are presented the main features of these segments.

THE ROMANIAN WINE TOURISM

If in countries like France, Italy, Spain or Germany the wine tourism is a concept that works very well, Romania is at the beginning, despite of the existent potential. Our country has failed to attract tourists from the West as effective as its neighbours, so our efforts to develop a wine route is low at present. Wine tourism has no success because few tourists hear talk about such offers.

They are too invisible in the catalogs of travel agencies, they are not advertised elsewhere. The lack of a defining brand in the vineyards and winery tourism leads to lack of promotion in the domain. One solution would be a wine festival like National Holiday, as it exists in the Republic of Moldova or the inclusion of wine in Romania's tourism promotion programmes. Extremely important for any touristic area is the existence of the infrastructure. The accommodations are very few, related activities are lacking, so the tourist is attracted no less to stay or to stay longer. But, first, to get to the accommodation units is necessary a adequate transport infrastructure. To attract tourists in the wine origin countries, it must be involved the wines with agro-tourism, with nice pensions and restaurants, where they can drink and eat, and also, it must have a transport infrastructure that will bring tourists to vineyards and wineries. According to NATA (National Association of Travel Agencies), the first who showed interest in a vacation in the vineyards were foreign tourists. Thus, wine tourism is primarily intended for connoisseurs and for foreigners (the Romanians usually visit those areas only in conditions which they are still in vacation or nearly). There is presented to them a programme that offers the opportunity to visit the cellars and vineyards, to taste wine, to participate in vintage and to take part in production of the wine. Some wine producers offer to guests accommodation in hostels. The number of tourists visiting Romanian vineyards and cellars is very small. Even if the number of tourists increases every year, they come mainly for curiosity and not for passion for the art of the wine. The key to this type of tourism is the promotion, which is lacking in the case of Romania. It is necessary that government together with private wine enterprises develop a national promotional strategy as it exist in Australia. Another important aspect is investment in the infrastructure.

In 2011, in the city Buzau Finþe°ti has inaugurated Lacerta Winery cellar, an Austrian investment of 8 million in wine tourism and wine industry. It is highlighted ancient Romanian architect Ion Mincu mansion, built 110 years ago and restored by Austrian specialists, and the unique beauty of the area or potential vineyard. The Lacerta Group management estimates that by the end of the investment will generate over one million euro. Also in 2011, there were invested 61 million lei for the rehabilitation of the wine route from Arad (it is the rehabilitation of 20 km). This investment involves beneficent economic effects at the national economy level such as creating work places. Both investments were made by accessing European funds.

Reconversion of Romanian vineyards and wineries' modernization were financed by European funds. The wine tourism can be a very profitable industry in Romania if there is a longterm national strategy for development of this sector. Romania has a great potential regarding the wine tourism development because it has favorable climatic conditions and winemaking tradition, history, culture, natural landscapes and beautiful vineyards. There are seven wine regions in the country: Podisul Transilvaniei, Dealurile Moldovei, Dealurile Munteniei si Olteniei, Dealurile Banatului, Dealurile Crisanei si Maramuresului, Dealurile Dobrogei, Terasele Dunării. Romania has nine famous vineyards offering wine tasting itineraries and consistently for visitors in general: Murfatlar, Urlateanu Cellar, Seciu, Stefanesti, Minis, Jidvei, Panciu, Bucium, Recas.

There are also museums of wine: Murfatlar, Dragasani Stefanesti, Husi, Odobesti, Minis, Hârlău. A number of tour operators offer specialized wine itineraries.

CONCLUSIONS

The wine purchasing, the wine tasting, the beauty of the Romanian winescapes, landscapes present a high potential of attractiveness for wine tourists. These attributes are factors of success in attracting the tourists. But Romania still needs at least another ten years to reach a comparable wine tourism from countries with tradition in this domain. The wine tourism is an important collateral activity to wine industry that can contribute to the development of this industry. Analyzing in this paper the nowadays situation of the Romanian wine making tourism, we identified three major obstacles in developing this area namely: the lack of a defining brand, lack of the transport infrastructure, accommodation and the lack of promotion. Even if the number of tourists increases every year, they come mainly for curiosity and not for passion for the art of the wine. This paper may become the inception of achievement of a certain research with an applicative character regarding the wine tourism, for example the elaboration of a national strategy of development in this area.

2

Introduction

AN OVERVIEW

Wine is an alcoholic beverage, typically made of fermented grape juice. The natural chemical balance of grapes is such that they can ferment without the addition of sugars, acids, enzymes or other nutrients. Wine is produced by fermenting crushed grapes using various types of yeast. Yeast consumes the sugars found in the grapes and converts them into alcohol. Different varieties of grapes and strains of yeasts are used depending on the type of wine being produced.

Although other fruits such as apples and berries can also be fermented, the resultant wines are normally named after the fruit from which they are produced and are generically known as fruit wine or country wine. Others, such as barley wine and rice wine, are made from starch-based materials and resemble beer and spirit more than wine, while ginger wine is fortified with brandy. In these cases, the use of the term "wine" is a reference to the higher alcohol content, rather than production process. The commercial use of the English word "wine" is protected by law in many jurisdictions.

Wine has a rich backdrop dating back to around 6000 BC and is thought to have originated in areas now within the borders of Georgia and Iran. Wine probably appeared in Europe at about 4500 BC in what is now Bulgaria, and Greece, and was very common in ancient Greece, Thrace and Rome. Wine has also played an important role in religion throughout backdrop. The Greek god Dionysus and the Roman equivalent Bacchus represented wine, and the drink is also used in Catholic Eucharist ceremonies and the Jewish Kiddush.

BACKDROP OF WINE

Archaeological evidence suggests that the earliest known production of wine, made by fermenting grapes, took place in sites in Georgia and Iran, from as early as 6000 BC. These locations are all within the natural area of the European grapevine *Vitis vinifera*. A 2003 report by archaeologists indicates a possibility that grapes were used together with rice to produce mixed fermented beverages in China in the early years of 7000 BC. Pottery jars from the Neolithic site of Jiahu, Henan were found to contain traces of tartaric acid and other organic compounds commonly found in wine. However, other fruits indigenous to the region, such as hawthorn, could not be ruled out. If these beverages, which seem to be the precursors of rice wine, included grapes rather than other fruits, these grapes were of any of the several dozen indigenous wild species of grape in China, rather than from *Vitis vinifera*, which were introduced into China some 6000 years later.

The oldest known evidence of wine production in Europe is dated to 4500 BC and comes from archaeological sites in Greece. The same sites also contain the world's earliest evidence of crushed grapes. In Ancient Egypt, six of 36 wine amphoras were found in the tomb of King Tutankhamun bearing the name "Kha'y", a royal chief vintner. Five of these amphoras were designated as from the King's personal estate with the sixth listed as from the estate of the royal house of Aten. Traces of wine have also been found in central Asian Xinjiang, dating from the second and first millennia BC.

In medieval Europe, the Roman Catholic Church was a staunch supporter of wine since it was necessary for the celebration of Mass. Monks in France made wine for years, storing it underground in caves to age. There is an old English recipe which survived in various forms until the nineteenth century for refining white wine using Bastard—bad or tainted *bastardo* wine. Wine was forbidden during the Islamic Golden Age, until Jâbir ibn Hayyân and other Muslim chemists pioneered its distillation for cosmetic and medical uses.

GRAPE VARIETIES

Wine is usually made from one or more varieties of the European species *Vitis vinifera*, such as Pinot Noir, Chardonnay, Cabernet Sauvignon, Gamay and Merlot. When one of these varieties is used as the predominant grape, the result is a *varietal*, as opposed to a *blended*, wine. Blended wines are not necessarily considered inferior to varietal wines; some of the world's most expensive wines, from regions like Bordeaux and the Rhone Valley, are blended from different grape varieties of the same vintage.

Wine can also be made from other species of grape or from hybrids, created by the genetic crossing of two species. *Vitis labrusca*, *Vitis aestivalis*, *Vitis rupestris*, *Vitis rotundifolia* and *Vitis riparia* are native North American grapes usually grown for consumption as fruit or for the production of grape juice, jam, or jelly, but sometimes made into wine.

Hybridization is not to be confused with the practice of grafting. Most of the world's vineyards are planted with European *V. vinifera* vines that have been grafted onto North American species rootstock. This is common practice because North American grape species are resistant to phylloxera, a root louse that eventually kills the vine. In the late 19th century, most of Europe's vineyards were devastated by the bug, leading to massive vine deaths and eventual replanting. Grafting is done in every wine-producing country of the world except for Argentina, the Canary Islands and Chile, which are the only ones that have not yet been exposed to the insect.

In the context of wine production, *terroir* is a concept that encompasses the varieties of grapes used, elevation and shape of the vineyard, type and chemistry of soil, climate and seasonal conditions, and the local yeast cultures. The range of possibilities here can result in great differences between wines, influencing the fermentation, finishing, and aging processes as well. Many wineries use growing and production methods that preserve or accentuate the aroma and taste influences of their unique *terroir*. However, flavour differences are not desirable for producers of mass-market table wine or other cheaper wines, where consistency is more important. Such producers will try to minimize differences in sources of grapes by using production techniques such as micro-oxygenation, tannin filtration, cross-flow filtration, thin film evaporation, and spinning cones.

CLASSIFICATION OF WINE

Regulations govern the classification and sale of wine in many regions of the world. European wines tend to be classified by region, while non-European wines are most often classified by grape. More and more, however, market recognition of particular regions is leading to their increased prominence on non-European wine labels. Examples of non-European recognized locales include Napa Valley in California, Willamette Valley in Oregon, Columbia Valley in Washington, Barossa Valley and Hunter Valley in Australia, Central Valley in Chile, Vale dos Vinhedos in Brazil, Hawke's Bay and Marlborough in New Zealand, Okanagan Valley and Niagara Peninsula in Canada.

Some blended wine names are marketing terms, and the use of these names is governed by trademark law rather than by specific wine laws. For example, Meritage is generally a Bordeaux-style blend of Cabernet Sauvignon and Merlot, and may also include Cabernet Franc, Petit Verdot, and Malbec. Commercial use of the term "Meritage" is allowed only via licensing agreements with an organization called the "Meritage Association".

European Classifications

France has various appellation systems based on the concept of terroir, with classifications ranging from Vin de Table at the bottom, through Vin de Pays and Appellation d'Origine Vin Délimité de Qualité Supérieure (AOVDQS) up to Appellation d'Origine Contrôlée (AOC) or similar, depending on the region. Portugal has something similar and, in fact, pioneered this technique back in 1756 with a royal charter which created the "Demarcated Douro Region" and regulated wine production and trade. Germany did likewise in 2002, although their system has not yet achieved the authority of those of the other countries'. Spain, Greece and Italy have classifications which are based on a dual system of region of origin and quality of product.

Besides Europe

New World wine—wines from outside of the traditional wine growing regions of Europe tend to be classified by grape rather than by *terroir* or region of origin, although there have been non-official attempts to classify them by quality.

TASTING

Wine tasting is the sensory examination and evaluation of wine. Wines are made up of chemical compounds which are similar or identical to those in fruits, vegetables, and spices. The sweetness of wine is determined by the amount of residual sugar in the wine after fermentation, relative to the acidity present in the wine. Dry wine, for example, has only a small amount of residual sugar. Inexperienced wine drinkers often tend to mistake the taste of ripe fruit for sweetness when, in fact, the wine in question is very dry. The red wines have Resveratrol which is a anti ageing compound.

Individual flavours may also be detected, due to the complex mix of organic molecules such as esters and terpenes that grape juice and wine can contain. Tasters often can distinguish between flavours characteristic of a specific grape and flavours that result from other factors in wine making, either intentional or not. The most typical intentional flavour elements in wine are those that are imparted by aging in oak casks; chocolate, vanilla, or coffee almost always come from the oak and not the grape itself.

Banana flavours are the product of yeast metabolism, as are spoilage aromas such as sweaty, barnyard, band-aid, and rotten egg. Some varietals can also have a mineral flavour, because some salts are soluble in water and are absorbed by the wine.

Wine aroma comes from volatile compounds in the wine that are released into the air. Vaporization of these compounds can be sped up by twirling the wine glass or serving the wine at room temperature. For red wines that are already highly aromatic, like Chinon and Beaujolais, many people prefer them chilled.

COLLECTING

Outstanding vintages from the best vineyards may sell for thousands of dollars per bottle, though the broader term fine wine covers bottles typically retailing at over about $US 30-50. "Investment wines" are considered by some to be *Veblen goods*—that is, goods for which demand increases instead of decreases as its price rises. The most common wines purchased for investment include those from Bordeaux, Burgundy, cult wines from Europe and elsewhere, and Vintage port.

Characteristics of highly collectible wines include:

- A proven track record of holding well over time
- A drinking window plateau that is many years long
- A consensus amongst experts as to the quality of the wines
- Rigorous production methods at every stage, including grape selection and appropriate barrel-aging

Investment in fine wine has attracted fraudsters who prey on their victims' ignorance of this sector of the wine market. Wine fraudsters often work by charging excessively high prices for off-vintage or lower-status wines from famous wine regions, while claiming that they are offering a sound investment unaffected by economic cycles. Like any investment, proper research is essential before investing.

PRODUCTION OF WINE

Table. Wine Production by Country 2006

Rank	Country	Production (tonnes)
1	France	5,349,333
2	Italy	4,711,665
3	Spain	3,643,666
4	United States	2,232,000
5	Argentina	1,539,600
6	Australia	1,410,483
7	China	1,400,000
8	South Africa	1,012,980
9	Chile	977,087
10	Germany	891,600

Table. Wine production by country 2007

Rank	Country	Production (tonnes)
1	Italy	5,050,000
2	France	4,711,600
3	Spain	3,645,000
4	United States	2,300,000
5	Argentina	1,550,000
6	China	1,450,000
7	South Africa	1,050,000
8	Australia	961,972
9	Germany	891,600
10	Chile	827,746

Wine grapes grow almost exclusively between thirty and fifty degrees north or south of the equator. The world's southernmost vineyards are in the Central Otago region of New Zealand's South Island near the 45th parallel south, and the northernmost are in Flen, Sweden, just north of the 59th parallel north.

Exporting Countries of Wine

Table. Top Ten Wine Exporting Countries in 2006

Rank	Country	1000 tonnes
1	Italy*	1,793
2	France	1,462
3	Spain*	1,337
4	Australia	762
5	Chile*	472
6	United States	369
7	Germany	316
8	Argentina	302
9	Portugal	286
10	South Africa	272
World**		8,353

Note:

* Unofficial figure.

** May include official, semi-official or estimated data.

Table. 2006 Export Market Shares

Rank	Country	Market share (% of value in US$)
1	France	34.9%
2	Italy	18.0%
3	Australia	9.3%
4	Spain	8.7%
5	Chile	4.3%
6	United States	3.6%
7	Germany	3.5%
8	Portugal	3.0%
9	South Africa	2.4%
10	New Zealand	1.8%

The UK was the world's biggest importer of wine in 2007.

USES OF WINE

Wine is a popular and important beverage that accompanies and enhances a wide range of European and Mediterranean-style cuisines, from the simple and traditional to the most sophisticated and complex. Wine is important in cuisine not just for its value as a beverage, but as a flavour agent, primarily in stocks and braising, since its acidity lends balance to rich savory or sweet dishes. Red, white, and sparkling wines are the most popular, and are known as *light wines* because they are only 10–14 per cent alcohol-content by volume. Apéritif and dessert wines contain 14–20 per cent alcohol, and are sometimes fortified to make them richer and sweeter.

Some wine labels suggest opening the bottle and letting the wine "breathe" for a couple of hours before serving, while others recommend drinking it immediately. Decanting—the act of pouring a wine into a special container just for breathing—is a controversial subject in wine. In addition to aeration, decanting with a filter allows one to remove bitter sediments that may have formed in the wine. Sediment is more common in older bottles but younger wines usually benefit more from aeration.

During aeration, the exposure of younger wines to air often "relaxes" the flavours and makes them taste smoother and better integrated in aroma, texture, and flavour. Older wines generally *fade*, or lose their character and flavour intensity, with extended aeration. Despite these general rules, breathing does not necessarily benefit all wines. Wine should be tasted as soon as it is opened to determine how long it should be aerated, if at all.

Religious Uses

Ancient Religions

The use of wine in religious ceremonies is common to many cultures and regions. Libations often included wine, and the religious mysteries of Dionysus used wine as a sacramental entheogen to induce a mind-altering state.

Judaism

Wine is an integral part of Jewish laws and traditions. The *Kiddush* is a blessing recited over wine or grape juice to sanctify the Shabbat or a Jewish holiday. On Pesach during the Seder, it is a Rabbinic obligation of men and women to drink four cups of wine. In the Tabernacle and in the Temple in Jerusalem, the libation of wine was part of the sacrificial service. Note that this does not mean that wine is a symbol of blood, a common misconception which contributes to the myth of the blood libel.

Christianity

In Christianity, wine is used in a sacred rite called the Eucharist, which originates in Gospel accounts of the Last Supper in which Jesus shared bread and wine with his disciples and commanded his followers to "do this in remembrance of me". Beliefs about the nature of the Eucharist vary among denominations.

While most Christians consider the use of wine from the grape as essential for validity of the sacrament, many Protestants also allow unfermented, pasteurized grape juice as a substitute. Wine was used in Eucharistic rites by all Protestant groups until an alternative arose in the late 1800s. Methodist dentist and prohibitionist Thomas Bramwell Welch applied new pasteurization techniques to stop the natural fermentation process of grape juice. Some Christians who were part of the growing temperance movement pressed for a switch from wine to grape juice, and the substitution spread quickly over much of the United States and to other countries to a lesser degree. There remains an ongoing debate between some American Protestant denominations as to whether wine can and should be used for the Eucharist or allowed as an ordinary beverage.

Islam

All alcohol is strictly forbidden under Islamic law. It is only permitted for medicinal reasons. Iran and Afghanistan used to have a thriving wine industry that disappeared after the Islamic Revolution in 1979 and earlier in Afghanistan. However, people of Nuristan in Afghanistan have produced wine since ancient times and still do so. In Greater Persia, *Mei* has been a central theme of poetry for more than a thousand years.

PACKAGING

Most wines are sold in glass bottles and are sealed using corks. An increasing number of wine producers have been using alternative closures such as screwcaps, or synthetic plastic "corks". In addition to being less expensive, alternative closures prevent cork taint, although they have been blamed for other problems such as excessive reduction.

Some wines are packaged in heavy plastic bags within cardboard boxes, and are called *box wines*, or cask wine. These wines are typically accessed via a tap on the side of the box. Box wine can maintain an acceptable degree of freshness for up to a month after opening, while bottled wine will more rapidly oxidize, and is considerably degraded within a few days.

Environmental considerations of wine packaging reveal benefits and drawbacks of both bottled and box wines. Glass used to make bottles has a decent environmental reputation, as it is completely recyclable, whereas plastics as used in box wines are typically considered to be much less environmentally friendly.

However, wine bottle manufacturers have been cited for Clean Air Act violations. A New York Times editorial suggested that box wine, being lighter in package weight, has a reduced carbon footprint from its distribution. Boxed wine plastics, even though possibly recyclable, can be more labour-intensive to process than glass bottles. And while a wine box is recyclable, its plastic wine bladder most likely is not.

STORAGE

Wine cellars, or *wine rooms* if they are above-ground, are places designed specifically for the storage and aging of wine. In an *active* wine cellar, temperature and humidity are maintained by a climate control system. *Passive* wine cellars are not climate-controlled, and so must be carefully located. Wine is a natural, perishable food product; when exposed to heat, light, vibration or fluctuations in temperature and humidity, all types of wine, including red, white, sparkling, and fortified, can spoil. When properly stored, wines can maintain their quality and in some cases improve in aroma, flavour, and complexity as they age. Some wine experts contend that the optimal temperature for aging wine is 55 °F (13 °C), others 59 °F (15 °C), Wine refrigerators offer an alternative to wine cellars.

They are available in capacities ranging from small 16-bottle units to furniture pieces that can contain 400 bottles. Wine refrigerators are not ideal for aging, but rather serve to chill wine to the perfect temperature for drinking. These refrigerators keep the humidity low, usually under 50 per cent, which is the optimal humidity of 50 per cent to 70 per cent. Lower humidity levels can dry corks out over time, allowing oxygen to enter the bottle and reduce the wine's quality.

Related professions:

Name	Description
Cooper	Craftsman of wooden barrels and casks. A cooperage is a company that produces such casks.
Garagiste	An amateur wine maker, or a derogatory term used for small scale operations of recent inception, usually without pedigree and located in Bordeaux.
Négociant	A wine merchant, most specifically those who assemble the produce of smaller growers and winemakers and sells them under their own name.
Oenologist	Wine scientist or wine chemist; a student of oenology. A winemaker may be trained as oenologist, but often hires a consultant instead.
Sommelier	A restaurant specialist in charge of assembling the wine list, educating the staff about wine, and assisting customers with their wine selections.
Terroir	Someone with special knowledge of the interplay specialist between the environmental factors such as soil, climate and topography—also known as terroir—and wine grape quality or wine character.
Vintner, Winemaker	A wine producer; a person who makes wine.
Viticulturist	A person who specializes in the science of grapevines. Can also be someone who manages vineyard pruning, irrigation, and pest control.

AGING OF WINE

The aging of wine, and its ability to potentially improve in quality, distinguishes wine from most other consumable goods. While wine is perishable and capable of deteriorating, complex chemical reactions involving a wine's sugars, acids and phenolic compounds can alter the aroma, colour, mouthfeel and taste of the wine in a way that may be more pleasing to the taster. The ability of a wine to age is influenced by many factors including grape variety, vintage, viticultural practices, wine region and winemaking style.

The condition that the wine is kept in after bottling can also influence how well a wine ages and may require significant time and financial investment.

Backdrop

The Ancient Greeks and Romans were aware of the potential of aged wines. In Greece, early examples of dried "straw wines" were noted for their ability to age due to their high sugar contents. These wines were stored in sealed earthenware amphorae and kept for many years. In Rome, the most sought after wines—Falernian and Surrentine—were prized for their ability to age for decades. It is noted that "old wine" was valued over "new wine". The Greek physician Galen wrote that the "taste" of aged wine was desirable and that this could be accomplished by heating or smoking the wine though, in Galen's opinion, these artificially aged wines were not as healthy to consume as naturally aged wines.

Following the Fall of the Roman Empire, appreciation for aged wine was virtually non-existent. Most of the wines produced in northern Europe were light bodied, pale in colour and with low alcohol. These wines did not have much aging potential and barely lasted a few months before they rapidly deteriorated into vinegar. The older a wine got the cheaper its price became as merchants eagerly sought to rid themselves of aging wine. By the 16th century, sweeter and more alcoholic wines were being made in the Mediterranean and gaining attention for their aging ability. Similarly, Riesling from Germany with its combination of acidity and sugar were also demonstrating their ability to age. In 17th century two innovations occurred that radically changed the wine industry's view on aging.

One was the development of the cork and bottle which allowed producers to package and store wine in a virtually air-tight environment. The second was the growing popularity of fortifying wines such as Port, Madeira and Sherries. The added alcohol was found to act as a preservative, allowing wines to survive long sea voyages to England, The Americas and the East Indies. The English, in particular, were growing in their appreciation of aged wines like Port and Claret from Bordeaux. Demand for matured wines had a pronounced effect on the wine trade. For producers, the cost and space of storing barrels or bottles of wine was prohibitive so a merchant class evolved with warehouses and the finances to facilitate aging wines for a longer period of time. In regions like Bordeaux, Oporto and Burgundy, this situation dramatically increased the balance of power towards the merchant classes.

What Wine can Age?

Despite the well known saying that *"All wine improves with age"*, only a few wines will actually have the ability to significantly improve with age. Master of Wine Jancis Robinson notes that only around the top 10 per cent of all red wine and top 5 per cent of all white wines can improve significantly enough with age to make drinking more enjoyable at 5 years of age than at 1 year of age. Additionally, Robinson estimates, only the top 1 per cent of all wine has the ability to improve significantly after more than a decade. It is her belief that more wine is consumed too old, rather than too young, and that the great majority of wines start to lose appeal and fruitiness after 6 months in the bottle.

In general, wines with a low pH have a greater capability of aging. With red wines, a high level of flavour compounds, such as phenolics, will increase the likelihood that a wine will be able to age. Wines with high levels of phenols include Cabernet Sauvignon, Nebbiolo and Syrah. The white wines with the longest aging potential tends to be those with a high amount of extract and acidity. The acidity in white wines plays a similar role that tannins have with red wines in acting as a preservative. The process of making white wines, which include little to no skin contact, means that white wines have a significantly fewer amounts of phenolic compounds. Similarly, the minimal skin contact with rosé wine limits their aging potential.

After aging at the winery most wood-aged Ports, Sherries, *Vins doux naturels, Vins de liqueur*, basic level Ice wines and sparkling wines are bottled when the producer feels that they are ready to be consumed. These wines are ready to drink upon release and will not benefit much from aging. Vintage Ports and other bottled-aged Ports and Sherries will benefit from some additional aging, as can vintage Champagne. In 2009, a 184-year-old bottle of Perrier-Jouët was opened and tasted, still drinkable, with notes of "truffles and caramel".

Wines with Little to No Aging Potential

A guideline provided by Master of Wine Jancis Robinson:

- German QBAs
- Asti and Moscato Spumante
- Rosé and blush wines like White Zinfandel
- Branded wines like Yellow Tail, Mouton Cadet, etc
- European table wine
- American jug and box wine
- Inexpensive varietals
- The majority of *Vin de pays*
- All Nouveau wines
- Vermouth
- Basic Sherry, Ports

Wines with Some Aging Potential

A guideline provided by Master of Wine Jancis Robinson. Note that vintage, wine region and winemaking style can influence a wine's aging potential so Robinson's suggestion of years are very rough estimates of the most common examples of these wines.

- Botrytized wines (5–25 yrs)
- Chardonnay (2–6 yrs)

- Riesling (2–30 yrs)
- Hungarian Furmint (3–25 yrs)
- Loire Valley Chenin blanc (4–30 yrs)
- Hunter Valley Semillon (6–15 yrs)
- Cabernet Sauvignon (4–20 yrs)
- Merlot (2–10 yrs)
- Nebbiolo (4–20 yrs)
- Pinot noir (2–8 yrs)
- Sangiovese (2–8 yrs)
- Syrah (4–16 yrs)
- Zinfandel (2–6 yrs)
- Classified Bordeaux (8–25 yrs)
- Grand Cru Burgundy (8–25 yrs)
- Aglianico from Taurasi (4–15 yrs)
- Baga from Bairrada (4–8 yrs)
- Hungarian Kadarka (3–7 yrs)
- Bulgarian Melnik (3–7 yrs)
- Croatian Plavac Mali (4–8 yrs)
- Russian Saperavi (3–10 yrs)
- Madiran Tannat (4–12 yrs)
- Spanish Tempranillo (2–8 yrs)
- Greek Xynomavro (4–10 yrs)

Factors and Influences

The ratio of sugars, acids and phenolics to water is a key determination of how well a wine can age. The less water in the grapes prior to harvest, the more likely the resulting wine will have some aging potential. Grape variety, climate, vintage and viticultural practice come into play here. Grape varieties with thicker skins, from a dry growing season where little irrigation was used and yields were kept low will have less water and a higher ratio of sugar, acids and phenolics. The process of making Eisweins, where water is removed from the grape during pressing as frozen ice crystals, has a similar effect of decreasing the amount of water and increasing aging potential.

In winemaking, the duration of maceration or skin contact will influence how much phenolic compounds are leached from skins into the wine. Pigmented tannins, anthocyanins, colloids, tannin-polysaccharides and tannin-proteins not only influence a wine's resulting colour but also act as preservatives. During fermentation adjustment to a wine's acid levels can be made with wines with lower pH having more aging potential. Exposure to oak either during fermentation or after during barrel aging will introduce more phenolic compounds to the wines. Prior to bottling, excessive fining or filtering of the wine could strip the wine of some phenolic solids and may lessen a wine's ability to age. The storage condition of the bottled wine will influence a wine's aging. Vibrations and heat fluctuations can hasten a wine's deterioration and cause adverse effect on the wines. In general, a wine has a greater potential to develop complexity and more aromatic bouquet if it is allowed to age slowly in a relatively cool environment.

The lower the temperature, the more slowly a wine develops. On average, the rate of chemical reactions in wine double with each 18 °F (8 °C) increase in temperature. Wine expert Karen MacNeil, recommends keeping wine intended for aging in a cool area with a constant temperature around 55°F (13°C). Wine can be stored at temperatures as high as 69°F (20°C) without long term negative effect. Cornelius Ough of the University of California, Davis believes that wine could be exposed to temperatures as high as 120 °F (49 °C) for a few hours and not be damaged. However, most experts believe that extreme temperature fluctuations would be detrimental to the wine. The ultra-violet rays of direct sunlight should also be avoided because of the free radicals that can develop in the wine and result in oxidation.

Wines packaged in large format bottles, such as magnums and 3 litre Jeroboams, seem to age more slowly than wines packaged in regular 750 ml bottles or half bottles. This may be because of the greater proportion of oxygen exposed to the wine during the bottle process. The advent of alternative wine closures to cork, such as screw caps and synthetic corks have opened up recent discussions on the aging potential of wines sealed with these alternative closures. Currently there is no conclusive results and the topic is the subject of ongoing research.

Bottle Sickness

One of the short-term aging needs of wine is a period where the wine is considered "sick" due to the trauma and volatility of the bottling experience. During bottling some oxygen is exposed to the wine, causing a domino effect of chemical reaction with various components of the wine. The time it takes for the wine to settle down and have the oxygen fully dissolve and integrate with the wine is considered its period of "bottle shock". During this time the wine could taste drastically different than it did prior to bottling or how it will taste after the wine has settled. While many modern bottling lines try to treat the wine as gently as possible and utilize inert gases to minimize the amount of oxygen exposure, all wine goes through some period of bottle shock. The length of this period will vary with each individual wine.

Dumb Phase

During the course of aging a wine may slip into a "dumb phase" where its aromas and flavours are very muted. In Bordeaux this phase is called the age ingrat or "difficult age" and is likened to a teenager going through adolescence.

The cause or length of time that this "dumb phase" will last is not yet fully understood and seems to vary from bottle to bottle.

Effects on Wine

As red wine ages, the harsh tannins of its youth gradually give way to a softer mouthfeel. An inky dark colour will eventually fade to a light brick red. These changes occur due to the complex chemical reactions of the phenolic compounds of the wine. In processes that begin during fermentation and continue after bottling, these compounds bind together and aggregate. Eventually these particles reach a certain size where they are too large to stay suspended in the solution and precipitate out. The presence of visible sediment in a bottle will usually indicate a mature wine. The resulting wine, with this loss of tannins and pigment, will have a paler colour and taste softer, less astringent. The sediment, while harmless, can have an unpleasant taste and is often separated from the wine by decanting.

During the aging process, the perception of a wine's acidity may change even though the total measurable amount of acidity is more or less constant throughout a wine's life. This is due to the esterification of the acids, combining with alcohols in complex array to form esters. In addition to making a wine taste less acidic, these esters introduce a range of possible aromas. Eventually the wine may age to a point where other components of the wine are less noticeable themselves, which will then bring back a heightened perception of wine acidity. Other chemical processes that occur during aging include the hydrolysis of flavour precursors which detach themselves from glucose molecules and introduce new flavour notes in the older wine and Aldehydes become oxidized. The interaction of certain phenolics develop what is known as tertiary aromas which are different from the primary aromas that are derived from the grape and during fermentation.

As a wine starts to mature, its bouquet will become more developed and multi-layered. While a taster may be able to pick out a few fruit notes in a young wine, a more complex wine will have several distinct fruit, floral, earthy, mineral and oak derived notes. The lingering finish of a wine will lengthen. Eventually the wine will reach a point of maturity, when it is said to be at its "peak". This is the point when the wine has the maximum amount of complexity, most pleasing mouthfeel and softening of tannins and has not yet started to decay. When this point will occur is not yet predictable and can vary from bottle to bottle. If a wine is aged for too long, it will start to descend into decrepitude where the fruit tastes hollow and weak while the wine's acidity becomes dominant.

Artificial Aging

There is a long backdrop of man using artificial means to try to accelerate the natural aging process. In Ancient Rome a smoke chamber known as a fumarium was used to enhance the flavour of wine through artificial aging. Amphorae were placed in the chamber, which was built on top of a heated hearth, in order to impart a smoky flavour in the wine that also seemed to sharpen the acidity. The wine would sometimes come out of the fumarium with a paler colour just like aged wine. Modern winemaking techniques like micro-oxygenation can have the side effect of artificially aging the wine. In the production of Madeira and rancio wines, the wines are deliberately exposed to excessive temperatures to accelerate the maturation of the wine. Other techniques used to artificially age wine include shaking the wine, exposing it to radiation, magnetism or ultra-sonic waves. More recently, experiments with artificial aging through high-voltage electricity have produced results before the remaining techniques, as assessed by a panel of wine tasters.

WINE BAR

A wine bar is a tavern-like business focusing on selling wine, rather than liquour or beer. A typical feature of many wine bars is a wide selection of wines available by the glass. Some wine bars are profiled on wines of a certain type of origin, such as Italian wine or Champagne. While many wine bars are private "stand alone" establishments, in some cases, wine bars are associated with a specific wine retailer or other outlet of wine, to provide additional marketing for that retailer's wine portfolio. In countries where licensing regulations allow this, some wine bars also sell the wines they serve, and effective function as a hybrid between a wine shop and a wine bar.

COATES LAW OF MATURITY

Coates Law of Maturity is a principle used in wine tasting relating to the aging ability of wine. Developed by the British Master of Wine, Clive Coates, the principle states that a wine will remain at its peak drinking quality for a duration of time that is equal to the time of maturation required to reach its optimal quality. During the evolution of a wine certain flavours, aromas and textures appear and fade. Rather than developing and fading in unison, these traits each operate on a unique evolutionary path and time line. The principle allows for the subjectivity of individual tastes because it follows the logic that positive traits that appeal to one particular wine taster will continue to persist along the principle's guideline while for another taster these traits might not be positive and therefore not applicable to the guideline. Wine expert Tom Stevenson has noted that there is logic in Coates' principle and that he has yet to encounter an anomaly or wine that debunks it.

Example

An example of the principle in practice would be a wine that someone discovers at 10 years of age. The drinker may find this wine very pleasing in texture, aroma and mouthfeel. Under the *Coates Law of Maturity* the wine will continue to be drinking at an optimal level for that drinker until it has reached 20 years of age at which time those positive traits that the drinker perceives will start to fade.

GLOBALIZATION OF WINE

"Globalization is the expansion of brands across nations and into other continents. In food and wine it refers to the whole problem of making the product global. The primary issue is scaling production while reducing the costs of goods with processes. In marketing it refers to wearing the mantle of fine food and wine, and increasing 100-point scores. In sales it refers to capturing the growth".

California winemaker Leo McCloskey.

Backdrop

Wine has been traded internationally since ancient times. And in the wake of the amphoras came winemakers, winemaking techniques, and cuttings of grapevines. Many grapes that are considered 'traditional' in Western Europe were in fact brought by ancient trade routes from the Eastern Mediterranean and the Black Sea region. The Phoenicians, the Greeks, the Romans, the Turks all brought grapes to new homes.

There was a second wave of migration, to the New World, under the European empires of the 16th-19th centuries—by the early 18th century South Africa was exporting Constantia to Europe, made with muscat grapes that originated in Egypt. Subsequent immigrants have brought their native wines and grapes wherever they have gone—the Italian influence on Argentine and Californian winemaking is particular noteworthy. Wines from Portugal and Madeira were fortified to survive journeys across the world, and left their mark on wines in the colonies that aped their style and were named after them.

The phylloxera epidemic of the late 19th century also had a big influence, destroying traditional field blends of indigenous grapes in vineyards, which were often replaced by monocultures of fashionable grapes such as the Bordeaux varieties—grafted, of course, onto rootstocks from North America. Vignerons faced a stark choice, either adopt the new techniques, or choose another profession. Phylloxera was the stimulus for the development of a new infrastructure of government breeding programmes and exchange of plant material and techniques.

After the Second World War, a number of countries developed bland wines for the export market, with an emphasis on uniformity and branding, such as Mateus Rose and Blue Nun. These were welcomed by a mass market—and the multiple retailers who served them—and those same factors have helped similar brands to gain more power, although changes in fashion mean that the names have changed. The modern equivalents come from industrial irrigated vineyards in the New World, in regions such as Murray Darling in southern Australia and Worcester in South Africa. Such moves reflect changes in the general scale of food production in industrialised countries.

Another aspect of this is the rise of varietal labelling, which has made the big companies less tolerant of blends of obscure grapes, instead preferring to market 'big name' varietals such as Cabernet Sauvignon, Merlot, Pinot Noir, Syrah, Chardonnay, Sauvignon Blanc and Riesling.

Another growing trend has been the practice of the blending of bulk wine from other countries with local wine. In some cases, a wine marketed as a local product may be sourced entirely from elsewhere. Regulations on this practice vary widely, depending on the jurisdiction.

The Judgement of Paris in 1976 and subsequent wine competitions helped winemakers throughout the New World realize that they could make wines equal to the very best produced anywhere in the world as well educating some markets about the potential of wine outside Europe. This process was much easier in some countries like the United Kingdom, with little indigenous production and a centuries-old tradition of importing wine from around the world, than it was in other countries. Further competitions brought to international attention other great wines from around the world, some of which like Penfolds Grange had already been made for decades.

A major influence has been the wine critic Robert M. Parker, Jr. among consumers in the United States. His approval can make a massive difference to sales of a wine in the United States, and some winemakers in some parts of the world have been accused of chasing this market by changing their wines to suit his personal taste. This effect is the main subject of the documentary film *Mondovino*. His points system is influential, particularly among retailers as a substitute for staff training.

ORGANIC WINE

At its most basic level, organic wine is made from grapes that have been grown without the use of chemical fertilizers, pesticides, fungicides and herbicides. The main categories are Sustainable, Organic and Biodynamic.

Sustainable

Sustainable winemaking means growers abstain from using man-made chemicals and artificial fertilizers to improve life in their vineyards and in the wines they create. Some of the components of sustainable winemaking practices consist of using natural fertilizers, composting and the cultivation of plants that attract insects that are beneficial to the health of the vines. Sustainable practices in these vineyards also extend to actions that have seemingly little or nothing to do with the production of grapes such as providing areas for wildlife to flourish near vineyard sites and allowing weeds and wildflowers to grow between the vines and using bio-diesel for tractors in the vineyards.

In short, sustainable winemaking means doing everything to limit the carbon footprint in the vineyard. Ultimately, sustainable winemaking encompasses the eco-system surrounding the vineyard with the goal that all the natural elements within the vineyard work in harmony with nature.

Organic Winemaking

Applying all the basics of sustainable winemaking and taking them one step further into organic winemaking you'll find some very significant differences, both in the winemakers approach and the end result in the bottle. Grape growing like any other farming is organic by origin. However, like most other methods of farming the vast majority of vineyards today are not organic. For many winemakers, especially at large wineries, it isn't cost effective to farm organically, and far too many things can go wrong throughout the year that can easily destroy crops.

Chemical fertilizers promote large yields and chemicals can easily wipe-out vineyard destroying diseases. Vines that are chemically fertilized and regularly sprayed for various diseases with chemicals are absorbed through the roots into the vine's sap and passed through leaves, stems, fruit and finally, into your glass. Not only do one eventually ingest these chemicals, but by using them it also drastically reduces the natural terroir of the wine and diminish the wine's fruit profile in your glass. Organic wines are produced by using only organically grown grapes. No pesticides, herbicides, fungicides, chemical fertilizers, or synthetic chemicals of any kind are allowed on the vines or in the soil of the vineyards claiming to be organic. Strict rules govern the winemaking process such as hand-harvesting, the types of yeasts that can be used during fermentation and storage conditions in the vineyards of all imported and domestic wines that acquire certification.

Organic winemakers abstain from all chemical substances used to stabilize conventional wines such as sulfites. It is important to remember that sulfites are a natural byproduct of the fermentation process and that it is impossible for any wine to be completely free of sulfites. Wines that are completely free of sulfites are an accident of nature–fermenting yeasts present on all grape skins generates naturally occurring sulfites. Organic wines may have naturally occurring sulfites, but the total sulfite level must be less than 20 parts per million in order to receive organic certification.

The stricter government regulations for organic wine and the rejection of using added sulfites are, for all intents and purposes, the two key differences between organic and sustainable winemaking.

Biodynamic Winemaking

Biodynamic winemaking is much more than a simple agricultural system;

it is a worldview that greatly impacts the practice of winemaking in many ways. To make biodynamic wine one have to think biodynamically, which has its roots in a series of lectures delivered by Rudolf Steiner in 1924. Steiner's life-long goal was to bridge the gap between the material and spiritual world through his "spiritual science" of anthroposophy. This science postulates the existence of an objective, intellectually comprehensible spiritual world one is able to directly access through cultivating a form of thinking that is independent of sensory experience. Very late in Steiner's life he turned to agriculture and his eight lectures, entitled Spiritual Foundations for the Renewal of Agriculture, were delivered a year before his death. These lectures are the cornerstone of biodynamic winemaking; in fact, all modern biodynamic practices are built upon Steiner's theories.

The key to understanding biodynamic winemaking is to consider the vineyard as a living system that is closed and self-sustaining. Organic and biodynamic winemaking shares many of the same attributes; biodynamic wines are produced by using only organically grown grapes. No pesticides, herbicides, fungicides, chemical fertilizers, or synthetic chemicals of any kind are allowed on the vines or in the soil of the vineyards. The grapes are harvested by hand, the vineyards are plowed by hand or horses, and only indigenous yeasts are used during fermentation. However, biodynamic winemakers see their vineyards in a much broader context that connects their vines and the year-long growing cycle with lunar and cosmic rhythms. In these vineyards the soil is not simply material for plant growth, but a living organism. The idea of using synthetic fertilizers or pesticides would, in the biodynamic winemaker's view, poison many key components that promote the health and longevity of their vineyards. These growers use a series of special preparations to enhance the life of the soil, which are applied at appropriate times throughout the year in keeping with the lunar and cosmic rhythms of nature.

Organic Certification and Natural Wines

"Organic," in countries with organic regulation, it means the wine has met certain standards that are set by a government agency. Different nations have their own certification criteria, so what's organic in one country may not be so in another. In the United States, the U.S. Dept of Agriculture certifies organic wine as being "USDA Organic".

Many wineries that are technically organic still choose not to be certified. There are many reasons for this. Some do not want the added costs and bureaucracy of registering. Others may disagree with their government's standards. It can also be a marketing decision. Whatever the case, in countries with organic regulation, they are not allowed to use "organic" on their labels.

Some think that organic certification standards are inappropriate, and that although grapes can be grown organically, winemaking itself is not organic.

The process can tend to little or no manipulation of wines by reverse osmosis, excessive filtration, or flavour additives, use of wild yeasts for fermentation. Some winemakers, although not meeting organic criteria, think their methods are superior and choose to label themselves as "natural" wines instead.

Sulfites

Organic wines are not necessarily sulfite-free. The use of added sulfites is debated heavily within the organic winemaking community. Many vintners favour their use, in extremely small quantities, to help stabilize wines, while others frown on them completely.

In the United States, wines labeled "organic" cannot contain added sulfites. Wines that have added sulfites, but are otherwise organic, are labeled "wine made from organic grapes."

WINE RATING

A wine rating is a score assigned by one or more wine critics to a wine tasted as a summary of that critic's evaluation of that wine. A wine rating is therefore a subjective quality score, typically of a numerical nature, given to a specific bottle of wine. In most cases, wine ratings are set by a single wine critic, but in some cases a rating is derived by input from several critics tasting the same wine at the same time. A number of different scales for wine ratings are in use. Also, the practices used to arrive at the rating can vary. Over the last couple of decades, the 50-100 scale introduced by Robert M. Parker, Jr. has become commonly used. This or numerically similar scales are used by publications such as Wine Enthusiast, Wine Spectator, and Wine Advocate. Other publications or critics, such as Jancis Robinson and Michael Broadbent, may use a 0-20 scale, or a 0-5 scale either with or without half-star steps.

In recent years, with the advent of aggregated user-generated ratings, there has also proliferated group rating systems, such as the one employed by CellarTracker, using input from non-professional wine tasters who taste under differing conditions. In addition to a simple numerical score, most wine ratings are meant to supplement the wine tasting notes, which are brief descriptions of the wine critics overall impression of the wine including its flavour qualities. However, often the emphasis is on the score applied by a critic rather than on the total wine tasting note.

Backdrop

While the composition of tasting notes and other forms of wine literature has existed throughout the backdrop of wine, the widespread use of numerical rating systems is a relatively recent phenomenon. During the mid 20th century, as American interest in wine was developing, consumers found themselves being introduced to a wide assortment of wines from across the globe. This surplus of available options created a niche market for critics who could provide a service in reviewing wines and making recommendations that could make the buying process easier for consumers. Following a pattern similar to the product reviews of such consumer magazines like *Consumer Reports* and *Which?*, American critics began writing more condensed wine reviews that consumers could scan through briefly to identify wines of interest. The popularization of numerical scoring is widely credited to the American wine critic Robert Parker who patterned his system of numerical ratings on the American standardized grading system in the 1970s.

Under Parker's system, wines were evaluated on a 50-100 scale that roughly correlated to an A-F "grade" on the wine. A wine was considered "good" if it got a score of at least 85 points. Readers of wine rating magazines such as Parker's *The Wine Advocate*, or its later imitators such as *Wine Spectator* and *The Wine Enthusiast*, could quickly at glance see a review of several dozen or even hundreds of available wines broken down into numerical evaluations. These consumers could isolate a range of scores to concentrate their buying purchase on without ever having to try a wine before hand. Similarly, wine retailers and merchants found themselves with a ready made marketing tool that didn't even require them to research or sample the wine before they put it on sale. The popularity of numerical wine ratings became a boon for the wine retailing industry. Wines that received scores classified as "outstanding" were essentially guaranteed favorable sales in the market. Wines that received "extraordinary" or "classic" ratings of 95-100 began to develop cult followings that, coupled with the limited production, helped to skyrocket their prices. A segment of wine investing emerged that aimed to capitalize on the speculation and eventual price increase surrounding highly scoring wines. The influence of wine ratings was particularly keen in the developing wine markets of Asia, Russia and South America at the turn of the 21st century.

Criticism

The numerical wine rating system has been heavily criticized. It has been considered a driving force in the globalization of wine and the down playing of the influence of *terroir* and individuality in wine making. Critics of the wine rating system contend that the economic and marketing power of receiving favorable scores by influential critics has steered global winemaking towards producing a homogeneous style that is perceived as appealing to the critics. These critics point to what they contend is an inherent flaw in sampling a wide assortment of wines at once. When compared together, wines that have deep colours, full bodied, stronger, concentrated flavours and smooth mouthfeel tend to stand out from the assortment more than wines with more subtle characteristics. These wines tend to receive more favorable wine ratings which has led to an increase in the proliferation of these styles of wines on the market.

3

Classification of Wine

INTRODUCTION

The classification of wine can be done to various methods including, but not limited to, place of origin or appellation, vinification methods and style, sweetness and vintage, or varietal used. Practices vary in different countries and regions of origin, and many practices have varied over time. Some classifications enjoy official protection by being part of the wine law in their country of origin, while other have been created by, for example, grower's organizations without such protection.

BY APPELLATION

Historically, wines have been known by names reflecting their origin, and sometimes style: Bordeaux, Rioja, Mosel and Chianti are all legally defined names reflecting the traditional wines produced in the named region. These naming conventions or "appellations" dictate not only where the grapes in a wine were grown but also which grapes went into the wine and how they were vinified. The appellation system is strongest in the European Union, but a related system, the American Viticultural Area, restricts the use of certain regional labels in America, such as Napa Valley, Santa Barbara and Willamette Valley. The AVA designations do not restrict the type of grape used.

In most of the world, wine labeled Champagne must be made from grapes grown in the Champagne region of France and fermented using a certain method, based on the international trademark agreements included in the 1919 Treaty of Versailles. However, in the United States, a legal definition called semi-generic has enabled U.S. winemakers to use certain generic terms if there appears next to the term the actual appellation of origin.

More recently, wine regions in countries with less stringent location protection laws such as the United States and Australia have joined with well-known European wine producing regions to sign the Napa Declaration to Protect Wine Place and Origin, commonly known as the Napa Declaration on Place. This is a "declaration of joint principles stating the importance of location to wine and the need to protect place names". The Declaration was signed in July 2005 by four United States winegrowing regions and three European Union winegrowing regions. The signatory regions from the US were Napa Valley, Washington, Oregon and Walla Walla, while the signatory regions from the EU were: Champagne, Cognac, Douro and Jerez. The list of signatories to the agreement expanded in March 2007 when Sonoma County, Paso Robles, Chianti Classico, Tokay, Victoria, Australia and Western Australia signed the Declaration at a ceremony in Washington, DC.

Regional Wine Classifications

Many Regional wine classifications exist as part of tradition or appellation law. The most common of these is based on vineyard sites and include the Bordeaux Wine Official Classification of 1855, though some regions classify their wines based on the style like the German wine classification system. Vineyard classification has a long history dating from some early examples in Jurançon in the 14th century, in 1644 when the council of Würzburg ranked the city's vineyards by quality, and the early five-level designation of vineyards based on quality in Tokaj-Hegyalja in 1700.

Other well known classifications include:

- Classification of Saint-Émilion wine of Bordeaux
- Classification of Graves wine of Bordeaux
- Cru Bourgeois of Bordeaux
- Classified estates of Provence

The follow regions are classified by vineyards, not estate:

- Grand cru of Burgundy and Alsace

By Vinification Methods and Style

Wines may be classified by vinification methods. These include classifications such as red or white wine, sparkling, semi-sparkling or still, fortified and dessert wines. The colour of wine is not determined by the juice of the grape, which is almost always clear, but rather by the presence or absence of the grape skin during fermentation. Grapes with coloured juice, for example alicante bouchet, are known as teinturier. Red wine is made from red grapes, but its red colour is bestowed by a process called maceration, whereby the skin is left in contact with the juice during fermentation. White wine can be made from any colour of grape as the skin is separated from the juice during fermentation. A white wine made from a very dark grape may appear pink or 'blush'. A form of Rosé is called *Blanc de Noirs* where the juice of red grapes are allowed contact with the skins for a very short time.

Sparkling and Still Wines

Sparkling wines such as champagne, contain carbon dioxide which is produced naturally from fermentation or force-injected later. To have this effect, the wine is fermented twice, once in an open container to allow the carbon dioxide to escape into the air, and a second time in a sealed container, where the gas is caught and remains in the wine. Sparkling wines that gain their carbonation from the traditional method of bottle fermentation are labelled "Bottle Fermented", *"Méthode Traditionelle"*, or *"Méthode Champenoise"*. The latter designation was outlawed for all wines other than Champagne in Europe in 1994.

Other international denominations of sparkling wine include Sekt or Schaumwein, Cava, and Spumante. Semi-sparkling wines are sparkling wines that contain less than 2.5 atmospheres of carbon dioxide at sea level and 20 °C. Some countries such as the UK impose a higher tax on fully sparkling wines. Examples of semi-sparkling synonym terms are *Frizzante* in Italy, *Vino de Aguja* in Spain and *Petillant* in France. In most countries except the United States, champagne is legally defined as sparkling wine originating from a region in France. Still wines are wines that have not gone through the sparkling wine methods and have no effervescence.

Dessert and Fortified Wine

Dessert wines range from slightly sweet to incredibly sweet wines. Late harvest wines such as Spätlese are made from grapes harvested well after they have reached maximum ripeness. Dried grape wines, such as Recioto and Vin Santo from Italy as well as Vinsanto from Santorini Greece, are made from grapes that have been partially raisined after harvesting. Botrytized wines are made from grapes infected by the mold Botrytis cinerea or noble rot.

These include Sauternes from Bordeaux, numerous wines from Loire such as Bonnezeaux and Quarts de Chaume, Tokaji Aszú from Hungary and Tokaj from Slovakia, and Beerenauslese from Germany and Austria. Eiswein is made from grapes that are harvested while they are frozen, and are commonly from the Niagara and Okanagan regions in Canada, Germany, and Austria. Fortified wines are often sweeter, and generally more alcoholic wines that have had their fermentation process stopped by the addition of a spirit, such as brandy, or have had additional spirit added after fermentation. Examples include Port, Madeira and Sherry.

Other Styles

Table wines may have an alcohol content that is no higher than 14 per cent in the U.S.. In Europe, light wine must be within 8.5 per cent and 14 per cent alcohol by volume. Thus, unless a wine has more than 14 per cent alcohol, or it has bubbles, it is a table wine or a light wine. Table wines are usually classified as "white," "red," or "rosé," depending on their colour. In Europe 'vins de table', 'vino da tavola', 'Tafelwein' or 'vino de mesa', which translate to 'table wine' in English, are cheaper wines that often on the label do not include the information on the grape variety used or the region of origin.

Cooking wine or Cooking sherry refers to inexpensive grape wine or rice wine. It is intended for use as an ingredient in food rather than as a beverage. Cooking wine typically available in North America is treated with salt as a preservative and food colouring. When a wine bottle is opened and the wine is exposed to oxygen, a fermentative process will transform the alcohol into acetic acid resulting in wine vinegar. The salt in cooking wine inhibits the growth of the microorganisms that produce acetic acid. This preservation is important because a bottle of cooking wine may be opened and used occasionally over a long period of time. Cooking wines are convenient for cooks who use wine as an ingredient for cooking only rarely. However, they are not widely used by professional chefs, as they believe the added preservative significantly lowers the quality of the wine and subsequently the food made with that wine. Most professional chefs prefer to use inexpensive but drinkable wine for cooking, and this recommendation is given in many professional cooking textbooks as well as general cookbooks. Many chefs believe there is no excuse for using a low quality cooking wine for cooking when there are quality drinkable wines available at very low prices.

Cooking wine is considered a wine of such poor quality, that it is unpalatable by itself and intended for use only in cooking. There is a school of thought that advises against cooking with any wine one would find unacceptable to drink.

By Vintage or Varietal

A vintage wine is one made from grapes that were all, or primarily, grown in a single specified year. Consequently, it is not uncommon for wine enthusiasts and traders to save bottles of an especially good vintage wine for future consumption. However, there is some disagreement and research about the significance of vintage year to wine quality. Most countries allow a vintage wine to include a portion of wine that is not from the labeled vintage.

A varietal wine is wine made from a dominant grape such as a Chardonnay or a Cabernet Sauvignon. The wine may not be entirely of that one grape and varietal labeling laws differ. In the United States a wine needs to be composed of at least 75 per cent of a particular grape to be labeled as a varietal wine. In the European Union, a minimum of 85 per cent is required if the name of a single varietal is diplayed, and if two or more varietals are described, these varietals combined must make up 100 per cent and they must be listed in descending order. *E.g.*, a mixture of 70 per cent Chardonnay and 30 per cent Viognier must be called Chardonnay-Viognier rather than Viognier-Chardonnay.

ALEXIS LICHINE'S CLASSIFICATION OF BORDEAUX WINE

In considering the Bordeaux Wine Official Classification of 1855, Alexis

Lichine held the opinion that the list, some hundred years after the selection was made, no longer expressed the whole truth concerning the ranking of Bordeaux wine. Working for a reevaluation and change of structure of the classification of Bordeaux estates, he ended up spending much of his professional life on a campaign that lasted more than thirty years to accomplish a revision. Having published his *Classification des Grands Crus Rouges de Bordeaux* in 1962, with several revisions over the following years, Lichine came to be viewed as "the doyen of unofficial classification compilers".

Reclassification

In 1959, a committee of which Lichine was a member as well as leading Bordeaux growers, shippers and brokers, was formed to decide what was to be done about reclassifying the work of 1855. Investigations revealed to what extent parcels of land had exchanged hands, some were considered insignificant but in other cases important transfers of terrain had taken place. It is acknowledged that at the time the list was compiled in great haste, primarily on the basis of which estates had consistently commanded the highest prices. While there was widespread agreement the 1855 classification had flaws, a general view remained that it was impossible to improve upon it.

The committee made a formal request to proceed with the revision in 1960. Opting for three categories instead of five, removing 18 chateaux and adding 13 new ones with updates every five years provoked reactions of outrage among those who faced great loss, "Château owners demoted or entirely deleted... condemned the ranking as malicious, incompetent and unjust." The *Institut National des Appellations d'Origine* (INAO) was called to arbitrate, but it became decided that the jurisdiction of INAO was too limited to resolve a mater of this complexity.

After two years of efforts, the Bordeaux Chamber of Commerce and *Académie des Vins de Bordeaux* also became involved in the debate surrounding the reforms. Recognising that the process would take a great deal of time, Lichine decided to publish his own classification.

Goals

In agreement with the committee, Lichine believed that, just as the principal philosophy behind the 1855 classification, *price* would be the most reliable indicator, but a revision could not let the transfer of first-rate soil go unchallenged. It was also important to identify cases where highly classified estates had become surpassed by those rated Fifth Growth or *Cru Bourgeois*, and addressing the 1855 classification's neglect of properties from other areas than Médoc, namely those of Graves, Saint-Émilion and Pomerol. Attempting to bring these areas together under one classification was considered unique to the Lichine rating.

Lichine also believed that no classification could be planned for a shorter span than 25-50 years since frequent changes would create consumer confusion and loss of public confidence, but saw the 1855 classification as evidence that no ruling can remain valid indefinitely.

Lichine was convinced that rankings of "first", "second", etc. were a mistake that should not be repeated, unfairly implying that there was, for instance, something second-rate about a Second Growth. Choosing to adapt and expand on the ranks used in the classifications of Graves and Saint-Émilion, Lichine arrived at the categories: *Outstanding Growths, Exceptional Growths, Great Growths, Superior Growths* and *Good Growths*.

Among the most visible changes was the elevation of Château Mouton Rothschild from its second growth status to *Cru Hors Classe*, which was the only of his suggestions ever to be realised. Mouton Rothschild was promoted to *Premier Cru* status in 1973.

AUSBRUCH

Ausbruch or sometimes Ausbruchwein is an Austrian wine term for a quality level in the *Prädikatswein* category. It is situated between Beerenauslese and Trockenbeerenauslese in requirements, which makes it a sweet dessert wine typically made from grapes affected by noble rot. The minimum must weight requirements for Ausbruch is 27 degrees KMW. The Ausbruch Prädikat exists only in Austria, not in Germany. The category was introduced into Austrian wine legislation in 1970, as a legalization of the production method allegedly already used in the area of Rust. *Ruster Ausbruch* are still the most common Ausbruch wines to encounter; in many other Austrian regions, producers classify their wines as Beerenauslese if they fall short of the Trockenbeerenauslese requirements.

Wine Production

The term Ausbruch initially designated a wine made from mixing grapes strongly affected by noble rot with must from less concentrated grapes, in the Spätlese to Beerenauslese range. This filled the purpose of dissolving crystallized sugars in the grapes in order to speed up the fermentation and make it more efficient.

This has also been called to "break out" the sugar, which is how the term was coined. This is the same as *Aszú* method of the Tokaji Aszú wines are produced in Austria's neighbouring country Hungary, although a classification system with several levels is used there.

However, in difference from the *Aszú* method, Ausbruch wines are not required to be made by mixing the two components, and in reality almost all present-day Austrian Ausbruch wines are produced in the same way as a Trockenbeerenauslese, but subject to a 27 °KMW rather than 30 °KMW requirement.

Grape Varieties

Historically the Hungarian grape Furmint was used in Ausbruch production but today it is rarely found in Austria. Most producers use a mix of grape varieties with Chardonnay, Pinot blanc, Traminer and Welschriesling being the most popular.

AUSLESE

Auslese is a German language wine term for a late harvest wine and is a riper category than Spätlese in the *Prädikatswein* category of the Austrian and German wine classification. The grapes are picked from selected very ripe bunches in the autumn and have to be hand picked. Generally Auslese wine can be made in only the best harvest years that have been sufficiently warm. A small proportion of the grapes may be affected by noble rot in some regions although this never dominates the character of the wine. Rheingau winemaker Schloss Johannisberg is generally credited with discovering Auslese wine in 1787.

Auslesen are sometimes considered a German dessert wine, especially the wines made from botrytis infected bunches, though it is not as sweet as Eiswein, Beerenauslese, or Trockenbeerenauslese dessert wines.

Auslesen can be enjoyed by themselves but are usually best accompanied with food, particularly those that exhibit the hearty characteristics of German cuisine.

The term in Alsace most closely corresponding to Auslese in terms of must weight requirements is *Vendange tardive*, even though this French term is linguistically equivalent to the German term *Spätlese*.

Requirements

The minimum must weight requirements for Auslese is as follows:

- In German wine, 83 to 100 degrees Oechsle, depending on the region and grape variety.
- In Austrian wine, 21 degrees KMW, corresponding to 105 °Oechsle.

Chaptalisation may not be used. The requirements are part of the wine law in both countries. Many producers, especially top-level producers, exceed the minimum requirements by a wide margin, resulting in richer and sweeter Auslesen that may even exceed the minimum requirements for Beerenauslese, the next *Prädikat* in order. In Germany, it is common to add stars on the wine label, *Fuder* numbers or a golden capsule, to indicate this.

Dry Auslese

The wines are occasionally made dry in some areas, such as Palatinate but are more typically sweeter, as the very high alcohol levels in dry examples can make them unbalanced particularly when young. The typical must weight for an Auslese is 90° Oechsle. These wines, particularly when made from the riesling grape can age for very long periods of time, often ten years or more.

With the recent introduction of the new classifications of top dry German wines, Erstes Gewächs and Grosses Gewächs, the Verband Deutscher Prädikats- und Qualitätsweingüter has discouraged the continued use of Auslese trocken, as it has been seen as confusing for the consumer to have sweet and powerful dry wines with the same Prädikat.

Red Wine Auslese

As German Wine makers try to carve out a niche in developing red wine, the Auslese ripeness classification has come into play as the ideal level to produce Spätburgunder, particularly in the Rheingau, Pfalz, and Baden regions. Winemakers are experimenting with grapes at Auslese level ripeness with Burgundian style production methods involving oak and a higher extraction of tannin levels.

These wines are also increasingly labelled Erstes Gewächs and Grosses Gewächs rather than Auslese.

BEERENAUSLESE

Beerenauslese is a German language wine term for a dessert wine-style late harvest wine. Beerenauslese is a category in the *Prädikatswein* category of the Austrian and German wine classifications. Beerenauslese wines, often called "BA" for short, are usually made from grapes affected by noble rot, *i.e.* "botrytized" grapes. The grapes for *Beerenauslese* wines are those that have been individually picked. These wines are typically very sweet and rich, and most age very well. The finest Beerenauslese wines are generally considered to be made from the Riesling grape variety, as this retains significant acidity even with the extreme ripeness, which results in a wine where the sweetness is balanced and which has great longevity and which often will improve for decades. These wines are produced in very small quantities when the weather is suitable for the noble rot to form and only in vineyards with appropriate conditions, so they tend to be very expensive.

An exception to this is Beerenauslesen produced from more eaily ripening grapes such as Ortega or Huxelrebe which have extremely high sugar content, but less noble rot character and less acidity, and therefore tends to come across as less elegant and usually without the potential to improve with cellaring. In Alsace, the term most closely corresponding to Beerenauslese is Sélection de Grains Nobles.

Requirements

The minimum must weight requirements for Beerenauslese is as follows:

- For German wine, 110 to 128 degrees Oechsle, depending on the region and grape variety.
- In Austrian wine, 25 degrees KMW, corresponding to 125 °Oechsle.

Chaptalisation may not be used. The requirements are part of the wine law in both countries. Many producers, especially top-level producers, exceed the minimum requirements, resulting in richer and sweeter wines that can exceed the minimum requirements for Trockenbeerenauslese, the next *Prädikat* in order. In Germany, it is common to add a golden capsule to indicate a superior wine.

BORDEAUX WINE OFFICIAL CLASSIFICATION OF 1855

The 57 appellations of Bordeaux are not classified in a single official ranking. But the Médoc, Sauternes and Barsac, Graves, and Saint-Emilion districts do have their own official internal classification systems. Pomerol, one of Bordeaux's greatest assets, was not included in the 1855 Classification, and remains unclassified to this day. However, Château Pétrus is often included with the First Growths of the 1855 Classification.

Much like our World's Fair today, Napoléon III's 1855 Expositon Universelle de Paris was a chance for France to display its very best for the world to see. The Gironde Chamber of Commerce requested that a classification system be devised to accompany their display of the fine wines of Bordeaux. The Bordeaux Wine Brokers' Union went to work on the project and came up with what we now refer to as the Classification of 1855.

They came up with a five-class ranking system of the red wines from the Médoc region, with the exception of Château Haut-Brion from Graves, which had to be included due to its renown. The white wines of Sauternes and Barsac were also included in a two-class ranking. The list reflected the market's view of the relative quality between the wines in terms of the selling price and reputation of the various châteaux. Within each category, the châteaux were ranked in order of quality — or selling price. Considering the fact that many châteaux have changed hands and with them the managment, thereby possibly effecting the quality of the wines for better or worse, the classification has held up remarkably well. The classification has only undergone one significant change in the last almost 150 years. By decree, on June 21, 1973, Château Mouton-Rothschild was promoted from a deuxieme cru to a premeir cru. At the same time, the premeir crus were to be listed in alphabetical order.

The 1855 Official Classification of the MÉDOC

First Growths (Premiers Crus) Commune:

- Château Lafite-Rothschild (Pauillac)
- Château Margaux (Margaux)
- Château Latour (Pauillac)
- Château Haut-Brion Pessac (Graves)
- Château Mouton-Rothschild (Pauillac)

Second Growths (Deuxièmes Crus) Commune:

- Château Rausan-Ségla (Margaux)

- Château Rauzan-Gassies (Margaux)
- Château Léoville-Las Cases (Saint-Julien)
- Château Léoville-Poyferré (Saint-Julien)
- Château Léoville-Barton (Saint-Julien)
- Château Durfort-Vivens (Margaux)
- Château Gruaud-Larose (Saint-Julien)
- Château Lascombes (Margaux)
- Château Brane-Cantenac Cantenac (Margaux)
- Château Pichon-Longueville-Baron (Pauillac)
- Château Pichon-Longueville, Comtesse de Lalande (Pauillac)
- Château Ducru-Beaucaillou (Saint-Julien)
- Château Cos d'Estournel (Saint-Estèphe)
- Château Montrose (Saint-Estèphe)

Third Growths (Troisièmes Crus) Commune:

- Château Kirwan Cantenac (Margaux)
- Château d'Issan Cantenac (Margaux)
- Château Lagrange (Saint-Julien)
- Château Langoa-Barton (Saint-Julien)
- Château Giscours Labarde (Margaux)
- Château Malescot Saint-Exupéry (Margaux)
- Château Boyd-Cantenac Cantenac (Margaux)
- Château Cantenac-Brown Cantenac (Margaux)
- Château Palmer Cantenac (Margaux)
- Château La Lagune Ludon (Haut-Médoc)
- Château Desmirail (Margaux)
- Château Calon-Ségur (Saint-Estèphe)
- Château Ferrière (Margaux)
- Château Marquis d'Alesme-Becker (Margaux)

Fourth Growths (Quatrièmes Crus) Commune:

- Château Saint-Pierre (Saint-Julien)
- Château Talbot (Saint-Julien)
- Château Branaire-Ducru (Saint-Julien)
- Château Duhart-Milon-Rothschild (Pauillac)
- Château Pouget Cantenac (Margaux)
- Château La Tour-Carnet Saint-Laurent (Haut Médoc)
- Château Lafon-Rochet (Saint-Estèphe)
- Château Beychevelle (Saint-Julien)
- Château Prieuré-Lichine Cantenac (Margaux)
- Château Marquis-de-Terme (Margaux)

Fifth Growths (Cinquièmes Crus) Commune:

- Château Pontet-Canet (Pauillac)
- Château Batailley (Pauillac)

- Château Haut-Batailley (Pauillac)
- Château Grand-Puy-Lacoste (Pauillac)
- Château Grand-Puy-Ducasse (Pauillac)
- Château Lynch-Bages (Pauillac)
- Château Lynch-Moussas (Pauillac)
- Château Dauzac Labarde (Margaux)
- Château Mouton-Baronne-Philippe (Pauillac)
- Château du Tertre Arsac (Margaux)
- Château Haut-Bages-Libéral (Pauillac)
- Château Pédesclaux (Pauillac)
- Château Belgrave Saint-Laurent (Haut-Médoc)
- Château de Camensac Saint-Laurent (Haut-Médoc)
- Château Cos-Labory (Saint-Estèphe)
- Château Clerc-Milon (Pauillac)
- Château Croizet-Bages (Pauillac)
- Château Cantemerle Macau (Haut-Médoc)

The Graves Classification

Other than Haut-Brion, the clasification of 1855 did not take into account the châteaux of Graves. It was first classified in 1953, but the classification did not became official until the 1959 ranking. The one class list is divided bewteen red wines and white wines, which means that some châteaux are described twice, once in each category. To avoid disputes the châteaux within each category, are not ordered by quality.

The 1959 Official Classification of the GRAVES

Classified Red Wines of Graves Commune:

- Château Bouscaut (Cadaujac)
- Château Haut-Bailly (Léognan)
- Château Carbonnieux (Léognan)
- Domaine de Chevalier (Léognan)
- Château de Fieuzal (Léognan)
- Château d'Olivier (Léognan)
- Château Malartic-Lagravière (Léognan)
- Château La Tour-Martillac (Martillac)
- Château Smith-Haut-Lafitte (Martillac)
- Château Haut-Brion (Pessac)
- Château La Mission-Haut-Brion (Talence)
- Château Pape-Clément (Pessac)
- Château Latour-Haut-Brion (Talence)

Classified White Wines of Graves Commune:

- Château Bouscaut (Cadaujac)

- Château Carbonnieux (Léognan)
- Château Domaine de Chevalier (Léognan)
- Château d'Olivier (Léognan)
- Château Malartic Lagravière (Léognan)
- Château La Tour-Martillac (Martillac)
- Château Laville-Haut-Brion (Talence)
- Château Couhins-Lurton (Villenave d'Ornan)
- Château Couhins (Villenave d'Ornan)
- Château Haut-Brion (Pessac) (added in 1960)

The St-Émilion Classification

Saint-Émilion was omitted from the 1855 classification. As a result, the local Wine Growers' Union decided to formally draw up a Classification of St-Émilion in 1955. It was to be revised every ten years to keep it from becoming to rigid and outdated. Although this is not happening on schedule, it has been revised twice, most recently in 1985.

The classification was based on soil, a tasting of the wine, and the reputation of the vineyard. Work on a new revision is being done now and should be published any time.

CRU (WINE)

Cru is a French wine term which means "growth place". More specifically, *cru* is often used to indicate a specifically named growth place, rather than any vineyard. The term is also used to refer to the produce of such a growth place, *i.e.*, the wine. The term *cru* is often used within classification of French wine. By implication, a wine which displays the name of its *cru* on its wine label is supposed to be a terroir wine characteristic of this *cru*. The terms *Premier Cru* and *Grand Cru* are often translated into English as First Growth and Great Growth.

Premier Cru

Premier Cru is a French language wine term corresponding to "First Growth", and which can be used to refer to classified vineyards, wineries and wines, with different meanings in different wine regions:

- For Bordeaux wine, the term is applied to classified wineries:
  - In the Bordeaux Wine Official Classification of 1855, *Premier cru* or *Premier cru classé* is the highest level of five within the "*Grand cru classé*" designation for red wines from the Médoc and Graves, and the second-highest of three in Sauternes where the highest is *Premier Cru Supérieur*. These wines are often referred to as First Growths in English.
  - In the Classification of Saint-Émilion wine, the highest level is

Premier grand cru classé A and the second-highest *Premier grand cru classé B*. The term *Saint-Émilion Grand cru* refers to wineries or wines below the overall *Grand cru classé* level, and is integrated within the appellation rules.

- For Burgundy wine, the term is applied to classified vineyards, with *Premier cru* being the second-highest classification level, below that of *Grand cru* and above the basic *village* AOCs. For Burgundy wines, the terms Premier Cru or 1er Cru are usually kept rather than being translated into English.

Grand Cru

Grand cru is a regional wine classification that designates a vineyard known for its favorable reputation in producing wine. Although often used to describe grapes, wine or cognac, the term is not technically a classification of wine quality per se, but is intended to indicate the potential of the vineyard or terroir. It is the highest level of classification of AOC wines from Burgundy or Alsace. The same term is applied to Châteaux in Saint-Émilion, although in that region it has a different meaning and does not represent the top tier of classification. In Burgundy the level immediately below grand cru is known as premier cru, sometimes written as 1er cru.

History in Burgundy

Early Burgundian wine history is distinctly marked by the work of the Cistercians with the Catholic Church being the principal vineyard owner for most of the Middle Ages. Receiving land and vineyards as tithes, endowments and as exchanges for indulgences the monks were able to studiously observe the quality of wines from individual plots and over time began to isolate those areas that would consistently produce wine of similar aroma, body, colour and vigour and designate them as *crus*.

CRU BOURGEOIS

The Cru Bourgeois classification lists some of the high quality wines from the Left Bank Bordeaux wine regions that were not included in the 1855 Classification of Classed Growths, or *Grands Crus Classés*. As the classification of Classed Growths had only one change since 1856, it came to be widely regarded as outdated, and many wine writers agree that there is considerable overlap in quality between the Classed Growths and the Cru Bourgeois.

The first Cru Bourgeois list was drawn up by the Bordeaux Chamber of Commerce and Chamber of Agriculture in 1932, selecting 444 estates for the classification. A 2003 revision of the classification was overturned by the French government in 2007, resulting in a ban of all use of the term, set to be lifted by 2009.

Classification

The 2003 Cru Bourgeois classification proposed a system of 247 wines classified in three tiers:

Crus Bourgeois Exceptionnels	Appellation
Château Chasse-Spleen	(Moulis-en-Médoc)
Château Haut-Marbuzet	(Saint-Estèphe)
Château Labégorce Zédé	(Margaux)
Château Les Ormes-de-Pez	(Saint-Estèphe)
Château de Pez	(Saint-Estèphe)
Château Phélan Ségur	(Saint-Estèphe)
Château Potensac	(Médoc)
Château Poujeaux	(Moulis-en-Médoc)
Château Siran	(Margaux)

(Total:9) Crus Bourgeois Supérieurs

(Total:87) Crus Bourgeois

(Total 151) As with any such classification system, there was controversy over these rankings, and some very highly regarded wines such as Château Gloria and Château Sociando-Mallet did not apply for classification.

Annulment

In February 2007, the French courts overturned the 2003 revision based on an appeal by dissatisfied producers. In essence the court ruled that four of the panel had conflicting interests, as owners of relevant wineries, and could not be seen as independent. Additionally, some vineyards were listed with both its *Grand vin* and second wine. The classification was at that point reverted to the 1932 classification, with the tiers Exceptionnel and Supérieur removed, and the original 444 estates equally classified Cru Bourgeois.

In July of that year, the suspension was officially amended and all use of the term Cru Bourgeois became illegal. As the 2005 vintages were already bottled and with further anticipated delays, the ruling was expected to be enforced starting with the 2007 vintage. The ban applies to all wines, also extending to those wineries in Sauternes, Côtes-de-Bourg and Blaye who use the term.

The Alliance des Crus Bourgeois responded by taking a new motion to the government, to create a new certification adopting the term *Label Cru Bourgeois* from the 2007 vintage to be released in 2009, "not as a classification, but as a mark of quality" open to all Médoc wines, based on production and quality standards.

In February 2008, however, a format for the classification to be reintroduced in 2009 was agreed by 180 estates from the defunct 2003 ranking, along with 95 new entrants. The revision demands that estates adhere to a new set of production rules and independent quality testing in order to remain in the classification, and at this stage the terms *Cru Bourgeois Supérieur* or *Cru Bourgeois Exceptionnel* would be no longer used.

DENOMINACIÓN DE ORIGEN

Denominación de Origen is part of a regulatory classification system primarily for Spanish wines but also for other foodstuffs like honey, meats and condiments. In wines it parallels the hierarchical system of France and Italy although Rioja and Sherry preceded the full system.

In foods it performs a similar role, namely regulation of quality and geographical origin among Spain's finest producers. There are five other designated categories solely for wine and a further three specifically covering food and condiments, all recognised by the European Union. In Catalonia, two further categories—Q and A—cover traditional Catalonian artisan food produce, but were not recognised by the EU as of 2007.The Spanish Ministry of Agriculture, Fisheries and Food regulates the quality of Spanish foodstuffs via a labelling system which establishes, among other things, a *Denominación de Origen* for the country's highest quality produce.

A semi-autonomous governing body exists for each region and for each food type, comprising skilled, impartial members who investigate the quality, ingredients and production process of each product, ensuring they attain specific quality levels.

They report to a central council at national government level but are normally based in the largest population centre of a given region and are responsible for enforcing its geographical limits. Products labelled *Denominación de Origen*, apart from being of superior quality, are expected to carry specific characteristics of geographical region or individual producer and be derived from raw materials originating within the region. Like most of these designations, a fundamental tenet of a DO label is that no product outside of that region is permitted to bear the name.

Product Types

Denominaciones de Origen status can be applied to a wide range of foods and condiments, specifically:

- Olive oil
- Rice
- Bread, cakes and pastries
- Cheese and butter Fresh meat
- Prepared meats and sausages
- Cured ham
- Fish, molluscs and crustaceans Vegetables
- Fruit
- Honey

- Condiments and spices Cider
- *VCPRD* wines
- *Vinos de la Tierra*
- Distilled alcoholic drinks

Quality foods may be designated a range of classifications, of which *Denominación de Origen* is the recognition of superior quality, with identifiable characteristics and specific ingredients, derived from an identifiable and verifiable source. Other classifications, not necessarily mutually exclusive, are as follows, under the general heading of *Alimentos de Calidad Diferenciada*:

- Denominación de Origen Protegida (DOP, or Protected Denomination of Origin)—An EU designation referring to food products specific to a particular region or town conveying a particular quality or characteristic of the designated area.
- Indicación Geográfica Protegida (IGP, or Protected Geographical Indicator)—Similar to DOP but relating to a wider, less specific, geographical region.
- Especialidades Tradicionales Garantizadas (ETG, or Traditional Specialty Guaranteed)—Products made using traditional ingredients, recipes or methods.
- Artisan Food Product Stamp (A)—Recognizing small, family-run food businesses with high quality, distinctive produce overseen by a qualified artisan (Catalonia only, not recognized by the EU).
- Food Quality Stamp (Q)—Foods with superior quality composition, production methods or presentation (Catalonia only, not recognized by the EU).
- Producción Agricultura Ecológica (PAE, or Organic Agricultural Production)—A stamp guaranteeing natural, environmentally-friendly production methods.

Wine

Wine region classification in Spain takes a quite complex hierarchical form in which the *Denominación de Origen* is a mid-range grading. As of 2009, Spain has over 120 identifiable wine regions under some form of geographical classification regulatory code which Spain formally adopted in 1986, upon accession to the EEC.

The Spanish appellation hierarchy for wines takes the following form:

- Denominación de Pago—Individual single-estates with an international reputation.
- Denominación de Origen Calificada: top-quality wine regions.
- Denominación de Origen—mainstream quality-wine regions.
- Vino de Calidad Producido en Región Determinada—less stringent regulation with specific geographical origin.

- Vinos de la Tierra—"country wine" areas which do not have EU QWPSR status but which may use a regional name.
- Vino de Mesa—Table wine, production of which has been in decline in recent years.

The 9 DO de Pago estates are:

- Dehesa del Carrizal;
- Dominio de Valdepusa;
- Finca Élez;
- Guijoso;
- Señorío de Arínzano;
- Prado de Irache;
- Otazu;
- Campo de la Guardia; and
- Pago Florentino.

The 2 DOCA/DOQ regions are:

- Priorat; and
- Rioja.

The more prominent DO regions include:

- Jumilla is a very successful DO producing notable wines from ungrafted, pre-phylloxera Monastrell vines.
- Campo de Borja has recently become more prominent. It features a number of cooperatives who produce Garnacha and Tempranillo.
- Jerez-Xérès-Sherry.
- Penedès is notable not only for the production of the sparkling wine Cava, but popular red wines from Tempranillo, Garnacha and Carinena grapes.
- Rías Baixas is known for its Albarino varietals, Spain's number one white wine. Other whites grown here include Treixadura, Loureira, Caino Blanco, and Torrontes. Popular red grapes in this region include Caino Tinto and Souson.
- Ribera del Duero challenges Rioja for the best red wines produced in Spain. Almost all of its wines are made from the Tempranillo grape.
- Rueda located west of Ribera del Duero, producing notable reds and whites typically less expensive than those of its more famous neighbours.
- Priorat and Rioja are the two highest-regarded wine producing regions in Spain and carry the special *Denominación de Origen Calificada*.
- Toro located between provinces of Zamora and Valladolid, along de River Duero, producing notable reds, from Tinta de Toro, a type of grape coming from Tempranillo.

DENOMINAZIONE DI ORIGINE CONTROLLATA

Denominazione di origine controllata is an Italian quality ensurance label for food products and especially wines. It is modelled after the French AOC. It was instituted in 1963 and overhauled in 1992 for compliance with the equivalent EU law on Protected Designation of Origin, which came into effect that year.

There are two levels of labels:

- *DOC*: Denominazione di Origine Controllata
- *DOCG*: Denominazione di Origine Controllata e Garantita

DOCG seal on a bottle of *Chianti Classico Riserva 1995* Both require that a food product be produced within the specified region using defined methods and that it satisfies a defined quality standard.

DOCG regions are subterritories of DOC regions that produce outstanding products that may be subject to more stringent production and quality standards than the same products from the surrounding DOC region.

The need for a DOCG identification arose when the DOC denomination was, in the view of many Italian food industries, given too liberally to different products. A new, more restrictive identification was then created, as similar as possible to the previous one so that buyers could still recognize it, but qualitatively different.

A notable difference for wines is that DOCG labelled wines are analysed and tasted by government–licensed personnel before being bottled. To prevent later manipulation, DOCG wine bottles then are sealed with a numbered governmental seal across the cap or cork.

Italian legislature additionally regulates the use of the following qualifying terms for wines:

- *Classico*: is reserved for wines produced in the region where a particular type of wine has been produced "traditionally". For the Chianti classico, this "traditional region" is defined by a decree from July 10, 1932.
- *Riserva*: may be used only for wines that have been aged at least two years longer than normal for a particular type of wine.

Wines labelled DOC or DOCG may only be sold in bottles holding at most 5 liters.

DENOMINAÇÃO DE ORIGEM CONTROLADA

The Denominação de Origem Controlada is the system of protected designation of origin for wines, cheeses, butters, and other agricultural products from Portugal.

Wines

Portuguese wine regions, as well as producers of several other products, established this system following Portugal's entry into the European Union in 1986. It is similar to the French *Appellation d'origine contrôlée*, the Italian *Denominazione di origine controllata* and the Spanish *Denominación de Origen* systems. The DOC system replaced the earlier *Região Demarcada* system of distinguishing Portuguese appellations developed in the early 20th century.

Regulation

In addition to protecting the designation of origin, the DOC also establishes regulations aimed at maintaining the quality level of the wines associated with a particular wine region. This includes establishing permitted grape varieties, regulating maximum yields at harvest, establishing minimum alcohol content, and periods of bottle or oak aging. Producers are required to submit finished wine samples to a regulating body to ensure compliance with DOC standards.

Other Levels

In addition to the top-level DOC designation, there are two secondary tiers: *Indicação de Proveniencia Regulamentada* and *Vinho Regional.* IPRs are similar to DOC "in training" and indicate regions that have established their own regulating bodies but have not yet established an internationally recognizable identity for their wines. It is similar to the French *Vin Délimité de Qualité Superieure* system. Vinho Regional is similar to the French *Vin de pays* and is sort of a "catchall" classification for wines that do qualify under the DOC or IPR designations.

EUROPEAN UNION WINE REGULATIONS

European Union wine regulations are common legislation related to wine existing within the European Union, the member states of which account for almost two-thirds of the world's wine production. These regulations form a part of the Common Agricultural Policy of EU, and regulate such things as the maximum vineyard surface allowed to individual EU member states, allowed winemaking practices and principles for wine classification and labelling. The wine regulations exist to regulate total production in order to combat overproduction of wine and to provide an underpinning to Protected designations of origin, among other things. In a sense, the wine regulations therefore try to protect both the producer and the consumer.

The EU wine regulations, as a part of CAP, do not include regulations on age limits for buying or drinking alcohol, regulations on wine advertising or retailing and other aspects of national social or public health policies of the individual EU member states.

While a large bulk of the text of the regulations is concerned with winemaking practices and the like, much of the history of the EU wine regulations has been linked to the issue of market imbalances and overproduction of wine.

In the early days of the CAP, the wine sector of the then-European Economic Community was in reasonable equilibrium for a rather short period of time. During this time, there were no regulations as to plantations and few interventions into the market, as this was not needed. However, the early post-World War II saw the introduction of many technological innovations within viticulture, which soon led to increased production, while the demand stayed constant. This resulted in a surplus of wine. The answer from EEC was to intervene in the market to make some guarantee as to sales, while still keeping the freedom to plant new vineyards, which aggravated rather than solved the problem of overproduction. While looking like a very illogical policy in hindsight, this was in keeping with the view that what the EEC was aiming to do was to balance variations in production from year to year.

After the realisation that the surplus was a structural one rather than a temporary variation, the wine regulations were changed to be more interventionist in 1978, with a ban on additional vineyard plantations, which means that a system of planting rights was introduced to regulate replantations. Also, requirements to distil the surplus wine into industrial alcohol were introduced, a procedure often referred to as "emergency distillation", although it has remained in force for decades.

At about the same time, domestic wine consumption of simpler wine qualities started to drop within the larger wine producing countries of Europe, making it even harder to return to the previous state of market equilibrium. From the 1980s, this has meant a marked reduction in the total demand, in terms of quantity, despite the fact that the wine-importing countries of northern Europe have increased their consumption.

Increasing wine exports from the New World, often in a style arrived at by market research rather than long tradition, also meant increased competition and changing tastes among wine consumers. As a result, the reduced total demand also included a shift in the demand towards higher quality level. Since it was realised that the vineyards in some locations would be unlikely to yield wines of the necessary quality, increased financial incentives for giving up vineyards, so-called grubbing-up schemes or vine pull schemes, were introduced in the late 1980s. This led to reduced overproduction, but a complete balance has so far never been achieved.

In the mid to late-1990s, much of CAP was overhauled and the legislation was simplified. A major revision was done in 1999, and it has been stated several times since then that the ambition is to phase out interventions such as emergency distillation, since they are "artificial outlets" for wine. However, this aim has proven difficult to achieve.

The latest round of reforms was announced in 2006 and led to agreed legal documents in 2008.

Some of the key points were:

- The system of planting rights to be abolished by 2015, with the possibility to keep them on a national level until 2018

- Distillation measures to be phased out after four years with progressively less money allowed to be allocated to these measures for each year.
- A three year voluntary grubbing-up scheme for up to 175,000 hectares of vineyards.
- Introduction of "national financial envelopes" whereby it becomes a national responsibility to choose the right balance of incentives.

Many of the reforms were less sweeping than what had initially been proposed, and the implementation of several items delayed.

Documents

The central document of the EU wine regulations is entitled Council Regulation on the common organisation of the market in wine and it is supplemented by several Commission regulations. The former document has been adopted by the Council of the European Union through the member states' ministers of agriculture, while the Commission regulations are written by the European Commission in collaboration with the Wine Management Committee, where the member states are represented.

Aspects Regulated

The aspects regulated by EU fall mainly into the categories winemaking practices, classification and labelling, wine-production potential, documentation of wine industry activities, imports from non-EU countries, and duties of enforcement agencies.

Classification and Labeling

The wines produced within EU are divided into two quality categories, Table wines and Quality Wines Produced in Specified Regions, where QWpsr is the higher category. Rules for winemaking practices and labelling are different for TW and QWpsr. The similar categories also exist for sparkling wine.

The TW and QWpsr categories are translated into different national wine classification for each member state. Thus, some member states may have more than two levels of classification, but all national levels correspond to either TW or QWpsr and are subject to the common minimum standards set out in the EU wine regulations.

As an example, France uses four levels of classification. *Vin de table* and *Vin de pays* are both EU Table wines, while *Vin Délimité de Qualité Supérieure* and *Appellation d'origine contrôlée* wines are QWpsr.

- Labelling information is divided into compulsory and optional information. Information not listed as part of either of these two categories may not be displayed on the bottle. To some extent, this information varies with the quality category.

- The labelling regulations include requirements for how grape varieties and vintage may be described on the label.
- Requirements and procedures for protected designations of origin for wine.
- Label indications of sweetness—from dry to sweet—are regulated in terms of which residual sugar levels they correspond to.
- Certain traditional bottle types may only be used for wines of certain origins; these are the Bocksbeutel and the Clavelin, as well as the Flûte d'Alsace, the use of which is only regulated within France.

Winemaking Practices

Perhaps most importantly, the regulations define wine as "the product obtained exclusively from the total or partial alcoholic fermentation of fresh grapes, whether or not crushed, or of grape must". Furthermore, wine can only be made from grape varieties listed as allowed, and only those vine varieties may be planted for commercial purposes. Each EU member state draws up such lists of varieties, which may only contain purebred *Vitis vinifera* varieties, and certain crosses between *V. vinifera* and other species of the *Vitis* genus. Thus, uncrossed so-called American vines, such as *Vitis labrusca*, may not be used for wine and are not allowed in EU vineyards.

Many winemaking practices depend on the classification of the wine—TW or QWpsr. Some practices also depend on where within EU the grapes are grown, since typical challenges to winemakers in colder or hotter climates are somewhat different. The definied European Union wine growing zones are used to regulate these practices, but some leeway is given for authorising deviations in vintages of exceptional climatic conditions.

- Minimum ripeness of grapes to be used for wine.
- Minimum alcohol content for wine, and maximum alcohol content of non-fortified wine.
- Chaptalisation and related forms of enrichment, the term used by the regulations. An upper limit is set, dependent on the wine growing zone, both on the extent of chaptalisation and the maximum alcohol level that may be achieved by chaptalisation.
- Deacidification, dependent on the wine growing zone.
- The use of sweet reserve, which is more restricted if the wine is also chaptalised.
- The amount of sulphur dioxide in the wine, the allowable amount of which depends on the colour and sweetness of wine.

EU Regulations and National Wine Laws

The reason why these regulations exist on the EU level is because of the common market inside the EU, which has led to a need to harmonise regulations for various products which traditionally have been regulated on a national level. The EU wine regulations form a framework for the wine laws of the European Union member states. Since national wine laws have a much longer history than the EU wine regulations, the EU regulations have been designed to accommodate existing regulations of several member states. In particular, the existing regulations concerning French wine, with its detailed appellation laws, formed a basis, while also making room for the very different German wine classification system. In general, the EU wine regulations provide for minimum standards across EU, while making it possible for individual member states to enact stricter standards in certain areas in their national wine laws.

An example comparing a French and two German wine types made from the same grape variety bring what the EU wine regulations stipulate, and how the individual countries have applied various stricter regulations than the minimum for these "quality wines".

Regulated aspect	EU regulation (minimum standard)	France: Alsace AOC labelled "Riesling"	German: Riesling Qualitätswein ("QbA")	German: Riesling Prädikatswein (e.g. a Kabinett)
Grape varieties	If the label indicates a single variety, minimum 85 per cent of that variety	100 per cent Riesling required	Minimum 85 per cent Riesling	Minimum 85 per cent Riesling
Minimum grape maturity required	Depends on wine growing zone. For Zone A, 5 per cent potential alcohol, for zone B, 6 per cent potential alcohol.	Minimum 8.5 per cent potential alcohol	Minimum grape maturity depends on the wine region, but is at least 6 per cent potential alcohol	Minimum grape maturity depends on the Prädikat and the wine region, but is at least 8.7 per cent potential alcohol
Chaptalisation	Maximum amount of chaptalisation depends on wine growing zone. For Zone A, corresponding to 3 per cent additional alcohol, for zone B, 2 per cent.	Generally allowed up to 2 per cent, but the regional committee may set a lower limit for a certain vintage	Chaptalisation allowed up to the maximum, up to 2 per cent additional alcohol in Baden and 3 per cent in the other regions	No chaptalisation allowed for any Prädikatswein

In a sense, the EU wine regulations as such are rather invisible to the wine consumers and the wine trade, since the details of quality classifications and labelling practices are generally part of the national wine laws, which provide the visible front-end.

EUROPEAN UNION WINE LABEL INFORMATION

The European Union is home to the world's largest wine economy with an average of 70 per cent of world production and 60 per cent of world consumption. Since the EU includes so many different countries with their own and unique wine laws and legislations, the general classification rules have been designed to maintain consistency across the entire economic zone. In simple terms, the wines produced within the EU fall under two broad categories—Table Wine and Quality Wine, which is technically known as Quality Wine Produced in a Specified Region. All levels of national wine classification systems within the EU correspond to either the TW or the QWPSR level.

Table wines are basically cheap blends made from wines sourced different regions. Most countries use a term in their official language to describe these wines like the French *Vin de Table*, German *Tafelwein*, Italian *Vino da Tavola* and so on. Typically, these wines are not permitted to disclose the region of production or the vintage on the labels.

The QWPSR on the other hand is a catch all term to denote wines of higher quality with protected geographical indications. To qualify as QWPSR, a wine has to pass the minimum standards of production methods, including vineyard practices and must come from one of the defined geographical locations. Every country has its own regulations regarding quality wines and the terms that appear on the labels fall within the EU laws as a framework. Some of the common QWPSR terms from the main producers are:

- *France*: 'AOP' Appellation d'Origin Protegée, formerly AOC where the 'origin' is the geographical location and 'VDQS' or Vin Délimité de Qualité Supérieure.
- *Italy*: 'DOCG' or Denominazione di Origine Controllata e Garantita and 'DOC' or Denominazione di Origine Controllata.
- *Spain*: 'DOCa' or Denominacion de Origen Calificada and 'DO' or Denominación de Origen.
- *Germany*: 'QmP' or Qualitätswein mit Prädikat and 'QbA' or Qualitätswein bestimmter Anbaugebiete. The higher level QmP wines are further classified to the level of ripeness of the grapes during harvest.

These are:

- *Kabinett*: Earliest harvested grapes among the QMP wines and are the driest.
- *Spätlese*: Means 'late harvest'.
- *Auslese*: Means 'select harvest'. Only the ripest grapes are selected during harvest.
- *Beerenauslese*: Means 'berry selection'. Individual berries that are affected by the Botrytis rot, shrivelled and hence are sweeter are picked later than Auslese wines.
- *Eiswein*: Means 'ice wine'. These wines are made from naturally frozen grapes. The water inside the berry freezes concentrating the sugar.
- *Trockeneerenauslese*: Means 'dry berry selection'. The berries that have been left on the vine for the longest period of time and have

naturally shrivelled to an extent that the sugar content as well as flavour components are highly concentrated, are used to make this wine. These are the sweetest and most expensive of all German wines.

- *Portugal*: 'DOC' or Denominacao de Origem Controlada.

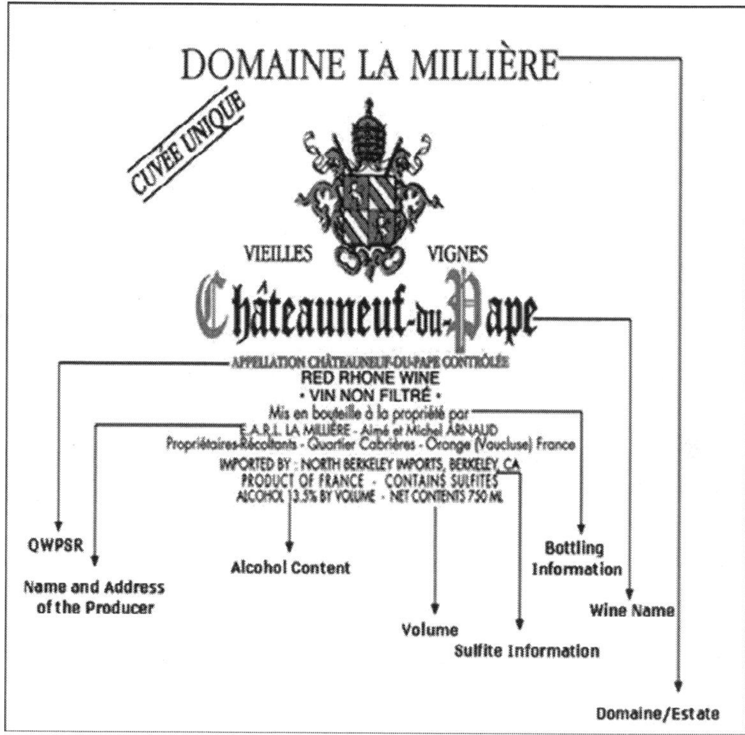

FIRST GROWTH

First Growth status refers to a classification of wines primarily from the Bordeaux region of France.

The Graves Classification

After the Second World War the omission of wines of Graves from the official classification was having a negative effect on the price and desirability of wines from the region. To improve marketing the region announced in 1953 its own classification of red wines and one white wine, with more white wines added in 1959.

Sixteen wines were given special classification:

- Château:Bouscaut (red and white)
- Château Carbonnieux (red and white)
- Château Couhins (white)
- Château Couhins-Lurton (white)

- Domaine de Chevalier (red and white)
- Château de Fieuzal (red)
- Château Haut-Bailly (red)
- Château Haut-Brion (red)
- Château La Mission Haut-Brion (red)
- Château La Tour Haut-Brion (red)
- Château Latour-Martillac (red and white)
- Château Laville Haut-Brion (white)
- Château Malartic-Lagravière (red and white)
- Château Olivier (red and white)
- Château Pape Clément (red)
- Château Smith Haut Lafitte (red)

The Saint-Émilion Classification

Missing from the 1855 list, the Bordeaux region of Saint-Émilion offered its own classification in 1955 to improve market demand and prices. The Classification of Saint-Émilion wine differs from the 1855 list in that it is updated approximately every ten years based on new assessments of quality. For each new release of the classification, wines may be promoted or demoted within the list. A wine may even be removed entirely, while other unclassified wines may be added. In 2006, for example, 11 wines were removed from the list, 6 new wines added, and 2 existing wines promoted to a higher division.

The Saint-Émilion Classification currently labels 15 wines as First Growths. These *Premiers Grands Crus Classés*, subdivided into two further classes: *A* and *B*. A further 55 wines are currently classified as *Grands Crus Classés*.

Premiers Grands Crus Classés A

- Château Ausone
- Château Cheval Blanc

Premiers Grands Crus Classés B

- Château Angélus
- Château Beauséjour (Duffau-Lagarrosse)
- Château Beau-Séjour Bécot
- Château Belair
- Château Canon
- Château Figeac
- Château La Gaffelière
- Château Magdelaine
- Château Pavie
- Château Pavie-Macquin
- Château Troplong Mondot

- Château Trottevieille
- Clos Fourtet

GERMAN WINE CLASSIFICATION

German wine classification consists of several quality categories and is often the source of some confusion, especially among non-German speaking wine consumers. The official classification is set down in the wine law of 1971, although some changes and amendments have been made since then. The classification is based on several factors, including region of origin, whether sugar has been added, and the ripeness of the grapes. The system is quite different from the French Appellation d'Origine Contrôlée system, or the systems in most other countries. In addition, German wine labels can be confusing for non-German speakers, although they give much information to those who are able to read them.

In recent years, the official classification has been criticised by many of the top producers, and additional classifications have been set down by wine growers' organisations such as VDP, without enjoying legal protection. The two main reasons for criticism are that the official classification does not differentiate between better and lesser vineyards and that the quality levels are less appropriate to high-quality dry wines.

An Overview of Categories

Two of the basic parameters in the classification of German wines is sweetness and quality. Wine quality is to some extent is a subjective judgement, and within the framework of any formal wine classification, different producers achieve very different results. However, the different quality categories used in classification of German wines are to some extent related to varying wine-making practices that generally are associated with different levels of quality:

- The EU category "quality wines" is by definition supposed to be superior to the category "table wines".
- A category that allows chaptalization is generally inferior to a category that does not allow chaptalization, if wines that are "true to terroir" are to be produced.
- A category that may only be produced in certain vineyard sites is generally superior to a category which may be produced anywhere.
- A category that requires the grapes or the wine to fulfill quality criteria that are so stringent that they can not be met by most vineyard sites in most vintages, can also be considered superior to categories which can be produced from almost any vineyard in almost any vintage.

Applying these distinctions to the categories in German wine classification gives the following overview. The table is primarily drawn up with wines produced from riesling grapes in mind.

Sweetness	Indicative sugar level	Typical quality level			
	grams per liter	Low	Medium	Medium to high	High
		Chaptalization allowed		Chaptalization not allowed	
		Table wine (EU)	Quality wine (EU)	From any vineyard in any vintage	Only from classified vineyards or Usually not possible to produce in any vineyard in any vintage
Intensely sweet	>150, sometimes >200				Trockenbeerenauslese (Eiswein)
Sweet	100-150				Eiswein Beerenauslese Auslese (Especially if Goldkapsel or *** has been added)
Semi-sweet	30-60	Tafelwein	QbA Liebfraumilch	Spätlese Kabinett	Auslese (Especially from Mosel) Erste Lage Spätlese Erste Lage Kabinett
Off-dry Can taste "internationally dry" if the acid level is sufficient	10-20	Tafelwein Landwein	QbA feinherb QbA halbtrocken Classic	Spätlese feinherb Kabinett feinherb Spätlese halbtrocken Kabinett halbtrocken	Auslese feinherb Auslese halbtrocken Charta
Dry	0-9	Landwein	QbA trocken Classic	Spätlese trocken Kabinett trocken	Grosses Gewächs Erstes Gewächs Erste Lage QbA Selection Auslese trocken

Quality Categories

The 1971 German wine law defines four overall quality categories:

1. *Deutscher Tafelwein*, or 'German table wine'

This is the equivalent to *vin de table*. It must be produced exclusively from allowed German-grown grape varieties in one of the five Tafelwine regions. Region or subregion must be indicated on the label. The grapes must reach a must weight of 44°Oe on the Oechsle scale in most regions, with the exception of Baden where 50°Oe must be reached. The alcohol content of the wine must be at least 8.5 per cent by volume, and concentration or chaptalization can be used to reach this level. They must reach a total acidity of at least 4.5 grams/ litre. *Tafelwein* can be a so-called Euroblend, a table wine made from grapes grown in several European countries.

2. *Deutscher Landwein*, or 'German country wine'

This is the equivalent to *vin de pays*, and was introduced with the 1982 harvest. Regulations are similar to those for Deutscher Tafelwein, but must come from one of the 19 Landwein regions, the grapes must reach 0.5 per cent higher potential alcohol, and the wine must be dry or off-dry in style, *i.e.* may not be semi-sweet. "Landwein" can also refer to German fruit wines.

3. *Qualitätswein bestimmter Anbaugebiete*, or quality wine from a specific region

These wines must be produced exclusively from allowed varieties in one of the 13 wine-growing regions and the region must be shown on the label.

The grapes must reach a must weight of 51°Oe to 72°Oe depending on region and grape variety. The alcohol content of the wine must be at least 7 per cent by volume, and chaptalization is allowed. QbA range from dry to semi-sweet, and the style is often indicated on the label. There are some special wine types which are considered as special forms of QbA. Some top-level dry wines are officially QbA although they would qualify as Prädikatswein. It should be noted that only *Qualitätswein* plus the name of the region, rather than the full term *Qualitätswein bestimmter Anbaugebiete* is found on the label.

4. *Prädikatswein*, recently renamed from *Qualitätswein mit Prädikat* (QmP)

The top level of the classification system. These prominently display a Prädikat from Kabinett to Trockenbeerenauslese on the label and may not be chaptalized. Prädikatswein range from dry to intensely sweet, but unless it is specifically indicated that the wine is dry or off-dry, these wines always contain a noticeable amount of residual sugar. Prädikatswein must be produced from allowed varieties in one of the 39 subregions of one of the 13 wine-growing regions, although it is the region rather than the subregion which is mandatory information on the label. The required must weight is defined by the Prädikat, and the alcohol content of the wine must be at least 7 per cent by volume for Kabinett to Auslese, and 5.5 per cent by volume for Beerenauslese, Eiswein and Trockenbeerenauslese.

Under the European Union wine quality grouping, Tafelwein and Landwein belong to the group of table wines, while QbA and Prädikatswein belong to the group of quality wines or VQPRD. In 2005, Tafelwein and Landwein only accounted for 3,6 per cent of total production, QbA 49,6 per cent and Prädikatwein 46,8 per cent. In most European countries, table wines make up a much higher proportion of the total production. While there are many German wines of excellent quality, the difference in comparison to other countries lie more in the national wine law and how it is applied by the growers. A case in point is Liebfraumilch, which foreign wine drinkers often see as the "simplest" German wine, but which is considered to be a special form of QbA and therefore a quality wine!

Prädikat Designations

The Prädikatswein category of the classification contains most high-quality German wines, with the exception of some top-quality dry wines. The different Prädikat designations differ in terms of the required must weight, the sugar content of the grape juice, and the level required is dependent on grape variety and wine-growing region and is defined in terms of the Oechsle scale. In fact the must weight is seen as a rough indicator of quality. The Prädikat system has its origin at Schloss Johannisberg in Rheingau, where the first Spätlese was produced in 1775 where wines received different colour seals based on their must weight.

The different Prädikat designations used are as followed, in order of increasing sugar levels in the must:

Kabinett: Fully ripened light wines from the main harvest, typically semi-sweet with crisp acidity, but can be dry if designated so.

Spätlesel—meaning "late harvest": Typically semi-sweet, often sweeter and fruitier than Kabinett. Spätlese can be a relatively full-bodied dry wine if designated so. While Spätlese means late harvest the wine is not as sweet as a dessert wine.

Auslese—meaning "select harvest": Made from selected very ripe bunches or grapes, typically semi-sweet or sweet, sometimes with some noble rot character. Sometimes Auslese is also made into a powerful dry wine, but the designation Auslese trocken has been discouraged after the introduction of Grosses Gewächs. Auslese is the Prädikat which covers the widest range of wine styles, and can be a dessert wine.

Beerenauslese—meaning "select berry harvest": Made from individually selected overripe grapes often affected by noble rot, making rich sweet dessert wine.

Eiswein: Made from grapes that have been naturally frozen on the vine, making a very concentrated wine. Must reach at least the same level of sugar content in the must as a Beerenauslese. The most classic Eiswein style is to use only grapes that are not affected by noble rot. Until the 1980s, the Eiswein designation was used in conjunction with another Prädikat but is now considered a Prädikat of its own.

Trockenbeerenauslese—meaning "select dry berry harvest" or "dry berry selection": Made from selected overripe shrivelled grapes often affected by noble rot making extremely rich sweet wines.

The minimum must weight requirements for the different Prädikat designations are as follows. Many producers, especially top-level producers, exceed the minimum requirements by a wide margin.

Prädikat	**Minimum must weight**	**Examples of requirements**		**Minimum alcohol level in the wine**
	Dependent on grape variety and wine-growing region	Riesling from Mosel	Riesling from Rheingau	
Kabinett	67-82°Oe	70°Oe	73°Oe	7 per cent
Spätlese	76-90°Oe	76°Oe	85°Oe	7 per cent
Auslese	83-100°Oe	83°Oe	95°Oe	7 per cent
Beerenausle se, Eiswein	110-128°Oe	110°Oe	125°Oe	5.5 per cent
Trockenbee -renauslese	150-154°Oe	150°Oe	150°Oe	5.5 per cent

This does not necessarily determine the sweetness of the final wine, because the winemaker may choose to ferment the wine fully or let some residual sugar remain.

Additional Designations

Wines can bear additional designation based on their sugar content or colour.

Sweetness of the Wine

The sugar content in the finished wine can be indicated by the following designations for QbA and Prädikatswein. For sparkling wines, many of the same designations are used, but have a different meaning.

Designation	**English translation**	**Maximum sugar level allowed**		
		Low acid wines	Medium acid wines	High acid wines
Trocken	Dry	4 grams per liter	Acid level in grams per liter + 2	9 grams per liter
Halbtrocken	Half-dry	12 grams per liter	Acid level in grams per liter + 10	18 grams per liter
Feinherb	Off-dry	Unregulated designation, slightly sweeter than halbtrocken		
Lieblich, mild or restsüss	Semi-sweet	Usually not specially marked as such on the label. Follows by default from their Prädikat in the absence of the above designations.		
Süss or edelsüss	Sweet	Usually not specially marked as such on the label. Follows by default from their Prädikat in the absence of the above designations.		

Colour

There are also colour designations that can be used on the label:

- *Weißwein—white wine*: May be produced only from white varieties. This designation is seldom used.
- *Rotwein—red wine*: May be produced only from red varieties with sufficient maceration to make the wine red. Sometimes used for clarification if the producer also makes rosés from the same grape variety.
- *Roséwein—rosé wine*: Produced from red varieties with a shorter maceration, the wine must have pale red or clear red colour.
- *Weißherbst—rosé wine or blanc de noirs:* A rosé wine which must conform to special rules: must be QbA or Prädikatswein, single variety and be labelled with the varietal name. There are no restrictions as to the colour of the wine, so they range from pale gold to deep pink.

Weißherbst wines also range from dry to sweet, such as rosé Eiswein from Spätburgunder.

Extra Ripeness or Higher Quality

Some producers also use additional designations to denote quality or ripeness level within a Prädikat. Especially for Auslese, which can cover a wide range of sweetness levels, the presence of any of these designations tends to indicate a sweet dessert wine rather than a semi-sweet wine. These designations are all unregulated.

Goldkapsel—gold capsule: A golden capsule or foil on the bottle. Denotes a wine considered better by the producer. Usually means a Prädikatswein that is sweeter or more intense, or indicates an auction wine made in a very small lot.

*Stars *, ** or ****: Usually means that a Prädikatswein has been harvested at a higher level of ripeness than the minimum required, and can mean that the wine is sweeter or more intense.

Fuder (vat) numbers: Usually indicated for better wines and often the numbers are arranged in some logical order, although the same numbers need not return in each vintage. This practice seems to be most common for semi-sweet and sweet wines in the Mosel region.

Special and Regional Wine Types

There are also a number of specialty and regional wines, considered as special version of some quality category.

Here are some of them:

- *Liebfraumilch or Liebfrauenmilch*: A semi-sweet QbA from the Rheingau, Nahe, Rheinhessen or Pfalz, consisting at least 70 per cent of the varieties Riesling, Müller-Thurgau, Silvaner or Kerner. In practice there is very little Riesling in Liebfraumilch since varietally labelled Riesling wines tend to fetch a higher price. Liebfraumilch may not carry a varietal designation on the label. Liebfraumilch is probably Germany's most notorious wine type, and is in principle a medium-quality wine designation although more commonly perceived to be a low-quality wine both at home and on the export market.
- *Moseltaler*: An off-dry/semi-sweet QbA cuvée from Mosel made from the following white grape varieties: Riesling, Müller-Thurgau, Elbling and Kerner. May not carry a varietal designation on the label, and sold under a uniform logotype. Must have a residual sugar of 15-30 grams per litre and a minimum acidity of 7 grams per litre. Basically a Liebfraumilch-lookalike from Mosel.
- *Riesling Hochgewächs—Riesling high growth*: A varietally pure Riesling QbA with at least 1.5 per cent higher potential alcohol than the minimum requirements for QbA in the region. Must also receive a higher grade in the mandatory quality testing.

- *Rotling*: A wine produced from a mixture of red and white varieties. A Rotling must have pale red or clear red colour
- *Schillerwein*: A Rotling from the Württemberg wine-growing region, which must be QbA or Prädikatswein.
- *Badisch Rotgold*: A Rotling from the Baden wine-growing region, which must be QbA or Prädikatswein. It must be made from Graubur-gunder and Spätburgunder and the varieties must be specified on the label.

New Classes for Dry Wines

There are three classes for dry wines with official status:

- *Classic*: Introduced with the 2000 vintage, Classic is in principle a dry or slightly off-dry QbA that conforms to slightly higher standards intended to make it food-friendly. It must be made from varieties considered classical in its region, have a potential alcohol of 1 per cent above the minimum requirements for its variety and region, and have an alcohol level of minium 12.0 per cent by volume, except in Mosel, where the minium level is 11.5 per cent. Maximum sugar level is twice the acid level, but no more than 15 grams per litre.
- *Selection*: In pricinple a Spätlese trocken from a selected site.
- *Erstes Gewächs*: a designation used only in Rheingau for top-level dry wines from selected sites.

The following designations are not official, but have become increasingly used in recent years:

- *Grosses Gewächs*: A designation used by VDP members in all regions except Mosel and Rheingau to designate top-level dry wines from selected sites. Used by the organisation Bernkasteler Ring for the same purpose in Mosel.
- *Erste Lage*: A designation used by VDP to denote selected sites suitable for Erstes Gewächs and Grosses Gewächs wines. Also used by VDP in Mosel in conjunction with a Prädikat to design top-level wines from these selected sites. Erste Lage QbA is used for the dry wines.
- *Charta Riesling*: A 100 per cent Rheingau Riesling of QbA or Prädikat quality with a residual sugar ranging from 9-18 grams/litre and a minimum acidity of 7.5 grams/litre. The wines must achieve higher starting must weights than required by law and undergo sensory testing by a special panel.

Historical Classifications no Longer in Use

Several terms went out of use with the 1971 wine law, but since many riesling wines can be successfully cellared for many decades, some of these designations may still be encountered on bottles.

Cabinet, or sometimes Kabinettwein: A better wine that has been set aside by the producer for later sale, corresponding to the use of the term Reserve in many countries. Often used in conjunction with a prädikat, so terms like "Trockenbeerenauslese Cabinet", which makes no sense whatsoever under the 1971 wine law, can be found on older bottles. The term Kabinett was not used in its later-day sense before the 1971 wine law.

Naturwein or Naturrein; natural wine or naturally pure: Designates a wine that has not been chaptalized. If no prädikat is used, it corresponds roughly to a post-1971 Kabinett, but can sometimes be drier.

Edelbeerenauslese: Corresponds to Trockenbeerenauslese. Strangely enough, although Edelbeeren means noble berries, and Trockenbeeren means dry berries, Edelbeerenauslese has been used for sun-dried grapes rather than grapes affected by noble rot. Eiswein Kabinett, Eiswein Spätlese, Eiswein Auslese, Eiswein Beerenauslese, Eiswein Trockenbeerenauslese: Before 1982, Eiswein was used together with another Prädikat, which denoted the must weight of the grapes before they froze. Since 1982, Eiswein is a Prädikat in its own right, with minimum must weights applied after freezing.

Geographic Classification

The geographic classification is different for Tafelwein, Landwein, QbA and Prädikatswein.

Geographic Classification for Tafelwein and Landwein

There are four Tafelwein regions: Rhein-Mosel, Bayern, Neckar and Oberrhein. These are divided into a number of subregions, which in turn are divided into 19 Landwein regions. Names of individual vineyards are not used for Tafelwein or Landwein.

Geographic Classification for QbA and Prädikatswein

There are four levels of geographic classification, and any level of classification can be used on the label of QbA and Prädikatswein:

- *Anbaugebiet*, wine growing regions, of which there are 13. Anbaugebiet is always indicated on the label of QbA and Prädikatswein.
- *Bereich*, district, of which there are 39. Each Anbaugebiet is divided into one or more Bereiche.
- *Großlage*, collective site, which is a collective name for a number of single vineyards, and which number about 170.
- *Einzellage*, single vineyard, of which there are about 2 600.

The names of Großlagen and Einzellagen are always used together with the name of a wine village, because some Einzellage names, such as *Schlossberg* are used in several villages. Unfortunately, it is not possible to tell a Großlage from an Einzellage just by looking at the wine label.

A few examples of how the names appear on labels:

- The vineyard Sonnenuhr in the village Wehlen along the Mosel is designated as Wehlener Sonnenuhr.
- The neighbouring village Zeltingen also has a vineyard called Sonnenuhr, and will appear on the label as Zeltinger Sonnenuhr.
- Both these vineyards belong to Großlage Münzlay, which is assigned to the village Wehlen. A wine from any of these vineyards, or a blend from both of them, can be sold under the name Wehlener Münzlay.
- These vineyards lie within Bereich Bernkastel, which provides an additional choice for labelling.
- It is also possible to simply label the wine as a wine from Anbaugebiet Mosel.

The are a few exceptions to the rule that a village must be indicated together with the vineyard name, those are a handful of historical vineyards known as *Ortsteil im sinne des Weingesetzes*. Examples are Schloss Johannisberg in Rheingau and Scharzhofberg along the Saar. They are of the same size as a typical Einzellage and could be thought of as Einzellagen which were so famous that they were excused from displaying the village name.

Labels

Additional information found on the label include the A.P. number, *Amtliche Prüfungsnummer*, which is the number documenting when and where the wine was given its classification.

CLASSIFICATION OF GRAVES WINE

The wines of Graves in the wine-growing region of Bordeaux were classified in 1953 by a jury appointed by Institute Nacional des Appellations d'Origine, and approved by the Minister of Agriculture in August of that year. The selection was revised with a few additions in February 1959. The classification concerns both red and white wines, and all chateaux belong to the appellation Pessac-Léognan, which eventually came into effect on September 9, 1987.

I.G.T.—INDICAZIONE GEOGRAFICA TIPICA

The new wine classification introduced in 1992 as a part of a general reorganization of the D.O.C. Italian wine law. I.G.T. was to be a new controlled quality level just below the D.O.C., to create a home for wines that, for many reasons, did not met the D.O.C., requirements, but had regional character.

Predictably, the introduction of the I.G.T. has been a mere sneeze as far as consumers are concerned — and a great example of a bureaucratic shell game. The creation of I.G.T., was made necessary by the inadequacies of the D.O.C., regulations and by the widespread revolt against them by many famous and politically powerful wine producers. These producers were being forced to give their top wines, often internationally styled ones that did not follow D.O.C., rules, the lowly Vino da Tavola designation.

Vino da Tavola had been the catch-all category for everyday wines until the super-Tuscan revolution hit Chianti and Maremma. Famous wines like Le Pergole Torte, Tignanello, and Sassicaia, which did not meet D.O.C., requirements, had to compete internationally against the world's finest wines with this common name on their labels. To further confuse the matter, the phrase "table wine" in the US is a legal designation set by the government to denote all wines of less than 14.5 per cent alcohol.

The end result is that I.G.T. has basically replaced the Vino da Tavola category for exported wines and does not provide much more of a guarantee of quality than Vino da Tavola did. Aa-choo!

There are oceans of "Veneto I.G.T." wine arriving in the USA now so let's look at those regulations. The wines can be white, red, or rose produced in lightly sparking or novella style. There are 39 permitted grape varieties and the grapes can come from any of 7 provinces. Pretty demanding requirements, right? So now exceptional wines made by great Veneto producers like Anselmi and Inama still carry the same designation as bulk wines made at the cooperatives. Exactly the same situation as before. To be fair the I.G.T., regulations are more stringent than those for Vino da Tavola and they do restrict the wine named to be at least of a defined region, while Vino da Tavolo could be produced from wines produced anywhere in Italy — and sometimes Italy seemed to mean the borders of the Roman Empire. However, the reality of the situation is that I.G.T. is a shallow marketing tool: a fancier name for almost the same thing.

I.G.T., wines are basically divided into three groups, all labeled the same: industrial grade, good solid country wines, and hyper-expensive superstars. One can't tell the players without a scorecard. Unfortunately, price is the first giveaway. Neil Empson offers Monte Antico, a reliable value in I.G.T. Toscano. What makes this wine reliable is the Empson name on the bottle. This same is true also for a wine like Castel di Salve, Santi Medici, Salento I.G.T. imported by Vin Divino, another very reliable importer. There are many poor Salento I.G.T. and Toscano I.G.T. wines, but when selected by a dedicated importer one have a much better chance of finding a good wine, and a good value.

Italian wine law is bursting at the seams from its own rich diet. Italy is overwhelmed by excellent wines, but they just don't fit well into the few categories and the constrictions of D.O.C.G., D.O.C. and I.G.T.

KABINETT

Kabinett or sometimes Kabinettwein is a German language wine term for a wine which is made from fully ripened grapes of the main harvest, typically picked in September, and are usually made in a light style. In the German wine classification system, Kabinett is the lowest level of *Prädikatswein*, lower in ripeness than Spätlese. A German Kabinett is semi-sweet by default, but may be dry or off-dry if designated so.

In Austria, Kabinett is subcategory of *Qualitätswein* rather than a *Prädikatswein*, and the term always designates a dry wine.

The term Kabinett, originally often written as Cabinet initially signified a better wine that has been set aside by the producer for later sale, corresponding to the use of the term Reserve in many countries. The term originated with the cistercian monks at Eberbach Abbey in Rheingau, where the first recorded use of the term Cabinet occurred in 1712. The abbey's best wines were set aside to be stored in a special cellar built in 1245, and it was later known as the Cabinet cellar, or *Cabinet-Keller*.

In the 1971 German wine law, Kabinett was given its current meaning of the "lightest" non-chaptalized wines, which is quite different from its origins as a reserve wine. Before 1971, the term Cabinet or Kabinett was often used in conjunction with a Prädikat, so terms like "Trockenbee-renauslese Cabinet", which makes no sense whatsoever under the 1971 wine law, can be found on older bottles.

The pre-1971 German wine term most closely corresponding to post-1971 Kabinett was Naturwein or Naturrein, which designated a non-chaptalised wine, where no other designation, such as Spätlese or Auslese, applied.

Requirements

The minimum must weight requirements for Kabinett is as follows, and the requirements are part of the wine law in both countries:

- In German wine, 67 to 82 degrees Oechsle, depending on the region and grape variety. Just as for other Prädikatsweine, Chaptalisation may not be used.
- In Austrian wine, 17 degrees KMW, corresponding to 85 °Oechsle. The alcohol content may be maximum 13 per cent, the residual sugar a maximum of 9 grams per litre, and the wines may not be chaptalized, which is an exception from the rules for other *Qualitätsweine*.

Style of German Kabinett Wine

Since Kabinett wines may not be chaptalized, in difference to German Qualitätswein and lower categories, they tend to be the German wines lowest in alcohol, despite the fact that the requirements on the grapes are higher than for QbA. The lightweight elegance of these wines are the most pronounced in Kabinett from the colder German wine regions, such as Mosel, and in wines made from the grape variety Riesling, which dominates many of the coldest

German regions. Typically, a Riesling Kabinett from Mosel shows a high acidity and flowery aromas together with hints of slate and minerality. For semi-sweet wines the alcohol level can be 7-8 per cent, and for dry Kabinett perhaps 10-11 per cent.

For other combinations of regions and grape varieties, the situation may be different. For example, a dry Kabinett made in Baden or the Palatinate made from Pinot varieties can easily reach 13 per cent alcohol.

Though these many of the classical German Kabinett wines may best be enjoyed in their youth, some better examples can be aged for 10 years or more.

LANGTON'S CLASSIFICATION OF AUSTRALIAN WINE

Langton's Classification of Australian Wine first released in 1991, is a grouping of high-end Australian wines compiled by the Melbourne- and Sydney-based auction house Langton's. The Classification is a ranking of the best performing wines based on market demand and vintages made. The Langton's Classification is split into four categories; Exceptional, Outstanding, Excellent and Distinguished. The classification is currently made up of 101 of Australia's finest wines, to be listed in the Classification a wine must have a minimum of ten vintage years and also achieve high secondary market values.

- *Exceptional*: Most highly sought after and prized Australian wines on the market
- *Outstanding*: Benchmark quality wines with a strong market following
- *Excellent*: High performing wines of exquisite quality achieving slightly lower market strength
- *Distinguished*: Popular secondary market or emerging classics, sometimes undervalued by the market.

LIEU-DIT

Lieu-dit is a French wine term which in its typical usage translates as "vineyard name" or "named vineyard". Typically, a *lieu-dit* is the smallest piece of land which has a traditional vineyard name assigned to it. In most cases, this means that a *lieu-dit* is smaller than an *appellation d'origine contrôlée* (AOC).

In some cases, *lieux-dits* appear on wine labels, in addition to the AOC name. This is most commonly seen for Alsace wine and Burgundy wine. It may not always be easy for consumers to tell if a name on a wine label is a *lieu-dit* or a cuvée name created by the producer.

The only case of mandatory mention of a *lieu-dit* is in Alsace, for Alsace Grand Cru AOC. The Grand Cru designation may only be used if a *lieu-dit* is indicated. *Lieux-dits* may also be indicated on regular Alsace AOC wines, but is not mandatory.

In Burgundy, the term *climat* is used interchangeably with *lieu-dit*. The use of the *lieu-dit* varies with the level of classification of the wine. Although the Grand Cru burgundies are in generally considered to be classified on the vineyard level and defined as separate AOCs, some Burgundy Grand Crus are in fact divided into several *lieux-dits*. For village level burgundies, the *lieu-dit* may only be indicated in smaller print than the village name to avoid confusion with Premier Cru burgundies, where the village and vineyard name are indicated in the same size print.

In Rhône, *lieux-dits* are most commonly seen for some of the top wines of the region. An example is the *lieu-dit* La Mouline within Côte-Rôtie.

ST EMILION CLASSIFICATION

The 1855 classifications of the Médoc and Sauternes did not even take into account the ancient domaines of Graves, just to the south of Bordeaux, so it is perhaps not surprising that the numerous estates around Libourne, some way to the east on the right bank of the Dordogne, were similarly excluded. Nearly a century had passed before the *Syndicat Viticole* considered the creation of a St Emilion classification to be a worthwhile undertaking, and indeed the fruit of their subsequent labours was published exactly one hundred years after the more famous classification of the chateaux of the left bank.

The *Syndicat Viticole* began to lay out plans for the classification as early as 1930, but it did not really take shape until the INAO agreed to oversee its creation, beginning with a governing decree published on October 7th, 1954. The system laid out was for two broad categories, the upper tier being *Premier Grand Cru Classé* and the lower being *Grand Cru Classé*. The classification they devised would depend on submitted requests for inclusion, rather than the system in 1855 where properties were ranked by local merchants, and the ranking would be based on a tasting of ten vintages from the estate in question rather than pure market value, which was the key factor one hundred years before. Crucially, it would be open to reassessment every ten years or so, setting it apart from the seemingly immutable 1855 classifications.

The initial classification was published on the 16th June 1955 and subsequently amended by decree the following August and October, the final list having 12 properties ranked as *Premier Grand Cru Classé* and 63 as *Grand Cru Classé*. The system was then revised in 1969, and again in 1986 and 1996, by which time the number of properties in the top tier was very similar at 13, but the second group had contracted somewhat, down to just 55. The most recent revision in 2006, however, saw the numbers at the top swell to 15, and lower down the numbers decreased even further to 46.

Controversy in 2006

There were eleven properties demoted from the *Grand Cru Classé* rung in the 2006 revision. For the sake of completeness it is worth noting that two other properties also disappeared, although not through demotion; these were

Chateau Curé-Bon, which was purchased by the Chanel team and subsequently absorbed into Chateau Canon in 2000, and Chateau La Clusière, which in a similar fashion was absorbed into a greater name, in this case Chateau Pavie.

Those that were demoted, however, were as follows:

- Chateau Bellevue
- Chateau Cadet-Bon
- Chateau Faurie-de-Souchard
- Chateau Guadet St-Julien
- Chateau La Marzelle
- Chateau Petit-Faurie-de-Soutard
- Chateau Tertre-Daugay
- Chateau La Tour-du-Pin-Figeac
- Chateau La Tour-du-Pin-Figeac
- Chateau Villemaurine
- Chateau Yon-Figeac

It was these demotions that were responsible for what was perhaps the greatest and certainly the most surprising controversy ever to beleaguer any Bordeaux classification, even though the 2006 revision came only three years after a hotly disputed reclassification of the Cru Bourgeois chateaux of Bordeaux. A number of proprietors listed before, who all faced demotion from the *Grand Cru Classé* ranking, in particular the owners of Chateau Cadet-Bon, Chateau Guadet St-Julien, Chateau La Tour du Pin Figeac and Chateau La Marzelle, decided to take the *Syndicat Viticole* to court over the new listing. It seemed as though they had a strong case, as an inspection of the credentials of the members of the INAO panel allegedly suggested lack of impartiality, and an administrative tribunal in Bordeaux was quick to suspend the classification pending review, leaving all the chateaux of the appellation, including greats such as Ausone and Cheval-Blanc, effectively without any formal ranking at all.

The stuttering resolution to this situation began in November 2007, when the Conseil d'Etat, the highest administrative court in France, ended the suspension having stated that this prior action had no legal justification. Although the inferences of the court did not dismiss the issues raised by the four complainants, it did state that they were not of a nature that warranted the permanent annulment of the classification. So it seemed as though the 2006 classification would stand, that was until it was again deemed void by a court in Bordeaux in July 2008.

Then in a bizarre development the following week the court, under pressure from the INAO, effectively reinstated the 1996 classification, to be applicable to the 2006-2009 vintages. This was of course great news for the four properties that brought the action, represented in court by lawyer Philippe Thévenin, but it was a grave disappointment for those that had benefited from the new system, namely those estates that had been promoted, and with this new development now saw themselves pushed back to their 1996 standings. This latter point was the next to be addressed in this complex clean-up, a process that was looking more and more like prolonged damage limitation than anything like a wine classification. A finance law amendment submitted by senators Gérard César and Philippe Dominati in December 2008 would have allowed the estates that missed out on the 2006 promotions to regain their new positions. So Pavie-Macquin and Troplong-Mondot would return to *Premier Grand Cru Classé* level, while Bellefond-Belcier, Destieux, Fleur-Cardinale, Grand Corbin and Grand Corbin-Despagne would regain the *Grand Cru Classé* accolade. In January 2009 the case, which was based on an argued loss of revenue, was thrown out. The 1996 classification was standing firm, and in March 2009 the French Court of Appeal hammered the final nail in the coffin of the 2006 ranking with a terminal judgement, ending any hope that it could be revived. Well, maybe....

The only workable solution was to find a ranking that would keep everybody content; reinstate the promoted chateaux to their new rankings, but conveniently overlook the fact that a number of properties should/would/could have been demoted. In truth it makes a farce of the classification, but no more so that the legal disputes that have been slowly strangling the system for the last three years. It was what the December 2008 law would have achieved, but clearly the government council that dismissed it failed to realise that. In May 2009, however, a new law concerning the classification was passed, with a convenient footnote reinstating the previously promoted chateaux within the 1996 classification. Result? The promoted are promoted and are thus happy, the demoted haven't been demoted after all and are thus happy, and everybody can get on with making wine.

Until the next time, of course, which is guaranteed to come. The current state of play—the 1996 classification with 2006 promotions superimposed—remains legal until 2011, when it must be reviewed.

St Emilion 1996 Classification with 2006 Promotions

The following is valid until 2011. The 2006 promotions are marked by *, those that escaped demotion through maintaining the 1996 listing by †. Note during this process two chateaux have been renamed, namely Belair, now part of the Moueix portfolio and rechristened Bélair-Monange, and also the La Tour-du-Pin-Figeac portion that belonged to the Giraud-Bélivier family and which was to have been demoted in 2006. This property is now under the same administration as neighbour Cheval-Blanc, and no doubt to reduce confusion with Figeac, another near neighbour, has been renamed La Tour-du-Pin.

Premiers Grands Crus Classés—A:

- Chateau Ausone
- Chateau Cheval-Blanc

Premiers Grands Crus Classés—B:

- Chateau Angélus
- Chateau Beau-Séjour Bécot
- Chateau Beauséjour
- Chateau Bélair-Monange
- Chateau Canon
- Chateau Figeac
- Clos Fourtet
- Chateau La Gaffelière
- Chateau Magdelaine
- Chateau Pavie
- Chateau Pavie-Macquin*
- Chateau Troplong-Mondot*
- Chateau Trottevieille

Grands Crus Classés:

- Chateau L'Arrosée
- Chateau Balestard-La-Tonnelle
- Chateau Bellefont-Belcier*
- Chateau Bellevue†
- Chateau Bergat
- Chateau Berliquet
- Chateau Cadet-Bon†
- Chateau Cadet-Piola
- Chateau Canon-la-Gaffelière
- Chateau Cap-de-Mourlin
- Chateau Chauvin
- Chateau La Clotte
- Chateau Corbin
- Chateau Corbin-Michotte
- Chateau La Couspaude
- Couvent des Jacobins
- Chateau Dassault
- Chateau Destieux*
- Chateau La Dominique
- Chateau Faurie-de-Souchard†
- Chateau Fleur-Cardinale*
- Chateau Fonplégade
- Chateau Fonroque
- Chateau Franc-Mayne
- Chateau Grand-Corbin*
- Chateau Grand-Corbin-Despagne*
- Chateau Grand-Mayne

- Chateau Grand-Pontet
- Chateau Les Grandes-Murailles
- Chateau Guadet St-Julien†
- Chateau Haut-Corbin
- Chateau Haut Sarpe
- Clos des Jacobins
- Chateau Laniote
- Chateau Larcis-Ducasse
- Chateau Larmande
- Chateau Laroque
- Chateau Laroze
- Chateau La Marzelle†
- Chateau Matras
- Chateau Monbousquet*
- Chateau Moulin-du-Cadet
- Clos de l'Oratoire
- Chateau Pavie-Decesse
- Chateau Petit-Faurie-de-Soutard†
- Chateau Le Prieuré
- Chateau Ripeau
- Chateau St-Georges-Côte-Pavie
- Clos St-Martin
- Chateau La Serre
- Chateau Soutard
- Chateau Tertre-Daugay†
- Chateau La Tour-du-Pin†
- Chateau La Tour-du-Pin-Figeac†
- Chateau La Tour Figeac
- Chateau Villemaurine†
- Chateau Yon-Figeac†

Besides the Classifications

Beyond the *Premier Grand Cru Classé* and the *Grand Cru Classé* properties of the St Emilion classification, there are many unclassified properties which may bear the grand sounding accolade of *Grand Cru* on the label. As a final point of interest in this rundown of the St Emilion ranking, one should make clear that this is not part of the classification. The distinction between a chateau that describes itself as *Grand Cru*, and one that does not, is a differentiation enshrined in appellation law. It does not necessarily denote a wine of great quality or from exalted *terroir*, and as such the term is rather a misnomer. Nevertheless, there are good wines to be found at this level if one knows where to look; estates such as Teyssier and Faugères do at least deserve a mention.

SPÄTLESE

Spätlese is a German language wine term for a wine from fully ripe grapes, the lightest of the late harvest wines. Spätlese is a riper category than Kabinett in the *Prädikatswein* category of the German wine classification and is the lowest level of *Prädikatswein* in Austria, where Kabinett is classified in another way. In both cases, Spätlese is below Auslese in terms of ripeness. The grapes are picked at least 7 days after normal harvest, so they are riper and have a higher must weight. Because of the weather, waiting to pick the grapes later carries a risk of the crop being ruined by rain. However, in warm years and from good sites much of the harvest will reach Spätlese level.

The wines may be either sweet or dry; it is a level of ripeness that particularly suits rich dry wines from Riesling, Weißer Burgunder and Grauer Burgunder grapes for example, as at Auslese levels the alcohol levels may become very high in a dry wine leaving the wine unbalanced, making wines with at least some residual sweetness preferable to most palates. However, most German wines are traditionally dry. Dry German wines can be very balanced and usually get higher rates from German wine journalists than a comparable wine with more sugar.

Many Spätlese wines will age well, especially those made from the Riesling grape.

Characteristics

- Greater Intensity and strength than Kabinett
- High level of acidity that curbs any overt sweetness
- Fleshy and intensely flavoured
- Often tastes of apple, pear and honeysuckle
- Elegant nose with highly detectable aromas

Requirements

The minimum must weight requirements for Spätlese are as follows:

- In German wine, 76 to 90 degrees Oechsle, depending on the region and grape variety.
- In Austrian wine, 19 degrees KMW, corresponding to 95 °Oechsle.

Chaptalisation may not be used. The requirements are part of the wine law in both countries. Many producers, especially top-level producers, regularly exceed the minimum requirements.

TABLE WINE

Any wine that isn't FORTIFIED or SPARKLING. 2. In the United States, the official definition for table wine is a wine that contains a minimum of 7 per cent alcohol and a maximum of 14 per cent. This definition does not define quality in any way, although some connote table wine with lower-quality, inexpensive wine. That's a mistake because many wines that simply say "Red Table Wine" or "White Table Wine" are excellent and not at all inexpensive. 3. The EUROPEAN UNION has developed a meaning that indentifies table wine as something that doesn't qualify as a quality wine under the various APPELLATION rules. In most cases, this means that table wine is probably of lower quality, but some independent producers feel the appellation rules are too restrictive. They produce some very high-quality wines labeled as table wine that just don't happen to be made exactly as the rules dictate. European synonyms for table wine include Germany's DEUTSCHER TAFELWEIN France's VIN DE TABLE Italy's VINO DA TAVOLA Portugal's VINHO DE MESA and Spain's VINO DE MESA.

THE LIV-EX BORDEAUX CLASSIFICATION

The Liv-ex Bordeaux Classification is a classification of Bordeaux wine compiled by the British internet and phone-based wine exchange, London International Vintners Exchange in March 2009, with an aim to recreate the Bordeaux Wine Official Classification of 1855 in a modern economic context, 154 years after the original compilation.

Based entirely on the level of prices, with the criteria of wines to be from the Left Bank and be produced in quantities of more than 2,000 cases, and not taking into account any second wines, the Liv-ex classification lists 60 estates, one less than that of 1855. The tiers were sectioned by the First Growths in the range of £2,000 a case and above, the Second Growths from £500 to £2,000, the Third Growths from £300 to £500, the Fourth Growths from £250 to £300 and the Fifth Growths from £200 to £250. The price averages were calculated from the period 2003–2007.

Among the chief differences from the 1885 classification is the placement of Château La Mission Haut-Brion among the First Growths, Château Lynch-Bages elevated from the fifth tier to the second, Château Palmer promoted a tier to become the top Second Growth, and while there are nine additions to the list, ten wines are removed.

Jack Hibberd of Liv-ex stated that the second wines of the estates were a complicating factor, "They obviously didn't exist in 1855, so we decided to classify each property on the basis of their first wine. It is interesting to note, however, that if they were included as separate chateaux, 12 would make the cut, with Carruades de Lafite and Forts de Latour reaching the level of second growths."

TROCKEN

Trocken is the German word for dry, and used within the classification of German wine. It is used on wine labels to indicate those which are dry rather than off-dry, sweeter or sweet. Technically trocken wines are not completely devoid of residual sugar, but have at most a few grams per litre, a level which can be perceptible but is not overtly sweet. Trocken is also used as a designation for Austrian wine, but more rarely than in Germany, since many quality categories of Austrian wines are dry by default.

Somewhat confusingly, for *Sekt* and other sparkling wines, *trocken* indicates a higher level of sugar than it does for non-sparkling wines. A *Sekt trocken* is best described as off-dry or semi-sweet, while a *Sekt brut* is completely dry.

Requirements

The maximum amount of sugar allowed for a *trocken* designation depends on the level of acid in the wine. For wine low in acid, a maxium of 4 grams per litre sugar is allowed. If the acid level exceeds 2 grams per litre, the sugar may exceed the acid level by 2 grams per litre, up to a maximum of 9 grams of sugar per litre. Most high-quality German white wines have a high enough acidity to be allowed up to 9 grams per litre of sugar under the *trocken* level. When used, the requirements in Austria are exactly the same.

Sparkling Wines

When used for sparkling wine, the term *trocken* actually means 17 to 35 grams per litre of sugar. This parallels the use of the term *sec* in French, which indicates a sparkling wine of the same sugar level as *trocken*. Drier wines are designated *extra trocken* at 12 to 20 grams of sugar per litre, while completely dry sparkling wines are given the designation *brut* or *extra brut*.

TROCKENBEERENAUSLESE

Trockenbeerenauslese is a German language wine term for an intensely sweet dessert wine-style wine.

Trockenbeerenauslese is the highest category in the *Prädikatswein* category of the Austrian and German wine classifications. *Trockenbeerenauslese* wines, often called "TBA" for short, are made from individually selected grapes affected by noble rot, *i.e.* "*botrytized*" grapes.

This means that the grapes have been individually picked and are shrivelled with noble rot, often to the point of appearing like a raisin. They are therefore very sweet and have an intensely rich flavour, frequently with a lot of caramel and honey bouquet, rock fruits note such as apricot and distinctive aroma of the noble rot. The finest examples are made from the Riesling grape, as this retains plenty of acidity even at the extreme ripeness. Other grape varieties are also used, such as Scheurebe, Ortega, Welschriesling, Chardonnay, and *Gewürztraminer* and many are more prone to noble rot than Riesling since they ripen earlier.

These wines are rare and expensive due to the labour-intensive method of production, and the fact that very specific climatic conditions are required to create botrytized grapes. Some of the best wines of this type are sold almost exclusively at the various German wine auctions. They are usually golden to deep golden in colour, sometimes even dark caramel. The body is viscous, very thick and concentrated, and arguably can be aged almost indefinitely due to the preservative powers of its high sugar content. Although TBA has very high residual sugar level, the finest specimens are far from being cloying due to high level of acidity.

Trockenbeerenauslesen have also been in common production since the 1960s in Austria. Most TBA wines from Austria come from Neusiedlersee, Burgenland. On both sides of lake Neusiedl those wines are produced. East of the lake, the village of Illmitz is known for the production of "liquid gold". At the western side of the lake in Rust and St. Margarethen, wine of exceptionally good quality can be found. This region is known for its wide and shallow lakes which can lose more than half their volume due to evaporation. The mists created by these lakes provide a very conducive climate for Noble Rot to shrivel grapes.

The style is similar to, but much more concentrated than, *Sélection de Grains Nobles* from Alsace.

In comparison to Sauternes, the wines are considerably sweeter, have a lower alcoholic strength and are usually not oaked.

As with most other premium grade dessert wines, *Trockenbeerenauslese* is to a large extent sold in half bottles of 375 ml.

The minimum must weight requirements for Trockenbeerenauslese is as follows:

- For German wine, 150 to 154 degrees on the Oechsle scale, depending on the region and grape variety.
- In Austrian wine, 30 degrees KMW, corresponding to 154 °Oechsle.

The requirements are part of the wine law in both countries. Many producers, especially top-level producers, exceed the minimum requirements, resulting in richer and sweeter wines. In Germany it is common to add a golden capsule to indicate a superior wine. The sweetness of a TBA that just comes up to the minimum requirements may be 150 grams per litre, but in exceptional circumstances, the wines may contain more than 300 grams of sugar per litre and may approach the very rare *Tokaji Eszencia* in concentration.

VIN DÉLIMITÉ DE QUALITÉ SUPÉRIEURE

Vin Délimité de Qualité Supérieure usually abbreviated as VDQS, is the second highest category of French wine, below *Appellation d'Origine Contrôlée* in rank, but above *Vin de pays*. VDQS is sometimes written as AOVDQS, with AO standing for *Appellation d'Origine*. VDQS wines are subject to restrictions on yield and vine variety, among others.

There are relatively few VDQS, as they typically move onto AOC status after a number of years, so VDQS represents a small part of the total French wine production. In 2005, VDQS wines made up 0.9 per cent of the total wine production, which meant 409,472 hectoliter. 42.3 per cent of the VDQS wines produced in that year were white, with 57.7 per cent being either red or rosé. By 2011, the VDQS category will be eliminated altogether.

VIN DE PAYS

Vin de pays is a French term meaning “country wine”. Vins de pays are a step in the French wine classification. Legislation on the *Vin de pays* terminology was created in 1973 and passed in 1979, allowing producers to distinguish wines that were made using grape varieties or procedures other than those required by the AOC rules, without having to use the simple and commercially non-viable table wine classification. Unlike table wines, which are only indicated as being from France, *Vin de pays* carries a geographic designation of origin, the producers have to submit the wine for analysis and tasting, and the wines have to be made from certain varieties or blends. Regulations regarding varieties and labelling practices are typically more lenient than the regulations for AOC wines.

Taxonomy

There are three tiers of Vin de Pays: *regional, departmental* and *local.*

There are six regional Vin de Pays, which cover large areas of France. The most voluminous contributor to this category of wines is Vin de Pays d’Oc, from the Languedoc-Roussillon area in Mediterranean France. The second largest volume of Vin de Pays wines is produced as Vin de Pays du Jardin de France, a designation that applies to wines from the whole Loire Valley. The other ones are: Vin de Pays du Comté Tolosan, Vin de Pays de Méditerranée and Vin de Pays des Comtés Rhodaniens.

Two further regional Vin de Pays designations, Vin de Pays de l’Atlantique and Vin de Pays Vignobles de France were approved by French authorities in 2007, but remain disputed and as of July 2009, they remained unpublished in the Official Journal of the European Union due to actions taken by other French wine producers.

Each regional Vin de Pays is divided into several departmental Vins de Pays, of which there are about 50. The names are derived from the French departments in question and the limits exactly the same than the department’s borders. For example, Vin de Pays du Gard is one of the Vins de Pays produced within Vins de Pays d’Oc using grapes from the Gard department and the Vin de Pays de Charente-maritime is produced in the Cognac area. Approximately one third of the French departments don’t produce *Vin de Pays*, for example Côte d’Or in Burgundy and Gironde in Bordeaux, or because the climate is not suited to produce wine at all, like the Bretagne, Normandy and Nord-Pas de Calais regions.

The local, or zone-defined Vin de pays are numerous, and may take its name from some historical or geographical phenomenon, such as Vin de Pays des Marches de Bretagne or Vin de Pays des Coteaux de l'Ardeche, or even a more locally specific variant. The boundaries of a zone may reflect a consistent terroir, rather than an administrative convenience, and could potentially in the long run achieve the status of an AOC.

Production Rules

The conditions to respect to be allowed to use the classification Vin de pays are the following:

- The yield must be less less than 90 hectoliters per hectare for white wines, and less than 85 hl for red and rosé wines.
- Only wine producers with a total yield of less than 100 hl/ha can qualify.
- The minimum alcoholic strength depends on the region and is 10 per cent in Le Midi, 9.5 per cent in South-west France area and the Centre East area, and 9 per cent for the Loire Valley and the East area.
- The allowed amount of sulfur dioxide allowed in the wines are 125 mg/l for red wines and 150 mg/l for white and rosé wines. For wines with sugar content of at least 5 g/l, the quantity of sulfur dioxide is slightly higher: 150 mg/l for red wines and 175 mg/l for white and rosé wines.
- The acidity in terms of pH values are also regulated, with some Vin de Pays areas having stricter rules than other.
- The wines must be kept and produced separately from other wines and are subject to quality monitoring by an official regional committee.

VINO DE LA TIERRA

Vino de la Tierra is a quality of Spanish wine that designates the rung below the mainstream quality wine indication of Denominación de Origen. It is the equivalent of the French vin de pays. It covers not only still wine but also sparkling wine and fortified wine.

It represents a higher quality than table wine. The labels of *Vino de la Tierra* wines are allowed to state the year of vintage and the grape varieties used in its production. In 2008 there were 43 registered *Vino de la Tierra* wines in Spain.

Similar Wine Classifications in Europe

Levels corresponding to Vino de la Tierra in other countries are:

- *Indicazione geografica tipica* for equivalent quality wines from Italy.
- *Landwein* for equivalent quality wines from Germany, Austria and South Tirol.

- *Landwijn* for equivalent quality wines from Netherlands.
- *Regional wine* for equivalent quality wines from the United Kingdom.
- *Vin de pays* for equivalent quality wines from France, Luxemburg and Val d'Aosta.
- *Vinho regional* for equivalent quality wines from Portugal.
- *Vi de la terra* for equivalent quality wines from Catalan-speaking regions in Spain.
- *Tradicional name or Regional wine for equivalent quality wines from Greece.*

QUINTA CLASSIFICATION OF PORT VINEYARDS IN THE DOURO

The Quinta classification of Port vineyards in the Douro is a system that grades the *terroir* and quality potential of vineyards in the Douro wine region to produce grapes suitable for the production of Port wine. In Portuguese, a *quinta* is a wine producing estate, which can be a winery or a vineyard. While other wine classification systems may classify the winery, the Douro quinta classification is based upon the physical characteristics of the vineyard.

The classification system is run by the *Instituto dos Vinhos do Douro e Porto* and shares some similarities to the classification of Champagne vineyards in that one of the purposes of the system is to ensuring that vineyards producing grapes with the highest quality potential receive a high price. A secondary function of the quinta classification is the establishment of permitted yields for production. Quintas with a higher classification are permitted to harvest more grapes than a vineyard which receiver a lower classification.

Ratings

Quintas are given numerical ratings in several categories-Age of the vines, altitude, aspect, vine density, gradient, granite content of the soil, schist content of the soil, types of grape varieties planted, overall location of the vineyard, microclimate, mixture, vineyard soil type, vine productivity and vineyard maintenance.

Vineyards that have favorable attributes in a particular category are award points while negative attribute receive point deduction. The totals are added up and the vineyard is then given an A-F rating with A being the best possible rating and F being the worst. The higher a quinta's rating, the more grapes the vineyard is permitted to harvest and the higher a price they can expect to receive for their wine.

- A rating- 1,200+ points
- B rating- 1,001-1,199 points
- C rating-801-1,000 points
- D rating-601-800 points

- E rating-400-600 points
- F rating-399 and below

Criteria

Category	Maximum awarded points possible	Maximum deduction	Comments
Age of vines	60	0	Vines that are older are more highly valued due to their naturally lower yields and more concentrated grapes.
Altitude	150	(-900)	Vineyards at lower altitudes are preferred.
Aspect	250	(-1000)	
Density of planting	50	(-50)	Vineyards with a lower density of planting are preferred.
Gradient	100	(-100)	Vineyards planted on steeper gradients are preferred.
Granite content	0	(-350)	Vineyards with more schistous soils, instead of granite, are preferred.
Grape varieties planted	150	(-300)	Vineyards planted with more the grapes officially recognized as being "Very Good" for Port production, such as Touriga Nacional, Touriga Francesa and Tinta Roriz, are favored.
Location	600	(-50)	
Microclimate	60	0	Evaluation of general terroir characteristics such as how sheltered the vineyard is from detrimental winds, etc.
Mixture	0	(-150)	
Schist content	100	0	Vineyards with higher schist content are preferred.
Soil types	100	(-350)	
Vine productivity	120	(-900)	Vines with a propensity for lower yields are preferred.
Vineyard maintenance	100	(-500)	

CLASSIFICATION OF CHAMPAGNE VINEYARDS

The classification of Champagne vineyards developed in the mid 20th century as a means of setting the price of grapes grown through the villages of the Champagne wine region. Unlike the classification of Bordeaux wine estates or Burgundy Grand cru vineyards, the classification of Champagne is broken down based on what village the vineyards are located in. A percentile system known as the *Échelle des Crus* acts as a pro-rata system for determining grape prices. Vineyards located in villages with high rates will receive higher prices for their grapes than vineyards located in villages with a lower rating. While the *Échelle des Crus* system was originally conceived as a 1-100 point scale, in practice, the lowest rated villages are rated at 80 per cent. *Premier crus* villages are rated between 90 and 99 per cent while the highest rated villages, with 100 per cent ratings are *Grand crus*.

4

Packaging and Storage of Wine

WINE PACKAGING

Commercially traded wine containers have evolved over thousands of years from primitive goatskins and earthen jars to modern polyethelene bag-in-box and glass bottles. Although relatively heavy and fragile, glass has long held the distinct advantages for wine packaging of being both chemically inert, preventing contamination, and impervious to oxygen, preventing spoilage.

LUSCIOUS LITTLE BOTTLES

Historical credit for invention of glass blowing goes to the Romans, although glass was essentially a luxury item for centuries. The oldest wine bottle ever found has been dated to 321 A.D. In 1821, an English company patented a machine to mold bottles that were uniform in size and shape. Selling wine already bottled, however, was illegal in England until 1860, due to both the political influence of pub owners and the lack of both labeling standards and means of authenticating the fill volume.

Wine was sold by the measure and bottled after the sale, with the customer providing their own bottles, often identified with a personal seal. Alois Senefelder, a German actor and playwright frustrated by printing costs, invented "stone printing" in 1796. Popularly known later as *lithography*, the process revolutionized printing economy and made mass-labeling of consumer products practical. Simple paper labels identifying the contents, usually by type only, began in the early 1800s in Germany; printed wine labels for widespread commercial application came after 1860.

Shape

Shapes for wine bottles evolve primarily from area tradition. There are "classic" shapes in general use by the majority of producers from any given area and "modern" shapes that are essentially more "artsy" variations of the classics. Although Old World wine producers rely heavily upon tradition to select their bottles, there are no appellation laws dictating bottle shape. It mostly is a matter of precedent and personal taste. Some marketing groups insist on particular bottle shapes and even sometimes offer a proprietary bottle mold to share with the membership, an expense that only the most well-financed estates would undertake on their own. These sometimes include a crest, coat-of-arms, or other design. There are also proprietary bottle molds owned by the glass company, rather than the producer. Italians seem to have the most variations, such as the tall bottles of fanciful shapes that sometimes hold Chianti, or the "fish" bottle of Verdicchio.

There are really three basic shapes in general commercial use; all other bottles are variations. The burgundy profile, for example, is slope-shouldered and used for both red, pink, and white wines. Bottles used for wines in Chablis, the Loire, and the Rhone are quite similarly shaped. Champagne uses a bottle that is made of thicker glass and includes a wide ring at the neck to hold the cage in place, et essentially the same profile. The flute, riesling, or hock bottle is also slope-shouldered, but taller, narrower, more drawn out. It is used almost exclusively for white or pink wines. The Bordeaux or claret bottle has some practicality to its design; the more distinct shoulder can serve as a catch basin for sediment when decanting.

There are also fairly wide variations in glass colours, from crystal clear through various shades of green and brown to nearly opaque, occasionally some blue as well. Light, whether natural or artificial, speeds wine spoilage. Darker bottle colours and certain shades protect wine from light, but producers generally select glass colour based upon packaging appeal, rather than solar security.

Every bottle has a bottom that may be either flat or "punted". The punt evolved as a pushed-up section of varying depth in the center of the bottom. This indentation was formed as a "handle" for glass blowers to turn their creation. So that bottles could stand upright, it was much easier to form an even plane by pushing up on the center of the bottom, rather than turning one that was perfectly flat. The punt forms a handle for Champagne riddlers and strengthens and spreads the pressure over more surface area to prevent sparkling wine bottles from bursting. Although they are more aesthetic than functional on still wine bottles, punts may serve as convenient thumb handles for strong-wristed servers and also help somewhat to direct deposits of sediment as bottles age. The punted bottle, by rendering the shape taller or wider, also gives the illusory impression that it contains more than a flat bottom bottle; it doesn't.

Every bottle also has a neck where the bottle narrows and the cork is inserted to seal the contents. On the classic shapes, necks vary slightly in length. For most American consumers, this is inconsequential, since 95 per cent of all wine sold in this country is consumed within 24 hours. It is, however, an important feature for collectors to observe the bottle neck and its level of fill or "ullage". A high fill is desirable, because this means there is less oxygen trapped in the bottle to hasten spoilage. However, a fill that is too high can be too sensitive to small changes in temperature and be prone to leakage. The condition of older wines can be estimated by ullage.

Some variations will occur, because bottle capacities commonly differ by one per cent, equal to a quarter ounce in a standard size bottle, not much, but often observable in the narrow neck. To overcome this, some sophisticated bottling lines actually "visualize" the fill level with light beams, rather than measure the quantity injected.

Until the 1970s, wine bottle sizes varied from about 650 to 850 milliliters, each appellation had their own standard. The European Union established standards that have been adopted worldwide. The "standard size" wine bottle is now 750 milliliters which the United States adopted, along with the rest of the Metric system, in 1979. One size does not necessarily fit all, however, and so various smaller and larger sizes are often available.

Table. wine • bottle • sizes • and • desi Table. wine • bottle • sizes • and • designations gnations

Measure	Size equivalence	* Servings	Popular name
187 milliliters	quarter bottle	1	Split
375 milliliters	half bottle	2	Tenth (often wrongly referred to as a "Split")
500 milliliters	two-thirds bottle	3 –	Half Liter
750 milliliters	standard bottle	4 +	Fifth
1.5 liter	two bottles	8 +	Magnum
3 liter	four bottles	17 +	Double Magnum, Jeroboam (sparkling wine ONLY)
4.5 liter / 5 liter	six / six + two thirds bottles	25 / 28	Jeroboam (claret shape) Jeroboam (burgundy shape)
6 liter	eight bottles	34	Imperial Magnum (claret shape) Methuselah (sparkling or burgundy shape)
9 liter	twelve bottles (one "case")	50 +	Salmanazar
12 liter	sixteen bottles	67 +	Balthazar
16 liter	twenty bottles	112 +	Nebuchadnezzar (sparkling wines)
± 12 liter to 16 liter	± sixteen to twenty bottles	90 to 112 +	Nebuchadnezzar (table wines)
± Size depends upon producer and origin		* @ 6 oz.	

Larger bottles are not only impressive, festive, and convenient for serving more guests, they are also demonstrably better at preserving the wine and extending the window of drinkability beyond that of smaller bottles. This may occur because the greater volume of wine makes the amount of trapped air, as well as the cork seal, proportionately smaller. Another factor may be that larger volumes of liquid change temperature more slowly and are therefore more resistant to potentially damaging fluctuations.

Seal of Approval

Keeping wine in the bottle until consumption is another concern. The dual purposes of any closure for wine are *containment* and *preservation*. Wine is sensitive to oxygen and will spoil before it has time to evaporate, so the latter purpose is the more critical. It is, however, much easier to keep wine from escaping bottles than to keep air from invading them.

In ancient times, when little was known of wine chemistry devices such as tightly bundled straw or oil-soaked twisted rags may have been stuffed into bottles to prevent spilling. Although glass bottles appear smooth-surfaced, they are actually imperfect, with shallow "hills and valleys", especially inside the neck, so these closures were only marginally effective for containment and not-at-all for preservation.

Eventually, stoppers made from bark of the cork oak, *quercus suber*, were discovered to be excellent closures, because of their elasticity and their apparent impenetrability to both moisture and oxygen.

A cork oak is not harvested the first time until it is 50 years old or more. After that virgin harvest, the bark is only taken every eight to twelve years. Trees may live for more than 200 years and are never cut down. It is the only tree species known to regenerate its bark. Forests of cork oaks grow all around the Mediterranean Sea, but the majority of all wine corks come from Portugal, which generates 60 per cent of cork production world-wide.

Cork bark is harvested by hand, using axes, going about halfway up the trunk. For eight to twelve months the cork is left to dry and season outdoors. After seasoning, the raw sheets of cork are boiled at fairly high temperatures for 50-75 minutes. This removes tannin, contaminants and impurities and swells the cork. The pieces are allowed to cool and dry somewhat for 2-4 days, then initially graded for thickness, followed by gradings for density and quality. After grading, the material is sent to the appropriate processing facility. Wine corks are punched from the top-graded sheets, then treated with peroxide to remove surface contaminants.

Only about 20-30 per cent of the total harvest is useful for making wine corks. Although more than 70 per cent of cork production by weight is used for other purposes, such as automotive gaskets, sandals, construction materials, and various stoppers of other kinds, more than 70 per cent of cork production value comes from wine corks. This may seem like the producers are over-charging for wine corks, but most wine corks are the "filet" of the cork bark, made from actual whole and unflawed pieces of thick bark that has grown many seasons between harvesting, while most other cork products are either the "ground beef" from chopped up pieces or from thin, younger bark. Corks may be quite good as wine bottle closures, but they are far from perfect. Since corks come from living plants, they are subject to the quality variability of all harvested commodities. All corks are not created equal. They suffer the same variety of grain, density, imperfections and susceptibility to defects from disease or boring insects as any wood product.

Cork, much like human skin, loses elasticity and moisture over time and shrinks; for this reason wine closed with cork should be stored laying down, so the cork remains wet. Serious collectors and producers of Port, Bordeaux, and other wines that are candidates for improvement with long aging often re-cork their bottles every 10 or 20 years. Some producers of expensive wines even conduct promotional tours around the world to offer this re-corking service to private collectors of their wines.

An increasing problem in wine corks has become contamination by the chemical compound 2,4,6-Trichloroanisole, or *TCA*. A result of the reaction between chlorine used to sterilize and process the corks and a mold that is present in many wood products, TCA produces a distinctive foul, musty, medicinal odour that can ruin wine. This problem is not exclusive to corks; all wood products in wineries are susceptible, including barrels, barrel racks, tanks, walls, scaffolding, shipping pallets, cardboard boxes and containers, etc. Any winery still using bleach as routine disinfectant is at extremely high risk. Both the cork and the wine industries are trying to develop solutions.

Natural cork stoppers have been the traditional seals for fine wines since the 18th Century. Wine consumers enjoy the ritual of carefully removing the cork from a bottle. The industry has long promoted the idea that superior wine comes only in cork-finished bottles and that wine in screwcap or screwtop bottles is inferior.

Wine dogma historically touts "the minute exchange of oxygen that corks allow in order for wines to properly age." Recent research that compared the same wines closed with both corks and screwcaps has shown that wine will age, with or without oxygen, and that wine in screw-capped bottles will age with both greater consistency and greater safety from spoilage.

The Australian Wine Research Institute tested and compared various wine closures over a total period of 40 months to evaluate their ability to preserve wine. Although the tests are ongoing and incomplete and despite historic idolatry for corks, screwcaps are most likely superior to corks for keeping wine contained and preserved in glass bottles. They have gained increasing acceptance in a very short time with the Australian wine industry, it will probably take much longer for wine consumers of the world to accept them.

Storing Wine

For any wine lover, storing wine well is very important. There are a few simple principles that need to be understood in order to select proper wine storage conditions. We can logically break down the process into just 3 categories: storing wine for the short haul, storing wine for long term aging and storing wines that have already been opened.

Short Term Storage

This is wine you will consume within 6 months. These may be bottles that are just home from the store and destined to be consumed shortly or bottles that have been pulled from longer storage to be accessible for spur of the moment consumption.

The closer you can duplicate the conditions required for long term storage, the better. However, in many situations, keeping the wines in a box in an interior closet is a satisfactory solution.

Keep the bottles stored so that:

- The cork stays moist.
- The wines are at the lowest stable temperature possible.
- The location is free of vibration.
- The location is not a storage area for other items that have a strong odour.

Stay away from those little 9 bottle racks that end up on top of the refrigerator; it's hot, close to the light and vibrates from the refrigerator compressor.

Long Term Storage

This is wine that you will keep for more than 6 months before consumption. A good storage location for wine is generally dark, is free of vibration, has high humidity and has a low stable temperature.

Generally accepted 'ideal' conditions are 50 to 55 degrees farenheight and 70 per cent humidity or higher. The high humidity is important because it keeps the corks from drying and minimizes evaporation. The only problem with even higher levels of humidity is that it brings on growth of mold on the labels or the loosening of labels that have water soluble glue.

Temperatures lower than 55 degrees only slow the aging of the wines. There have been wines found in very cold cellars of castles in Scotland that are perfectly sound and are much less developed that those kept at 'normal' cellar temperature. A near constant temperature is preferable to one that fluctuates.

With regard to light, most modern bottles have ultraviolet filters built into the glass that help protect the contents from most of the effects of UV rays. Despite the filters in the glass, long term storage can still allow enough rays in to create a condition in the wine that is referred to as 'light struck'. The result is that the wine picks up the taste and smell of wet cardboard. This is especially noticeable in delicate white wines and sparkling wines. The condition can be created by putting a bottle of champagne near a fluorescent light for a month.

Regular or constant vibrations from pumps, motors or generators should be avoided since the vibrations they cause are thought to negatively affect the evolution of the wines. One additional factor to avoid is storing other items with very strong odors near the wine. There have been many reports of wines picking up the aromas of items stored nearby.

If you do not have a suitable wine cellar, there are many types of 'wine refrigerators' that will work as well. They differ from common refrigerators in that they work at higher temperatures and they do not remove humidity from the air. There are kits available that will convert regular refrigerators into suitable wine storage units.

Storage after Opening

This is storage for bottles of table wine that have been opened but not completely consumed. There are many methods for prolonging the life of opened table wines but even the best can only slow the degradation of the wine. These methods are for still table wines. Sparkling wines and fortified dessert wines have different characteristics and requirements.

Gas Systems: Sparging the bottle with a gas can be very effective but it is expensive and one never known anyone who actually used a gas system over a long period of time. They just seem to ultimately be more trouble than they are worth. If you do elect to try such a system, stay away from carbon dioxide since it will mix into solution with the wine.

- *Vacu-vin*: An item came on the market a few years ago called a Vacu-vin. This consists of rubber bottle stoppers that hold a weak vacuum created by a hand pump that comes with the system. While some people swear by them, there is a consistent complaint that wines treated with a Vacu-vin seem 'stripped' of aromas and flavour. They actually create a lower pressure environment instead of an actual vacuum. This means they don't remove all the oxygen and oxidation of the wine will still occur.
- *Half bottles, marbles and progressive carafes*: These are all ways of limiting the amount of air in contact with the wine.

Conditions Affecting Wine

In wine storage conditions, there are three factors that have the most pronounced efect on the wine: light, humidity and temperature. Direct light, whether it be sunlight or incandescent, can adversely react with phenolic compounds in the wine and create potential wine faults. Delicate, light-bodied white wines run the greatest risk from light exposure and are often packaged in darkly tinted wine bottles that offer some protection from the light.

Wines packaged in clear, light green and blue coloured bottles are the most vulnerable to light and may need extra precautions for storage. For example, the Champagne house of Louis Roederer uses cellophane wrap to protect its premium *cuvee* Cristal from light, the wine being packaged in a clear bottle. In the cellar, wines are stored in corrugated boxes or wooden crates to protect the wines from direct light.

Some degree of humidity is required in order to keep wines with cork enclosures from drying out. Even when wine bottles are stored on their sides, one side of the cork is still exposed to air. If the cork begins to dry out, it can allow oxygen to enter the bottle, filling the ullage space and possibly causing the wine to spoil or oxidize. Excessive humidity can also pose the risk of damaging wine labels, which may hinder identification or hurt potential resale value. Wine experts such as Jancis Robinson note that 75 per cent humidity is often cited as ideal but there is very little significant research to definitively establish an optimal range. Concern about humidity is one of the primary reasons why wine experts such as Tom Stevenson recommends that wine should not be kept in a refrigerator since the refrigeration process often includes dehumidifying, which can quickly dry out corks.

Some wine experts debate the importance of humidity for proper wine storage. In the *Wine Spectator*, writer Matt Kramer cites a French study which claimed that the relative humidity within a bottle is maintained at 100 per cent regardless of the closure used or the orientation of the bottle. However, Alexis Lichine contends that low humidity can still be detrimental to premium wine quality due to the risk of the cork drying out. As a way of maintaining optimal humidity, Lichine recommends spreading half an inch of gravel on the floor of a wine cellar and periodically sprinkling it with some water.

Temperature and other Factors

Wine is very susceptible to changes in temperature, with temperature control being an important consideration in wine storage. If the wine is exposed to too high a temperature for long periods of time, it may become spoilt or "cooked" and develop off flavours that taste raisiny or stewed. The exact length of time that a wine is at risk of exposure to high temperatures will vary depending on the wine, with some wines being able to sustain exposure to high temperatures more easily than other, more delicate wines.

If the wine is exposed to temperatures that are too cold, the wine can freeze and expand, causing the cork to be pushed out; this will allow more oxygen to be exposed to the wine. Dramatic temperature swings can also cause adverse chemical reactions in the wine that may lead to a variety of wine faults. Most experts, such as Jancis Robinson, recommend that wine be kept at constant temperatures between 50 and 59 °F. Tom Stevenson speculates that 52 °F may be the most ideal temperature for storage and aging.

The storage condition of the bottled wine will influence a wine's aging. Vibrations and heat fluctuations can hasten a wine's deterioration and cause adverse effect to it. In general, a wine has a greater potential to develop complexity and a more aromatic bouquet if it is allowed to age slowly in a relatively cool environment. The lower the temperature, the more slowly a wine develops. On average, the rate of chemical reactions in wine doubles with each 18 °F increase in temperature. Wine expert Karen MacNeil, recommend keeping wine intended for aging in a cool area with a constant temperature around 55 °F. Wine can be stored at temperatures as high as 69 °F without long-term negative effect. Cornelius Ough of the University of California, Davis believes that wine can be exposed to temperatures as high as 120 °F for a few hours and not be damaged.

Orientation of the Bottle

Most wine racks are designed to allow a wine to be stored on its side. The thinking behind this orientation is that the cork is more likely to stay moist and not dry out if it is kept in constant contact with the wine. Some wineries package their wines upside down in the box for much the same reason. Research in the late 1990s suggested that the ideal orientation for wine bottles is at a slight angle, rather than completely horizontal.

This allows the cork to maintain partial contact with the wine in order to stay damp but also keeps the air bubble formed by a wine's ullage at the top rather than in the middle of the bottle if the wine is lying on its side. Keeping the ullage near the top, it has been argued, allows for a slower and more gradual oxidation and maturation process. This is because the air bubble that is the ullage space expands and contracts depending on temperature fluctuation. When exposed to higher temperatures the bubble expands, and if the wine is tilted at an angle, this expansion will diffuse through the cork and not harm the wine.

If the wine is completely on its side then this expansion will cause the bubble located in the middle of the bottle to push towards the cork, ejecting some wine in the process. When temperatures drop, the bubble contracts and forms a vacuum that brings more oxygen into the wine, speeding up the oxidation process. While most wines can benefit from lying on their side, Champagne and other sparkling wines tend to age better if they are kept upright. This is because the internal pressure caused by the trapped carbonic gas provides enough humidity and protection from oxygen. The preference for upright storage of Champagne is shared by the *Comité Interprofessionnel du Vin de Champagne* (CIVC) who conducted an extensive study of Champagnes that were stored in various conditions and orientations. This study found that Champagne stored on its side aged more quickly because oxygen was allowed to seep in after the Champagne corks lost their elasticity due to contact with the moist wine.

Alternative Wine Closures

Storing wine that is bottled with alternative wine closures other than cork have many of the same considerations in regards to temperature and light sensitivity. While humidity and concerns about oxidation are not as pronounced, the relative recent popularity and increased usage of these closures have not given much opportunity for much research into the storage and aging potential of wines that use these closures.

Places to Store Wine

Since the end of the 20th century, there has been growth in industries relating to wine storage. Some wine connoisseurs may elect to store their wine at home in a dedicated room or closet. Other options involve purchases and rentals at off-site wine storage facilities that are specifically designed for the task.Some of these industries focus on the construction of home wine cellars and wine caves, small rooms or spaces in which to store wine. Others produce smaller wine accessories, such as racks and wine refrigerators.

These appliances can feature adjustable temperature interfaces, two chambers for red and white wines, and materials which protect the wine from the sun and ambient environment.

WINE BARRELS

The use of wine barrels to store and age wine is a centuries old tradition. Wine aged in oak barrels is enhanced with the addition of vanilla and oak overtones. Wooden Wine Barrels also allow for a small amount of evaporation of the contents during the aging period.

Fig. Wine Barrels

French Oak was considered especially desirable wood for making wine barrels for many years. Most French Oak comes from one or more of the forests that were planted in the days of Napoleon for shipbuilding. Since the days of sailing ships have come and gone, those French forests have become ongoing forestry operations. Five primary forests used for wine barrel production are Allier, Limousin, Nevers, Trancais and Vosges. Each of these forests produces wood with distinctive characteristics involving tightness of the wood grain as well as the amount of oak flavours that are imparted to the wine. Tight grained wood tends to impart the Oak characteristics much more slowly than wood with looser grain. Winemakers select wood for their wine barrels from different forests for the effect on the finished wine. Early experiments with American Oak were not very successful since the amount of influence that the barrel had on the taste of the wine was too great. At first it was thought that the problem was with the wood itself. Now we know that most of the difficulties were caused by the way the wood was prepared and the way the barrel was constructed. As coopers began using traditional French barrelmaking techniques on 'foreign' oak, the results improved dramatically.

Perhaps the two most significant differences in wood preparation and barrel construction techniques were the seasoning of the wood and the way the staves were prepared. The French Coopers always let the wood air-dry for at least 24 months to attain proper seasoning. The American barrel makers were more used to building whiskey barrels and used a kiln-dry method to season the wood. The staves for whiskey barrels were also sawn rather than split. The French barrel makers split the wood along the grain of the wood to make the staves. Splitting rather than sawing produced staves that had more subtle effects on the wine.

Once the French barrel building techniques were applied to Oak from other countries, the results improved substantially. It is now common to find American Oak as well as that of several other countries including Hungary in the construction of wine barrels. Barrels made from American Oak typically cost less than half the price of French Oak Barrels and are now capable of achieving similar results.

During the construction of the barrel, a step takes place where the partially assembled barrel is placed over a small wood fire. During this step, the inside of the barrel is charred or 'toasted'. The amount of char in the barrel has an effect on the wine that is aged in it. Winemakers can normally order their barrels with Light Toast, Medium Toast or Heavy Toast. The 'toast' decision will be made based on the grape variety to be used in the barrel as well as the style of wine to be produced.

There are a wide variety of additional options available to the winemaker when it comes to wine barrels. Many winemaking regions have traditional shapes. There are also many sizes of barrels as well as variations in the thickness of the staves and the way the barrels are finally constructed.

It is most common for wines to be fermented in temperature-controlled Stainless Steel tanks before they are placed in oak barrels for aging. Some grape varieties, such as Chardonnay and Pinot Noir, may be fermented and aged in the same Oak barrel. Since new barrels impart more flavours to the wine than previously used barrels, the percentage of new barrels used by a winery each year is an important piece of information. By the time a barrel is about 5 years old, it is virtually neutral as far as its influence on the taste of the wine.

Various techniques have been developed to extend the use of barrels or to gain the benefits of oak aging without actually going to the time or expense of the traditional methods. One method involves shaving the inside of used barrels and inserting new thin inner staves that are toasted. Another procedure is to use oak shavings in a large 'tea bag' that is placed inside stainless steel tanks of wine. None of these cost saving techniques has been able to achieve the results of traditional barrel aging.

ALTERNATIVE WINE CLOSURES

Alternative wine closures are substitute closures used in the wine industry for sealing wine bottles in place of traditional cork closures. The emergence of these alternatives has grown in response to quality control efforts by winemakers to protect against "cork taint" caused by the presence of the chemical Trichloroanisole (or TCA).

The closures debate, chiefly between supporters of screw caps and natural corks, has increased the awareness of post-bottling wine chemistry, and the concept of winemaking has grown to continue after the bottling process, because closures with different oxygen transmission rates may lead to wines that taste different when they reach consumers.

The cork-industry group APCOR cites a study showing a 0.7-1.2 per cent taint rate. In a 2005 study of 2800 bottles tasted at the *Wine Spectator* blind-tasting facilities in Napa, California, 7 per cent of the bottles were found to be tainted.

Synthetic Corks

Synthetic corks are made from plastic compounds designed to look and "pop" like natural cork, but without the risk of TCA contamination. Disadvantages of some wine synthetic corks include a risk of harmful air entering a bottle after only 18 months, as well as the difficulty in extracting them from the bottle and using the plastic cork to reseal the wine. James Laube of *Wine Spectator* notes that some can also impart a slight chemical flavour to the wine.

Unlike natural corks, many wine synthetic corks are made from material that is not biodegradable but recyclable as either in many communities. There are two main production techniques for synthetic wine closures: injection molding and extrusion. Methods also exist which are claimed to combine the two techniques of injection and extrusion. A 2007 study by Victor Segalen Bordeaux 2 University showed that injection molded synthetic corks allowed the highest levels of oxygen permeation in when compared to natural cork and screw caps, offering the lowest protection against oxidation of the wine. A new generation of injection molded synthetic closures have developed a system of nano-cells as to perfectly replicate the cellular structure of natural cork and by exactly duplicating the permeability values of the top-quality-one-piece natural corks.,

Screw Caps

A screw cap is a metal cap that screws onto threads on the neck of a bottle, generally with a metal skirt down the neck to resemble the traditional wine capsule. A layer of plastic, cork, rubber, or other soft material is used as wad to make a seal with the mouth of the bottle. Its use as an alternative wine closure is gaining increasing support as an alternative to cork for sealing wine bottles.

Benefits and Concerns

In Brief, Compared to Cork:

- Screw caps prevent the wine faults of oxidation and of cork taint, and are easier to open; there are concerns about long-term aging.
- Cork is traditional, viewed by customers as higher-end, and has a proven track record.

Traditionally associated in the US with extremely inexpensive jug wines or even "skid row" wines, the screwcap is making a comeback due to concern about premature oxidation and cork taint. Screwcaps have a much lower failure rate than cork, and in theory will allow a wine to reach the customer in perfect condition, with a minimum of bottle variation. Cork, of course, has a centuries-old tradition behind it, and there are also concerns about the impact of screwcaps on the aging of those few wines that require decades to be at their best. Some argue that the slow ingress of oxygen plays a vital role in aging a wine, while others argue that this amount is almost zero in a sound cork and that any admitted oxygen is harmful. Various studies are underway, although one data point is that producers in Champagne have aged their wines under crown cap for quite some time with no apparent outcry. Even though most wine is consumed within a year of production, it may be advantageous to use screwcaps due to the relatively high incidence of cork taint.

Stelvin Screw Caps

The most known brand of wine screw caps is Stelvin, a brand developed by Rio Tinto Alcan, and recently sold to Amcor. The brand is so common that it is genericized in common use, with many in the wine trade referring to screw caps as "Stelvin closures", regardless of brand.

The distinguishing features of wine screw caps, in particular Stelvin brand ones, are:

- A long outside skirt, for aesthetics: to resemble the traditional wine capsule;
- The use of the plastic PVDC as a neutral liner on the inside wadding.

The Stelvin was developed in the late 1960s and early 1970s, and commercialized in the 1970s. It was developed by French company *La Bouchage Mecanique,* thence acquired by Pea-Pechiney, which became part of Alcan, now Rio Tinto Alcan. It was developed at the 1964 behest of Peter Wall, Production

Director of the Australian Yalumba winery, working with other companies. It was preceded as a closure by a Stelcap/cork combination: the Stelcap was also a long-skirted screw cap, but with a different inner lining.

It was originally trialled in 1970/71 with the Swiss wine Chasselas, which was particularly affected by cork taint, and first used commercially in 1972 for the Swiss winery Hammel. It was adopted commercially in Australia in late 1976/early 1977. For noble wines, wines from the 1971/72 vintage were sealed with Stelvin, then tasted in 1978, and found similar to cork-closed wines.

Adoption

Screw caps met with customer resistance in Australia and New Zealand, and were phased out in the early 1980s, only to be reintroduced gradually in the 1990s. They were widely adopted in the 1980s by Swiss winemakers, and have shown increasingly wide adoption in the succeeding years.

In New Zealand, adoption went from 1 per cent in 2001 to 70 per cent in 2004. Screw cap adoption in fine wines is proceeding in fits and starts. In July 2000, a group of producers of Clare Valley Rieslings bottled a portion of their wines in screwcap, and earlier that year PlumpJack Winery announced it would bottle half its production of US$130 1997 Reserve Cabernet Sauvignon in screwcap. Other announcements have followed, including one from Bonny Doon Vineyard in July 2002 that 80,000 cases of its "Big House" red and white wine would be bottled under screwcaps - followed by almost all the rest of their production by late 2004.Domaine Laroche in Chablis, France has been bottling their Chablis, Premier crus and Grand Crus on Screwcap since 2001 vintage. In July 2004 Corbett Canyon became the first million plus case brand to switch to screwcaps for their entire production, shipping just over three million cases a year. Other notable producers that have switched to screwcaps are R.H. Phillips in 2004, Hogue Cellars in 2004 and Villa Maria, also in 2004.

Fig. Glass-Stopper Compared with Corkstopper

Vino-Seal

Vino-Seal, or Vino-Lok, is a plastic/glass closure released by Alcoa. Since its introduction into the European market in 2003, over 300 wineries have utilized Vino-Seal. Using a glass stopper with an inert o-ring, the Vino-Seal creates a hermetic seal that prevents oxidation and TCA contamination. A disadvantage with the Vino-Seal is the relatively high cost of each plug and cost of manual bottling due to the lack of compatible bottling equipment outside of Europe. The design has won a *Worldstar Award for Packing Excellence* from the World Packaging Organization.

Zork

Invented by Conor McKenna and developed by John Brooks in Adelaide, South Australia, Zork is an alternative wine closure that seals like a screw cap and pops like a cork. The Zork closure consists of three parts; an outer cap providing a tamper evident clamp that locks onto the European CETIE band of a standard cork mouth bottle, an inner metal foil which provides an oxygen barrier similar to a screw cap, and an inner plunger which creates the 'pop' on extraction and reseals after use.

Fig. A Bottle of Wine Sealed with a Zork

Crown caps

The traditional crowned bottle cap has been used in the sparkling wine industry as a closure during the bottle fermentation process. Normally the cap is replaced with a cork before shipping, though recently some producers are releasing wines using the crown cap as their closure.

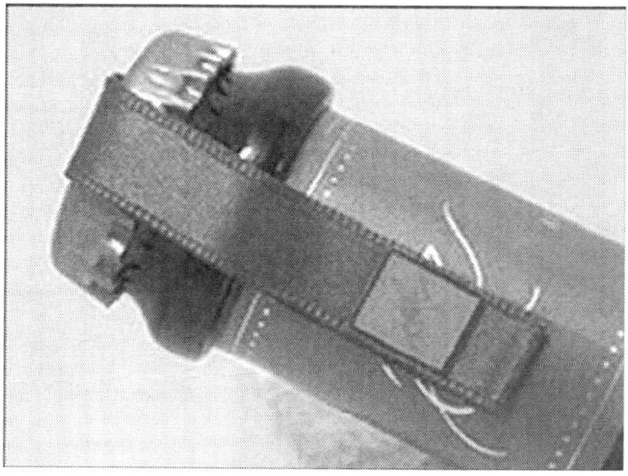

Fig. Crown Cap Closure on a Sparkling Wine

The crown caps provide a tight seal without risking cork-taint. Although easier to open, crown caps eliminate part of the ceremony and mystique of opening a sparkling wine.

Opposition

There is continuing opposition to the use of alternative closures in some parts of the winemaking industry. In March 2006, the Spanish government outlawed the use of alternative wine closures in 11 of Spain's wine producing regions as part of their D.O. regulations. Opposition due to the environmental impact of synthetic stoppers is also growing, because synthetic stoppers are not as biodegradable as cork, but the main reason is that cork 'farms' have great biodiversity and some of the species are unique to cork-growing areas, however with the commercial demand for cork reduced, many of these farms are being removed to grow more profitable crops.

AMPHORA

An amphora is a type of ceramic vase with two handles and a long neck narrower than the body. The word *amphora* is Latin, derived from the Greek *amphoreus* an abbreviation of *amphiphoreus* a compound word combining *amphi-* plus *phoreus*, from *pherein*, referring to the vessel's two carrying handles on opposite sides.

Amphora dated to around 4800 BCE have been found in Banpo, a Neolithic site of the Yang Shao Culture in China. In the West, Amphorae first appeared on the Syrian coast around 3500 BCE and spread around the ancient world, being used by the ancient Greeks and Romans as the principal means for transporting and storing grapes, olive oil, wine, oil, olives, grain, fish, and other commodities. They were produced on an industrial scale from Greek times and used around the Mediterranean until about the 7th century. Wooden and skin containers seem to have supplanted amphorae thereafter.

They are of great benefit to maritime archaeologists, as amphorae in a shipwreck can often indicate the age of the wreck and geographic origin of the cargo. They are occasionally so well preserved that the original contents are still present, providing invaluable information on the eating habits and trading systems of the ancient Mediterranean peoples. Amphorae were too cheap and plentiful to return to their origin-point and so, when empty, they were broken up at their destination. In Rome this happened in an area named Testaccio, close to Tiber, in such a way that the fragments, later wetted with Calcium hydroxide, remained to create a hill now named Monte Testaccio 45 meters tall and more than 1 km circumference. High-quality painted amphorae were produced in significant numbers for a variety of social and ceremonial purposes. Their design differs significantly from the more functional versions; they are typified by wide mouth and a ring base, with a glazed surface and decorated with geometric shapes. Such amphorae were often used as prizes. Some examples, bearing the inscription "I am one of the prizes from Athens", have survived from the Panathenaic Festivals held between the 6th century BC to the 2nd century BC. Painted amphorae were also used for funerary purposes. The *loutrophoros*, a type of amphora, was used principally for funeral rites. Outsize vases were also used as grave markers, while some amphorae were used as containers for the ashes of the dead.

Fig. Large late Geometric Attic Amphora, ca. 725 BC – 700 BC.

Forms and Sizes

Two principal types of amphorae existed: the *neck amphora*, in which the neck and body meet at a sharp angle; and the *one-piece amphora*, in which the neck and body form a continuous curve. Neck amphorae were commonly used in the early history of ancient Greece but were gradually replaced by the one-piece type from around the 7th century BC onwards.

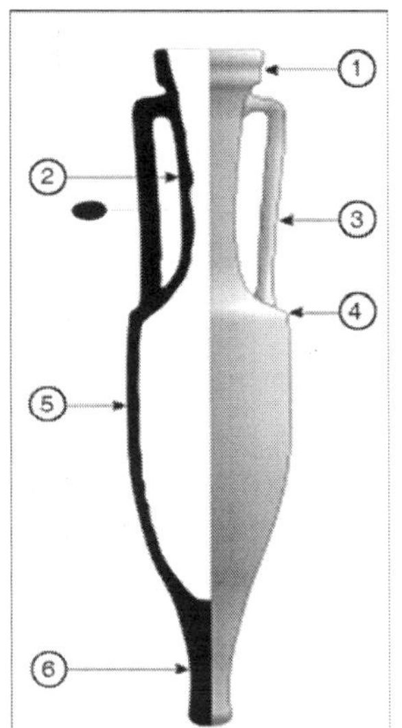

Fig. Dressel 1B Type Amphora

Key: 1: rim - 2: neck - 3: handle - 4: shoulder - 5: belly *or* body - 6: foot.

Most were produced with a pointed base to allow them to be stored in an upright position by being partly embedded in sand or soft ground. This also facilitated transport by ship, where the amphorae were tightly packed together, with ropes passed through their handles to prevent breaking or toppling during a rough sea voyage.

Amphorae varied greatly in height. The largest could stand as much as 1.5 metres high, while some were under 30 centimetres high - the smallest were called amphoriskoi. Most were around 45 centimetres high. There was a significant degree of standardisation in some variants; the wine amphora held a standard measure of about 39 litres giving rise to the amphora quadrantal as a unit of measure in the Roman Empire. In all, around 66 distinct types of amphora have been identified.

BAG-IN-BOX

The Bag-In-Box packaging system offers a complex solution to the problem of packaging of liquid and paste-textured foodstuffs: wine, water, sauces, syrups, liquid eggs and dairy products, vegetable and fruit purees, juice concentrates, fruit and vegetable additives to yogurts, oils, fats, etc.

Bag-In-Box is a specially designed bag with a tap or pressure plug fitment, filled with the product and placed into an outer container.

We offer bags ranging in size from 2 to 1200 litres. Depending on the product, customer requirements concerning oxygen barriers, the shipping distance and storage conditions, the bags are made of two or more layers of laminated and metallised film.

The filled bag is placed into an outer container, which is manufactured from a selection of materials depending on the bag volume and final product application:

- For 2 - 20 litre bags - carton boxes are used.
- For 220 litre bags - metal conical drums are utilised.
- For 1000 - 1200 litre bags - containers manufactured from plastic, metal or wood are used.

The bag protects the product from coming into contact with air/oxygen, odours and light, while the outer container facilitates transportation and protects the bag from mechanical damage.

In the recent years Flexitanks are becoming more widely used worldwide. These flexible containers ranging in volume from 16 to 24 thousand litres are used for the transportation of wine materials and juice concentrates over substantial distances.

Flexitanks are placed into a standard 20" container. Such packaging system significantly simplifies the process of shipment of liquids and reduces the transportation costs.

Commercial Uses

The first commercial Bag-in-Box was invented by William R. Scholle in 1955 for the safe transportation and dispensing of battery acid. Scholle Packaging is still the worldwide leading Bag-In-Box manufacturer to this day with manufacturing facilities spread around the world.

The BiB has many common commercial applications. The most ubiquitous uses of BiBs by commercial users are to supply syrup to soft drink fountains and to dispense bulk supplied condiments such as ketchup or mustard in the foodservice context. And BiB technology is still used for its original application of dispensing sulfuric acid for filling lead-acid batteries in garages and dealerships.

For commercial syrup applications, the customer tears a pre-scored opening at one end of the box and connects a compatible nozzle to a built-in port on the bag to pump out its contents. The port itself contains a one-way valve which opens only with pressure from the attached nozzle and which prevents contamination of the syrup in the bag. For consumer applications like box wine, there is a tap already present on the bag, so all the consumer has to do is locate the tap on the outside of the box.

After the contents are exhausted, the box and bag within are typically discarded rather than refilled, although both bag and box are fully recyclable.

Advantages

Bag in a box packaging is liked by producers because it is inexpensive. Seen from the environmental perspective, a bag also has benefits. The bag allows a contents of 3-1000l, so that less packaging or labelling is required. The material it is made from is lighter than the alternatives, which reduces pollution caused by transport.

Wine Cask

The 'wine cask' was invented by Thomas Angove of Angove's, a winemaker from Renmark, South Australia, and patented by the company on April 20, 1965. Polyethelene bladders of 1 gallon were put into cardboard boxes for sale to consumers. The original design required that the consumer cut the corner off the bladder inside the box, pour out the desired quantity of wine and then reseal it with a special peg.

In 1967 Charles Henry Malpas and Penfolds Wines patented a plastic, air-tight tap welded into a metallised bladder, making storage much more convenient for consumers. All modern wine casks now utilise some sort of plastic tap, which is exposed by tearing away a perforated panel on the box.

The main advantage to bag-in-a-box packaging is that it prevents oxidation of the wine during dispensing. After opening, wine in a bottle it is oxidised by air in the bottle which has displaced the wine poured; wine in a bag is not touched by air and thus not subject to oxidation until it is dispensed. Cask wine is not subject to cork taint or spoilage due to slow consumption after opening.

However, the bag is not hermetically sealed and has an unopened shelf life shorter than bottled wine. Most casks will have a best-before date stamped. As a result, it is not intended for cellaring and should be drunk within the prescribed period.

Bag in a box packaging is also preferred by producers of more economical wines because it is less expensive than glass bottles. A bag of wine, once removed from the box, will float on water; this allows quick cooling of a white wine by immersion in an ice bath.

BARREL

A barrel or cask is a hollow cylindrical container, traditionally made of vertical wooden staves and bound by wooden or metal hoops. Traditionally, the barrel was a standard size of measure referring to a set capacity or weight of a given commodity. For example, a beer barrel was originally a 36 gallon capacity while an ale barrel was a 32 gallon capacity. Wine was shipped in 31.5 gallon barrels. Barrels are one size of cask. Other cask sizes include, but are not limited to, pins, firkins, kilderkins, puncheons, rundlets, tierces, pipes, butts, and tuns. Someone who makes barrels is a *cooper*. Modern barrels are also made of aluminium, stainless steel, and plastic.

In Asia/Europe in ancient times liquids like oil and wine were carried in vessels, for instance amphora, sealed with pine resin. The Romans began to use barrels in the 3rd century AD, as a result of their commercial and military contacts with the Gauls, who had been making barrels for several centuries.

For nearly 2,000 years barrels were the most convenient form of shipping or storage container for those who could afford the superior price. All kinds of bulk goods, from nails to gold coins, were stored in them. Bags and most crates were cheaper, but they were not as sturdy and they were more difficult to manhandle for the same weight. Barrels slowly lost their importance in the 20th century, with the introduction of pallet-based logistics and containerization.

Starting in the late 19th century, barrels were largely superseded by corrugated fibreboard boxes for storage and transport of dry goods, and in the mid 20th century, steel drums began to be used for the storage and transport of fluids such as water, oils and hazardous waste. Barrels are still used today for artistic presentation of merchandise in many stores, although these barrels are often merely decorative, and not made water-tight.

Usage

Barrels are used for the storage of liquids, from simple water to ferment wine, to age wine and whiskey.

For Storage of Water

Water barrels are often used to collect the rainwater from dwellings. This usage, known as rainwater harvesting requires, an adequate roof-covering and an adequate rain pipe.

For Storage of Oil

The standard barrel of crude oil or other petroleum product is 42 US gallons. This measurement originated in the early Pennsylvania oil fields, and permitted both British and American merchants to refer to the same unit, based on the old English wine measure, the tierce.

Earlier, another size of whiskey barrel was the most common size; this was the 40 US gallons barrel for proof spirits, which was of the same volume as 5 US bushels. However, by 1866 the oil barrel was standardized at 42 US gallons.

Oil has not actually been shipped in barrels since the introduction of oil tankers, but the 42-US-gallon size is still used as a unit for measurement, pricing, and in tax and regulatory codes. Each barrel is refined into about 19.74 US gallons of gasoline, the rest becoming other products such as jet fuel and heating oil, using fractional distillation. The current standard volume for barrels for chemicals and food is 55 US gallons.

For Aging of Beverages

Some wine is fermented "in barrel," as opposed to a neutral container such as a steel or concrete tank. Wine can also be fermented in large wooden tanks, often called "open-tops" because they are open to the atmosphere. Other wooden cooperage for storing wine or spirits are called "casks", and they are large with either elliptical or round heads.

Other Uses

Due to the traditional barrel's distinctive shape and construction method, the term has been used to describe a variety of other related or similar objects, such as the gun barrel and barrel organ.

Some kinds of food, such as pork, were stored in barrels in larders before the era of refrigerators. This practice generated a political term, pork barrel, in which earmarks for particular people or locations were labeled "pork-barrel" spending.

Shape

Barrels often have a convex shape, bulging at the middle. This constant bulge makes it easier to roll a well-built wooden barrel on its side, changing directions with little friction. It also helps to distribute stress evenly in the material by making the container more spherical. Casks used for ale or beer have shives and keystones in their openings. Before serving the beer a spile is hammered into the shive and a tap into the keystone. The "chine hoop" is the iron hoop nearest the end of a wooden barrel, the "bilge hoops" those nearest the bulge, or centre. The stopper used to seal the hole in a barrel is called the bung.

Sizes

English Traditional, Wine

Table. English Casks of Wine

Gallon	Rundlet	Barrel	Tierce	Hogshead	Firkin, puncheon, tertian	Pipe, butt	Tun	
							1	Tun
						1	2	Pipes, butts
					1	1½	3	Firkins, puncheons, tertians
				1	1⅓	2	4	Hogsheads
			1	1½	2	3	6	Tierces
		1	1⅓	2	2⅔	4	8	Barrels
	1	1¾	2⅓	3½	4⅔	7	14	Rundlets
1	18	31½	42	63	84	126	252	Gallons (US/wine)
3.79	68.14	119.24	158.99	238.48	317.97	476.96	953.92	Litres
1	15	26¼	35	52½	70	105	210	Gallons (imperial)
4.55	68.19	119.3	159.1	238.7	318.2	477.3	954.7	Litres

Pre-1824 definitions continued to be used in the US, the wine gallon of 231 cubic inches being the standard gallon for liquids. In Britain that gallon was replaced by the Imperial gallon. The tierce later became the petrol barrel. The tun was originally 256 gallons, which explains where the *quarter*, 8 bushels or 64 gallons, comes from.

Sizes for UK Beer

Although it is common to refer to draught beer containers of any size as barrels, in the UK this is strictly correct only if the container holds 36 imperial gallons.

The terms "keg" and "cask" refer to containers of any size, the distinction being that kegs are used for beers intended to be served using external gas cylinders. Cask ales undergo part of their fermentation process in their containers, called casks.

Casks are available in several sizes, and it is common to refer to "a firkin" or "a kil" instead of a cask.

Sizes for US Beer and Ale

The modern US beer barrel is 31 US gallons, half a gallon less than the traditional wine barrel.

Table. English casks of ale and beer

Gallon	Firkin	Kilderkin	Barrel	Hogshead	(Butt)	(Tun)		Year designated
						1	tuns	
					1	1¾	butts	
				1	3	5¼	hogsheads	
			1	1½	4½	7⅞	barrels	
		1	2	3	9	15¾	kilderkins	
	1	2	4	6	18	31½	firkins	
1	8	16	32	48	144	252	ale gallons (ale)	(1454)
= 4.62	= 36.97	= 73.94	= 147.88	= 221.82	= 665.44	= 1164.52	litres (ale)	
1	9	18	36	54	162	283½	ale gallons (beer)	
= 4.62	= 41.59	= 83.18	= 166.36	= 249.54	= 748.62	= 1310.09	litres (beer)	
1	8½	17	34	51			ale gallons	1688
= 4.62	= 39.28	= 78.56	= 157.12	= 235.68			litres	
1	9	18	36	54			ale gallons	1803
= 4.62	= 41.59	= 83.18	= 166.36	= 249.54			litres	
1	9	18	36	54			imperial gallons	1824
= 4.55	= 40.91	= 81.83	= 163.66	= 245.49			litres	

BOCKSBEUTEL

The Bocksbeutel is a type of wine bottle with the form of a flattened ellipsoid. It is commonly used for wines from Franconia in Germany, but is also used for some Portuguese wines, in particular rosés, where the bottle is called cantil, and in rare cases for Italian wine and Greek wine.

Fig. Bocksbeutel

This bottle shape is derived from that of field bottles, which were known already in antiquity, and which were manufactured with a flattened shape for practical purposes, for example to keep the bottle from rolling away on uneven ground.

The Bocksbeutel has been used for wine from Franconia at least since the early 18th century, initially for the wines from the region's most famous vineyard, the Würzburger Stein, and later for other Franconian wines, in particular those of better quality. The city council of Würzburg decided in 1728 that the best wines from the city's own winery, the *Bürgerspital*, should be filled in Bocksbeutel bottles. There are two conflicting claims of the origin of the name Bocksbeutel, although the *Beutel*-part stands for "container" in both cases. Another claim is that the term actually means "goat's scrotum", which is supposed to be of similar shape as the bottle. This explanation is given as early as 1690 in a dictionary by Kaspar von Stieler. The term *Bokesbudel* with this meaning is said to have existed in the Early Middle Age.

Protected Bottle Shape

Within the European Union, the Bocksbeutel enjoys the status of a protected bottle shape. The regulations describe the Bocksbeutel as a short-necked glass bottle, pot-bellied but flattened in shape, with the base and the cross-section of the bottle at the point of greatest convexity ellipsoidal in shape. The ratio between the long and short axes of the ellipsoidal cross-section is approximately 2:1, and the ratio of the height of the convex body to the cylindrical neck of the bottle is approximately 2.5:1.

The Bocksbeutel may be used for the following wines:

- German wines of QbA and Prädikatswein quality from.
  - Franconia.
  - Certain parts of Baden, in the district known as Tauberfranken and around Baden-Baden.
- *Certain wines from Northern Italy at the DOC and DOCG level*:
  - Santa Maddalena.
  - Valle Isarco, if made from Silvaner or Müller-Thurgau.
  - Terlaner, if made from Pinot blanc.
  - Bozner Leiten.
  - Alto Adige, if made from Riesling, Müller-Thurgau, Pinot noir, Moscato giallo, Silvaner, Lagrein, Pinot blanc or Moscato rosa.
  - Greco di Bianco.
  - Trentino, if made from Moscato.
- Certain Greek wines.
  - Agioritiko.
  - Rombola Kephalonias.
  - Wines from the island of Kefalonia.
  - Wines from the island of Paros.
  - Wines from the Peloponnese.
- Certain Portuguese wines. The use is limited to rosé wines and those other quality wines and *vinho regional* which can prove that they have traditionally been bottled in *cantil*-type bottles before they received their present classification.

BOTA BAG

A bota bag is a traditional Spanish wine skin. Typically, it is made of leather, and is used to carry wine, although any liquid will do. Traditionally, bota bags were lined with tree sap or other resins to prevent liquids from seeping through. Modern bota bags have a latex liner. It was very handy for Spanish travellers. A goatskin is a container for wine, so called for being traditionally made of goatskin. In the Basque Country, the goatskin is known as a zahato.

The zahato is the traditional wineskin bottle of the Basque shepherds. With its narrow nozzle, it is possible to drink "zurrust", *i.e.* intercepting the jet without touching the bottle. The name of *zahato* or *zahako* is a diminutive *zahat-to/-ko* of *zahagi* 'big goatskin bottle'. Its manufacturer is a *zahatogile*.

The zahato is made of two pieces of tanned and close-cropped goatskin. Softened, they are cut out on a last and are sewn on their sides. Then the bottle is turned up, seam and hair inside. After drying, it is inflated, then coated with pitch to make it impermeable. The nozzle, traditionally in horn, is fixed by a red collar. The zahato is carried across the shoulder with the red cord which surrounds it along the seam.

WINE BOTTLES

The shape of wine bottles can communicate a great deal about the taste of the wine inside. In Europe, many wine producing areas developed unique wine bottle shapes that became the traditional bottle for wines of that region. As winemaking spread around the world, new wineries often adopted those traditional European bottle shapes in order to communicate with their consumers.

The high shouldered 'Bordeaux Bottle' is used by most wineries for Cabernet Sauvignon, Merlot, Malbec and most Meritage or Bordeaux blends. This is because those are the key grape varieties that are allowed for use in red wines from the Bordeaux region.

The Bordeaux bottle is also generally used for Sauvignon Blanc and Semillon.

These are the primary grape varieties allowed in the production of white wines in Bordeaux.

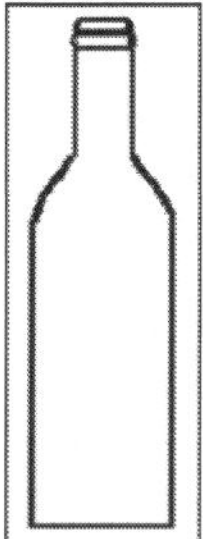

The slope shouldered 'Burgundy Bottle' is generally used for Chardonnay and Pinot Noir around the world. These are the two key grape varieties used in the Burgundy region of France for white and red wine production.

This shape is also used for many Loire Valley wines.

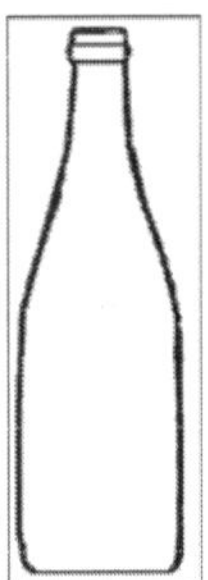

The tall 'Hoch Bottle' is used in Germany and also in Alsace.

It is used by wineries in many parts of the world for several grape varieties including Riesling, Gewurztraminer and Muller-Thurgau.

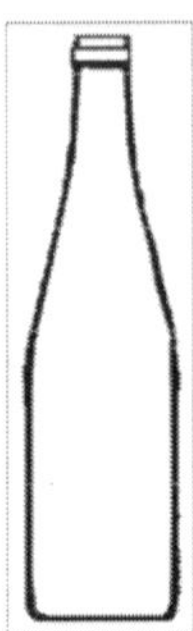

Wine Bottle Sizes

Metric Wine Bottle Sizes to Imperial Wine Bottle Sizes

Table. Wine Bottle Sizes

Bottle Sizes	Equivalent fluid ounces	Bottles per case	Liters per case	U.S. Gallons per case	Corresponds to
3 liters	101 Fl. Oz.	4	12.00	3.17004	4/5 Gallon
1.5 liters	50.7 Fl. Oz.	6	9.00	2.37753	2/5 Gallon
1.00 liters	33.8 Fl. Oz.	12	12.00	3.17004	1 Quart
750 milliliters	25.4 Fl. Oz.	12	9.00	2.37753	4/5 Quart (Old U.S. Fifth)
500 milliliters	16.9 Fl. Oz.	24	12.00	3.17004	1 Pint
375 milliliters	12.7 Fl. Oz.	24	9.00	2.37753	4/5 Pint
187 milliliters	6.3 Fl. Oz.	48	8.976	2.37119	2/5 Pint
100 milliliters	3.4 Fl. Oz.	60	6.00	1.58502	2, 3 & 4 Oz.
50 milliliters	1.7 Fl. Oz.	120	6.00	1.58502	1, 1.6 & 2 Oz.
Official Conversion Factor: 1 Liter = 0.26417 U.S. Gallon					

Standard Wine Bottle Sizes

Table. These are Traditional Standard Bottle Sizes for Champagne.

Split	1/4 bottle	18.7 cl
Half	1/2 bottle	37.5 cl
Bottle	1 bottle	750 ml
Magnum	2 bottles	1.5 l
Jeroboam	4 bottles	3 l
Methuselah	8 bottles	6 l
Salmanazar	12 bottles	9 l
Balthazar	16 bottles	12 l
Nabuchadnezzar	20 bottles	15 l

Shapes

Wine producers in Portugal, Italy, Spain, France and Germany follow the tradition of their local areas in choosing the shape of bottle most appropriate for their wine.

- *Port, sherry, and Bordeaux varieties*: Straight-sided and high-shouldered with a pronounced punt. Port and sherry bottles may have a bulbous neck to collect any residue.
- *Burgundies and Rhône varieties*: Tall bottles with sloping shoulders and a smaller punt.
- *Rhine, Mosel, and Alsace varieties*: Narrow and tall with little or no punt.
- *Champagne and other sparkling wines*: Thick-walled and wide with a pronounced punt and sloping shoulders.
- *German wines from Franconia*: The Bocksbeutel bottle.
- The Chianti and some other Italian wines: the *fiasco*, a round-bottomed flask encased in a straw basket.

Many North and South American, South African, and Australasian wine producers select the bottle shape they wish to associate their wines with. For instance, a producer who believes his wine is similar to Burgundy may choose to bottle his wine in Burgundy-style bottles. Other producers have chosen idiosyncratic bottle styles for marketing purposes. Pere-Anselme markets its Châteauneuf-du-Pape in bottles that appear half-melted. The Moselland company of Germany has a riesling with a bottle in the shape of a house cat. The home wine maker may use any bottle, as the shape of the bottle does not affect the taste of the finished product. The sole exception is in producing sparkling wine, where thicker-walled bottles should be used to handle the excess pressure.

Colours

The traditional colours used for wine bottles are:

- *Bordeaux*: Dark green for reds, light green for dry whites, clear for sweet whites.

- *Burgundy and the Rhone*: Dark green.
- *Mosel and Alsace*: dark to medium green, although some producers have traditionally used amber.
- *Rhine*: Amber, although some producers have traditionally used green.
- *Champagne*: Usually dark to medium green. Rosé champagnes are usually a colorless or green.

Clear bottles have recently become popular with white wine producers in many countries, including Greece, Canada and New Zealand. Most red wine worldwide is still bottled in green glass.

Capsules

Most wine bottles finished with a cork have a protective sleeve called a capsule covering the top of the bottle. Capsules were historically made of lead, and protected the cork from being gnawed away by rodents or infested with cork weevil. Because of research showing that trace amounts of toxic lead could remain on the lip of the bottle and mix with the poured wine, lead capsules were slowly phased out, and by the 1990s, most capsules were made of tin, heat-shrink plastic or aluminium. Sealing wax is sometimes used, or the capsule can be omitted entirely, since it is not needed with some modern stoppers. In the US, the FDA finally officially banned lead foil capsules on domestic and imported wine bottles as of 1996.

Punts

A punt, also known as a kick-up, refers to the dimple at the bottom of a wine bottle. There is no consensus explanation for its purpose.

The more commonly cited explanations include:

- It is a historical remnant from the era when wine bottles were free blown using a blowpipe and pontil. This technique leaves a punt mark on the base of the bottle; by indenting the point where the pontil is attached, this scar would not scratch or make the bottle unstable.
- It had the function of making the bottle less likely to topple over—a bottle designed with a flat bottom only needs a small imperfection to make it unstable—the dimple historically allowed for a larger margin of error.
- It consolidates sediment deposits in a thick ring at the bottom of the bottle, preventing much/most of it from being poured into the glass;
- It increases the strength of the bottle, allowing it to hold the high pressure of sparkling wine/champagne.
- It holds the bottles in place on pegs of a conveyor belt as they go through the filling process in manufacturing plants.
- It accommodates the pourer's thumb for stability and ease of pouring.
- They often knew more than their master about what was happening

in town, and with a thumb up the punt they could show their master whether a guest was reliable or not.

- It provides a grip for riddling a bottle of sparkling wine manually in the traditional champagne production process.
- It simply takes up some of the volume of the bottle, giving the impression that you're getting more wine for your money than is actually the case.
- Taverns had a steel pin set vertically in the bar. The empty bottle would be thrust bottom-end down onto this pin, puncturing a hole in the top of the punt, guaranteeing the bottle could not be refilled.
- The punt acts as a lens, refracting the light to make the colour of the wine more appealing.
- Prevents the bottle from resonating as easily, decreasing the likelihood of shattering during transportation.
- Allows bottles to be more easily stacked end to end.

Environmental Impact

Glass retains its colour on recycling, and the United Kingdom has a large surplus of green glass because it imports a large quantity of wine but produces very little. 1.4 million tonnes are sent to landfill annually.

Glass is a relatively heavy packing material and wine bottles use quite thick glass, so the tare weight of a full wine bottle is a relatively high proportion of its gross weight. This has led to suggestions that wine should be exported in bulk from producer regions and bottled close to the market. This would reduce the cost of transportation and its carbon footprint, and provide a local market for recycled green glass. Less radically, box wine is sold in large-size light cardboard and foil containers, though its use has been restricted to cheaper products in the past and as such retains a stigma. Some wine producers are exploring more alternative packagings such as plastic bottles and tetra packs.

BOTTLING LINE

Bottling lines are production lines that fill a product, generally a beverage, into bottles on a large scale.

The first step in bottling wine is *depalletising*, where the empty wine bottles are removed from the original pallet packaging delivered from the manufacturer, so that individual bottles may be handled. The bottles may then be rinsed with filtered water or air, and may have carbon dioxide injected into them in attempt to reduce the level of oxygen within the bottle. The bottle then enters a *filler* which fills the bottle with wine and may also inject a small amount of inert gas on top of the wine to disperse oxygen.

The bottle then travels to a corking machine where a cork is compressed and pushed into the neck of the bottle. Whilst this is happening the corker vacuums the air out of the bottle to form a negative pressure headspace. This removes any oxygen from the headspace, which is useful as O_2 can ruin the quality of the product by oxidation. A negative pressure headspace will also counteract pressure caused by the thermal expansion of the wine, preventing the cork from being forced from the bottle.

Some bottling lines incorporate a *fill height detector* which reject under or over-filled bottles, and also a metal detector.

After filling and corking, a plastic or tin capsule is applied to the neck of the bottle in a *capsular*. Next the bottle enters a labelling machine where a label is applied. To ensure traceability of the product, a *lot number*, generally the date and time of bottling, may also be printed on the bottle. The product is then packed into boxes and warehoused, ready for sale.

BOX WINE

A box wine is a wine packaged as a Bag-In-Box. Such packages contain a plastic bladder protected by a box, usually made of corrugated fibreboard.

The 'wine cask' was invented by Thomas Angove of Angove's, a winemaker from Renmark, South Australia, and patented by the company on April 20, 1965. Polyethelene bladders of 1 gallon were put into corrugated boxes for sale to consumers. The original design required that the consumer cut the corner off the bladder inside the box, pour out the desired quantity of wine and then reseal it with a special peg.

In 1967 Charles Henry Malpas and Penfolds Wines patented a plastic, air-tight tap welded into a metallised bladder, making storage much more convenient for consumers. All modern wine casks now utilise some sort of plastic tap, which is exposed by tearing away a perforated panel on the box.

The main advantage to bag-in-a-box packaging is that it prevents oxidation of the wine during dispensing. After opening, wine in a bottle it is oxidised by air in the bottle which has displaced the wine poured; wine in a bag is not touched by air and thus not subject to oxidation until it is dispensed. Cask wine is not subject to cork taint or spoilage due to slow consumption after opening.

However, the bag is not hermetically sealed and has an unopened shelf life shorter than bottled wine. Most casks will have a best-before date stamped. As a result, it is not intended for cellaring and should be drunk within the prescribed period.

Bag in a box packaging is also preferred by producers of more economical wines because it is less expensive than glass bottles. A bag of wine, once removed from the box, will float on water; this allows quick cooling of a white wine by immersion in an ice bath.

The packaging first found commercial success in the land of its invention Australia, and while it has since established a steady market across Europe, in the U.S. the boxed wine has found difficulty in overcoming a down-market image.

Pros and Cons

Bag-in-box packaging is not inferior to bottles, but is preferred by some wineries because it is far less expensive, lighter and more environmentally friendly than bottled wine and far easier to handle and transport. Boxed wine is typically cheaper than bottled varieties.

Unlike bottled wine which goes bad a few days after opening, boxed wine stays fresh for weeks after opening since the vacuum-sealed pouch does not allow the wine to be exposed to air. However, unopened boxed wines do have a shorter shelf life than bottled wines so most boxes will have a best-before date stamped on them. As a result, the product is not intended for cellaring and should be consumed within the prescribed period. Deterioration may be quite noticeable by 12 months after filling.

Manufacturers of 'higher class' bottled wines have complained about the cheapness of 'cask' wines, arguing that they provide a cheap means for alcoholics to become inebriated. In particular, the lower level of alcohol excise levied on cask wine in Australia has been criticised as encouraging binge drinking. Cask wine in Australia is colloquially referred to as "goon" or "boxy", in reference to its low price and high alcohol content.

Box wine is considered to have benefits from an environment protection point of view. The bag allows a contents of 2-10 litres, so that far less packaging mass is required. The material it is made from is very light, which reduces greenhouse gas emissions caused by transport.

CARBOY

A carboy is a rigid container with a typical capacity of 5 to 15 gal. Carboys are primarily used for transporting fluids such as water, chemicals. etc. They are also used for in-home fermentation of beverages, often wine.

Brewing

In brewing, a carboy is also known as a demijohn. It is a glass or plastic vessel used in fermenting beverages such as wine, mead, and beer. Usually it is fitted with a rubber stopper and a fermentation lock to prevent bacteria and Oxygen from entering during the fermentation process.

During the homebrewing process, a primary carboy is used for fermentation. Once primary fermentation is complete, the beer is either transferred to a secondary carboy for conditioning or it can be transferred directly to bottles for conditioning.

Polypropylene carboys are also commonly used in laboratories to transfer purified water. They are typically filled at the top and have a spigot at the bottom for dispensing.

The word carboy is from the Persian *qarabah*, from Arabic *qarraba*, "big jug". Carboys come in various volumes ranging from 1 gallon to 6.5 gallons.

The term carboy used on its own will generally refer to a 5 gallon carboy, unless otherwise noted. A one gallon carboy is usually called a jug. A 15 gallon carboy is often called a demijohn. "Demijohn" is an old word that formerly referred to any glass vessel with a large body and small neck, enclosed in wickerwork. The word is said to derive from the name of a Persian town, Damaghan, but this is not supported by any historical evidence. *The Oxford English Dictionary* the word comes from the French *dame-jeanne*, literally "Lady Jane", as a popular appellation. This is in accordance with the historical evidence at present known, since the word occurred initially in France in the 17th century, and no earlier trace of it has been found elsewhere.

In Britain, demijohn refers to a one-gallon glass brewing vessel. In Southeast U.S. slang, a demijohn jug, of any size, is referered to as a jimmyjohn. The name is sometimes misspelled as "carboil," "carbuoy," or "carble."

Laboratory

In modern laboratories, carboys are usually made of plastic, though traditionally were made of feric glass or other shatter-resistant glasses immune to acid corrosion or halide staining common in older plastic fomulations. They are used to store large quantities of liquids, such as solvents or deionized water. In these applications, a tap may be included for dispensing. Carboys are also used to collect and store waste solvents. Collecting waste solvents in plastic carboys is preferable to reusing glass Winchesters due to the lesser chance of breakage if a solution is placed in an incorrectly labeled carboy.

CELLARTRACKER

CellarTracker is a web site that stores information about wines and wine collections. Created in 2003 by Eric LeVine, a former Microsoft programme manager. As of May 2009, CellarTracker, it has more than 80,000 users, and entries for over 12 million individual bottles. On the site, users can track wines they have purchased and consumed, input tasting notes, value their collections, and share their information with others.

CellarTracker is free to use, but donations are encouraged; in 2006 Levine predicted the site would gross $225,000 in revenue in 2007. LeVine, that he designed CellarTracker to save wine collectors from having to enter the same information twice, which addressed a "fatal flaw" that he saw in other wine software utilities at the time.

CLOSURE (WINE BOTTLE)

Closure is a term used in the wine industry to refer to a stopper, the object used to seal a bottle and avoid harmful contact between the wine and oxygen.

They include:

- Traditional natural cork closures.

- Alternative wine closures, such as screw caps, synthetic closures, glass closures.
- Historical applications no longer in use, such as wooden stoppers with cloth or wax.

The choice of closure depends on issues such as the risk of cork taint, oxygen permeability and desired life of the wine. Another factor is consumer reaction, with the wine-buying public in Australia and New Zealand positive to alternative closures, while opinion is divided among consumers of the United States. In Europe, perceptions that associate screw caps with low-quality wine may be declining.

Screw Cap Closures

Screw caps have been associated with cheap wines in the past and have had some serious perception hurdles to hop; however, they are definitely on the rise with many winemakers in the U.S. and abroad experimenting with them on select wines. New Zealand is leading the wine industry with the majority of wineries converting from cork to cap. Wineries in Australia, Spain, South Africa, South America, Canada, the U.S. and France are all testing the capping trend as well.

Currently there are three ways to close a bottle of wine: natural cork, synthetic cork and screw caps.

Natural cork closures have a centuries-long heritage. A "corked" bottle has a musty smell and taste that stems from TCA-a substance used to sanitize the natural cork prior to bottling. The result is a flat, moldy flavour devoid of fruit-filled taste and aroma. It is estimated that about 5-10 per cent of wines available on merchants' shelves are "corked."

Synthetic corks, derived from plastic, appeared to be a viable alternative to traditional corks. However, their track record has been tarnished due to their inability to keep oxidation at bay for any real length of time, significantly decreasing the shelf life of a wine and short-changing the maturing process of select wines.

Screw caps provide the best seal for bottled wines, and eliminate the "corked" and oxidation problem in one fell swoop. Hogue Cellars completed a 30-month study comparing natural and synthetic cork closures with the Stelvin screw caps, their findings suggest significant benefits in utilizing screw caps over either natural or synthetic cork closures. While, screw caps do diminish the drama and romance of bottle opening it is well worth the sacrifice to ensure a taint-free wine that offers consistent aging, maintained flavour and freshness with optimum quality control.

The Stelvin screw cap appears to be the industry's cap closure of choice. With producers such as Hogue Cellars, Beringer, Bonny Doon, Penfolds and many others utilizing the Stelvin screw cap closure for wines of all price ranges.

We are sure to look this trend take hold as winemakers and wine enthusiasts alike place a higher priority on overall quality and less on "corked" tradition.

CORK MATERIAL

Cork material is an impermeable, buoyant material, a prime-subset of generic cork tissue that is harvested for commercial use primarily from Quercus suber that is endemic to southwest Europe and northwest Africa. Cork is composed of suberin, a hydrophobic substance, and because of its impermeability, buoyancy, elasticity, and fire resistance, it is used in a variety of products, the most common of which is for wine stoppers. Portugal produces approximately 50 per cent of cork harvested annually worldwide.

There are about 2,200,000 hectares of cork forest worldwide; 33 per cent in Portugal, and 23 per cent in Spain. Annual production is about 340,000 tons; 52 per cent from Portugal, 32 per cent from Spain, 6 per cent Italy.

Once the trees are about 25 years old the cork is stripped from the trunks every nine years. The trees live for about 200 years. The first two harvests produce poorer quality cork.

The cork industry is generally regarded as environmentally friendly. The sustainability of production and the easy recycling of cork products and by-products are two of its most distinctive aspects. Cork oak forests also prevent desertification and are the home of various endangered species.

Carbon footprint studies committed by Corticeira Amorim, Oeneo Bouchage of France and the Cork Supply Group of Portugal concluded that cork is the most environmentally friendly wine stopper. The Corticeira Amorim's study, in particular was developed by PricewaterhouseCoopers, to ISO 14040 and ISO 14044 standards.

Cork oak forests comprise the majority of habitat for the Iberian lynx, one of the most endangered cat species in the world. Its decline has been a function of a loss of habitat due to development of housing as well as the introduction of a virus to control the rabbit population which was the lynx's primary prey.

Properties and Uses

Cork's elasticity combined with its near-impermeability makes it suitable as a material for bottle stoppers, especially for wine bottles. Cork stoppers represent about 60 per cent of all cork based production.

Cork's low density makes it a suitable material for fishing floats and buoys, as well as handles for fishing rods.

Sheets of cork, often the by-product of more lucrative stopper production, are used to make bulletin boards, and when used as floor tiles and other building materials, because it is a good insulator, it can reduce the energy required for heating. Granules of cork can also be mixed into concrete. The composites made by mixing cork granules and cement have low thermal conductivity, low density and good energy absorption. Some of the property ranges of the composites are density, compressive strength and flexural strength.

Use for wine Bottle Closures

As late as the mid-1600s, French vintners did not use cork stoppers, using oil-soaked rags stuffed into the necks of bottles instead.

Wine corks can be made of either a single piece of cork, or composed of particles, as in champagne corks; corks made of granular particles are called "technical corks". Natural cork closures are used for about 80 per cent of the 20 billion bottles of wine produced each year. After a decline in use as wine-stoppers due to the increase in the use of cheaper synthetic alternatives, cork wine-stoppers are making a comeback and currently represent approximately 60 per cent of wine-stoppers today.

Cork is a suitable material for use as a bottle stopper. Because of the cellular structure of cork, it is easily compressed upon insertion into a bottle and will expand to form a tight seal. The interior diameter of the neck of glass bottles tends to be inconsistent, making this ability to seal through variable contraction and expansion an important attribute. However, unavoidable natural flaws, channels, and cracks in the bark make the cork itself highly inconsistent. In a 2005 closure study 45 per cent of corks showed gas leakage during pressure testing both from the sides of the cork as well as through the cork body itself.

Since the mid-1990s, a number of wine brands have switched to alternative wine closures such as synthetic plastic stoppers, screwcaps, or other closures. In some countries, screwcaps are often seen as a cheap alternative destined only for the low grade wines, however in Australia, for example, the majority of non-sparkling wine production now uses these caps as a cork alternative. These alternatives to real cork have their own properties, some advantageous and others controversial.

For example, while screwtops are generally considered to offer a trichloroanisole free seal they reduce the oxygen transfer rate to almost zero, which can lead to reductive qualities in the wine. TCA is one of the primary causes of cork taint in wine. However, in recent years major cork producers have developed methods that remove most TCA from natural wine corks. Natural cork stoppers are important because they allow oxygen to interact with wine for proper aging, and are best suited for bold red wines purchased with the intent to age.

The study "Analysis of the life cycle of Cork, Aluminum and Plastic Wine Closures," commissioned by cork manufacturer Amorim and made public in

December 2008, concluded that cork is the most environmentally responsible stopper, in a one-year life cycle analysis comparison with the plastic stoppers and aluminum screwcaps.

Other Uses

Cork is used in musical instruments, particularly woodwind instruments, where it is used to fasten together segments of the instrument, making the seams airtight. Conducting baton handles are also often made out of cork.

Cork can be used as bricks for the outer walls of houses, as in Portugal's pavilion at Expo 2000. On November 28, 2007, the Portuguese national postal service CTT issued the world's first postage stamp made of cork.

Cork is used as the core of a baseball. Replacing the interior of a baseball bat with cork—a practice known as corking—was historically a method of cheating at baseball; the efficacy of the practice is now discredited.

Cork in Automotive Industry

The buoyance of natural cork is used to good effect in petrol and oil level gauges, but the most important application of cork in the automotive industries is in cork-and-rubber gaskets. Today, these are as essential as petrol or diesel fuel to the car and truck industries. The material used combine the compressibility and resilience of cork with the high mechanical strength and dimensional stability of rubber, making them the best substances of such automotive applications as oil pan gaskets, valve cover gaskets and timing gear cover gaskets.

Another important application of cork-and-rubber is as a seal to retain lubricants in crank shaft bearings when pressure is applied, the air within cork cells is compressed, thus exerting a reverse pressure on the restraining faces.

This is termed 'fight back' and is a primary requirement in all good gasket materials. Cork-and-rubber can be cut easily, and because it is strong and flexible, it can be used for making gaskets with narrow flanges. A wide variety of formulations used for making gaskets with narrow flanges. A wide variety of formulations using different types of rubber like Natural Rubber, Synthetic Rubber, Nitrile, Neo-prene, EPDM Silicone and sizes of cork granuals are available to meet the industry's various requirements.

Cork in Electrical Industry

Special cork-and-rubber have been developed to prevent leakage of the very searching cooling fluids used in modern electrical transformer, similar material are also widely used in switch gear circuit breakers, lightning arresters, and other transmission equipment, as well as in conduit fittings, gear cases and cover plates in washing machines.

Mechanical Properties	GR/GCS-R&B (Moderate Oil Resistant)			GR/GCS-S&P (Good Oil Resistant)			GR/GCS-I&II (Very good Oil Resistant)		
Grade	RC-50	RC-70	RC-80	RC-50B	RC-70B	RC-80B	RC-50C	RC-70C	RC-80C
Hardness IRDH	50±5	70±5	80±5	50±5	70±5	80±5	50±5	70±5	80±5
Dimensional change percent max.	1.5	1.5	1.5	1.5	1.5	1.5	1.5	1.5	1.5
Tensile Strength Kg/Cm^2 (KPa*) Min.	6.63 (650)	9.18 (900)	12.75 (1250)	7.14 (700)	12.75 (1250)	15.50 (1550)	12.75 (1250)	15.50 (1550)	19.50 (1900)
Compressibility at 28 Kg/Cm^2 (2800 KPa) Percent	45-60	35-50	25-35	45-60	35-50	25-35	35-45	25-35	15-25
Recovery Percent Min.	80	80	80	80	80	80	80	80	80
Compression Set Percent Max.	80	85	90	80	85	90	80	85	90
Chemical Test on water extracts									
a. pH where b. applicable	5.0 to 8.5			5.0 to 8.5			5.0 to 8.5		
c. Chloride content d. (as chloride ion)	0.2 Percent Max.			0.2 Percent Max.			0.2 Percent Max.		
e. Sulphate content (as sulphate ion)	0.2 Percent Max.			0.2 Percent Max.			0.2 Percent Max.		
Volume change after immersion in ASTM Oil No.3 for 70 hours at 100°C Temp.	40 Percent Max.			25 Percent Max.			15 Percent Max.		

- 1 Kg/cm^2=98.0665 KPa
- Variation in thickness at any point on the sheet is ± 10 per cent for thickness upto 2.50 mm and ±0.25 mm for thickness above 2.50 mm

CORK TAINT IN WINE

The waiter reluctantly returns a bottle of opened wine to the kitchen. "The gentleman out there told this wine is corked, and wants another one," he told to the manager.

The manager looks at the wine, and grudgingly replies, "What's he on about, there's no bits of cork in there! Give him another one we don't want a scene." I'm sure this scenario is played out daily in restaurants and cafes throughout the world. Such is the lack of understanding surrounding cork taint or corkiness in wine. So what is cork taint?

It is the biggest peril bottled wine buyers face. It strikes sporadically, randomly and often very ferociously. No wine, regardless of its pedigree or price, is immune. What is worse is that it forms in the wine after bottling, and cannot be detected until it is opened. It is the serial killer of wine. So exactly what is it, and how prevalent is it?

Cork taint is in fact a set of very undesirable aroma and flavour characters that are imparted to bottled wines following contact with their cork. Six chemical compounds have been found to contribute to cork taint. These are guaiacol, geosmin, 2-methylisoborneol (MIB), octen-3-ol and octen-3-one; and the most important of them all 2,4,6 trichloroanisole. TCA as it is affectionately known is a small and chemically simple molecule. With the exception of guaiacol, these compounds are sensorially very potent. TCA can be detected in dry white wine and sparkling wines at levels around two parts per trillion and in red and port wines at around five parts per trillion.

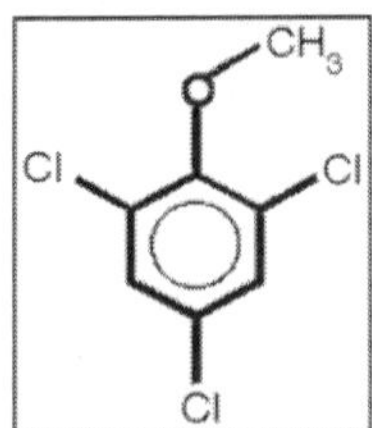

Fig. The Chemical Structure of 2,4,6 Trichloroanisole

Such low concentrations are difficult to conceptualise but it is analogous to one teaspoon in a couple of thousand olympic sized swimming pools or one second in 32,000 years. A single gram of pure TCA could badly taint the entire volume of wine produced in Australia each vintage. The other less common contributors to cork taint are not much better having sensory thresholds of around 20 parts per trillion.

For particularly badly tainted wines it is relatively easy if you know what to look for. TCA which is implicated in more than 80 per cent of cork tainted wines typically has a musty, mouldy or wet hessian character. MIB and geosmin have an earthy/muddy aroma, guaiacol is smoky or medicinal, and octen-3-ol and octen-3-one smell distinctly of tinned mushrooms.

While most corked wines are musty or mouldy, occasionally one of the other characters predominates. Complex chemical mechanisms underlie the production of TCA. The one of most importance is the conversion of chlorophenols to chloroanisole by common microscopic fungi such as Aspergillus sp. and Pennicilium sp., in the presence of moisture. Chlorophenols have been used as pesticides and as wood preservatives and as such are common environmental pollutants. The uptake of the minutest amounts of chlorophenol by cork tree bark during any stage of its growth, or subsequent manufacture into cork will provide the potential for cork taint production.

Cork bleaching with hyperchlorite also provide a ready source of chlorophenols for use by these micro-organisms. TCA can also be formed in packing materials and wooden shipping container floors. It can then pass either through the air or by direct contact to previously unaffected corks. For similar reasons TCA is a major contaminant of many other foods and beverages.

The exact incidence of cork taint in Australian wines is hotly debated. Estimates range from one to seven per cent. Australian Wine Research Institute records of the incidence of cork taint seen by winemakers in thousands of bottles of wines opened as part of their Advanced Wine Assessment Course suggest that the figure is around five per cent.

Whatever the exact figure, it is indisputable that cork taint is responsible for adversely modifying the sensory properties of a great deal of bottled wine each year. Arguments by even experienced tasters often arise over whether a wine is corked. This is due to a number of reasons. The first is that people vary greatly in their sensitivity to aromas, taints included. A rule of thumb is that for a specific aroma compound, the most perceptive five per cent of the population are about 200 times more sensitive than the bottom five per cent.

Therefore when at low levels, you can be sure that not everyone will perceive the taint. Secondly, cork taint manifests itself differently depending on its degree. At low levels, while not being noticed in its own right, the TCA suppresses the wine's aroma and flavour. Under these circumstances, comparison with other bottles is the only way in which the taint can be confidently verified.

The taint compounds themselves also smell differently depending on their concentration. For example, MIB is somewhat earthy at lower concentrations but when present in large amounts has a camphorous aroma. These shifts in the way the taint compounds smell makes them hard to pin down in some wines. Finally to exacerbate these problems of identification, humans quickly become adapted to the musty aroma of TCA. Continued sniffing of a TCA affected wine can result in rapid reductions in its perceived mustiness. In fact TCA is one of the most strongly adaptive compounds known.

The upshot of this is if you think a wine is corked on the first sniff, it probably is. Subsequent sniffing is far less reliable. The question of whether a wine is corked is also complicated by the fact that the same taints can arise not from the cork but from wine storage in TCA-affected oak barrels. Winemakers describe this as musty oak, and typically associate the fault with poorly maintained old oak. However even relatively new barrels can be affected by TCA.

The wine from a single badly contaminated barrel when blended with hundreds of others, will significantly affect the entire blend. Such is the potency of these compounds. So if you open a bottle of corked wine what can you do about it? In short, nothing. Under wine conditions TCA is a very stable compound. After it leaches into the wine shortly after bottling it will remain there outliving the wine itself.

No amount of subsequent breathing will clean up the wine. The cork is simply part of the wine's packaging. If its failure results in the wine not being of merchandisable quality then you have the legal right to return it. Large wineries receive hundreds of returned bottles each year on the basis of them being 'off'. Most of these are subsequently found to be cork tainted. Alternatively you could choose to purchase wines with alternative stoppers such as Stelvin capsules or synthetics.

However for a range of other reasons, cork is still undeniably the stopper of choice for most consumers and producers, and remains an important component of the wine packaging mix.

Production

The production of TCA in cork or its transfer by other means in to wine is complex, but most results when naturally-occurring airborne fungi are presented with chlorophenol compounds, which they then convert into chloroanisole.

Chlorophenols taken up by cork trees are an industrial pollutant found in many pesticides and wood preservatives, which may mean that the incidence of cork taint has risen in modern times. Chlorophenols can also be a product of the chlorine bleaching process ironically used to sterilize corks, which has led to the increasing adoption of methods such as peroxide bleaching.

TCA is responsible for the vast majority of cases of cork taint, but other less common and less known compounds that can cause different varieties include guaiacol, geosmin, 2-methylisoborneol, octen-3-ol and octen-3-one - each has its own aroma, all of them considered objectionable in wine.

Estimated Occurrence of Cork Taint and Industry Response

The cork-industry group APCOR cites a study showing a 0.7-1.2 per cent taint rate. In a 2005 study of 2800 bottles tasted at the *Wine Spectator* blind-tasting facilities in Napa, California, 7 per cent of the bottles were found to be tainted.

Improvements in cork and winemaking methodology continue to strive to lower the incidence, but the media attention given to cork taint has created a controversy in winemaking, with traditional cork growers on one side and the makers of newer synthetic closures and screw caps on the other. Screw caps and synthetic corks, however, can be prone to another aroma taint: sulphidisation, which arises from the reduced oxygen supply which concentrates sulphurous smells arising from universal preservatives.

Systemic TCA

Systemic TCA tainting occurs when TCA has infiltrated a winery via means other than cork and can affect entire production of wine instead of just a few bottles. This occurs when wine barrels, drain pipes, wooden beams in the cellars, and rubber hoses are tainted by TCA. Sometimes entire cellars have to be rebuilt in order to extinguish all potential systemic TCA culprits. Rubber hoses or gaskets have a high affinity for TCA and therefore concentrate TCA from the atmosphere.

Wine or water that subsequently passes through infected hoses can become tainted with TCA. Another possible means of TCA contamination is through the use of Bentonite, a clay preparation used in treating wine for heat stability. Bentonite has a high affinity for TCA and will absorb TCA and related chemicals in the atmosphere. If an open bag of Bentonite is stored in an environment with a high TCA concentration, this TCA will be absorbed in the Bentonite and transferred to the wine lot to which the Bentonite is added. It is notable that often this systemic TCA will impart a trace to the wine, which itself is not detected by most consumers. However, with this high baseline level of TCA in bottled wine, even a relatively clean cork can elevate the TCA level in the wine above threshold levels rendering the wine "corked."

The primary chemical precursor to TCA is TCP, an anti-microbial agent used in processing wood. Molds are able to de-toxify TCP by methylating the -OH to -OCH_3, which is not toxic. Chlorinated phenols can form chemically when hypochlorous acid or chlorine radicals come in contact with wood. The use of chlorine or other halogen-based sanitizing agents is being phased out of the wine industry in favour of peroxide or peracetic acid preparations.

It should be noted that chlorine dioxide has not been shown to produce these spontaneous chlorophenols. *Wine Spectator* has reported that such California wineries as Pillar Rock Vineyard, Beaulieu Vineyard, E & J Gallo Winery and Chateau Montelena have had trouble with Systemic TCA.

Treatment

There are now filtration and purification systems available which attempt to remove the TCA from corked wine to make it drinkable again, though there are few means of reducing the level of TCA in tainted wine that are approved by the TTB.

One method of removing TCA from tainted wine is to soak polyethylene in the infected wine. The non-polar TCA molecule has a high affinity for the polyethylene molecule, thereby removing the taint from the wine. The surface area of polyethylene needed to reduce the taint to sub-threshold levels is based on the TCA level in the affected wine, temperature, and the alcohol level of the wine.

This can be done at home, as advocated by Andrew Waterhouse by pouring the wine into a bowl with a sheet of polyethylene plastic wrap. For ease of pouring, a pitcher, measuring cup, or decanter can be used instead. Effective within a few minutes, the 2,4,6-trichloroanisole molecule is chemically similar to polyethylene and will stick to the plastic.

Some vintners have used Half and Half to remove TCA from wine. The French company Boffin markets a product called "Dream Taste" which uses a copolymer shaped like a cluster of grapes to remove the TCA taint from commercial wine.

DECIMAL DOZEN

A decimal dozen is a design of cartons for bottled wine that holds two rows of five bottles, developed by the Helm Wines winery, Canberra, Australia, to replace traditional dozen-bottle cartons. The quoted motivation is that demographics reports show that females buy more than 50 per cent of wine in Australia. The OH&S regulations, a female should not lift more than 15 kilograms, which is only the minimum gross weight of a standard 12-bottle carton, which can weigh up to 20 kg for some types of bottles. In 2005 it was a nominee for the ACT Occupational Health and Safety Award in the category "Best Solution to an Identified Workplace Health and Safety Issue" for addressing "the manual handling issues by introducing a ten bottle carton in a 2 × 5 configuration".

PUNCHEON

Puncheon is a tool or instrument for piercing or punching, such as those used for impressing designs onto coin dies. The "barrel" meaning is thought to derive from the fact that it would have been marked by use of a punch to denote its contents.

SOLERA

Solera is a process for aging liquids such as wine, beer, vinegar, and brandy, by fractional blending in such a way that the finished product is a mixture of ages, with the average age gradually increasing as the process continues over many years. A *solera* is literally the set of barrels or other containers used in the process. Products which are often *solera* aged include Sherry, Madeira, Port wine, Marsala, Mavrodafni, Muscat, and Muscadelle wines; Balsamic, Commandaria, and Sherry vinegars; Spanish brandy; and rums.

Fig. Sherry Solera

Solera Process

In the *solera* process, a succession of containers are filled with the product over a series of equal aging intervals. One container is filled for each interval. At the end of the interval after the last container is filled, the oldest container in the *solera* is tapped for part of its content, which is bottled. Then that container is refilled from the next oldest container, and that one in succession from the second-oldest, down to the youngest container, which is refilled with new product. This procedure is repeated at the end of each aging interval. The transferred product mixes with the older product in the next barrel. No container is ever drained, so some of the earlier product always remains in each container.

This remnant diminishes to a tiny level, but there can be significant traces of product much older than the average, depending on the transfer fraction. In theory traces of the very first product placed in the *solera* may be present even after 50 or 100 cycles.

Aging

The age of product from the first bottling is the number of containers times the aging interval. As the *solera* matures, the average age of product asymptotically approaches the initial age, divided by the fraction of a container which is transferred or bottled.

For instance, suppose the *solera* consists of four barrels of wine, and half of each barrel is transferred once a year. At the end of the fourth year, half the fourth barrel is bottled. This first bottling is aged four years. The second bottling will be half four years old and half five years old, for an average age of four and a half years.

The third bottling will be: one fourth wine that was six years in the fourth barrel, one fourth wine that was four years in the third barrel and one year in the fourth barrel, one fourth that was three years in the third barrel and two years in the fourth barrel, and one fourth that was two years in the second barrel, one year in the third, and one year in the fourth: average age five years. After 20 years, the output of the *solera* would be a mix of wine from 4 to 20 years old, averaging slightly under 8 years. The average age asymptotically converges on eight years as the *solera* continues.

Solera Production

The output of the *solera* is the fraction of the last container taken off for bottling each cycle. The amount of product tied up in the *solera* is usually many times larger than the production. This means that a *solera* is a very large capital investment for a winemaker. If done with actual barrels, the producer may have several *soleras* running in parallel. For a small producer, a *solera* may be the largest capital investment, and a valuable asset to be passed down to descendants. Wine produced from a solera cannot formally have a vintage date because it is a blend of vintages from many years. However, some bottlings are labeled with an age for marketing reasons. It is unclear whether such age indications denotes the average age, or the age of the oldest batch.

STOPPER (PLUG)

A stopper plug for sealing the tap hole of a molten metal receptacle is formed of refractory materials, fibrous substances, and consumable-disintegrable materials in a hollow conical plug that is expandable in a tap hole by movement of a wedge-shaped member therein, the expanded stopper plug being capable of effectively sealing the tap hole for a predetermined time.

WINE CELLAR

A wine cellar is a storage room for wine in bottles or barrels, or more rarely in carboys, amphorae or plastic containers. In an *active* wine cellar, important factors such as temperature and humidity are maintained by a climate control system. In contrast, *passive* wine cellars are not climate-controlled, and are usually built underground to reduce temperature swings. An aboveground wine cellar is often called a *wine room*, while a small wine cellar is sometimes termed a *wine closet*.

Purpose

Wine cellars protect alcoholic beverages from potentially harmful external influences, providing darkness and a constant temperature. Wine is a natural, perishable food product. Left exposed to heat, light, vibration or fluctuations in temperature and humidity, all types of wine can spoil. When properly stored, wines not only maintain their quality but many actually improve in aroma, flavour, and complexity as they mature.

Conditions

Wine can be stored satisfactorily between 7–18 °C as long as any variations are gradual. A temperature of 13 °C, much like what is found in the caves used to store wine in France, is ideal for both short-term storage and long-term aging of wine. Note that wine generally matures differently and more slowly at a lower temperature than it does at a higher temperature. Between 10–14 °C, wines will age normally.

Active Versus Passive

Wine cellars can be either active or passively cooled. Active wine cellars are highly insulated and need to be properly constructed. They require specialized wine cellar conditioning and cooling systems to maintain the desired temperature and humidity.

In a very dry climate, it may be necessary to actively humidify the air, but in most areas this is not necessary. Passive wine cellars must be located in naturally cool and damp areas with minor seasonal and diurnal temperature variations—for example, a basement in a temperate climate. Passive cellars may be less predictable, but cost nothing to operate and are not affected by power outages.

Debate on Humidity

Some wine experts debate the importance of humidity for proper wine storage. In the *Wine Spectator*, writer Matt Kramer noted a French study which claimed that the relative humidity within a bottle is maintained 100 per cent regardless of the closure used or the orientation of the bottle. However, Alexis

Lichine told that low humidity can be a problem because it may cause organic corks to dry prematurely. An inch of gravel covering the floor periodically sprinkled with a little water was recommended to retain the desired humidity.

WINE CAVE

Wine caves are subterranean structures for the storage and aging of wine. They are an integral component of the wine industry world wide. The design and construction of wine caves represents a unique application of underground construction techniques. The storage of wine underground offers the benefits of energy efficiency and optimum use of limited land area. Wine caves naturally provide both high humidity and cool temperatures; key to the storage and aging of wine.

Humidity

High humidity minimizes evaporation. Wine makers consider humidity over 75 per cent for reds and over 85 per cent for whites to be ideal for wine aging and barrel storage. Humidity in wine caves ranges naturally from 70 to 90 per cent. In Northern California, wine barrel evaporation in a surface warehouse is on the order of 4 gallons per each 60 gallon barrel per year. In a wine cave, barrel evaporation is reduced to about 1 gallon per barrel per year. Since red wines are usually barreled and aged for two years, this represents a 10 per cent gross volume loss difference. For white wines, which are barreled and aged for about one year, a 5 per cent loss difference is realized, a significant savings.

Temperature

The wine industry has long considered a constant temperature between 55 °F and 60 °F to be optimal for wine storage and aging. The air temperatures in Northern California result in a uniform underground temperature of about 58 °F, optimal for wine caves. A surface warehouse requires energy to cool, heat, and humidify. While the most basic wine cave can cost over $100 per sq ft to construct, reduced energy costs result in a net savings over the long term.

Land Use

In the Napa-Sonoma wine growing region, as in many areas of California, land values are high. Non-agricultural development is often restricted. A storage warehouse reduces the land available to grow grapes, impacts open space and natural habitats, and precludes other land uses. Land-use regulation in California places limitations on the types and locations of land development. Many land use restrictions and permitting requirements do not apply to underground space. In Northern California there are an estimated 130 to 150 caves used for wine aging, barrel storage, and tasting rooms.

Marketing

Marketing is an important component of the modern wine industry, and many caves serve varied marketing and public relations functions. Recently constructed caves contain commercial and private kitchens, wine libraries, concert, staff offices, elevators, restrooms, and other amenities. Some have high-end interiors, including ceramic and stone flooring, masonry-lined walls and ceilings, sculpture and artwork, mood lighting, fountains, waterfalls, and chandeliers.

Wine Cave Construction

The challenge for the design and construction of most wine caves is to create a fairly wide span in weak rock with low cover. The size of a typical wine barrel storage cave is 13 to 18 ft wide and 10 to 13 ft high. Constructed caves, however, range up to 85 ft in width and 50 ft in height; difficult to achieve in poor quality rock. In areas of complex geology, good portal sites are hard to find. A typical wine cave is constructed with two or more portal sites, for safety and operational reasons. At least one portal leads directly outside, but in many cases at least one portal makes a direct connection to a winery building.

Most portals into the wine caves have rock/soil overburden heights less than 0.2 times their entrance heights and widths. The height of the portal face normally ranges from 12 to 20 ft. The portal areas are seldom stripped of the loose soil material and the portals are cut from the native ground surface using excavators. The side slopes of the portal are often laid back to 0.5H:1V or steeper, and the portal face is excavated to vertical or near vertical.

The construction of cave interiors can be complicated by the elaborate curves and labyrinth-style floor plans selected by some owners for their wine caves. As the ground surface slopes upward, providing more cover and usually sounder rock, caves can accommodate multiple drifts. Where possible, the cave is designed and constructed to provide at least 1.2 times their width of cover at intersections. Room and pillar layouts, similar to underground mine design, provide an economical construction arrangement. Tunnel legs are usually 30 to 100 ft in length and pillars are typically a minimum of 20 ft wide.

On most occasions, the New Austrian Tunneling Method which is also known now as Sequential Excavation Method, with minor innovative technology advances, is used to excavate and support wine caves. The caves are typically excavated in an inverted horseshoe shape with a crown radius and with straight or curved legs. The tunnels are usually excavated using a tunnel roadheader or a milling head attachment on an excavator. The spoils behind the roadheader conveyor belt are dumped on the invert and mucked out using a rubber-tired skid loader or a load-haul-dump (LHD) mining machine.

Initially, the excavation advance is likely to be limited to 2 ft without initial ground support. Once turned under, and depending on ground conditions, the unsupported advance may be increased to 4 ft, 6 ft and longer increments. The maximum advance without initial ground support may reach 20 ft or more in stable volcanic ash tuff. In sheared serpentinite, deeply weathered lava rock or wet clayey ground, however, unstable ground conditions may limit the unsupported advance to less than 2 ft. Shotcrete reinforcement and ground support is utilized at the tunnel portals and in the interior of the wine caves. At the portals, soil nail and shotcrete walls are typically used for permanent support and are constructed from the top down in lifts. Soil nails are installed 4 to 6 ft apart in the horizontal and vertical directions. The shotcrete is typically a minimum of 6 inches thick and reinforced with welded wire fabric. The typical 4,000 psi design strength mix is applied using the wet process.

Within the caves, the initial ground support is usually fibre-reinforced shotcrete. A minimum of 2 inches thickness of wet mix shotcrete is applied around the exposed ground perimeter following each day's advance. As cave dimensions and ground conditions require, additional layers of shotcrete and welded wire fabric follow on subsequent days. The shotcrete mix is a 4,000 psi compressive strength design. In some cases, pattern or spot rock bolts are also installed. Where wider and taller halls are used, modeling is employed to assist with the liner design. Interior finishing of the caves is an integral part of the construction process. Wet spots and water seeps are unsightly, and can cause maintenance and safety problems. Moisture vapor migration through the cave liner, however, is desirable to maintain humidity.

Most contractors install prefabrication drainage strips at regular intervals between the native ground and the shotcrete liner. The drain strips relieve the hydrostatic pressure, but have little effect on wet spots and water seeps. Where excessive groundwater is present, membranes placed between successive shotcrete layers have been used. Many new products, including admixtures and membranes, are being evaluated and tested to improve moisture conditions. The wine cave industry in Northern California is at the forefront of waterproofing technology implementation. After the cave complex has been completely excavated, waterproofed, and initially supported, a 2 inches thickness of final shotcrete or plain/coloured gunite is applied to the walls and arch. Utility conduits and piping are encased within the final layer of shotcrete in the walls and arch and placed under the concrete floor slab. Reinforced concrete slabs are usually 6 in. thick and are underlain by subdrain.

To support their varied uses, wine cave complexes may contain as many as 13 different utility systems. These include systems for hot and cold domestic water and processing water, electric power, lighting, sound and water features, battery emergency power, compressed gas systems, communications and radio relays, automatic ventilation, and computerized sensors and climate controls.

WINE LABELS

Every bottle of wine must have a label, and that label must provide certain information about the wine. Some of the information on a wine label is required by the country where the wine is *made.* Other items of information are required by the country where the wine is *sold.* When the requirements are different in the two places, life can get very, very complicated for label writers!

The Forward and Backward of Wine Labels

Many wine bottles have two labels. The front label names the wine and grabs your eye as you walk down the aisle, ranging from reallyhelpful suggestions like "this wine tastes delicious with food" to oh-so-useful data such as "this wine has a total acidity of 6.02 and a pH of 3.34." The U.S., requires certain information to appear on the front label of all wine bottles — basic stuff, such as the alcohol content, the type of wine and the country of origin — but they don't define *front label.* So sometimes producers put all that information on the smaller of two labels and call that one the front label. Then the producers place another larger, colourful, dramatically eye-catching label — with little more than the name of the wine on it — on the *back* of the bottle. Guess which way the back label ends up facing when the bottle is placed on the shelf?

The Mandatory Sentence

The federal government mandates that certain items of information appear on labels of wines sold in the U.S. Such items are generally referred to as *the mandatory.* These include

- A brand name.
- Indication of class or type.
- The percentage of alcohol by volume.
- Name and address of the bottler
- Net contents.
- The phrase *Contains Sulfites.*
- The government warning

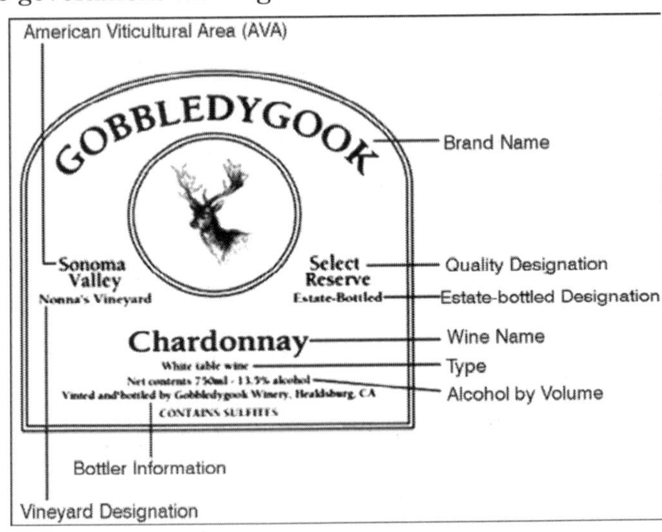

Fig. The Label of an American Varietal Wine.

Label Definitions

Here's some other terms you may find on the label of your favorite bottle of wine:

- *Vintage year*: The year in which the grapes for a particular wine were harvested.
- *Reserve*: Indicates that a wine has received extra aging at the winery before release.
- States that the company the bottled the wine also grew the grapes.

WINE RACKS

Wine racks can be decorative or utilitarian, but they all have one thing in common — they are designed to hold wine bottles to free up space.

Some wine racks are designed to safely store bottles, while others display wine. Storage racks, called *cellar style* wine racks, can be modular or stackable, so that one can buy as many or as few as needed. Wine racks that are used for storage are usually made of wood, often pine. They are rectangular frames without a front or back, that stand on a wide foot. The frames have vertical runners, evenly spaced, with horizontal ledges placed at even intervals inside the length of the runners, forming small square compartments. A wine bottle is laid on its side inside a compartment. These modular style wine racks can be stacked in a cellar or large kitchen to form a wall, or they can be used individually, placed on a counter. A small modular wine rack normally holds 10 bottles of wine.

More ornate wine racks are available in materials like wrought iron, crafted into various designs, such as a ribbon gracefully wrapping around itself. The "ribbon" might hold a single bottle of wine. A wine rack like this is purely decorative and kept on a counter.

Wine racks come in countless designs, limited only by the imagination. There are wine racks to fit every purpose, décor and personality. A wine rack can add ambiance to a room, protect wine in a cellar, or keep wine handy on the counter. Low-profile wine racks are even made for storing wine inside the refrigerator.

Materials

Wood

Wood is the most popular medium when it comes to wine rack construction. It is easily obtainable and very workable. Many types of wood are used. Cedar is popular choice because of the aroma is gives off. This aroma is also its downfall. It can penetrate the wine via the cork. Fir is another popular choice. It also is very strong and comes in a natural cream colour. Wood is also easily painted and sealed if individuals are looking for a more distinct look.

Metal

Metal is another popular choice for wine racks. Although it is not as easy to work with as wood, metal pieces tend to be more unique. With metal, more fluid and flowing shapes can be made, which is impossible with wood. Metal can also be painted to match any decor. Metal racks are a good idea for short-term wine storage. Since they tend to be smaller and hold fewer bottles, they are better for display than wine aging.

5

The Business of Wine

WINE BUSINESS IN AMERICA

American wine has been produced for over 300 years. Today, wine production is performed in all fifty states, with California leading the way in wine production followed by Washington State, Oregon and New York. The United States is the fourth largest wine producing country in the world after France, Italy, and Spain. The production in the U.S. State of California alone is more than double of the production of the entire country of Australia.

The North American continent is home to several native species of grape, including Vitis labrusca, Vitis riparia, Vitis rotundifolia, Vitis vulpina, and Vitis amurensis, but it was the introduction of the European Vitis vinifera by European settlers that led to the growth of the wine making industry. With more than 1,100,000 acres (4,500 km2) under vine, the United States is the fifth most planted country in the world after France, Italy, Spain and Turkey.

WINE REGIONS

There are nearly 3,000 commercial vineyards in the United States with at least one winery in all 50 States.

- *West Coast*: The majority of American wine production occurs in the states of California, Washington and Oregon.
- *Rocky Mountain Region*: Notably Idaho and Colorado
- *Southwestern United States*: Notably Texas and New Mexico
- *Midwestern United States*: Notably Missouri, Illinois and Minnesota
- *Great Lakes region*: Notably Michigan, northern New York and Ohio
- *East Coast of the United States*: Notably New Jersey, New York State, Pennsylvania, Virginia, and North Carolina

Appellation System

The early American appellation system was based on the political boundaries of states and counties. In September 1978 the Bureau of Alcohol, Tobacco and Firearms developed regulations to establish American Viticultural

Areas (AVA) based on distinct climate and geographical features. In June 1980, the Augusta AVA in Missouri was established as the first American Viticultural Area under the new appellation system. For the sake of wine labeling purposes, all the states and county appellations were grandfathered in as appellations. There were 187 distinct AVAs designated under U.S. law as of April 2007.

Appellation Labeling Laws

In order to have an AVA appear on a wine label, at least 85 per cent of the grapes used to produce the wine must be grown in the AVA.

With the larger state and county appellations the laws vary depending on the area. For a County Appellation, 75 per cent of the grapes used must be from that county. If grapes are from two or three contiguous counties, a label can have a multi-county designation so long as the percentages used from each county are clearly on the label. For the majority of U.S. States the State Appellation requires 75 per cent of the grapes in the wine to be grown in the state. Texas requires 85 per cent and California requires 100 per cent. If grapes are from two to three contiguous states a wine can be made under a multi-state designations following the same requirements as the multi-county appellation.

American wine or United States is a rarely used appellation that classifies a wine made from anywhere in the United States, including Puerto Rico and Washington, D.C.. Wines with this designation are similar to the French wine vin de table and can not include a vintage year. By law this is the only appellation allowed for bulk wines exported to other counties.

Semi-generic Wines

Current U.S. laws allow American made wines to be labeled as "American Burgundy" or "California champagne", even though these names are restricted in Europe. U.S. laws only restrict usage to include the qualifying area of origin to go with these semi-generic names. Other semi-generic names in the United States include Claret, Chablis, Chianti, Madeira, Malaga, Marsala, Moselle, Port, Rhine wine, Sauternes, Sherry and Tokay. European Union officials have been working with their U.S. counterparts through World Trade Organization negotiations to eliminate the use of these semi-generic names.

Fighting Varietals

Fighting varietal is a term that originated in California during the mid 1980s to refer to any inexpensive cork-finished varietal wine in a 1.5 litre bottle. Fighting varietals have largely replaced the jug wines that were often labeled with semi-generic names. Consumer demand for varietals has essentially dried up the market for semi-generic wines. The exception is very inexpensive sparkling wines that are sometimes labeled "California champagne."

Other U.S. Labeling Laws

In the United States, at least 95 per cent of grapes must be from a particular vintage for that year to appear on the label. Prior to the early 1970s, all grapes had to be from the vintage year. All labels must list the alcohol content based on percentage by volume. For bottles labeled by varietal at least 75 per cent of the grape must be of the varietal. In Oregon, the requirement is 90 per cent. American wine labels are also required to list if they contain sulfites and carry the Surgeon General's warning about alcohol consumption.

Three-tier Distribution

Following the repeal of Prohibition, the federal government allowed each state to regulate the production and sale of alcohol in their own state. For the majority of states this lead to the development of a three-tier distribution system between the producer, wholesaler and consumer. Depending on the state there are some exceptions, with wineries allowed to sell directly to consumers on site at the winery.

Some states allow interstate sales through e-commerce. In the 2005 case of Granholm v. Heald, the Supreme Court of the United States struck down state laws banning interstate shipments but allowing in-state sales. The outcome of the Supreme Court decision was that states could decide to allow out of states wine sales along with in state sales or ban both altogether.

Largest Producers

As of 2005 The largest producers of American wine.

- E & J Gallo Winery-Accounts for more than a quarter of all U.S. wine sales and is the second largest producer in the world.
- Constellation Brands-With foreign wine holdings Constellation is the largest producer in the world and includes Robert Mondavi Winery and Columbia Winery in its portfolio
- The Wine Group-San Francisco-based business which owns the Franzia box wine label, Concannon Vineyard and Mogen David kosher wine.
- Bronco Wine Company-Owners of the Charles Shaw wine "Two Buck Chuck" line which accounts for nearly 5 million of Bronco's annual average 9 million cases per year.
- Diageo-UK based company with American holdings in Sterling Vineyards, Beaulieu Vineyard and Chalone Vineyard.
- Brown-Forman Corporation-Owners of the Korbel Champagne Cellars brand.
- Beringer Blass-Australian based wine division of Foster's Group and owner of the Beringer wine and Stags' Leap Winery brands.
- Jackson Wine Estates-Owners of the Kendall-Jackson brand.

American Viticultural Area

An American Viticultural Area is a designated wine grape-growing region in the United States distinguishable by geographic features, with boundaries defined by the Alcohol and Tobacco Tax and Trade Bureau (TTB), United States Department of the Treasury. The TTB defines AVAs at the request of wineries and other petitioners. There were 193 AVAs as of February, 2009. Prior to the installation of the AVA system, wine appellations of origin in the United States were designated based on state or county boundaries. All of these appellations were grandfathered into federal law and may appear on wine labels as designated places of origin, but these appellations are distinct from AVAs.

American Viticultural Areas range in size from the Ohio River Valley AVA at 26,000 square miles (67,000 km2) across four states, to the Cole Ranch AVA in Mendocino County, California, at only 62 acres (25 ha). The Augusta AVA near the town of Augusta, Missouri was the first recognized AVA, gaining the status on June 20, 1980.

Unlike most European wine appellations of origin, an AVA specifies only a geographical location from which at least 85 per cent of the grapes used to make a wine must have been grown. AVAs are more similar to the Italian Indicazione Geografica Tipica than other European appellation of origin systems. American Viticultural Area designations do not limit the type of grapes grown, the method of vinification, or the crop yield. Some of those factors may, however, be used by the petitioner to justify uniqueness of place when proposing a new AVA.

Requirements

Current regulations impose the following additional requirements on an AVA:

- Evidence that the name of the proposed new AVA is locally or nationally known as referring to the area.
- Historical or current evidence that the boundaries are legitimate.
- Evidence that growing conditions such as climate, soil, elevation, and physical features are distinctive.

Petitioners are required to provide such information when applying for a new AVA, and are also required to use USGS maps to both describe and depict the boundaries.

Once an AVA is established, at least 85 per cent of the grapes used to make a wine must be grown in the specified area if an AVA is referenced on its label.

State or county boundaries-such as for Oregon or Sonoma County-are not AVAs, even though they are used to identify the source of a wine. AVAs are reserved for situations where a geographically defined area has been using the name and it has come to be identified with that area. A vineyard may be in more than one AVA. For example, the Santa Clara Valley AVA and Livermore

Valley AVAs are located within the territory of the San Francisco Bay AVA, which is itself located within the Central Coast AVA.

Current areas

The following is a listing of AVAs by region:

California AVAs

Central Coast and Santa Cruz Mountains

All of these AVAs are included in the geographic boundaries of the Central Coast AVA with the exceptions of Ben Lomond Mountain AVA and Santa Cruz Mountains AVA, which are surrounded by, but are specifically excluded from, the larger regional AVA.

- Arroyo Grande Valley
- Arroyo Seco
- Ben Lomond Mountain
- Carmel Valley
- Central Coast
- Chalone
- Cienega Valley
- Edna Valley
- Hames Valley
- Lime Kiln Valley
- Livermore Valley
- Monterey
- Mt. Harlan
- Pacheco Pass
- Paicines
- Paso Robles
- San Antonio Valley
- San Benito
- San Bernabe
- San Francisco Bay
- San Lucas
- San Ysidro District
- Santa Clara Valley
- Santa Cruz Mountains
- Santa Lucia Highlands
- Santa Maria Valley
- Sta. Rita Hills
- Santa Ynez Valley
- York Mountain

Central Valley

Unlike other regions of California, there is no large regional AVA designation that includes the entire Central Valley wine growing region.

- Alta Mesa
- Borden Ranch
- Capay Valley
- Clarksburg
- Clements Hills
- Cosumnes River
- Diablo Grande
- Dunnigan Hills
- Jahant
- Lodi
- Madera
- Merritt Island
- Mokelumne River
- River Junction
- Salado Creek
- Sloughhouse
- Tracy Hills

Klamath Mountains

These AVAs are located in the southern Klamath Mountains of far northwestern California.

- Seiad Valley
- Trinity Lakes
- Willow Creek

North Coast

All of these AVAs are included within the geographic boundaries of the six-county North Coast AVA.

- Alexander Valley
- Anderson Valley
- Atlas Peak
- Bennett Valley
- Benmore Valley
- Calistoga
- Chalk Hill
- Chiles Valley
- Clear Lake
- Cole Ranch
- Covelo

- Diamond Mountain District
- Dos Rios
- Dry Creek Valley
- Green Valley of Russian River Valley
- Guenoc Valley
- High Valley
- Howell Mountain
- Knights Valley
- Los Carneros
- McDowell Valley
- Mendocino
- Mendocino Ridge
- Mt. Veeder
- Napa Valley
- North Coast
- Northern Sonoma
- Oak Knoll District of Napa Valley
- Oakville
- Potter Valley
- Red Hills Lake County
- Redwood Valley
- Rockpile
- Russian River Valley
- Rutherford
- Solano County Green Valley
- Sonoma Coast
- Sonoma Mountain
- Sonoma Valley
- Spring Mountain District
- St. Helena
- Stags Leap District
- Suisun Valley
- Wild Horse Valley
- Yorkville Highlands
- Yountville

Sierra Foothills

All of these AVAs are contained entirely within the geographic boundaries of the Sierra Foothills AVA.

- California Shenandoah Valley
- El Dorado
- Fair Play

- Fiddletown
- North Yuba
- Sierra Foothills

South Coast

All of these AVAs are contained entirely within the geographic boundaries of the South Coast AVA.

- Cucamonga Valley
- Leona Valley
- Malibu-Newton Canyon
- Ramona Valley
- Saddle Rock-Malibu
- San Pasqual Valley
- South Coast
- Temecula Valley

Pacific Northwest AVAs

A list of American Viticultural Areas (AVAs) in the Pacific Northwest states of Oregon, Washington, and Idaho:

- Applegate Valley, Oregon
- Chehalem Mountains, Oregon
- Columbia Gorge, Oregon and Washington
- Columbia Valley, Washington and Oregon
- Dundee Hills, Oregon
- Eola-Amity Hills, Oregon
- Horse Heaven Hills, Washington
- Lake Chelan, Washington
- McMinnville, Oregon
- Puget Sound, Washington
- Rattlesnake Hills, Washington
- Red Hill Douglas County, Oregon, Oregon
- Red Mountain, Washington
- Ribbon Ridge, Oregon
- Rogue Valley, Oregon
- Snake River Valley, Idaho and Oregon
- Snipes Mountain AVA, Washington
- Southern Oregon, Oregon
- Umpqua Valley, Oregon
- Wahluke Slope, Washington
- Walla Walla Valley, Oregon and Washington
- Willamette Valley, Oregon
- Yakima Valley, Washington
- Yamhill-Carlton District, Oregon

East Coast AVAs

A list of American Viticultural Areas (AVAs) on the East Coast of the United States:

- Catoctin, Maryland
- Cayuga Lake, New York
- Central Delaware Valley, New Jersey and Pennsylvania
- Cumberland Valley, Maryland and Pennsylvania
- Finger Lakes, New York
- Haw River Valley, North Carolina
- Hudson River Region, New York
- Lake Erie, New York, Ohio, and Pennsylvania
- Lancaster Valley, Pennsylvania
- Lehigh Valley, Pennsylvania
- Linganore, Maryland
- Long Island, New York
- Martha's Vineyard, Massachusetts
- Monticello, Virginia
- Niagara Escarpment, New York
- North Fork of Long Island, New York
- North Fork of Roanoke, Virginia
- Northern Neck George Washington Birthplace, Virginia
- Outer Coastal Plain, New Jersey
- Rocky Knob, Virginia
- Seneca Lake, New York
- Shenandoah Valley, Virginia and West Virginia
- Southeastern New England, Connecticut, Massachusetts, and Rhode Island
- Swan Creek, North Carolina
- The Hamptons, Long Island, New York
- Virginia's Eastern Shore, Virginia
- Warren Hills, New Jersey
- Western Connecticut Highlands, Connecticut
- Yadkin Valley, North Carolina

Central US AVAs

A list of the remaining American Viticultural Areas (AVAs), not on the West or East Coasts:

- Alexandria Lakes, Minnesota
- Altus, Arkansas
- Arkansas Mountain, Arkansas
- Augusta, Missouri
- Bell Mountain, Texas

- Escondido Valley, Texas
- Fennville, Michigan
- Fredericksburg in the Texas Hill Country, Texas
- Grand River Valley, Ohio
- Grand Valley, Colorado
- Hermann, Missouri
- Isle St. George, Ohio
- Kanawha River Valley, West Virginia
- Lake Michigan Shore, Michigan
- Lake Wisconsin, Wisconsin
- Leelanau Peninsula, Michigan
- Loramie Creek, Ohio
- Mesilla Valley, New Mexico and Texas
- Middle Rio Grande Valley, New Mexico
- Mimbres Valley, New Mexico
- Mississippi Delta, Louisiana, Mississippi, and Tennessee
- Ohio River Valley, Indiana, Kentucky, Ohio, and West Virginia
- Old Mission Peninsula, Michigan
- Ozark Highlands, Missouri
- Ozark Mountain, Arkansas, Missouri, and Oklahoma
- Shawnee Hills, Illinois
- Shenandoah Valley, Virginia and West Virginia
- Sonoita, Arizona
- Texas Davis Mountains, Texas
- Texas High Plains, Texas
- Texas Hill Country, Texas
- Texoma, Texas
- Upper Mississippi Valley, Iowa, Minnesota, Illinois and Wisconsin
- West Elks, Colorado

Arbor Mist

Arbor Mist is the brand name of an alcoholic beverage which blends seasonal wines such as merlot, zinfandel and chardonnay with fruit flavourings. Its slogan is "Great Tasting Wine with a Splash of Fruit," describing the beverage. Arbor Mist has a lower alcohol content than most wines, and is usually cheaper than other similar alcoholic beverages. It is made by the Arbor Mist Winery in Canandaigua, New York, and is packaged by Constellation Brands.

Arbor Mist first appeared on store shelves in the United States in the summer of 1998, and was the best-selling wine debut since the 1970s. Originally appearing in just two different fruit varieties, Arbor Mist now makes twelve different varieties of their wine product. These flavours include: Blackberry Merlot, Cranberry Twist White, Merlot, and Orchard Fruits Chardonnay. Arbor

Mist now manufactures "wine blenders" as well. In 2009 Arbor Mist launched two new Sparkling products: Peach Sparkle and Raspberry Sparkle.

Charles Shaw Wine

Charles Shaw is a brand of "extreme value" wine. Largely made from California grapes, Charles Shaw wines currently include Cabernet Sauvignon, White Zinfandel, Merlot, Chardonnay, Sauvignon Blanc, Shiraz, Valdiguie in the style of Beaujolais nouveau, and limited quantities of Pinot Grigio. In 2009, an international version of Chardonnay from Australia was introduced in limited stores. These wines once sold for $1.99 exclusively at Trader Joe's grocery stores in California, which had the wines gaining the nickname "Two Buck Chuck."

Coombsville

Coombsville is an agricultural area located at the southeastern end of the Napa Valley's famed grape-growing appellation. Since the middle of the 20th century, it has gained recognition for its suitability for slow-ripening Bordeaux varietals such as cabernet sauvignon.

A geographic area shaped like a "cup and saucer," Coombsville is characterized by gently hilly terrain formed millions of year ago by shifting masses of earth. Part of the proposed Tulocay American Viticultural Area or AVA, Coombsville is distinguished from other parts of the Napa Valley by its slightly cooler climate and soil conditions, which are a mix of well-draining river rock and mineral-rich volcanic ash.

The area takes its name from Nathan Coombs who purchased the land from Nicholas Higuera's Rancho Entre Napa, an 1836 Mexican land grant. It was out this parcel that Coombs created the city of Napa in 1847.

Located east of Napa, Coombsville's agricultural orientation was initially focused on livestock and subsistence farming as opposed to vineyard development. It was only in the mid-20th century that the region began to attract attention from grape growers and vintners, including John Caldwell.

Today, it is home to several wineries and vineyards, including Caldwell Vineyard, Dolce Winery, Farella Vineyard, Marita's Vineyard, Porter Family Vineyards, Sodaro Estate Winery, and Tulocay Winery.

Franzia

Franzia is a brand of wine produced by The Wine Group, known for its box wines sold in 3 and 5-litre cartons. The Wine Group is the third largest wine company in the world, behind Constellation Brands and the DGP Wine Gallery. Franzia wines are quite inexpensive, and thus Franzia wine is popular among university students in the United States. The Franzia brand today has no relationship with Fred Franzia of the Bronco Wine Company, also known for its low-cost Charles Shaw wines. The Franzia family sold the brand to Coca-Cola in 1973, and it was sold to The Wine Group in 1981.

Manischewitz

Manischewitz is a leading brand of kosher products based in the United States, best-known for their matzo and wine. Founded in 1888 and under family control until 1990, it is the world's largest matzo manufacturer and one of America's largest kosher brands.

The B. Manischewitz Company, LLC was founded by Rabbi Dov Behr Manischewitz, in 1888 in Cincinnati, Ohio. The Company built a second factory in Jersey City, New Jersey in 1932, to better serve the large Jewish community of the New York metropolitan area, and the Cincinnati factory was eventually closed in 1958. In 1990 a $1 million fine was levied against the company for price fixing with its two main competitors at the time, Streit's and Horowitz. Ownership of the B. Manischewitz Company was maintained by the Manischewitz family until it was purchased by a group led by Kohlberg and company in 1990 for $42.5 million. In 2004 its name was changed to R.A.B. Food Group, LLC and today is known as The Manischewitz Company. Manischewitz remains the world's top matzo manufacturer and one of America's top kosher brands.

Foods

Manischewitz has revolutionized the way in which matzo is produced. By mass producing matzos they turned matzo making from a strictly local product into a national, and eventually international product. Manischewitz matzos were also the first to feature uniform texture, taste, and feel. When the company first began shipping matzos they also decided to make them square, whereas before matzos had been consistently round. Manischewitz's main innovation-making matzos with machines instead of by hand, aroused some initial controversy. Some rabbis of the era claimed that in order to be acceptable for religious use, the matzo had to have been made by a man and not a machine. Manischewitz was ultimately able to overcome these concerns, in part by demonstrating the meticulous adherence to the religious rules that were being demonstrated.

In addition to matzo, Manischewitz-labeled foods include cookies, pasta, and soups. Other well-known kosher brands associated with R.A.B. include Carmel, Elite, Mother's, Rokeach, Mrs. Adler's, and Tradition; many of these were acquired by R.A.B. after successful runs as independent kosher labels. Kosher foods such as these are staples of many supermarkets in the United States. R.A.B. is not involved with Manischewitz wine, however, except in name: it has, since 1986, licensed the Manischewitz brand name to the Manischewitz Wine Company, a subsidiary of Canandaigua Wine Company.

Wine

The Manischewitz winery is located in Naples, New York, and has since 1987 been the property of Constellation Brands, which continues to license the Manischewitz name from R.A.B. Foods. The Winery was founded by Leo Star and run by the Star family since 1927.

The Manischewitz winery is best known for its sweet concord wine, which is widely available in much of North America. Made from labrusca grapes, its aroma is unusual, and is combined with a large amount of residual sugar. As concord was popularized over the years by U.S. media as being the kosher wine, it is often the wine used by non-Orthodox Jews in celebrating Passover. However, Manischewitz's sweet Concord contains corn syrup, a sweetener derived from corn, which is a food forbidden for Passover. Manischewitz produces special Kosher for Passover bottling of their wine which are sweetened with cane sugar as opposed to the corn syrup used throughout the year.

It is also used as Communion wine: The sweetness of Manischewitz wine and other kosher wines is often the fodder of jokes. However, Kosher wine does not have to be sweet. One of the reasons for the prevalence of sweet kosher wine in the U.S., and in the Americas generally, dates back to the early days of Jews in America, when there was the need to locally produce kosher wine for the Kiddush ritual on the Shabbat and holidays. The combination of a limited choice of grape varieties that could grow in the areas where Jews had settled, along with limited time available to produce the wine and a market dominated by hard cider, yielded a bitter wine that had to be sweetened to make it palatable.

Indeed, so well-known is the sweet Manischewitz variety in the U.S. that the existence of a thriving kosher wine industry anchored by vineyards in France and Israel, along with a growing U.S. industry, is often a surprise to Americans unaccustomed to taking kosher wine seriously.

Meritage

Meritage is a proprietary term used to denote red and white Bordeaux-style wines without infringing on the Bordeaux region's legally protected designation of origin. Winemakers must license the Meritage trademark from its owner, the California-based Meritage Alliance. Member wineries are found principally in the United States, though increasingly elsewhere.

The Meritage Association was formed in 1988 by a small group of Napa Valley, California vintners increasingly frustrated by U.S. BATF regulations stipulating wines contain at least 75 per cent of a specific grape to be labeled as that varietal. As interest grew in creating Bordeaux-style wines, which by their blended nature fail to qualify for varietal status, members sought to create a recognizable name for their high-quality blended wines. In 1988, the association hosted a contest to conceive a proprietary name for these wines, receiving over

6,000 submissions. "Meritage", -a combination of merit and heritage, was selected and its coiner awarded two bottles of the first ten vintages of every wine licensed to use the brand.

By 1999 The Meritage Association had grown to 22 members. Shifting its focus from trademark policing to education and marketing resulted in swift growth. By 2003 the Association had over 100 members, including its first international participants.

In May of 2009, The Meritage Association announced that it has changed its name to The Meritage Alliance. As of August 2009, the Alliance had over 250 members.

Trademark Licensing and Wine Production

The Meritage agreement stipulates the blends that can be labeled "Meritage", a fee per case and various labeling restrictions.

Red Bordeaux is made principally from Cabernet Sauvignon and Merlot grapes, with lesser proportions of Cabernet Franc, Petit Verdot, and Malbec. A red Meritage must be made from at least two of these grapes with no varietal comprising more than 90 per cent of the blend.

White Meritage is a blend of at least two of the principal white Bordeaux grapes Sauvignon Blanc, Sémillon, and Muscadelle du Bordolais.

Although not stipulated by the licensing agreement, the Meritage Association strongly recommends that wineries label only their best blend Meritage and limit production to no more than 25,000 cases.

WINE BUSINESS IN ARGENTINE

The Argentine wine industry is the fifth leading producer of wine in the world. Argentine wine, as with some aspects of Argentine cuisine, has its roots in Spain. During the Spanish colonization of the Americas, vine cuttings were brought to Santiago del Estero in 1557, and the cultivation of the grape and wine production stretched first to neighbouring regions, and then to other parts of the country.

Historically, Argentine winemakers were traditionally more interested in quantity than quality with the country consuming 90 per cent of the wine it produces. Until the early 1990s, Argentina produced more wine than any other country outside Europe, though the majority of it was considered unexportable. However, the desire to increase exports fueled significant advances in quality. Argentine wines started being exported during the 1990s, and are currently growing in popularity, making it now the second biggest wine exporter in Latinamerica behind Chile.

The devaluation of the Argentine peso in 2002, following the economic collapse, further fueled the industry as production costs decreased and tourism significantly increased, giving way to a whole new concept of wine tourism in

Argentina. The past years have seen the birth of numerous tourist-friendly wineries with free tours and tastings. The Mendoza Province is now one of Argentina's top tourist destinations and the one which has grown the most in the past years.

The most important wine regions of the country are located in the provinces of Mendoza and San Juan and La Rioja. Salta, Catamarca, Río Negro and more recently Southern Buenos Aires are also wine producing regions. The Mendoza province produces more than 60 per cent of the Argentine wine and is the source of an even higher percentage of the total exports.

Due to the high altitude and low humidity of the main wine producing regions, Argentine vineyards rarely face the problems of insects, fungi, molds and other grape diseases that affect vineyards in other countries. This permits cultivating with little or no pesticides, allowing even organic wines to be easily produced.

There are many different varieties of grapes cultivated in Argentina, reflecting her many immigrant groups. The French brought Auxerrois, which became known as Malbec, which makes most of Argentina's best known wines. The Italians brought vines that they called Bonarda, although Argentine Bonarda appears to be the Corbeau of Savoie, also known as Charbono in California, which may be related to Dolcetto.

It has nothing in common with the light fruity wines made from Bonarda Piemontese in Piedmont. Torrontés is another typically Argentine grape and is mostly found in the provinces of La Rioja, San Juan, and Salta. It is a member of the Malvasia group that makes aromatic white wines. It has recently been grown in Spain. Cabernet Sauvignon, Syrah, Chardonnay and other international varieties are becoming more widely planted, but some varieties are cultivated characteristically in certain areas.

Backdrop

Viticulture was introduced to Argentina during the Spanish colonization of the Americas and later again by Christian missionaries. In 1541, Vitis vinifera vines were brought from Spain and planted along the Río de la Plata by the Atlantic coast. The vines did not thrive in the humid subtropical climate of the region and viticultural activity in the area was eventually abandoned. In 1542, dried grape seeds taken from vines in Peru were planted near what is now the Salta Province east of the Andes. Eight years later another expedition from Peru brought vine cuttings.

In 1556, cuttings from the Chilean Central Valley were brought to what is now the San Juan and Mendoza wine region which firmly established viticulture in Argentina. Ampelographers suspect that one of these cuttings brought the ancestor grape of the Chile's Pais and California's Mission grape. This grape was the forerunner of the Criolla Chica variety that would be the backbone of the Argentine wine industry for the next 300 years. The first recorded commercial vineyard was established at Santiago del Estero in 1557 by Jesuit missionaries which was followed by expansion of vineyard plantings in Mendoza in the early 1560s and San Juan between 1569 and 1589. During this time the missionaries and settlers in the area began construction of complex irrigation channels and dams that would bring water down from the melting glaciers of the Andes to sustain vineyards and agriculture. While a provincial governor, Domingo Faustino Sarmiento, instructed the French agronomist Miguel Aimé Pouget to bring grapevine cutting from France to Argentina. Of the vines that Pouget brought were the very first Malbec vines to be planted in country.

As the infantile Argentine wine industry became centralized in the western part of country among the foothills of the mountains, the population centers of the country developed in the east. Transporting wine by means of a long wagon journey put a crimp in the growth of the wine industry that would not be eased till the 1885 completion of the Argentine railway that connected the city of Mendoza to Buenos Aires. Don Tiburcio Benegas, governor of the province of Mendoza and owner of El Trapiche wine estate, was instrumental in financing and pushing through the construction, convinced that in order for the Argentine wine industry to survive it needed a market. The 19th century also saw the first wave of immigrants from Europe. Many of these immigrants were escaping the scourge of the phylloxera epidemic that ravaged vineyards in their homeland and they brought with them their expertize and winemaking knowledge to their new home.

Economic Troubles and Growth of Export Industry

In the 20th century, the development and fortunes of the Argentine wine industry were deeply influenced by the economic influences of the country. In the 1920s, Argentina was the eighth richest nation in the world with the domestic market feeding a strong wine industry. The proceeding global Great Depression dramatically reduced vital export revenues and foreign investment and lead to a decline in the wine industry. There was a brief revival in the economy during the presidency of Juan Perón but the economy declined soon again under the military dictatorship of the 1960s and 1970s. During this time the wine industry was sustained by the domestic consumption of cheap vino de mesa. By the early 1970s, the average Argentinian was consuming nearly 24 gallons of wine a year compared, a significantly higher amount than other countries such as the United Kingdom and United States which was averaging less than a gallon a person during the same period.

The 1980s saw a period of hyperinflation running at nearly 1000 per cent a year. Foreign investment was mostly stagnant. Under the presidency of Carlos Menem, the country saw some economic stability. The favorable exchange rate on the Argentine peso during the convertibility period saw an influx of foreign investment. However this period also saw a dramatic drop in domestic consumption. Following the example of neighbouring Chile, the Argentine wine industry started to more aggressively focus on the export market-particularly the lucrative British and American markets. The presence of Flying winemakers from France, California and Australia brought modern technical know how for viticultural and winemaking techniques such as yield control, temperature control fermentation and the use of new oak barrels. By the end of the 1990s, Argentina was exporting more 3.3 million gallons (12.5 million liters) to the United States with exports to the UK also strong. Wine experts such as Karen MacNeil noted that up to this point that the Argentine wine industry was considered a "sleep giant" that by the end of the 20th century was waking up.

Viticulture

The growing season in Argentina usually last from budbreak in October to harvest beginning sometime in February. The Instituto Nacional de Vitivinicultura (INV), the main government controlling body for the wine industry, declares the beginning date for harvest in a region with the harvest season sometimes lasting till April depending on the variety and wine region. A sizable population of itinerant laborers provides an abundance of grape pickers at low cost which has slowed the conversion to mechanical harvesting. After harvest, grapes often have to travel long distances over several hours from the rural vineyards to winemaking facilities located in more urban areas. In the 1970s, yields were reported as surpassing 22 tons per acre, a sharp contrast to the average yields in premium wine regions such as Bordeaux and Napa Valley of 2 to 5 tons an acre. As the Argentine wine industry continues to grow in the 21st century, several viticultural related trends will involve improvements in irrigation, yield control, canopy management and the construction of more winemaking facilities closer to the vineyards.

Argentina, like Chile, is unique in the wine world for the absence of the phylloxera threat that has devastated vineyards across the globe. Unlike Chile, the phylloxera louse is present in Argentina but is a particular weak biotype that doesn't survive long in the soil. When it does attack vines, the damage is not significant enough to kill the vine and the roots eventually grow back. Because of this most of the vineyards in Argentina are planted on ungrafted rootstock. There are many theories about why phylloxera has not yet reach this part of the world. The centuries old tradition of flood irrigation where water is allowed to deeply saturate the soil maybe one cause as is the high proportion of sand present in the soil. The relative isolation of Argentina is also cited as a potential benefit against phylloxera with the country's wine regions being bordered by mountains, deserts and oceans that create natural barriers against the travels of the louse. Despite the minimum risk of phylloxera, some producers are turning to grafted rootstock that provide better yield control.

Various methods of vine training was introduced to Argentina by European immigrants in the 19th and 20th century. The espaldera system combined the traditional method of using three wires to train the vines low to the ground. In the 1950s a new system known as parral cuyano was introduced where vines were trained high off the ground with the clusters allowed to hang down. This style was conducive to the high yielding varieties of Criolla and Cereza that were the backbone of the bulk wine producing industry that sprang up in response to the large domestic market. In the late 20th century, as the market turned to focus more on premium wine production, more producers switched back to the traditional espaldera system and began to practice canopy management in order to control yields.

Lrrigation

The intricate irrigation system used to bring water from melted snow caps in the Andes originated in the 16th century and has been a vital component of agriculture in Argentina. Water flows down from the mountain through a series of ditches and canals where it is stored in reservoirs for use by vineyards which can apply for government regulated water licenses that provide them access to the water. Newly planted vineyards on lands that do not have existing water rights will often use alternative water sources such as digging deep boreholes between 196-650 feet (60-200 meters) below the surface to retrieve water from underground aquifer. These water wells, though costly to build, can supply a vineyard with as much as 66,000 gallons (250,000 liters) of water an hour.

Historically, flood irrigation was the most common method used with large amounts of water are allowed to run across flat vineyard lands. While this method may have been a unwittingly preventive measurement against the advance of phylloxera, it does provide much control for the vineyard manager to limit yields and increase potential quality in the wine grapes. Later a method of furrow irrigation was developed where water is funneled into furrow channels that the vines are planted in. While providing a little more control, this method was still more conducive to producing high yields. In the late 1990s, drip irrigation started to become more popular. Though expensive to install, this method provides the maximize amount of control for the vineyard manager to facilitate yield control and increase potential quality in the grape by leveraging water stress on the vine.

Wine Regions

While there is some wine production in the provinces of Buenos Aires, Córdoba and La Pampa, the vast majority of wine production takes place in the far western expanse of Argentina leading up to the foothills of the Andes. The Mendoza region is the largest region and the leading producer, responsible for more than two-thirds of the country's yearly production, followed by the San

Juan and La Rioja regions to the north. In the far northeastern corner of the country are the provinces of Catamarca, Jujuy and Salta which includes some of the world's highest planted vineyards. In the southern region of Patagonia, the Río Negro and Neuquén provinces have traditionally been the fruit producing centers of the country but have recently seen growth in the planting of cool climate varietals.

Mendoza

Despite total acreage planted declining from 629,850 acres (255,000 hectares) in 1980 to 360,972 acres (146,081 hectares) in 2003, Mendoza is still the leading producer of wine in Argentina. As of the beginning of the 21st century, the vineyard acreage in Mendoza alone was slightly less than half of the entire planted acreage in the United States and more than the acreage of New Zealand and Australia combined. The majority of the vineyards are found in the Maipú and Luján departments. In 1993, the Mendoza sub region of Luján de Cuyo was the first controlled appellation established in Mendoza. Other notable sub-regions include the Uco Valley and the Tupungato department. Located in the shadow of Mount Aconcagua, the average vineyards in Mendoza are planted at altitudes 1,970-3,610 feet (600-1,100 meters) above sea level. The soil of the region is sandy and alluvial on top of clay substructures and the climate is continental with four distinct seasons that affect the grapevine, including winter dormancy.

Historically, the region has been dominated by production of wine from the high yielding, pink-skinned varieties of Cereza and Criolla Grande but in recent years Malbec has become the regions most popular planting. Cereza and Criolla Grande still account for nearly a quarter of all vineyard plantings in Mendoza but more than half of all plantings are now to premium red varietals which beyond Malbec include Cabernet Sauvignon, Tempranillo and Italian varieties. In the high altitude vineyards of Tupungato, located southwest of the city of Mendoza in the Uco Valley, Chardonnay is increasing in popularity. The cooler climate and lower salinity in the soils of the Maipú region has been receiving attention for the quality of its Cabernet Sauvignon. Wine producers in the region are working with authorities to establish a controlled appellation.

San Juan and La Rioja

After Mendoza, the San Juan region is the second largest producer of wine with over 116,000 acres (47,000 hectares) planted as of 2003. The climate of this region is considerably hotter and drier than Mendoza with rainfall averaging 6 inches (150 millimeters) a year and summer time temperatures regularly hitting 107°F (42°C). Premium wine production is centered around the Calingasta, Ullum and Zonda departments as well as the Tulum Valley. In addition to producing premium red varietals made from Syrah and Charbono, the San Juan region has a long antiquity of producing sherry-style wines, brandies and vermouth. The high yielding Cereza vine is also prominent here where it is used for blending and grape concentrate as well as for raisin and table grape consumption.

The La Rioja region was one of the first areas to be planted by Spanish missionaries and has the longest continued antiquity of wine production in Argentina. Though a relatively small region, with only 20,000 acres (8,000 hectares) planted as of 2003, the region is known for aromatic Moscatel de Alexandrias and Torrontés made from a local sub-variety known as Torrontés Riojano. Lack of water has curtailed vineyard expansion here.

Northwestern Regions

The vineyards of the northwestern provinces of Catamarca, Jujuy and Salta are located between the 24th parallel and 26th parallel south and include some of the highest elevated vineyards in the world with many vineyard planted more than 4,900 feet (1,500 meters) above sea level. Two vineyards planted by Bodega Colome in Salta are at elevations of 7,500 feet (2,250 meters) and 9,900 feet (3,000 meters). In contrast, most European vineyards are rarely planted above 1,600 feet (900 meters). Wine expert Tom Stevenson notes that the habit of some Argentine producers to tout the altitude of their vineyards in advertisements and on wine labels as if they were grand cru classifications. The soils and climate of the regions are very similar to Mendoza but the unique mesoclimate and high elevation of the vineyards typically produces grapes with higher levels of total acidity which contribute to the wines balance and depth. Of the three regions, Catamarca is the most widely planted with more than 5,800 acres (2,300 hectares) under vine as of 2003. In recent years the Salta region, and particularly its sub-region of Cafayate, have been gaining the most worldwide attention the quality of its full bodied whites made from Torrontés Riojano as well as its fruity reds made from Cabernet Sauvignon and Tannat.

Most of Cafayate region in Salta is located at 5,446 feet (1,660 meters) above sea levels in the river delta between the Rio Calchaqui and the Rio Santa Maria. The climate of the area experiences a foehn effect which traps rain producing cloud cover in the mountains and leaves the area dry and sunny. Despite its high altitude daytime temperatures in the summertime can reach 100°F (38°C) but at night the area experiences a wide diurnal temperature variation with night time temperatures dropping as low as 54°F (12°C). There is some threat of frost during the winter when temperatures can drop as low as 21°F (-6°C). Despite producing less than 2 per cent of Argentina's yearly wine production, the Cafayate region is increasing gaining in prestige and appearance on wine labels, as well as foreign investment from worldwide wine producers such as enologist Michel Rolland and California wine producer Donald Hess.

Patagonia

The southern Patagonia region includes the fruit producing regions of Río Negro and Neuquén which has a considerably cooler climate than the major regions to the north which provides a long, drawn out growing season in the chalky soils of the area. In the early 20th century, Humberto Canale imported vine cuttings from Bordeaux and established the first commercial winery in the region. While 9,300 acres (3,800 hectares) were planted as of 2003, the region is growing as more producers plant cool climate varietals like Chardonnay and Pinot noir as well as Malbec, Semillon and Torrontés Riojano. Many of the grapes for the Argentine sparkling wine industry are sourced from this area. Located more than 990 miles (1,600 kilometers) south of Mendoza, the vineyards of Bodega Weinert are noted as the southernmost planted vineyards in the Americas.

Grape Varieties and Wines

Under Argentine wine laws, if a grape name appears on the wine label, at least 80 per cent of the wine must be composed that grape variety. The backbone of the early Argentine wine industry was the high yielding, pink skin grapes Cereza, Criolla Chica and Criolla Grande which still account for nearly 30 per cent of all vines planted in Argentina today. Very vigorous vines, these varieties are able to produce many clusters weighing as much as 9 pounds (4 kg) and tend to produce pink or deeply coloured white wines that oxidize easily and often have noticeable sweetness. These varieties are often used today for bulk jug wine sold in 1 litre cardboard cartons or as grape concentrate which is exported worldwide with Japan being a considerably large market. In the late 20th century, as the Argentine wine industry shifted it focus on premium wine production capable for export, Malbec arose to greater prominence and is today the most widely planted red grape variety followed by Bonarda, Cabernet Sauvignon, Syrah and Tempranillo. The influence of Italian immigrants has brought a variety of Italian varietals with sizable plantings throughout Argentina-including Barbera, Dolcetto, Freisa, Lambrusco, Nebbiolo, Raboso and Sangiovese.

While the historic birthplace of Malbec is Southwest France where is still widely in Cahors and has some presence in Bordeaux, it is in Argentina where the grape receives most of it notoriety. The grape clusters of Argentine Malbec are different from its French relatives have smaller berries in tighter, smaller clusters. Malbec wine is characterized by deep colour and intense fruity flavours with a velvety texture. As of 2003 there were over 50,000 acres (20,000 hectares) of Malbec. The international variety of Cabernet Sauvignon is gaining in popularity and beside being made as a varietal, it used as a blending partner with Malbec, Merlot, Syrah and Pinot noir. Syrah has been steadily increasing in planting going from 1,730 acres (700 hectares) in 1990 to more than 24,710 acres (10,000 hectares) in 2003 with the San Juan region earning particular recognition for the grape. Tempranillo is often made by carbonic maceration those some premium, old vine examples are made in the Uco Valley. Red wine production accounts for nearly 60 per cent of all Argentine wine. The high temperatures of most regions contribute to soft, ripe tannins and high alcohol levels.

The Pedro Giménez grape is the most widely planted white grape varietal with more than 36,300 acres (14,700 hectares) planted primarily in the Mendoza and San Juan region. The grape is known for its fully bodied wines with high alcohol levels and is also used to produce grape concentrate. The next largest plantings are dedicated to the Torrontés Riojano variety followed by Muscat of Alexandria, Chardonnay, Torrontés Sanjuanino and Sauvignon blanc. Other white grape varieties found in Argentina include Chenin blanc, Pinot gris, Riesling, Sauvignonasse, Semillon, Ugni blanc and Viognier.

Torrontés produces some of the most distinctive white wines in Argentina, characterized by floral Muscat-like aromas and a spicy note. The grape requires careful handling during the winemaking process with temperature control during fermentation and a sensitivity to certain strains of yeast. The grape is most widely planted in the northern provinces of La Rioja and Salta, particularly the Calchaquí Valleys, but has spread to Mendoza. In response to international demand, plantings of Chardonnay have steadily increased. The University of California, Davis produced a special clone of the variety that, despite it propensity to develop millerandage, is still widely used in Argentina and Australia. Argentine Chardonnay has shown to thrive in high altitude plantings and is being increasing planted in the Tupungato region on vineyard sites located at altitudes around nearly 4,000 feet (1,200 meters).

Modern Wine Industry

By the turn of the 21st century there were over 1,500 wineries in Argentina. The two largest companies are Bodegas Esmeralda and Peñaflor. Between the two of them, these companies are responsible for nearly 40 per cent of all the wine made in Argentina. The Argentine wine industry is fifth worldwide in production and eighth in wine consumption. The continued trend of the industry is to increase quality and control yields. To some extent the results have been a mixed bag. Between the mid 1990s and early 21st century, Argentina had ripped up nearly a third of its vineyards but reduced yearly production only by 10 per cent. This meant there was an increase in yields from 66 hl/ha to 88 hl/ha.

Mendoza Wine

The Mendoza Province is one of Argentina's most important wine regions, accounting for nearly two-thirds of the country's entire wine production. Located in the eastern foothills of the Andes, in the shadow of Mount Aconcagua, vineyards are planted at the some of the highest altitudes in the world with the average site located 1,970-3,610 feet (600-1,100 meters) above sea level.

The principal wine producing areas fall into two main departments-Maipú and Luján which includes Argentina's first delineated appellation established in 1993 in Luján de Cuyo. The pink-skinned grapes of Criolla Grande and Cereza account for more than a quarter of all plantings but Malbec is the regions most important planting followed closely by Cabernet Sauvignon, Tempranillo and Chardonnay. Mendoza is considered the heart of the winemaking industry in Argentina with the vast majority of large wineries located in the provincial capital of Mendoza.

Wine Producing Areas

As of 2008, the Mendoza region contained more than 356,000 acres (144,000 hectares) of planted vineyards-producing nearly two-thirds of the entire Argentine wine production. The principal wine producing areas fall into two main departments - Maipú and Luján, which includes Argentina's first delineated appellation established in 1993 in Luján de Cuyo. With vineyards planted at altitudes between 2,640-3,630 feet (800-1,100 meters), the Luján de Cuyo region is known particular for its Malbec which seems to thrive in this region as a mean annual temperature of 58°F (15°C). Historically the San Rafael region to the south and San Martín region to the east of the city of Mendoza were important centers for wine production. San Rafael was also awarded DOC status in 1993. However the switch to premium wine production of international varieties has diminished their importance. One area of emerging importance in the Mendoza wine region is the Valle de Uco which includes the Tupungato Department featuring vineyards planted nearly 4000 feet (1,200 meters) above sea levels and is emerging as a source for premium quality white wine varietals such as Chardonnay.

In the Luján department, areas that may appear on wine labels include the towns of Anchoris, Agrelo, Carrodilla, Chacras de Coria, Las Compuertas, Mayor Drummond, Perdriel, Tres Esquinas, Ugarteche and Vistalba. In the Maipú department, areas that may appear on wine labels include the towns of Maipú, Coquimbito, Cruz de Piedra, Las Barrancas, Lunlunta and Russell.

Grape Varieties

The pink-skinned varieties of Cereza and Criolla Grande have historically formed the backbone of the Mendoza wine industry and today still account for around a quarter of all vineyard plantings. Used primarily for inexpensive jug wines and grape concentrate, their importance has steadily declined as the Mendoza region focuses more on the export of premium wine varietals. Malbec has emerged as the most important variety followed, in planted acreage, by Tempranillo, Cabernet Sauvignon and Chardonnay.

Buenos Aires Wines

The Buenos Aires Province has become a producer of premium wines during the first decade of the 21st century. Vineyards are located at the southern part of the province, specially around Médanos. The activity was pioneered in lands already dedicated to garlic and pastures. Wine from Médanos won a Silver Medal in the 2009 Decanter World Wine Awards, the world's largets wine contest celebrated in London.

Wine Regions

Médanos appellation is a geographic indication applied to wines produced in Médanos whose characteristics are a function and a direct result of the geographic area and the terroir in which the grapes are grown and the wines are produced and aged.

Médanos appellation wines include:

- Malbec
- Sauvignon Blanc
- Cabernet Sauvignon
- Cabernet Franc
- Tannat
- Chardonnay
- Petite Verdot
- Tempranillo

Wine from Médanos won a Silver Medal in the 2009 Decanter World Wine Awards, the world's largets wine contest celebrated in London.

Given its proximity to the Ocean, the Médanos terroir consists of sandy soil over a limestone plate with long sun hours and a resulting high termic amplitude during the day.

Médanos is the only Argentine terroir dedicated to production of premium wines with oceanic influence.

The closeness to the Ocean and the strong winds in the area develop thick skins in the grapes that contribute to complex wines with intense colours. This terroir has unique conditions for vineyards making its Malbec distinguishable and having weather conditions that produce outstanding wines, such as Chardonnay, Sauvignon Blanc and Cabernet Sauvignon which are better suited to this environment than to the traditional Argentine wine producing regions.

Wine Types

This terroir is producing premium wines that include Malbec, Cabernet Sauvignon, Merlot, Tannat, Chardonnay and Sauvignon Blanc.

Domaine Al Este

Domaine Al Este is a 290 hectares terroir located in Médanos, Buenos

Aires Province, Argentina. Developed by Al Este, it was the result of a careful analysis and screening of land in this new terroir that was particularly apt for the growth of vineyards dedicated to the production of premium wines.

The Médanos terroir, that had traditionally been dedicated to garlic and pastures, has striking similarities to Bordeaux, France in terms of its soil, weather conditions and proximity to the sea. More recently, the idea of starting a wine project in Médanos got reignited as a result of a trip to France which provided renewed confidence in the terroir's potential.

The Médanos terroir has proven itself. In its first submission to a wine contest with wine produced from young vines, Al Este has been awarded a Silver Medal in the 2009 Decanter World Wine Awards, the world's largets wine contest celebrated in London. Al Este's award winning wine is recommended by Decanter in sixth position as one of the top chardonnays in 2009

WINE BUSINESS IN ARMENIA

Avshar Wine Factory

Avshar Wine Factory is one of the leading producers of alcohol drinks in Armenia. From 1968 the factory began to performance as a state company but with the independence of Armenia and market economic transitions the factory was in need of radical change and since 1995 it was privatized. The factory is located in Ararat region, village Avshar, Republic of Armenia. This place is known as the heart of the country, which is rich in fruitful gardens and fields famous for incomparable types of fruits, vegetables and grained pulses. The region is known to have wine treatment antiquity even since BC, when just as to tradition- Noy came down from Ararat mountain, just where he planted the first wine field.

The founder of the company is Temur I. Grigoryan. He held the factory till 1994 after which the factory supervision was transferred to his son Arayik T. Grigoryan. After the factory's privatization a total reconstruction was realized. Now the factory is armed with modern equipments and technologies being under the constant control of professional workers. Starting from 1999 the factory exports its products to Germany, Belgium, Israel, CIS countries and USA. The factory's main products are brandy, wine and vodka.

AUSTRALIAN WINE BUSINESS

The Australian wine industry is the fourth-largest exporter in the world, exporting over 400 million litres a year to a large international export market that includes "old world" wine-producing countries such as France, Italy and Spain. There is also a significant domestic market for Australian wines, with Australians consuming over 400 million litres of wine per year. The wine industry is a significant contributor to the Australian economy through production, employment, export and tourism.

Vine cuttings from the Cape of Good Hope were brought to the penal colony of New South Wales by Governor Phillip on the First Fleet (1788). An attempt at wine making from these first vines failed, but with perseverance, other settlers managed to successfully cultivate vines for winemaking, and Australian made wine was available for sale domestically by the 1820s. In 1822 Gregory Blaxland became the first person to export Australian wine, and was the first winemaker to win an overseas award.

In 1830 vineyards were established in the Hunter Valley. In 1833 James Busby returned from France and Spain with a serious selection of grape varieties including most classic French grapes and a good selection of grapes for fortified wine production. Wine from the Adelaide Hills was sent to Queen Victoria in 1844, but there is no evidence that she placed an order as a result.

The production and quality of Australian wine was much improved by the arrival of free settlers from various parts of Europe, who used their skills and knowledge to establish some of Australia's premier wine regions. For example, emigrants from Prussia in the mid 1850s were important in establishing South Australia's Barossa Valley as a winemaking region.

Early Australian winemakers faced many difficulties, particularly due to the unfamiliar Australian climate. However they eventually achieved considerable success. "At the 1873 Vienna Exhibition the French judges, tasting blind, praised some wines from Victoria, but withdrew in protest when the provenance of the wine was revealed, on the grounds that wines of that quality must clearly be French." Australian wines continued to win high honours in French competitions. A Victorian Syrah competing in the 1878 Paris Exhibition was likened to Château Margaux and "its taste completed its trinity of perfection." One Australian wine won a gold medal "first class" at the 1882 Bordeaux International Exhibition and another won a gold medal "against the world" at the 1889 Paris International Exhibition. That was all before the destructive effects on the industry of the phylloxera epidemic.

In the decades following the devastation caused by phylloxera until the late 1970s, Australian wine production consisted largely, but not exclusively, of sweet and fortified wines. Since then, Australia has rapidly become a world leader in both the quantity and quality of wines it produces. For example, Australian wine exports to the US rose from 578,000 cases in 1990 to 20,000,000 cases in 2004 and in 2000 it exported more wine than France to the UK for the first time in antiquity.

The industry has also suffered hard times in the last 20 years. In the late 1980s, governments sponsored growers to pull out their vines to overcome a glut of winegrapes. Low grape prices in 2005 and 2006 have led to calls for another sponsored vine pull. Cleanskin wines were introduced into Australia during the 1960s as a means to combat oversupply and poor sales. In recent years organic and biodynamic wines have been increasing in popularity, following a worldwide trend. In 2004 Australia hosted the First International Biodynamic Wine Forum in Beechworth, Victoria which brought together biodynamic wine producers from around the globe. Despite the overproduction of grapes many organic and biodynamic growers have enjoyed continuing demand thanks to the premium prices winemakers can charge for their organic and biodynamic products, particularly in the European market.

Grape Varieties

Major grape varieties are Shiraz, Cabernet Sauvignon, Merlot, Chardonnay, Sauvignon Blanc, Sémillon, and Riesling. The country has no native grapes, and Vitis vinifera varieties were introduced from Europe and South Africa in the late 18th and early 19th centuries. Some varieties have been bred by Australian viticulturalists, for example Cienna and Tarrango.

Although Syrah was originally called Shiraz in Australia and Syrah elsewhere, its dramatic commercial success has led many Syrah producers around the world to label their wine "Shiraz".

About 130 different grape varieties are used by commercial winemakers in Australia. Over recent years many winemakers have begun exploring so called "alternative varieties". Many varieties from France, Italy and Spain for example Petit Verdot, Pinot Grigio, Sangiovese, Tempranillo and Viognier are becoming more common. Wines from many other varieties are being produced.

Australian winemaking results have been impressive and it has established benchmarks for a number of varietals, such as Chardonnay and Shiraz. Moreover, Australians have innovated in canopy management and other viticultural techniques and in wine-making, and they have a general attitude towards their work that sets them apart from producers in Europe. Australian wine-makers travel the wine world as highly skilled seasonal workers, relocating to the northern hemisphere during the off-season at home." They are an important resource in the globalisation of wine and wine critic Matt Kramer notes that "the most powerful influence in wine today" comes from Australia (Kramer).

Table. Red Grapes Planted

Grape	Area Ha (04)	Area Ha (05)	Area Ha (06)	Area Ha (07)	Area Ha (08)
Shiraz	39,182	40,508	41,115	43,417	43,977
Cabernet Sauvingnon	29,313	28,621	28,103	27,909	27,553
Merlot	10,804	10,816	10,593	10,790	10,764
Pinot Noir	4,424	4,231	4,254	4,393	4,490
Grenache	2,292	2,097	2,025	2,011	2,011

Mourvedre	1,040	963	875	794	785
Other Red	11,235	10,797	7,002	11,309	10,902

Table. White Grapes Planted

Grape	Area Ha (04)	Area Ha (05)	Area Ha (06)	Area Ha (07)	Area Ha (08)
Chardonnay	28,008	30,507	31,219	32,151	31,564
Sémillon	6,278	6,282	6,236	6,752	6,716
Sauvignon Blanc	3,425	4,152	4,661	5,545	6,404
Riesling	4,255	4,326	4,400	4,432	4,400
Other White	23,925	23,365	17,683	24,303	23,109

GSM Blends

GSM is a name commonly used in Australia for a red wine consisting of a blend of Grenache, Shiraz and Mourvèdre. This blend originated from those used in some Southern Rhône wines, including Châteauneuf-du-Pape. Grenache is the lightest of the three grapes, producing a pale red juice with soft berry scents and a bit of spiciness. As a blending component, it contributes alcohol, warmth and fruitiness without added tannins. Shiraz can contribute full-bodied, fleshy flavours of black fruits and pepper. It adds colour, backbone and tannins and provides the sense of balance such blends require. Mourvèdre contributes elegance, structure and acidity to the blend, producing flavours of sweet plums, roasted game and hints of tobacco.

Notable Production

Australia's most famous wine is Penfolds Grange. The great 1955 vintage was submitted to competitions beginning in 1962 and over the years has won more than 50 gold medals. The vintage of 1971 won first prize in Syrah/Shiraz at the Wine Olympics in Paris. The 1990 vintage was named 'Red Wine of the Year' by the Wine Spectator magazine in 1995, which later rated the 1998 vintage 99 points out of a possible 100. Wine critic Hugh Johnson has called Grange the only First Growth of the Southern Hemisphere. The influential wine critic Robert Parker, who is well known for his love of Bordeaux wines, has written that Grange "has replaced Bordeaux's Pétrus as the world's most exotic and concentrated wine".

Other red wines to garner international attention include Henschke Hill of Grace, Clarendon Hills Astralis, D'Arenberg Dead Arm, Torbreck Run Rig and other high-end Penfolds wines such as St Henri shiraz.

Australia has almost 2000 wine producers, most of whom are small winery operations. The market is dominated by a small number of major wine companies. After several phases of consolidation, the largest Australian wine company by sales of branded wine was Foster's Group in 2001-2003 and then in 2004 and 2005, Hardy Wine Company. Hardys, part of the world's biggest wine company Constellation Brands, had the largest vineyard area and the largest winegrape intake in the years 2001 - 2005.

Major Wine Regions

The information included on wine labels is strictly regulated. One aspect of this is that the label must not make any false or misleading statements about the source of the grapes. Many names are protected. These are divided into "South Eastern Australia", the state names, zones, regions, and subregions. The largest volume of wine is produced from grapes grown in the warm climate Murray-Darling Basin zones of Lower Murray, North Western Victoria and Big Rivers.

In general, the higher-value premium wines are made from smaller and cooler-climate regions:

South Australia wine regions:

- Southern Fleurieu
- Adelaide Hills
- Barossa Valley
- Clare Valley
- Coonawarra
- Eden Valley
- Langhorne Creek
- McLaren Vale
- Padthaway
- Riverland
- Wrattonbully

Victoria wine regions:

- Alpine Valleys
- Beechworth
- Goulburn Valley
- Grampians
- Heathcote wine region
- Henty
- Mornington Peninsula
- Pyrenees
- Rutherglen
- Yarra Valley
- King Valley

New South Wales wine regions:

- Hunter Valley
- Mudgee
- Riverina

- New England
- Southern Highlands

Western Australia wine regions:

- Margaret River
- Swan Valley
- Great Southern

The South Australian wine industry is responsible for more than half the production of all Australian wine.

In recent years, the Tasmanian wine industry has emerged as a producer of high quality wines. In particular, the Tamar Valley has developed a reputation for its Chardonnay and Pinot Noir, which are well suited to the cooler Tasmanian climate.

Queensland is also developing a wine industry with over 100 vineyards registered in the state. Some notable wines are produced in the high-altitude Granite Belt region in the state's extreme south, production is centred on the towns of Stanthorpe and Ballandean.

Export Markets

The Australian Wine export market was worth 2.8 billion Australian dollars (AU$) a year in June 2007, and was growing at 9 per centpa. Of this about AU$2 billion is accounted for by North America and the UK, and in this key latter market Australia is now the largest supplier of still wines. 2007 statistics for the North American market show that Australian wine accounted for a 17 per cent share of the total value of U.S. imported wine, behind France with 31 per cent and Italy with 28 per cent.

New marketing strategies developed for the key UK market encouraged customers to explore premium Australian brands, while maintaining sales of the lower-margin high-volume brands, following research that indicated a celebratory dinner was more likely to be accompanied by an inferior French wine than a premium Australian wine. This is partly due to exchange rate fluctuations, making Australian wines appear much cheaper than French wines in the UK and hence perceived as being of poorer quality. While this situation may be somewhat mitigated by the continued rise in the Australian dollar during 2010, the stronger currency threatens to weaken Australian exports to the crucial US market.

In 2009 the Australian wine initiative Australia's First Families of Wine was established as a multi-million-dollar venture aimed at resurrecting the fortunes of the AU$6 billion industry, by promoting the quality and diversity of Australian wine. First Families chairman and Tahbilk chief executive Alister Purbrick said: "We desperately need to change the global perception of Australian wine. We don't believe as individual companies we can stem the avalanche of news stories about Australia producing nothing but cheap industrial wines. But together we can present a powerful showcase of terrific regional wines of great diversity." Some industry commentators lay the blame for this negative opinion on the giant, publicly listed multinational corporations, such as Constellation Wines and Foster's, which have dominated the industry for years and concentrated on the cheap commodity end of the market, rather than building the reputation of Australia's finer, regionally distinctive wines. The twelve member companies are Brown Brothers, Campbells, Taylors, DeBortoli, McWilliam's, Tahbilk, Tyrell's, Yalumba, D'Arenberg, Howard Park, Jim Barry and Henschke.

Australian and New Zealand Wine Industry Journal

The Australian and New Zealand Wine Industry Journal publishes a wide range of substances from technical and scientific papers to practical advice and the latest news on research and development. The journal is issued six times a year and features practical winemaking, practical grape growing, substances on wine regions and wine styles, vintage reports, marketing, finance and management, research papers, and industry news and analyses.

Liqueur Muscat

A Liqueur Muscat is a fortified wine made in Australia from the Muscat Blanc à Petits Grains and Muscadelle grapes. The wine is sweet, dark, highly alcoholic Australian wine that has some similarities to Madeira and Malaga. The grape is most commonly produced in Victoria in the wine regions of Rutherglen and Glenrowan.Liqueur Muscat essentially starts out being a late harvest wine with the grapes allowed to stay on the vine till they are in a partially raisined state.

The grapes are then pressed and go through partial fermentation where it is halted by the addition grape spirits. The wine is then aged in oak in a system resembling the Sherry solera system. Similar to Madeira, the wines are often exposed to high temperatures.In the late 1990s, winemakers in Rutherglen established as voluntary classification and regulation system for their Liqueur Muscat wines.

At the lowest classification is the wine styled Rutherglen Muscat followed by Classic Muscat and Grand Muscat. At the highest end and meant to indicate a richer and more complex wine is the Rare Muscat.

Melbourne Food and Wine Festival

Launched in 1993, the annual Melbourne Food and Wine Festival is one of Victoria's hallmark events. Each March the festival celebrates Melbourne and Victoria's vibrant food and wine culture in a fortnight-long programme of over 250 events. Dates for 2010 are 12 - 23 March.

Operating on a not-for-profit basis, the festival's charter is to promote the quality produce, talent and lifestyle of Melbourne and Victoria, and to reinforce Melbourne as the food and wine capital of Australia.

Since its beginnings with a small programme of events, the festival has grown to become known for iconic events including Langham Melbourne MasterClass, World's Longest Lunch and Cellar Door at Southgate. For several years, the festival has recorded 300,000 visitors annually.

The festival is managed by a board of management and is supported by a small team who are responsible for the coordination of its iconic events, in close collaboration with Victoria's food and wine industry. Its creative direction is guided by a panel of three: Jill Dupleix, Tony Tan, and Ben Edwards. Celebrity food critic Matt Preston was already the festival's sole creative director, the 2009 Melbourne Food and Wine Festival being his last.

The Melbourne Food and Wine Festival commenced in 1993 with a simple programme of 12 events. Since its inception it has grown annually, with the 2007 Festival encompassing over 150 events over a two week period. On an annual basis the Festival attracts food and wine experts from across the world, including world-renowned chefs and winemakers, growers, purveyors, authors, food and wine commentators and critics to present alongside some of Australia's best. In 2009, the Festival hosted international culinary luminaries who numbered 30 Michelin stars among them, including The Fat Duck's Heston Blumenthal (3 stars), The French Laundry's Thomas Keller (7 stars) and Noma's Rene Redzepi (2 stars), as well as world-class winemakers such as the Rhone Valley's Michel Chapoutier and Champagne's Sophie and Pierre Larmandier.

Melbourne Food and Wine Festival 2010

In 2010, the Langham Melbourne MasterClass line-up includes chefs David Chang, Massimo Bottura and Claude Bosi and winemaker Gaia Gaja.

Beyond Langham Melbourne MasterClass, the festival has announced that its hallmark World's Longest Lunch will celebrate Melbourne's Chinese heritage and the return of Heat Beads® Hawkers' Market to Queen Victoria Market, featuring tasting plates from a dozen top Asian restaurants. Simultaneous to the World's Longest Lunch in Melbourne, the community of Marysville will host one of 19 Regional World's Longest Lunches one year on from the Black Saturday bushfires. The event forms part of the festival's programme of more than 70 regional events. The festival will also grow and install an urban food-producing garden - 'Metlink Edible Garden' - in Melbourne's City Square, exploring the food city dwellers can grow in their suburban backyards and the produce strengths of Victoria's regional 'backyard'.

Recognition

The Festival continues to receive both local and international acclaim.

Recent domestic award wins include the Melbourne Airport 2008 and 2009 Victorian Tourism Awards in the category of 'Major Festivals and Events' and 2008 Melbourne Awards in the category of 'Community Division - Contribution to Profile'; international award wins include 2008 International Festival and Events Awards Gold for 'Best Festival Program'.

Passion Pop

Passion Pop is an Iconic Australian alcoholic beverage, labeled as a carbonated 'passion flavoured' wine-based beverage. The product was created by Frank 'Pop' Miranda and Ron Potter in 1977-78 at Pop's winery; Mixed Berry and its newest addition Pink

Passion Pop is an Australian icon and has been a market leader in the Flavoured Sparkling Wine category for over 30 years. Passion Pop's low price made it very popular amongst Australian students and the younger generation. Passion Pop costs approx. AU$7.00 per bottle.

Passion Pop is produced by Australian Vintage. It is labelled as a carbonated 'flavoured' wine, and comes in 750 ml bottles. The drink is 9.5 per cent alcohol, meaning that one bottle contains 5.6 standard drinks. Passion Pop has just released a new flavour called Passion Pop Pink which is strawberry in flavour. To be opened, the drinks require skill to pop a champagne-like cork.

Passion Pop comes in a 750 mL glass "champagne-style" bottle. It was one of the first beverage products in Australia to utilise a plastic stopper. Passion Pop has recently modernized its packaging; deviating from the simple white label, to a fashionable one which contradicts the already home-brand appearance.

Penfolds Grange

Penfolds Grange is an Australian wine, made predominantly from the Shiraz grape and usually a small percentage of Cabernet Sauvignon. It is widely considered Australia's "first growth" and its most collectable wine. The term "Hermitage", the name of a French wine appellation, was commonly used in Australia as another synonym for Shiraz or Syrah. In 1953 two versions of Grange were made, one 87 per cent Shiraz and 13 per cent Cabernet Sauvignon, the other 100 per cent Cabernet Sauvignon.

The first vintage of Penfolds Grange was made on an experimental basis in 1951 by winemaker Max Schubert, while he was employed by Penfolds Wines. Having toured Europe in 1950, Schubert implemented wine-making techniques observed in Bordeaux upon his return, aiming to create a red wine able to rival the finest Bordeaux wines both in terms of quality and ageing potential.

Individual bottles of the 1951 vintage are still held by collectors; one sold at auction in 2004 for just over A$50,000. The first vintage to be commercially released was the 1952. Penfolds Grange was styled as a powerful still wine in an age when fortified wines were in fashion. Negative reviews by wine critics and poor commercial prospects for the wine led Penfolds management in 1957 to forbid Schubert from producing Penfolds Grange, but Schubert persisted in secret through 1959. As the initial vintages aged, however, their true value came to be appreciated, and in 1960 the management instructed Schubert to re-start production, oblivious to the fact that Schubert had not missed a vintage.

The great 1955 vintage was submitted to competitions beginning in 1962 and over the years has won more than 50 gold medals. The vintage of 1971 won first prize in Shiraz at the Wine Olympics in Paris. The 1990 vintage was named 'Red Wine of the Year' by the Wine Spectator magazine in 1995, which later rated the 1998 vintage 99 points out of a possible 100.

Penfolds Grange also carries a "Bin" designation, referring to its storage location in Penfolds cellars while aging. 1951 was Bin 1, 1952 was Bin 4, and later vintages carried various designations. By 1964 the designation was standardised as "Bin 95."

By the end of the 1980s the wine came to be regarded as a collector's item. The name "Hermitage" was dropped from the label with the 1990 vintage, following objections by the European Union authorities to the use of a French place-name, as no third-country wine entering EU may carry a geographical name recognized by European wine officials.

Listed in the 4th edition of Langton's Classification of Australian Wine at the "Exceptional" level, and have been at the top of the Langton classification since the first release 1991.

Unlike most expensive cult wines from the Old World, which are from single vineyards or even small plots within vineyards, Grange is made from grapes harvested over a wide area. This means that the precise composition of the wine will change from year to year and it is the branding and expertise of the winemaking which purchasers value, rather than the qualities of the specific places where the grapes are grown or the particular vines. The quantity of Penfolds Grange produced varies considerably from year to year and is a carefully guarded secret. Despite the vagaries of grape sourcing and vintage variation due to growing conditions, some believe that there is a consistent and recognisable "Penfolds Grange" style.

Yellow Tail (Wine)

Yellow Tail is a brand of wine produced by Casella Wines Pty Ltd. Casella wines is based in Yenda, Australia, which has a population of approximately 1000 people. The Casella family has produced wines since the 1820s in Italy. However in 1951 the Casella family, headed by Filippo Casella and his wife Maria, moved to Australia for a better life. YellowTail is a new wine brand and was a chance for the family winery to enter into the bottled wine market-having already supplied bulk wine to other wineries. YellowTail was developed around the year 2000, originally marketed to export countries and became the number one imported wine to the USA by 2003. In that time the family-owned winery expanded 10 times its original size. The winery has the capacity to have approximately 300 million litres on site with more wine produced and stored elsewhere. Yellow Tail's advertising campaign in the United States ranges from large scale billboards to ads on their delivery trucks.

The namesake of the brand, Yellow Tail, is the Yellow-footed Rock Wallaby, a relative of kangaroos.

Vineyard

The vineyard comprises approximately 3 per cent of all wine produced and is around 540 acres (2.2 km2), located in the Riverina, Griffith, region of Australia.

Wines

Approximately a third of the grapes that are harvested by Yellow Tail are from their vineyard in Riverina, Australia. The rest is from other vineyards in South Eastern Australia. All Yellow Tail wines have their own specific label colour. In addition to sparkling wines, Yellow Tail makes wine from the following varieties-

- Moscato
- Riesling
- Semillon
- Sauvignon Blanc
- Pinot Grigio
- Chardonnay
- Rosé
- Pinot Noir
- Merlot
- Grenache
- Shiraz
- Cabernet Sauvignon

International Sales

In 2000, the Casellas joined with W.J. Deutsch and Sons, a family-owned marketing and distribution firm, in order to distribute the Yellow Tail wines in the United States. In 2001, it sold 112,000 cases, a number that jumped to 7.5 million in 2005, helped by distribution through Costco.

Yellow Tail has enjoyed similar success in the UK which, in 2000, began importing more wine from Australia than from France for the first time in antiquity.

Both research and experience demonstrates that most consumers today, especially when buying New World wines, want to buy wine by variety and brand name. Young consumers in particular tend to avoid what they consider to be confusing and pretentious wine labels characteristic of some Old World wine bottles.

WINE BUSINESS IN AUSTRIA

Austrian wines are mostly dry white wines with some luscious dessert wines made around the Neusiedler See. About 30 per cent of the wines are red, made from Blaufränkisch, Pinot Noir and locally bred varieties such as Zweigelt. Four thousand years of winemaking antiquity counted for little after the "antifreeze scandal" of 1985, when it was revealed that some wine brokers had been adulterating their wines with diethylene glycol. The scandal destroyed the market for Austrian wine, but in the long term has been a force for good, compelling Austria to tackle low standards of bulk wine production, and reposition itself as a producer of quality wines that stand comparison with the best in the world. The country is also home to Riedel, makers of some of the most expensive wine glasses in the world.

There is archaeological evidence of grape growing in Traisental 4000 years ago. Grape seeds have been found in urns dating back to 700BC in Zagersdorf, whilst bronze wine flagons of the Celtic La Tène culture dating to the 5th century BC have been found at Dürrnberg in Salzburg state. Viticulture thrived under the Romans, once Probus had overturned the ban on growing grapes north of the Alps. Both Grüner Veltliner and Welschriesling appear to have been grown around the Danube since Roman times.

Viticulture suffered with the invasions of Bavarians, Slavs and Avars after the fall of the Roman empire, but from 788 the rule of Charlemagne saw considerable reconstruction of vineyards and introduction of new grape presses. Once Otto the Great had seen off the threat from Magyar incursions in 955, Austrian viticulture was nurtured by the Church and encouraged among the populace at large. The first vineyard names recorded are Kremser Sandgrube in 1208, and Steiner Pfaffenberg in 1230. Rudolf IV introduced the first wine tax, Ungeld, in 1359, as Vienna established itself as a centre for wine trading on the Danube.

The wine business boomed in the 16th century, but the Thirty Years War and others of the 17th century took their toll, as much due to the heavy taxation of the period as the direct disruption of war. Various drink taxes were unified in 1780, as part of a drive by Maria Theresa and Joseph II to encourage viticulture. An imperial decree of 17 August 1784 gave birth to the distinctive Austrian tradition of inns called Heurigen. Derived from the German for 'new wine', the decree allowed all winemakers to sell home-grown food with their wine all year round. Fir trees hung above the door alerted customers to the arrival of the new season's wine. The 19th century saw the arrival of all sorts of biological invaders. First there was powdery mildew and downy mildew. One response to these fungal diseases from North America was the founding in 1860 of what became the Federal Institute for Viticulture and Pomology at Klosterneuburg. Then the phylloxera root aphid arrived in 1872 and wiped out most of the vineyards of central Europe. Although it took several decades for the industry to recover, it allowed lower quality grapes to be replaced with better varieties, particularly Grüner Veltliner. After World War I, Austria was the third biggest wine producer in the world, much being exported in bulk for blending with wine from Germany and other countries.

However that intensification of viticulture sowed the seeds of its own destruction. During the twentieth century Austrian wine became a high-volume, industrialised business, with much of it being sold in bulk to Germany. A run of favourable years in the early 1980s saw massive yields of wines that were light, dilute and acidic, that nobody wanted. Wine brokers discovered that these wines could be made saleable by the addition of a little diethylene glycol, more commonly found in antifreeze, which imparted sweetness and body to the wine.

The adulteration was difficult to detect chemically-the 'antifreeze scandal' broke when one of them tried to claim for the cost of the chemical on his tax return. Although the amounts of glycol were less dangerous than the alcohol in the wine, and only a few middlemen were involved, exports collapsed and some countries banned Austrian wine altogether. The antifreeze jokes persist, but in fact the scandal was the saviour of the industry in Austria. Strict new regulations restricted yields among other things, producers moved towards more red wine and a dry style of white wine that was what the 1990s market would demand, and the middlemen went bust forcing producers to sell direct and encouraging the expression of local terroir.

Perhaps most importantly, there was a massive change in the culture of wine production in Austria towards an emphasis on quality, as opposed to the low standards that permitted the scandal to happen in the first place.

The Austrian Wine Marketing Board was created in 1986 as a response to the scandal, and Austria's membership of the European Union has prompted further revisions of her wine laws, notably the new DAC system of geographical appellations launched in 2002. Today Austria lies 17th in the list of wine producing countries by volume, but the wines are now of a quality that can take on-and beat-the best in the world.

Grape Varieties

Grüner Veltliner is the dominant white grape in Austria, producing generally dry wines ranging from short-lived Heuriger wines to Spätleses capable of long life. The ancient Welschriesling variety is used in the noble rot dessert wines of the Neusiedlersee; it also makes undistinguished dry wines for drinking young, as does Müller-Thurgau. Neuburger was supposedly found as flotsam in the Danube in the 1850s, but is now known to be a cross between

Silvaner and the ancient Roter Veltliner. Frühroter Veltliner is also known as Malvasier, suggesting a link to the Malvasia grape family of the Eastern Mediterranean.

Muscat Ottonel is used in dessert wines from the Neusiedlersee, as is Bouvier, which is related to the muscat family and is a parent of the Orémus grape used in Tokaji. There were high hopes for Goldburger, a cross between Welschriesling and Orangetraube bred in Klosterneuburg, but after an initial wave of planting enthusiasm has dimmed. Zierfandler and Rotgipfler are local grapes of the Thermenregion, and are often blended together as Spätrot-Rotgipfler. It's worth noting that Pinot gris is known as Ruländer in Austria, and sometimes as Grauburgunder; Pinot blanc is known as Weißburgunder or Weissburgunder, and Sauvignon blanc is called Muskat Sylvaner. Riesling plays a much smaller role than in Germany, but the relatively small amount grown is used for some of Austria's most appreciated dry white wines.

Zweigelt and Blauburger were bred at Klosterneuburg in the 1920s and now account for nearly half of Austria's red wine. The former can be made into powerful wines for ageing, the latter is easier to grow and is generally blended; both are also made into a lighter style for drinking young.

Blaufränkisch and Blauer Portugieser are the traditional red grapes of the region, being part of the blend of Hungary's Egri Bikavér. The former is the more 'serious' variety, Blauer Portugieser produces fresh, fruity red wines for drinking young. Saint Laurent came from France in the mid-19th century, and seems to have substantial Pinot noir parentage; St Laurent has a reputation for being problematic to grow, but can produce good quality wine. Blauer Wildbacher is probably an indigenous wild grape variety, used to make a cult rosé called Schilcher in western Styria. Rössler is the latest variety to be bred at Klosterneuburg.

Classification

As recently as 1999, Robert Parker described Austrian wine labels as "illegible and confusing". There's a lot of historical reasons for this, but since joining the EU the Austrians have made real efforts to improve matters. At present there are three systems-the traditional system based on the German plan, a different classification used only in the Wachau, and a new system of regional appellations called DACs that is being trialled in the Weinviertel.

National Classification

The existing system was based on the German system during World War II, but was modified after 1985. It is based on the Klosterneuberger Mostwaage (KMW), which measures the sugar content of the grapes at harvest in a way similar to the Öchsle scale, where 1°KMW is ~5°Oe.

- Tafelwein->10.7°KMW, can come from more than one region

- Landwein->14°KMW, >17g/litre dry extract, <11.5 per cent alcohol, <6g/l residual sugar. A Tafelwein that comes from just one region.
- Qualitätswein->15°KMW >9 per cent alcohol. Comes from a single wine district.
- Kabinett->17°KMW Qualitätswein with no chaptalisation, residual sugar <9g/litre, alcohol <12.7 per cent.
- Prädikatswein-covers the range from Spätlese to Eiswein, to which nothing can be added-no must, no chaptalisation. Most of the wines may not be released until the 1st May after harvest.
  - Spätlese->19°KMW, wine not released until 1 March after harvest
  - Auslese->21°KMW, bad grapes removed
  - Beerenauslese->25°KMW, bad grapes removed
  - Ausbruch->27°KMW, botrytised grapes, grape juice or late harvest wine may be added to assist the pressing operation.
  - Trockenbeerenauslese->30°KMW, completely botrytised grapes
  - Eiswein->25°KMW, further concentrated by being harvested and pressed when frozen.
  - Strohwein or Schilfwein->25°KMW, made from grapes dried on straw mats.

Wachau Classification

The "Vinea Wachau Nobilis Districtus" has three categories, all for dry wines:

- Steinfeder-maximum 11.5 per cent alcohol, mostly for local quaffing.
- Federspiel-11.5 per cent to 12.5 per cent alcohol and a minimum must weight of 17° KMW, roughly equivalent to Kabinett.
- Smaragd-minimum 12.5 per cent alcohol, with a maximum 9g/litre residual sugar; some of the best dry whites in Austria.

Districtus Austriae Controllatus (DAC)

The Latin for "Controlled District of Austria" is the new geographical appellation, equivalent to the French AOC or the Italian DOCG. Regional wine committees award the DAC to wines typical of their region. There are now 6 DACs:

- Weinviertel DAC
- Mittelburgenland DAC
- Traisental DAC
- Kremstal DAC
- Kamptal DAC
- Leithaberg DAC

Wine Regions

In 2005 Austria had 51,213 hectares of vineyard, almost all of it in the east of the country. 31,425ha are in the state of Niederösterreich and 15,386ha in Burgenland which together make up Weinland Österreich. Steirerland accounts for 3,749ha, Wien 621ha and there's 32ha in "the Austrian Mountains" which covers the rest of the country. The four main wine regions are split into 16 districts.

In 1985 Diethylene Glycol Wine Scandal

The 1985 diethylene glycol wine scandal involved a limited number of Austrian wineries that had illegally adulterated their wines using the mildly toxic substance diethylene glycol to make the wines appear sweeter and more full-bodied in the style of late harvest wines. Many of these Austrian wines were exported to Germany, some of them in bulk to be bottled at large-scale German bottling facilities. At these facilities, some Austrian wines were illegally blended into German wines by the importers, resulting in diethylene glycol ending up in some bulk-bottled German wines as well.

The scandal was uncovered by German wine laboratories performing quality controls on wines sold in Germany, and immediately made headlines around the world. The affected wines were immediately withdrawn from the market. A number of people involved in the scandal were sentenced to prison or heavy fines in Austria and Germany. Although potentially health-damaging in larger quantities, no recorded instances of injuries from the consumption of the adulterated wines are known.

The short-term effect of the scandal was a complete collapse of Austrian wine exports and a total loss of reputation of the entire Austrian wine industry, with significant adverse effects on the reputation of German wines as well. The long-term effect was that the Austrian wine industry focused their production on other wine types than already, primarily dry white wines instead of sweet wines, and increasingly targeted a higher market segment, but it took the Austrian wine industry over a decade to recover. Much stricter wine laws were also enacted by Austria.

At the time of the scandal, Germany was the most important export market for Austrian wine and had been so for a number of years, with an increasing trend. The Austrian wines exported to Germany were of a similar style to those produced by Germany itself, meaning semi-sweet and sweet white wines. However, much of these Austrian wines were focused on the low cost segment, and were priced lower than German wines at the corresponding level of sweetness.

The traditional sweet wines of Germany and Austria are produced from late harvest grapes, some of them affected by noble rot, and labelled in a hierarchy of Prädikat designations from Kabinett to Trockenbeerenauslese depending on the ripeness of the grapes. Although sweet reserve was allowed for the production of semi-sweet wines, no external sources of sugar were allowed for any wines with a Prädikat designation. Thus, the production of wines at higher Prädikat levels tends to vary from year to year depending on vintage conditions, and all wines with higher designations sell at a premium price.

As the sweet wines were more favoured at the time of the scandal than they have been in the 1990s and 2000s, and since the Prädikat designations were almost universally recognized throughout the German-speaking countries, a cheap Auslese or Beerenauslese was often identified as a "bargain" by many German consumers. Many of the cheap sweet wines exported from Austria were blends from different grape varieties, and several of them did not carry any varietal designations, in contrast to the more expensive Prädikat wines of Germany, which often were produced from Riesling grapes.

Some Austrian exporters had entered into long-term contracts with supermarket chains to supply large quantities of wine at a specified quality level in terms of Prädikat. Apparently these producers ran into problems in some weak vintages, where much of the grape harvest did not reach sufficient ripeness levels. At the levels of ripeness that were reached, the wines would be less sweet, less full-bodied and more acidic. One vintage plagued by these problems in Austria was 1982. It is believed that when this led to insufficient quantities of wine being available to fulfill the contracts, some producers started to search for methods, including illegal ones, to "correct" the wines. By itself, simple sweetening would not necessarily do the job, since it would not sufficiently correct the taste profile of the wine.

By using diethylene glycol, it was possible to affect both the impression of sweetness and the body of the wine. German wine chemists have stated that it is unlikely that an individual winemaker of a small winery had sufficient chemical knowledge to devise the plan, implying that the recipe must have been drawn up by a knowledgeable wine chemist consulting for a large-scale producer.

Diethylene Glycol

Diethylene glycol (DEG) was otherwise used as an industrial chemical or as antifreeze, although ethylene glycol is more common for that application. Adulteration of products with diethylene glycol has led to thousands of deaths world wide since the first recorded case: the Elixir sulfanilamide incident in 1937. Most of the wines contained up to a few grams of DEG per litre, which meant that dozens of bottles would have to be consumed in a limited period of time to reach the lethal dose of approximately 40 grams.

However, in one record-setting wine 48 grams per litre was detected, which meant that the consumption of a single bottle could have been lethal. Also, long-term consumption of DEG is known to damage the kidney, liver and brain.

Discovery

The first wine discovered to contain DEG was a 1983 Rüster Auslese from a supermarket in Stuttgart, analysed on June 27, 1985. Domestic wine fraud involving illegal sweetening had occurred earlier in Germany, and had led to investigations and prosecution of the winemakers involved. What made the 1985 finds very different was that a toxic compound had been used, and subsequent sampling indicated that a significant number of different bottlings were part of this toxic adulteration plan.

Therefore, unlike cases of simple sweetening, the 1985 DEG findings immediately took the proportion of a full-scale scandal requiring action by federal authorities in both Germany and Austria. On July 9, the Federal Ministry of Health in Bonn issued an official health warning against the consumption of Austrian wines. The findings immediately made headlines in German media, and from there were cabled out throughout the world.

Market Consequences

From mid-July 1985, it was almost impossible to sell Austrian wine on any export market. Some countries introduced a ban on the import and sale of all Austrian wines, and in many other countries Austrian wines were removed from shelves by wine dealers themselves.

From a pre-1985 level of around 45 million liters per year, exports immediately fell to one-tenth their already level, or around 4.4 million liters in 1986. They then stayed at approximately the same level until 1989, and were slightly higher in period 1990-1997, but still well under pre-1985 levels. Not until 2001 did the export volume, at just over 50 million liters, match the old level.

It thus took the Austrian wine industry 15 years to regain its former position in terms of export volume, despite optimistic predictions from some quarters in Austria that it would all be forgotten in other countries in one year's time.

Legal Consequences

In the weeks following the breaking of the scandal, several dozens of wine producers and wine dealers were arrested by Austrian authorities. The first prison sentence, of one and a half years, followed in mid-October.

Many of the adulterated wines were found to originate in Wagram in Lower Austria, where a consulting wine chemist was prosecuted. One of the convicted Wagram winemakers, Karl Grill, proprietor of Firma Gebrüder Grill, committed suicide after being sentenced.

A stricter wine law was enacted by the Parliament of Austria on August 29, 1985. Having seen the immediate collapse of Austrian wine exports, the Austrian government rushed this legislation through parliament in order for it to be in effect before the 1985 harvest.

In Germany, following a lengthy investigation, six former leading employees of the wholesale dealer and bottler Pieroth were sentenced to fines of one million Deutsche Mark by the Landgericht in Koblenz in April 1996. Many other legal actions took place over the coming years in Germany. The bottling firm Pieroth fought a legal action in the administrative courts in order to try to establish that the Federal Minister for Youth, Family and Health, Heiner Geißler (CDU) had exceeded his authority when his ministry had issued a blacklist containing all wines that had been found to contain DEG, and naming the bottler in each case.

The case went through all three tiers of the administrative courts, and was finally settled on October 18, 1990, when the Federal Administrative Court of Germany ruled against Pieroth and found that the minister had the right to issue the list. Pieroth's actions, which did not earn the company any sympathy with the public, were probably not meant as a measure to allow the further selling of adulterated wine, but as an attempt to put Pieroth in a position to recover money from customers who had refused to pay their outstanding bills following the scandal.

Other courts had ruled in civil law proceedings that deliveries of wines found to contain DEG were a form of non-fulfillment of a purchase contract that removed any obligation to pay, but that customers still had to pay if they only suspected that a wine contained DEG, and the wine was subsequently cleared of suspicion. Thus, the legal status of the blacklist was a crucial element in the many contract disputes.

Destruction of the Wine

As a consequence of the scandal, a total of 270,000 hectoliter of wine had to be destroyed by the German authorities, which had confiscated or otherwise collected the wine. Doing this in an environmentally acceptable way proved to be something of a challenge, because DEG was incompatible with sewage treatment plants. In the end, the wine was destroyed by being poured into the ovens of a cement plant as a cooling agent instead of water. `

Spätrot-Rotgipfler

Spätrot-Rotgipfler is a wine produced in the Thermenregion in Austria, particularly in the Gumpoldskirchen district. It is a blend of the two varieties Zierfandler and Rotgipfler. Zierfandler is said to contribute finesse, while Rotgipfler contributes with strength and a higher alcohol, and the wine often has asparagus aromas. Spätrot-Rotgipfler is often produced as Prädikatswein, with more or less pronounced sweetness, and is long-lived.

Uhudler

Uhudler is a unique wine from Austria, which originates in the Südburgenland region. In appearance it is often a rosé colour, but is also made as a white wine. It has intense flavours of strawberry and black currants, a characteristic taste often called "foxy" in wine parlance. The grape varieties used are highly resistant to phylloxera and other diseases; as a result they do not often have to be sprayed with pesticides. They also require little fertilization because of their vigorous growth.

Uhudler originates from the time of the large phylloxera infestations around 1860. The phylloxera aphid reached Europe in 1860 and Austria in around 1900. After the losses of the European grape varieties through phylloxera, many attempts were made to either exterminate the pest or use alternative, non-traditional viticultural practices which would prevail against infestation.

In time, disease resistant North American vines were imported to Europe and used to produce wine. Many crossings between native North American and European varietals were created at this time. The wine produced did not correspond in any way to the established taste trends in Europe. During the early 20th century, however, some fruit from North American vines were blended with that from Vitis vinifera to enhance the "fruitiness" of the wine.

After the discovery that grafting Vitis Vinifera onto native North American rootstocks was a solution to the phylloxera problem in Europe - and in order to allow European wine to regain its place in the first half of the 20th century - North American vines were forbidden under wine regulations across the European continent. In order to damage the reputations of wines produced from native North American varietals, it was also maintained that these wines contained a high content of methanol, and therefore were injurious to the health of the drinker. By the '70s in Austria, private drinking of the Uhudler was thus quite limited, but production for private consumption was permitted. However, prohibition led to the rising popularity of the beverage.

On the basis of the Austrian Wine Law uhudler can be marketed in 8 communities of the Burgenland. Uhulder is made from the varieties Concord, Delaware, Elvira und Ripatella.

Because of the enormous aggravation of the Austrian wine law due to the wine scandals of the middle of the 1980s, Uhudler was forbidden. This situation continued up to the beginning of the 1990s. During this time thousand of litres of Uhudler were destroyed by wine cellar supervisors.

Oenology

The grapes/clusters are usually red, but also white. The varieties used are inter-specific hybrids, which were developed from crossings between the European species Vitis vinifera with the native North American Vitis labrusca and Vitis riparia. It is Vitis Labrusca which lends the wine its characteristic "strawberry" flavouring. "Uhudler" can refer to several varieties and today it is disputed which varieties rank in the "Uhudlergruppe" and which do not. Some of the varieties used include the grapes Concord, Isabella, Elvira, Clinton, Ripadella and Noah.

WINE BUSINESS IN UK

Wine from the United Kingdom is generally classified as either English wine or Welsh wine, with reference to England or Wales as its respective origin. The term British wine is generally used for fermented imported grape juice or concentrate that can originate from anywhere in the world, and so is not used for wine in the usual sense. Traditionally seen as struggling with an unhelpfully cold climate, the English and Welsh wine industry has been helped by the warmer British summers over recent years and it is speculated that global warming may encourage major growth in the future.

The United Kingdom is a major consumer, but only a very minor producer of wine, with English and Welsh wine sales combined accounting for just 1 per cent of the domestic market.

In recent years, English sparkling wine has started to emerge as the UK wine style receiving the most attention. Theale Vineyard Sparkling Chardonnay 2003 beat off stiff competition from fine Champagnes and top sparkling wines to make it into the world's Top Ten Sparkling Wine at the world's only dedicated sparkling wine competition, French-based Effervescents du Monde 2007.

English Wine

At the last official count, the Wine Standards Board reported that there were just over 350 vineyards producing wine throughout England. The largest of these is Denbies Vineyard in Surrey which, as of mid-2007, has 265 acres (1.07 km2) of vines, although Chapel Down Wines near Tenterden in Kent, has the biggest winery and produces more wine, and will soon overtake Denbies. "English wine" is also a common generic term used in India meaning "Western spirits".

Welsh Wine

Wine Standards Board, there are currently 17 operational vineyards in Wales.

'British Wine'

The term British wine is commonly used to describe a drink which is made in Britain by fermenting imported grape juice or concentrate that can originate from anywhere in the world. The most common style is a medium or sweet high-strength wine that is similar to sherry.

Backdrop

Roman to 19th Century

The Romans introduced wine making to the United Kingdom, and even tried to grow grapes as far north as Lincolnshire. The British climate was too cold and too wet to grow grapes for making wine. Winemaking continued at least down to the time of the Normans with over 40 vineyards in England, although much of what was being produced was for making communion wine for the Eucharist.

From the Middle Ages, the English market was the main customer of clarets from Bordeaux, France, helped by the Plantagenet kingdom, which included England and large provinces in France. In the 18th century, the Methuen Treaty of 1703 imposed high duties on French wine. This led to the English becoming a main consumer of sweet fortified wines like sherry, port wine, and Madeira wine from Spain and Portugal. Fortified wine became popular because unlike regular wine, it does not spoil after the long journey from Portugal to England.

Later in the 19th century, many upper and upper-middle class people started to drink wines from many parts of Europe like France, Spain, Italy and Germany.

20th Century

Viticulture was revived in the 1970s onwards, possibly helped by a rising local temperature due to global warming, making many parts of Hampshire, Sussex, Kent, Essex, Suffolk, Berkshire and Cambridgeshire, dry and hot enough to grow grapes of high quality. The first English wines were influenced by the sweet German wines like Liebfraumilch and Hock that were popular in the 1970s, and were blended white and red sweet wines, called cream wine. The largest vineyard in England is Denbies Wine Estate in Surrey, which has 265 acres (1.07 km2) under vines, and a visitors' centre that is open all year round. The growth of English wine accelerated in the late 1990s, helped by popularity of wine from the new world, especially Australia, Chile, Argentina, New Zealand and South Africa which made consumers in the British Isles more accepting of wines that were not from the traditional wine growing regions of Europe. They were made popular by their single vintages, brand labels, and general non-fussiness of the wine. This influenced the English wine industry to copy what happened in the new world and produce good-quality wines with grapes like Chardonnay and Pinot Noir. In 2004 a panel judging European sparkling wines awarded most of the top ten positions to English wines-the remaining positions going to French Champagnes.

Winemaking has spread to the south-west, including Wiltshire, Dorset, Devon, Somerset, Cornwall and the Isle of Wight, and also to the Midlands and the north of England, with Yorkshire, Shropshire, Derbyshire, Leicestershire and Lancashire boasting at least one vineyard each as of 2007.

21st Century

Significant plantings have been happening across the south of the country with a number of farmers contract growing vines for some of the major English producers. Farmers are looking at the potential benefits of growing vines as the return per tonne for grapes over more traditional crops are not to be ignored. A field of wheat might yield 3 tonnes per acre at around £120 per tonne. Growing grapes could yield 3 to 4 tonnes per acre at around £950 to £1100 per tonne. It is a significant difference but growers will need to invest money for no initial return, as crops tend to come in the 3rd or 4th year.

Another explanation for the growth in viticulture in the UK, is the local food movement, and the desire by consumers to cut the amount of food miles connected with the produce that they buy, including locally produced wine.

Grape Varieties

As of 2004, Seyval Blanc was the most grown variety, with Reichensteiner next, with Müller-Thurgau and then Bacchus following closely behind. However, Müller-Thurgau, which was one of the first to be grown during the 20th century renaissance, has recently lost favour, dropping from 134.64 ha (1st) in 1996 to 81.1 ha (3rd) in 2004. Other widely grown varieties of white grape include Chardonnay, Madeleine Angevine, Schönburger, Huxelrebe and Ortega. Red varieties include Dornfelder, Pinot meunier and Pinot Noir, and a few others, but red grapes tend to be lesser grown, with 20184 hL of white wine and only 5083 hL of red wine made in 2006.

Effect on the British Economy

Most of the wine consumed in Britain is imported from other countries as it is usually hard to grow grapes due to the British climate. Now that English wine is being produced in larger quantities, more people in the British Isles are buying it as opposed to imported wines. The quantities produced are tiny compared to the volumes consumed, less than 1 per cent just as to DEFRA.

Rules of Wine Labeling

There are several official categories of wine in the UK. For still wines there are United Kingdom Table Wine, English Regional Wine, English Quality Wine, Welsh Regional Wine, Welsh Quality Wine. All but UK Table Wine have to go through a testing and tasting procedure before they can be so labelled. For sparkling wines the categories are English Sparkling Wine and English Quality Sparkling Wine with Welsh equivalents. These wines do not have to be tested or tasted before being so labelled.

WINE BUSINESS IN CANADIAN

Canadian wine is produced in mainly southern British Columbia and southern Ontario. There is also a growing number of small scale producers of grapes and wine in southern Quebec and Nova Scotia. The two largest wine-producing regions in Canada are the Okanagan Valley of British Columbia and the Niagara Peninsula of Ontario. Other wine-producing areas in British Columbia include the Similkameen valley, southern Fraser River valley, southern Vancouver Island and the Gulf Islands. Other areas in Ontario include the shores of Lake Erie and in Prince Edward County.

The Canadian wine industry also vinifies imported grapes and juice. These products are labeled Cellared in Canada and are not required to conform to the strict Vintners Quality Alliance content regulations.

Icewine, which can be produced reliably in most Canadian wine regions, especially the Okanagan Valley, is the most recognized product on an international basis. Canada produced 75.9 million litres of wine in 2002.

Canadian wine has been produced for over 200 years. Early settlers tried to cultivate Vitis vinifera grapes from Europe with limited success. They found it necessary to focus on the native species of Vitis labrusca and Vitis riparia along with various hybrids. However, the market was limited for such wines because of their peculiar taste which was often called "foxy". However, this became less apparent when the juice was made into Port- and Sherry-styled wines. For a period of time in the 1800s the export of these affordable wines to England made Ontario one of the largest wine exporters in North America.

During the first half of the twentieth century, the temperance movement and later consumer demand for fortified and sweet wines hampered the development of a quality table wine industry. However, during the 1960s consumer demand shifted from sweet and fortified wines to drier and lower alcohol table wines. At the same time, there were significant improvements in wine-making technology, access to better grape varieties and disease-resistant clones, and systematic research into viticulture.

After the repeal of alcohol prohibition in Canada in 1927, provinces strictly limited the number of licences to produce wine. A nearly 50-year moratorium on issuing new winery licences was finally dropped in 1974. During the same decade, demonstration planting began to show that Vitis vinifera could be successfully grown in Canada. Other growers found that high quality wines could be produced if Vitis vinifera vines were grown with reduced yields, new trellising techniques, and appropriate canopy management.

In 1988, three important events occurred: the free trade with the United States, the establishment of the Vintners Quality Alliance (VQA) standard, and a major grape vine replacement/upgrading programme. Each of these events served in one way or another to improve the viability of the wine industry in Canada.

During the 1990s, Canadian vintners continued to demonstrate that fine grape varieties in cooler growing conditions could potentially possess complex flavours, delicate yet persistent aromas, tightly focused structure and longer ageing potential than their counterparts in warmer growing regions of the world.

Market Share

Canadian wines have a less than 50 per cent share of the Canadian wine market, making Canada one of the few wine-producing countries where domestically produced wines do not hold a dominant share. Wine in general has been increasing its market share against other alcoholic beverages: since the late 1990s wine has increased its market share from 21 per cent to 28 per cent and since 2007 wine sales have increased by 9.5 per cent to $5 billion.

While there are many small Canadian wineries, the domestic wine market has long been dominated by two companies, Vincor International and Andres Wines. In 2006, Vincor International, which had grown aggressively in previous years by acquiring wineries in California, Australia and New Zealand, was itself acquired by Constellation Brands, a U.S. based company and one of the primary consolidators of the global wine business.

Exports

Some Canadian wine is exported to the United States, Europe or the Far East. Canada shipped US$4.9 million worth of wine to the United States in 2001. Icewine is a major export product for Canadian wineries. Much of the wine exported overseas is in the form of icewine. The largest importers are Asian countries, particularly China and Japan.

Cellared in Canada Controversy

In late 2009, local and international criticism of the "Cellared in Canada" practice and the LCBO emerged. Under the "Cellared in Canada" label, Canadian wine producers can import pre-fermented grape must from grapes grown in other countries to produce wines under their own wine label. In Ontario, producers are allowed to designated these wines as being made or "cellared" in Canada if they contain at least 30 per cent local Ontario grapes.

In British Columbia, growers do not need to have any local grapes at all in the wine. Grape growers in Ontario began protesting the practice as a threat to their livelihood claiming that thousands of tons of Canadian grapes are left rotting on the vine because producers are using imported grapes to make wine labeled as "Canadian". Wine producers who do not use the "Cellared in Canada" designation criticized the practice as tarnishing the reputation of Canadian wines and misleading consumers. Producers and growers in Canada have petitioned the government for several changes in the practices such as making the origin of grapes more clear on the wine label and increasing the visibility of 100 per cent Canadian wines produced by members of the Vintners Quality Alliance (VQA) in province run liquor stores.

As of August 2009, the province stores of the LCBO featured less than 2.5 per cent Canadian wine produced by VQA members with the vast majority of its wines produced under the "Cellared in Canada" designation with up to 70 per cent foreign grapes.

Association of B.C. Winegrowers

Association of British Columbia Winegrowers, or ABCW is an association of artisan winemakers located in the Canadian province of British Columbia. Most of the member wineries are small lot producers, family owned and operated. Their wines are all made from 100 per cent BC-grown fruit. The ABCW's 57 members account for over 70 per cent of the province's wineries.In 2007, the ABCW created BC WineCast an audio podcast devoted to exploring the hidden wineries of British Columbia. Each week, the ABCW Executive Director, Dr. David E. Bond, speaks with a different member winemaker about the passion behind their chosen craft.

British Columbia Wine

British Columbia wine is Canadian wine produced in the province of British Columbia. Wines made from 100 per cent British Columbia grapes can qualify for classification under one of British Columbia's two classification systems, depending on the varietal, the wine-making techniques employed, and various other restrictions.

Originally, the British Columbia Wine Institute handled regulation and marketing of the Vintners Quality Alliance (VQA), which is also an appellation system. More recently, the British Columbia Wine Authority was formed by the provincial government to regulate part of the industry. It created a second classification, "Wines of Distinction", to be also from 100 per cent British Columbia grapes, but with less stringent quality control. In practice, it has strengthened the VQA classification.

British Columbia is gaining recognition for its world-class premium VQA wines. Wines which are neither labelled VQA or Wine of Distinction, and from certain producers can use foreign bulk wine to produce a third category of wine which is labelled as Cellared in Canada. Significant parts of the wine industry, and respected wine writers in Canada and abroad, are quite concerned about this practice.

There are several classifications of winery, represented by numerous organizations. The smallest are known as "farmgate" wineries. "Land" wineries are mid-sized operations.

Varieties

The most prominent varieties of grapes grown in British Columbia are:

For red wine and rose production:

- Merlot
- Pinot Noir
- Cabernet Sauvignon
- Syrah
- Cabernet Franc

- Gamay
- Marechal Foch
- Malbec
- Petit Verdot
- Zweigelt

For white wines:

- Pinot Gris
- Chardonnay
- Gewürztraminer
- Sauvignon Blanc
- Pinot Blanc
- Riesling
- Viognier
- Ehrenfelser
- Semillon
- Bacchus

Growing Regions

Based on their unique terroir, there are five official viticultural areas in the province which are recognized by the VQA. Wines bearing the name of a viticultural area are produced from a minimum of 95 per cent of the grapes grown in the designated area.

- Okanagan Valley
- Similkameen Valley
- Fraser Valley
- Vancouver Island
- Gulf Islands

Lifford Wine Agency

The Lifford Wine Agency is a wine importer in Ontario, Canada which produces the plantatree is a brand of wine. There are three wines, Merlot, Cabernet Sauvignon and Chardonnay, distributed under this brand. For every bottle sold, the company donates $2.50 to Tree Canada to fund the planting of a tree. The brand is meant to be carbon positive, signifying that the carbon produced in making the product is offset, thus having a positive impact on one's carbon footprint. The wine is imported in bulk to Ontario from California and then bottled in lightweight PET bottles to be distributed only in Ontario with plans to distribute nationally.

WINE BUSINESS CHILEAN

Chilean wine is wine made in the South American country of Chile. The region has a long viticultural antiquity for a New World wine region dating to the 16th century when the Spanish conquistadors brought Vitis vinifera vines with them as they colonized the region. In the mid-18th century, French wine varieties such as Cabernet Sauvignon and Merlot were introduced. In the early 1980s, a renaissance began with the introduction of stainless steel fermentation tanks and the use of oak barrels for aging. Wine exports grew very quickly as quality wine production increased. The number of wineries has grown from 12 in 1995 to over 70 in 2005. Chile is now the fifth largest exporter of wines in the world, and the ninth largest producer. The climate has been described as midway between that of California and France. The most common grapes are Cabernet Sauvignon, Merlot and Carmenère. So far Chile has remained free of phylloxera louse which means that the country's grapevines do not need to be grafted.

European Vitis vinifera vines were brought to Chile by Spanish conquistadors and missionaries in the 16th century around 1554. Local legend states that the conquistador Francisco de Aguirre himself planted the first vines. The vines most likely came from established Spanish vineyards planted in Peru which included the "common black grape", as it was known, that Hernán Cortés brought to Mexico in 1520. This grape variety would become the ancestor of the widely planted Pais grape that would be the most widely planted Chilean grape till the 21st century. Jesuit priests cultivated these early vineyards, using the wine for the celebration of the Eucharist. By the late 16th century, the early Chilean historian Alonso de Ovalle described widespread plantings of "the common black grape", Muscatel, Torontel, Albilho and Mollar.

During the Spanish rule, vineyards were restricted in production with the stipulation that the Chilean should purchase the bulk of their wines directly from Spain itself. In 1641, wine imports from Chile and the Viceroyalty of Peru into Spain were banned, severely damaging the wine industry in the colony. The market loss caused the huge surplus of grapes to be made into pisco and aguardiente.

The concentration solely on pisco production, nearly eliminated wine production in Peru. For the most part the Chileans ignored these restrictions, preferring their domestic production to the oxidized and vinegary wines that didn't fare well during the long voyages from Spain. They were even so bold as to start exporting some of their wines to neighbouring Peru with one such export shipment being captured at sea by the English privateer Francis Drake. When Spain heard of the event rather than being outraged at Drake, an indictment was sent back to Chile with the order to uproot most of their vineyards. This order, too, was mostly ignored.

In the 18th century, Chile was known mostly for its sweet wines made from the Pais and Muscatel grapes. To achieve a high level of sweetness the wines were often boiled which concentrated the grape must. Following his shipwreck off the coast at Cape Horn, Admiral John Byron travelled across

Chile and came back to England with a glowing review of Chilean Muscatel comparing it favorably to Madeira. The 19th century wine writer André Julien was not as impressed, comparing Chilean wines to a "potion of rhubarb and senna".

Despite being politically linked to Spain, Chile's wine antiquity has been most profoundly influenced by French, particularly Bordeaux, winemaking. Prior to the phylloxera epidemic, wealthy Chilean landowners were influenced by their visits to France and began importing French vines to plant.Don Silvestre Errázuriz was the first, importing Cabernet Sauvignon, Merlot, Cabernet franc, Malbec, Sauvignon blanc and Sémillon. He hired a French oenologist to oversee his vineyard planting and to produce wine in the Bordeaux style. Errázuriz saw potential in Chile and even experimented with the German wine grape Riesling.In events that parallel those of the Rioja wine region, the entrance of phylloxera into the French wine world turned into a positive event for the Chilean wine industry. With vineyards in ruin, many French winemakers traveled to South America, bringing their experience and techniques with them.

Political instability in the 20th century, coupled with bureaucratic regulations and high taxes tempered the growth of the Chilean wine industry. Prior to the 1980s, the vast majority of Chilean wine was considered low quality and mostly consumed domestically. As awareness of Chile's favorable growing conditions for viticulture increased so did foreign investment in Chilean wineries. This period saw many technical advances in winemaking as Chile earned a reputation for reasonably priced premium quality wines. Chile began to export extensively, becoming the third leading exporter, after France and Italy, into the United States by the turn of the 21st century. It has since dropped to fourth in the US, being surpassed by Australia, but focus has switched to developing exports in the world's other major wine markets like the United Kingdom and Japan.

Wine Regions

In December 1994, the Republic of Chile defined the following viticultural regions:

- *Atacama, within the Atacama region*: Within it are two subregions, the Copiapó Valley and the Huasco Valley, both of which are coterminous with the provinces of the same names. The region is known primarily for its Pisco production. Atacama is also an important source of table grapes.
- *Coquimbo, within the Coquimbo Region*: It has three subregions: Elqui Valley, Limarí Valley, and the Choapa Valley. All subregions are coterminous with the provinces of the same names. Like the Atacama this region is primarily known for Pisco and table grapes.
- *Aconcagua, within the Valparaiso Region*: It includes two subregions,

the Valley of Aconcagua and the Valley of Casablanca. The Aconcagua Valley is coterminous with the province of that name. The Casablanca Valley is coterminous with the comuna of that name. The Panquehue commune is also gradually developing a reputation for high quality wine production. Casablanca is one of Chile's cooler wine regions and is often compared to the Californian wine region of Carneros and grows similar grape varietals like Chardonnay and Pinot noir. Casablanca's growing seasons last up to a month longer than other regions, typically harvesting in April. The northern region of Aconcagua is Chile's warmest wine region and is primarily planted with Cabernet Sauvignon and Merlot. The soil of this region is composed mainly of alluvial deposits left over from ancient river beds.

- Valle Central, which spans the O'Higgins Region (VI) and Maule Region (VII) Administrative Regions and the Administrative Metropolitan Region. Within it are four subregions: the Maipo Valley, the Rapel Valley, the Curicó Valley and the Maule Valley. This is Chile's most productive and internationally known wine region, due in large part to its close proximately to the country's capital Santiago. It is located directly across the Andes' from Argentina's most well known wine region Mendoza Province. The Maipo Valley is the most widely cultivated valley and is known for Cabernet Sauvignon. The Rapel wine region in the Colchagua Province is also known for it Cabernet. Curicó has both red and white wine varieties planted but is most widely known for it Chardonnay. The Maule Valley still has large plantings of the local Pais but is gradually being planted with better red wine varieties. The soil of Maipo Valley is noted for high salinity stemming from irrigation from the Maipo river and low potassium level which has some impact on the grapevines. Vineyards in the Maule also suffer from low potassium as well as deficient nitrogen levels. Advances in viticultural techniques have helped vineyards in these regions compensate for some of these effects.
- *Southern Chile, within the Bio-Bio Region (VIII).* Two subregions are included: Itata Valley and Bío-Bío Valley. The region is primarily known for its mass produce Pais box and jug wines though Concha y Toro Winery has experimented with Gewürztraminer from this region. The southern regions have more rainfall, lower average temperatures and fewer hours of sunlight than the northern wine regions.

Viticulture

Chile's natural boundaries has left it relatively isolated from other parts of the world and has served to be beneficial in keeping the phylloxera louse at bay. Because of this many Chilean vineyards do not have to graft their rootstock and incur that added cost of planting. Chilean wineries have stated that this "purity" of their vines is a positive element that can be tasted in the wine but most wine experts agree that the most apparent benefit is the financial aspect. The one wine region that is the exception to this freedom from grafting is Casablanca whose vines are susceptible to attack by nematodes. While phylloxera is not a problem, winemakers do have to worry about other grape diseases and hazards such as downy mildew, which was spread easily by El Niño influences and severely affected the 1997-1998 vintages. Powdery mildew and verticillium wilt can also cause trouble.

There is not much vintage variation due to the reliability of favorable weather with little risk of spring time frost or harvest time rains. The main exception, again, is Casablanca due in part to its closer proximately to the Pacific. For the Chilean wine regions in the Valle Central, the Andes and Coastal Ranges create a rain shadow affect which traps the warm arid air in the region. At night, cool air comes into the area from the Andes which dramatically drops the temperature. This help maintain high levels of acidity to go with the ripe fruit that grapes develop with the long hours of uninterrupted sunshine that they get during the day. The result is a unique profile of flavonoids in the wine which some Chilean wineries claim make Chilean wines higher in resveratrol and antioxidants. Harvest typically begins at the end of February for varieties like Chardonnay with some red wine varieties like Cabernet Sauvignon being picked in April and Carmenère sometimes staying on the vine into May.

The Andes also provide a ready source of irrigation which was historically done in flood plain style. Chilean vineyard owners would dig canals throughout their vineyards and then flood the entire surface area with water allowing some to seep into the ground and the run off to be funnel away through the canals. This encouraged excessive irrigation and high yields which had a negative effect on quality. During the wine renaissance of the 1980s and 1990s more vineyards converted to drip irrigation system which allowed greater control and helped reduce yields. The soil composition of Chile's vineyards varies from the clay dominated landscapes of Colchagua, which is thus heavily planted with the clay-loving Merlot, to the mixture of loam, limestone and sand found in other regions. In the southern Rapel and parts of Maule, tuffeau soil is present with volcanic soil being found in parts of Curico and Bio-Bio.

Winemaking

Chile has benefited from an influx of foreign investment and winemaking talent that begin in the late 20th century. Flying winemakers introduced new technology and styles that helped Chilean wineries produce more international recognized wine styles. One such improvement was the use of oak. Historically Chilean winemakers had aged their wines in barrels made from rauli beechwood which imparted to the wine a unique taste that many international tasters found unpleasant. Gradually the wineries began to convert to French and American oak or stainless steel tanks for aging.

Financial investment manifested in the form of European and American winemakers opening up their own wineries or collaborating with existing Chilean wineries to produce new brands.

These include:

- Robert Mondavi, collaboration with Viña Errázuriz to produce Sena.
- Miguel A. Torres, Catalan winemaker opened Miguel Torres Chile in 1979.
- Kendall-Jackson, opened Viña Calina.
- Château Lafite Rothschild, collaboration with Los Vascos.
- Bruno Prats, Owner of Château Cos d'Estournel, and Paul Pontallier, former winemaker of Chateau Margaux, opened Domaine Paul Bruno.
- Château Mouton Rothschild, collaboration with Concha y Toro Winery to produce Almaviva.

Wine Laws

Chile's wine laws are more similar to the US appellation system than to France's Appellation d'origine contrôlée that most of Europe has based their wine laws on. Chile's system went into effect in 1995 and established the boundaries of the countries wine regions and established regulations for wine labels. There are no restrictions of grape varieties, viticultural practices or winemaking techniques. Wines are required to have at least 75 per cent of a grape variety if its to listed on the label as well as at least 75 per cent from the designated vintage year. To list a particular wine region, 75 per cent is also the minimum requirement of grapes that need to be from that region. Similar to the United States, the term Reserve has no legal definition or meaning.

Grapes and Wines

Over twenty grape varieties are grown in Chile, mainly a mixture of Spanish and French varieties, but many wineries are increasing experimentation in higher amount. For most of Chile's antiquity, Pais was the most widely planted grape only recently getting passed by Cabernet Sauvignon. Other red wine varieties include Merlot, Carménère, Zinfandel, Petite Sirah, Cabernet franc, Pinot noir, Syrah, Sangiovese, Barbera, Malbec, and Carignan. White wine varieties include Chardonnay, Sauvignon blanc, Sauvignon vert, Sémillon, Riesling, Viognier, Torontel, Pedro Ximénez, Gewürztraminer and Muscat of Alexandria.

Chilean winemakers have been developing a distinct style for their Cabernet Sauvignon, producing an easy drinking wine with soft tannins and flavours of mint, black currant, olives and smoke. The country's Chardonnays are less distinctive, following more the stereotypical New World style. While sparkling wines have been made since 1879, they have not yet established a significant place in Chile's wine portfolio.

Merlot and Sauvignon Blanc

In the late 20th century as Chilean wines became more popular, wine tasters around the world began to doubt the authenticity of wines labeled Merlot and Sauvignon blanc. The wines lack many of the characteristics and typicity of those grapes. Ampelographers began to study the vines and found that what was considered Merlot was actually the ancient Bordeaux wine grape Carménère that was thought to be extinct. The Sauvignon blanc vines were found to actually be Sauvignonasse, also known as Sauvignon vert, or a mutated Sauvignon blanc/Sémillon cross. In response to these discoveries several Chilean wineries began to import true Merlot and Sauvignon blanc cuttings to where most bottle of wines labeled Merlot and Sauvignon blanc from vintages in the 21st century are very likely to truly be those varieties.

International Competitions

Chilean wines have ranked very highly in international competitions. For example, in the Berlin Wine Tasting of 2004, 36 European experts blind tasted wines from two vintages each of eight top wines from France, Italy and Chile. The first and second place wines were two Cabernet-based reds from Chile: Viñedo Chadwick 2000 and Sena 2001. The Berlin Wine Tasting of 2005 held in Brazil featured five Chilean wines in the top seven. In the Tokyo Wine Tasting of 2006, Chilean wines won four of the top five rankings.

Aguardiente

Aguardiente, aguardente, augardente/caña or oruxu, is the generic name for alcoholic drinks between 29 and 60 per cent alcohol, meaning "firewater", or, literally "burning water". The word itself is a compound word, combining the words for water and burning.

By definition, aguardientes are strongly alcoholic beverages, obtained by fermentation and later distillation of sugared or sweet musts, vegetable macerations, or mixtures of the two. This is the most generic level; by this definition aguardientes may be made from a number of different sources. Fruit-based aguardientes include those made from oranges, grapes, bananas, or madronho.

Grain-based ones may be made from millet, barley, or rice and tuber-based aguardientes from beet, manioc, or potato, and finally what are classed as "true" aguardientes from sugarcane and other sweet canes including some species of bamboo. Under this definition, many other distinct liquors could be called aguardientes, including Vodka, Sake, Pisco, and certain forms of hard Chicha. On 14 November 1996, it was concluded in analysis that Cane Aguardiente and

Cachaça are similar but distinct products. Cane Aguardiente was thereafter defined in Brazil as an alcoholic beverage of between 38 per cent and 54 per cent alcohol by volume, obtained by simple fermentation and distillation of sugarcane that has already been used in the sugar-production process, and which has distinct flavour similar to rum. Cachaça, on the other hand, is an alcoholic beverage of between 38 per cent and 48 per cent alcohol by volume, obtained by fermentation and distillation of sugar cane juice which may have added sugar up to 6 g/L.

Some histories state that the Egyptians were the first to use fermented liquors, as cures for diverse medical conditions. The ancient Greeks however, pioneered the process of creating and distilling ácqua ardens. Greek aguardientes were created by distilling wine; the Treaty of the Sciences, written by Pliny, contains a fragment of the original recipes as well as the process of distillation using Cedar balsam. Later, the Egyptians developed the first alembics, the designs of which adorn the walls of the temple at Memphis. The Arabic language gives us the words "alembic" and "alcohol". The expansion of the Roman Empire brought aguardiente to Europe and the Middle East and aguardiente became the base of alchemical elixirs such as the Elixir of Longevity.

In the Middle Ages, in a 1250 study of distillation by Arnaut de Villeneuve, he described the "spirit" of wine; later his contemporary, Raymond Lulle, through the process of distillation 3 or 4 times over very low heat, claimed to have discovered in wine the essences of the four elements, Earth, Air, Water, and Fire. By about 1730, ageing distilled aguardientes had become common practice, and now in the 20th century these are considered distinct from "pure" or "raw" aguardientes.

Regional Variations

Brazil

In Brazil, an aguardente known as cachaça or pinga, considered distinct from traditional aguardiente, is made from sugar cane. Cachaça, like rum, has two varieties: unaged (white) and aged (gold). White cachaça is usually bottled immediately after distillation and tends to be cheaper. It is often used to prepare caipirinha and other beverages in which cachaça is an ingredient. Dark cachaça, usually seen as the "premium" variety, is aged in wood barrels and is meant to be drunk pure. Traditionally no herbs are used to flavour the cachaça and its flavour is influenced by the fermentation agent, time spent in the cask or type of wood from which the barrel is made.

Colombia

In Colombia, aguardiente is an anise-flavoured liqueur derived from sugar cane, popular in the Andean region. Each department of Colombia holds the rights to produce it, but aguardiente produced in one region can be sold in another. By adding different amounts of aniseed, different flavours are obtained, leading to extensive marketing and fierce competition between brands. Aguardiente has a 29 per cent alcohol content.

Other anise-flavoured liqueurs similar to aguardiente but with a lower alcohol content are also sold. Aguardiente has maintained since the Spanish era the status of the most popular alcoholic beverage in the andean regions of Colombia with the notable exception of the Caribbean Region in which the Rum is king. Colombians in the andean regions drink it straight as individual shots and they rarely use it in cocktails.

Chile

In Chile, aguardiente is an alcoholic beverage of 45 per cent and higher alcohol content by volume. It is made, like Italian grappa, by distilling the grape residue, primarily the skins and pulp plus the stems and seeds, left over from winemaking after pressing the grapes.

It is used to make several other flavoured liquors like the murtado or enmurtillado, the enguindado and licor de oro. Dried mint, peeled walnuts, almonds, and other aromatic herbs are also used to flavour the aguardiente. It is mainly consumed by itself, or as a base to make cola de mono.

Ecuador

In Ecuador, aguardiente is also derived from sugarcane but unlike Colombia it is left largely unflavoured. It is then taken straight as shots, mulled with cinnamon and fruit juices to make the hot cocktail called canelazo, or mixed with the juice of agave masts and Grenadine syrup for the hot cocktail called Draquita. Locally or artisanally made aguardiente is commonly called Punta, and alcohol content can vary widely, from "mild" puntas of about 10 per cent to "strong" of about 40 per cent or higher.

The traditional distillation process produces aguardiente as strong as 60GL. Every Ecuadorian province has a slightly different flavour to the aguardiente produced there, and equally each province has a different recipe for canelazo. Commercially, aguardiente is marketed on a national scale by the companies Zhumir and Cristal, who both offer a number fruit-flavoured versions of the liquor along with the traditional flavourless variety. Both companies also offer sparkling coolers based on aguardiente that are similar to the vodka coolers available in North America. In Ecuador, aguardiente is the most commonly consumed strong alcohol.

Galicia

In Ecuador, aguardiente is also derived from sugarcane but unlike Colombia it is left largely unflavoured. It is then taken straight as shots, mulled with cinnamon and fruit juices to make the hot cocktail called canelazo, or mixed with the juice of agave masts and Grenadine syrup for the hot cocktail called Draquita. Locally or artisanally made aguardiente is commonly called Punta, and alcohol content can vary widely, from "mild" puntas of about 10 per cent to "strong" of about 40 per cent or higher.

The traditional distillation process produces aguardiente as strong as 60GL. Every Ecuadorian province has a slightly different flavour to the aguardiente produced there, and equally each province has a different recipe for canelazo. Commercially, aguardiente is marketed on a national scale by the companies Zhumir and Cristal, who both offer a number fruit-flavoured versions of the liquor along with the traditional flavourless variety. Both companies also offer sparkling coolers based on aguardiente that are similar to the vodka coolers available in North America. In Ecuador, aguardiente is the most commonly consumed strong alcohol.

Galicia

In Mexico in the state of Michoacan, charanda is a traditional rum-like sugarcane aguadiente.

Portugal

Portuguese aguardente has several varieties. Aguardente vínica is distilled from wine, either of good quality or undrinkable wines. It's mostly used to fortify wines like Port or aged to make aguardente velha, a kind of brandy. There is also aguardente bagaceira that is made of pomace as a way to prevent waste after the wine season. It is usually bootlegged, as most drinkers only appreciate it in its traditional 50 per cent to 80 per cent ABV. The most common way to drink it is added to espresso, in what is known as a café com cheirinho. In the Azores, this espresso-aguardente combination is commonly referred to as "café com música".

WINE BUSINES IN CHINA

Wine in China refers to grape wines that are produced in China. Grape wine has a long antiquity in China, along with other Chinese alcoholic beverages.

Beginning in 1980, French and other Western wines began to rise in prominence in the Chinese market, both in mainland China and Taiwan. French-taught Chinese winemakers introduced wine to a market dominated mostly by beer, and have quickly expanded in scale such that China, with its immense population, is set to become the largest wine market in the world.

The antiquity of Chinese grape wine has been dated back more than 4,600 years. In 1995, a joint Sino-USA archeology team including archaeologists from the Archeology Research Institute of Shandong University and American archaeologists under the leadership of Fang Hui investigated the two archaeological sites 20 km to the northeast of Rizhao, and discovered the remnants of a variety of alcoholic beverages including grape wine, rice wine, mead, and several mixed beverages of these wines. Out of more than two hundred ceramic pots discovered at the sites, seven were specifically used for grape wine. Remnants of grape seeds were also discovered.

Thus, grape wine is one of a range of traditional Chinese alcoholic beverages, with others made from sorghum, millet, rice, and fruits such as lychee or Asian plum.

Modern Chinese Wine

China's modern wine antiquity dates back more than a hundred years, to 1892. It is believed that Confucius drank the wines of the region that is now Shandong Province, but when Zhang Bishi, an overseas Chinese diplomat, decided to start his winery in Yantai, there was little to be found there but a few edible grapes. He imported more than 500,000 wine plants from the U.S. and from Europe. His company still exists, known as Changyu Pioneer Wine, and is believed to be the tenth largest winery in the world.

French wine was the first foreign wine imported into China. In 1980, at the beginning of Chinese economic reform, Rémy Martin ventured into China to set up the first joint-venture enterprise in Tianjin: the Dynasty Wine Ltd., which was also the second joint-venture enterprise in China. Over the years, the company developed over 90 brands of alcoholic beverages, and its products won numerous awards both domestically and abroad.

However, most of its products were exported abroad in the first two decades due to the low income of the local population, and it was not until after the year 2000 when the economic boom finally provided the domestic population with sufficient disposable income to support the domestic market; this relatively recent occurrence coincided with the increased popularity of French wine in China. Other companies, including China Great Wall Wine Co., Ltd, Suntime and Changyu, have also risen in prominence, and by 2005, 90 per cent of grape wine produced was consumed locally.

Also, as globalization has brought China onto the international economic scene, so to has its winemaking industry come onto the international wine scene. China has a long tradition of the fermentation and distillation of Chinese wine, including all alcoholic beverages and not necessarily grape wine, but is one of the most recent participants in the globalization of wine that started years ago in Paris, when several countries such as Canada realized that they may be able to produce wines as good as most French wine.

Quite recently, Chinese grape wine has begun appearing on shelves in California and in Western Canada. While some critics have treated these wines with the same type of disregard with which Chilean and Australian wines were once treated, others have recognized a new frontier with the potential to yield some interesting finds. Others have simply taken notice that China is producing drinkable table wines comparable to wines from other countries.

Regions

Xinjiang wine refers to wine produced in Xinjiang in western China. The use of grapes for making wine was first recorded by a Chinese emissary in 138 BC, although it is possible grapes were cultivated even earlier than this during the Shang era.

A cable car connects Xi Shan to Hui Shan. By the Yuan dynasty wine production based in Xinjiang was a notable industry and spread to other parts of China. By the Ming dynasty period, varieties such as the crystal, purple and seedless rabbit-eye grape were grown. Grapes are also sold in abundance at the marketplace in Urumqi.

Market

The Chinese domestic market for wine is projected to become the largest in the world in a few decades, even though the current annual per capita consumption of wine in China is only 0.35 litres. In 2008, wine merchant Berry Brothers and Rudd predicted that within 50 years the quality of Chinese wine will rival that of Bordeaux.

At the moment, a few large companies, such as Changyu Pioneer Wine, China Great Wall Wine Co., Ltd. and the Dynasty Wine Ltd., dominate the market. The total production of wine in 2004 was 370 thousand tons, a 15 per cent increase from the previous year. Total market grew 58 per cent between 1996 and 2001, and 68 per cent between 2001 and 2006. Notable wine-producing regions include Beijing, Yantai, Zhangjiakou in Hebei, Yibin in Sichuan, Tonghua in Jilin, Taiyuan in Shanxi, and Ningxia. The largest producing region is Yantai-Penglai, with its more than 140 wineries producing 40 per cent of China's wine production.

Statistics show that the main market for white wine is among females, who prefer it over beer, still the main alcoholic beverage for most males; red wine has become a symbol of the elite and rich and is usually used as a table wine. In 2005, 80 per cent of vineyards produce red wine and 20 per cent of vineyards produce white wine, while 90 per cent of wine consumed as of 2007 is red wine.

WINE BUSINESS IN CROTIA

Croatian wine has a antiquity dating back to the Ancient Greek settlers, and their wine production. Like other old world wine producers, many traditional grape varieties still survive here, perfectly suited to their local wine hills. Modern wine-production methods have taken over in the larger wineries, and EU-style wine regulations have been adopted, guaranteeing the quality of the wine. There are currently over 300 geographically defined wine regions, and a strict classification system to ensure quality and origin. The majority of Croatian wine is white, with most of the remainder being red, and only a small percentage is rosé wines. In 2005, Croatia ranked 21st in wine producing countries with 180,000 tonnes.

Wine is a popular drink in Croatia, and locals traditionally like to drink wine with their meals. Quite often, the wine is diluted with either still or sparkling water-producing a drink known as gemišt in the north, and bevanda in the south.

Like the rest of Central and Eastern Europe, viticulture in the present-day Croatia existed hundreds of years before the rise of the Roman Empire. Recent research has shown that the Illyrians living in Dalmatia during the Bronze Age and Iron Age may already have grown grapevines. However, the true beginning of grape cultivation and wine production in Croatia is related to the Ancient Greeks settlers, who arrived on the Croatian coast in the 5th century BC. The Greek writer Athenaeus wrote 22 centuries ago about the high quality wine produced on the Dalmatian islands of Vis, Hvar and Kor?ula. Coins from the period have motifs related to grape cultivation and wine, demonstrating the importance of wine in the economics of the ancient Greek colonies.

Under the Roman Empire, the production of wine grew, becoming more organized. Wine was exported to other parts of the empire. Artifacts from this time include stone presses from which wine was squeezed, amphoras from sunken Roman galleys, and decorations on numerous religious and household items bear witness to the wine-making culture.

As the Croatians arrived and settled the area, they learned from their predecessors, and wine production continued to expand. During the Middle Ages, there was a royal court official called the "royal wine procurer", whose responsibilities included the production and procurement of wine. Free towns adopted legal standards on winegrowing and protected it just as. For example, a statute of the town and island of Kor?ula in 1214 contains strict rules protecting the vineyards.

In the 15th century, the Ottoman Turks arrived in Eastern Europe, and imposed strict anti-alcohol laws as part of the new Islamic law. Fortunately, the Ottoman Empire was tolerant of Christianity, and Catholic church traditions involving wine are thought to have "saved" European wine production from complete extinction. Priests and monks were permitted to continue producing wine in order to provide for Church services.

In the 1700s, much of present-day Croatia came under control of the Habsburg Empire, where wine production flourished through the 19th and 20th centuries. But the antiquity of wine was to change dramatically in 1874, when phylloxera, a hazardous grapevine pest, started to appear in Europe. Wine production dropped, first in France and Germany, as the growers struggled to combat the blight. For a time, Croatian vineyards remained unaffected, and wine exports greatly increased to fill the extra demand. Some French companies even planted vines in Croatia with a view to expanding operations in the safe area. However, by the turn of the century, Croatian vines had also succumbed to phylloxera, leading to the destruction of the vineyards and the collapse of the local economy in many areas. Large amount of wine growing families moved to the new world, contributing to the growth of wine production there.

Under the communist system of Yugoslavia, wine production was centered in large cooperatives, and private ownership of vineyards was discouraged. Quantity rather than quality became the main focus. The Croatian War of Independence in the early 1990s saw many vineyards and wineries once again destroyed. However, with the move back to small, independent producers, Croatian wines are once again competing with the best in the world wine market.

Wine Styles

There are two distinct wine-producing regions in Croatia. The continental region in the north-east of the country, produces rich fruity white wines, similar in style to the neighbouring areas of Slovenia, Austria and Hungary. On the north coast, Istrian wines are similar to those produced in neighbouring Italy, while further south production is more towards big Mediterranean-style reds. On the islands and the Dalmatian coast, local grape varietals, microclimates and the rather harsh nature of the vineyards leads to some highly individual wines, and some of Croatia's best known.

The majority (67 per cent) of wine produced is white and produced in the interior, while 32 per cent is red and produced mainly along the coast. Rosé is relatively rare. Some special wines, such as sparkling wine and dessert wine are also produced.

Wine Regions

Croatia has two main wine regions: Continental and Coastal, which includes the islands. Each of the main regions is divided into sub-regions which are divided yet further into smaller vinogorje, and districts. Altogether, there are more than 300 geographically-defined wine-producing areas in Croatia.

Continental Croatia

The inland wine region, stretching from north-west to south-east along the Drava and Sava rivers, has a typical continental climate with cold winters and hot summers. Production is concentrated in white wine varieties. The best-known area within this region is Slavonia, and the most widely planted grape is Graševina, which yields light, crisp, refreshing, mildly aromatic wines.

The continental region is divided into the following sub-regions:

Sub-region	Winehills (Vinogorje)
Moslavina	Čazma, Voloder-Ivanić Grad
Plešivica	Krašić, Ozalj-Vivodina, Plešivica-Okić, Samobor, Sveta Jana
Podunavlje	Baranja, Erdut, Srijem
Pokuplje	Karlovac, Petrinja, Vukomeričke Gorice
Prigorje—Bilogora	Bilogora, Dugo Selo-Vrbovec, Kalnik, Koprivnica-Đurđevac, Zagreb, Sv. Ivan Zelina
Slavonia	Daruvar, Đakovo, Feričanci, Kutjevo, Nova Gradiška, Orahovica-Slatina, Pakrac, Požega-Pleternica, Slavonski Brod, Virovitica
Zagorje—Međimurje	Klanjec, Krapina, Ludbreg, Međimurje, Pregrada, Stubica, Varaždin, Zabok, Zlatar

Coastal Croatia

The coastal wine region runs from Istria in the north to Dalmatia to the south. The Mediterranean climate, with long, hot dry summers and mild, short, wet winters is particularly well suited to wine production. In Istria and the north coast, the focus is on fruity, dry white wines from a wide range of grape varieties, the best known of which are Malvazija and Graševina. Further south, in Dalmatia, the islands and hillsides have an infinite variety of microclimates resulting in a wine-growing area where terroir is a crucially important factor. A wide range of indigeous grape varietals are grown here, the best known being Plavac Mali, a close relative of Zinfandel.

The coastal region is divided into the following sub-regions:

Sub-region	Winehills (Vinogorje)
Istria	Western Istria, Central Istria, Eastern Istria
Croatian Coast	Opatija-Rijeka, islands Krk, Rab, Cres-Lošinj, Pag
Northern Dalmatia	Benkovac-Stankovci, Drniš, Knin, Pirovac-Skradin, Primošten, Promina, Šibenik, Zadar-Biograd
Dalmatian Interior	Imotski, Sinj-Vrlika, Vrgorac
Central and South Dalmatia	Kaštela-Trogir, Split-Omiš-Makarska, Neretva, Konavle, Pelješac peninsula, islands Brač, Hvar, Korčula, Lastovo, Mljet, Šolta, Vis

Classification

The Croatian Institute of Viticulture and Enology was set up in 1996 to oversee the country's wine industry, and be responsible for regulating wine-growing and wine production. Standards, similar to the EU wine regulations were set up, to ensure the consistent quality of the final product.

Croatian wines are classified by quality, which is clearly marked on the label:

- *Vrhunsko Vino*: Premium Quality Wine

- *Kvalitetno Vino*: Quality Wine
- *Stolno Vino*: Table Wine

In addition, wines may qualify for a geographical origin stamp, if it is produced from grapes grown in the same wine-growing region. The definition becomes stricter for higher quality classifications, so that a premium quality wine with geographical origin stamp must meet criteria for the type of grape, the position in the vinogorije with the distinct quality and characteristics for the varietal. If the wine has a grape varietal stamp, it must be at least 85 per cent of the grape type whose name it carries. Distinctive quality wines are the wines that have a special quality, attained in certain years, in special conditions of maturation, manner of harvesting and processing, and have to be produced only from the recommended sorts of grape for the particular wine-growing hills.

Wines qualifying for a vintage designation, must be kept in cellar conditions longer than its optimal maturation period, and not less than 5 years from the day of processing grape into wine, of which at least 3 years in a bottle.

- *Suho*: Dry
- *Polusuho*: Semi-dry
- *Slatko*: Sweet
- *Bijelo*: White
- *Crno*: Red
- *Rosa*: Rose
- *Prošek*: Dalmatian dessert wine made from dried *grapes*. Similar to Italian Vin Santo

BUSINESS OF CYPRIOT WINE

The Cypriot wine industry ranks 37th in the world in terms of total production quantity (37,500 tonnes)., and much higher on a per capita basis. Although, chronologically, Cyprus belongs to the old world of wine producing countries, the industry has gone through changes that place it more on par with the new world. The wine industry is a significant contributor to the Cypriot economy through cultivation, production, employment, export and tourism. Cyprus has been a vine-growing and wine-producing country for millennia. Internationally, it is best known for Commandaria wine. Most wine production remains based on a few varieties of local grapes such as Mavro and Xynisteri although international varieties are also cultivated.

Backdrop

The antiquity of wine in Cyprus can be broken down into four distinct periods.

Ancient

Exactly how far back wine production in Cyprus goes is unknown. Wine was being traded at least as early as 2300 BC, the date of a shipwreck carrying over 2,500 amphorae, discovered in 1999. Its origin and destination are unknown, but must have been along the trade route between Greece and Egypt.

More recently, two discoveries have put that date back by a few more years. The first was the discovery of a Bronze Age perfumery near the village of Pyrgos. Near this perfumery, an olive press, a winery, and copper smelting works were also discovered. Wine containers and even the seeds of grapes were unearthed.

The second discovery involved an intriguing sequence of events. Dr. Porphyrios Dikaios, in Cypriot archaeology and once curator of the Cyprus Museum, had carried out excavations on the outskirts of Erimi village between 1932 and 1935. During these excavations, several fragments of round flasks were unearthed. These pottery fragments ended up in the stores of the Cyprus Museum still unwashed in wooden boxes. They were dated to the chalcolithic period (between 3500BC-3000BC). In 2005, well after Dr Dikaios' death, the chemical signatures of 18 of these were examined by a team of Italian archaeologists led by Maria-Rosaria Belgiorno. Twelve of these showed traces of tartaric acid proving that the 5,500-year-old vases were used for wine.

Medieval to 1878

As expected, the antiquity of wine on the island closely relates to its political and administrative antiquity. During the Lusignan occupation, the island had close ties with the Crusader nations and especially the nobility of France. During this period, Commandaria wine won the Battle of the Wines, the first recorded wine tasting competition, which was staged by the French king Philip Augustus in the 13th century. The event was recorded in a poem by Henry d'Andeli in 1224.

During the Ottoman occupation of the island, wine production went into decline. This was attributed to two factors: Islamic tradition and heavy taxation. Indicative are reports written mainly by French and British travelers of the time; Cyrus Redding writes in 1851:the vine grower of Cyprus hides from his neighbour the amount of his vintage, and always buries part of his produce for concealment; the exactions of the government are so great, that his profit upon what he allows to be seen is too little to remunerate him for his loss in time and labour. The quality of the wine produced also lagged behind times with Samuel Baker referring to Cypriot wines in 1879 "It should be understood that no quality of Cyprus wines is suitable to the English palate".

1878-1980

1878 marked the handover of the island form Ottoman rule to the British Empire. British occupation brought a revival in the winemaking industry. Taxation rules changed and the local cottage industry began to expand. 1844 saw the foundation of one of the largest wineries surviving to date, that of ETKO by the Hadjipavlou family. The Chaplin family was Hadjipavlou's main competitor until the arrival of KEO a company formed by a group of prominent local businessmen. KEO bought the Chaplin winery in 1928. In 1943, following a strike, a breakaway of trade union members from ETKO created a cooperative, LOEL. In 1947 the vine-growers themselves created SODAP, a co-operative to "protect the rights of the growers". These "big four" wine producers dominated the industry scene and survive to date.

The first wave of expansion for Cypriot wines came with the misfortunes of the European viticulture sector. The phylloxera epidemic that affected mainland Europe in the late 19th century had destroyed the majority of wine producing vines. Cyprus, an island with strict quarantine controls managed to remain unaffected. As a consequence, demand for Cyprus grapes and wines coupled to the relatively high prices offered resulted in a mini boom for the industry. Further demand early in the early 20th century came from local consumption and from the regional forces of Britain and France in the Middle East. Cyprus produced quality cheap wine and spirits and the big four companies prospered as a result.

The next big export product came in the form of Cyprus Sherry. It was first marketed by that name in 1937 and was exported mainly to northern Europe. By the 1960s, Britain was consuming 13.6 million litres of Cyprus wines, half the island's production, mostly as sweet sherry. A British market research study of fortified wines in 1978 showed Emva cream was the leading Cyprus sherry in terms of brand recognition, and second in that market only to Harveys' Bristol Cream.

The island became the UK's third leading wine supplier behind France and Spain. A major factor was that Cyprus Sherry was more affordable than Spanish Sherry as British taxation favoured alcoholic beverages with an alcoholic content under the 15.5-18 per cent bracket. This competitive advantage was lost a few years later with the re-banding of the alcohol content taxation. The fortified wine market also began to shrink as a whole due to a change in consumer taste and as a result Cyprus sherry sales in the UK fell from their peak in the early 1970s by some 65 per cent by the mid 1980s. The final blow came when the EC ruled that as of January 1996 only fortified wine from Jerez could assume the title of sherry.

The other big market for Cyprus wine during the same period was the former Soviet bloc. Large volumes of low quality, mass produced, blended wines were sold to the eastern block with the cooperative wine producers taking the lion's share. This market began to dry up in the 1980s and vanished altogether with the fall of communism. Indicative of the industry's mass production tactics comes in a report by The Times in 1968 commenting on "the end of an underwater pipeline off the coast of Limassol linking to tankers taking on not gas or oil but wine-100 tons an hour of it-destined for about 40 countries throughout the world.

1980 Onwards

In response to the challenges faced by the industry the Cyprus vine-products commission began efforts to overhaul the sector in order to help it survive under the new circumstances. Reforms were intended to improve the quality rather than quantity of wine. Three initiatives were launched:

- Firstly, new varieties of grapes were introduced and incentives given for their cultivation. The varieties introduced were considered more suitable for quality wine production intended for wines more palatable to overseas markets. Examples include grapes such as Cabernet Sauvignon, Cabernet Franc, Carignan Noir and Palomino.
- Secondly, incentives were given to create small regional wineries with a production capacity of 50,000 to 300,000 bottles per year. This intended to promote better quality wines by reducing the distance grapes travelled from vineyard to winery. The big four wineries were located in the large port cities of Limassol and Paphos so vine growers were forced to transport their harvest for miles in the summer heat. This had an effect on the quality of wine as the fermentation process had already begun during transport. The knock on effect of this incentive also helped maintain the village population in the vine cultivating regions.
- Thirdly a new Appellation of Origin was launched in 2007.

Quality Levels and Appellation System

The Cyprus vine products council has based wine denominations on European Union law and is responsible for enforcing the regulations. Currently there are three accepted categories:

- *Table wine*: This is similar to the Vin de Table in France or Vino di Tavola in Italy.
- Local wine which follows in similar fashion to the French Vin de pays and the Italian Indicazione Geografica Tipica. Regulations state that 85 per cent of the grapes used in the production of such wine originates from the specific geographical regions and from the registered vineyards. Vines must be more that 4 years old with a controlled annual yield per cultivated hectare. Red wine must have a minimum of 11 per cent alcohol content whilst rose and white wine a minimum of 10 per cent. There are four such designated areas: Lefkosia, Lemesos, Larnaca and Paphos.
- Protected designation of origin is the most prestigious designation and in theory indicates a higher quality product. It is modelled on

the French Appellation d'origine contrôlée, whereas the Italian equivalent is the Denominazione di origine controllata. Wines with this designation must originate from registered vineyards of an altitude above 600 or 750 meters depending on location. Vines should be more than 5 years old and yield is restricted to 36 or 45 hl per hectare depending on grape variety. There are further regulations dictating the grape composition and ageing process.

Grape Varieties

The climate allows for cultivation of most grape varieties. However local varietals constitute the bulk of current plantations. Maratheftiko is an ancient grape varietal that is currently being revived.

Table showing areas and quantities cultivated by Vines for Wines by variety:

	Variety	2004 Cultivation	2004 Quantity (kg)	% of total	2003 Quantity (kg)	% of total
1	Mavro	92,140	35,690,050	49.6	33,124,678	52.5
2	Xynisteri	26,573	11,102,700	15.4	6,750,800	10.7
3	Carignan Noir	26,573	8,894,350	12.4	7,609,261	12.1
4	Cabernet	8,129	2,446,508	3.4	1,435,575	2.3
5	Malaga	3,786	1,501,930	2.1	1,551,251	2.5
6	Mataro	2,331	1,196,940	1.7	1,946,431	3.1
7	Shiraz	1,968	149,750	0.2	60,656	0.1
8	Ofthalmo	1,843	1,119,800	1.6	1,122,278	1.8
9	Palomino	1,800	2,509,350	3.5	2,189,155	3.5
10	Grenache Noir	1,768	960,611	1.3	1,007,031	1.6
11	Alicante Bouschet	1,509	589,105	0.8	527,685	0.8
12	Oeillade	1,281	526,735	0.7	500,540	0.8
13	Marathefti ko	1,249	204,660	0.3	185,961	0.3
	Total	159,076	71,996,587		63,083,177	

Limassol Wine Festival

The Limassol Wine festival is an annual event aimed to celebrate Cyrpus's rich viticulture. Since the first festival in 1961, it is organised annually in late August to early September. It is organised by the municipality of the city of Limassol at the grounds of the municipal gardens.

It has an annual attendance in excess of 100,000 visitors that include locals and many tourists. The four big wine cooperatives along with many smaller independent producers offer free tasting of their wine portfolio.

BUSINESS OF FRENCH WINE

French wine is produced in several regions throughout France, in quantities between 50 and 60 million hectolitres per year, or 7-8 billion bottles. France has the world's second-largest total vineyard area, behind Spain, and competes with Italy for the position of being the world's largest wine producer. French wines accounted for 17.6 per cent of world exports in 2005. French wine traces its antiquity to the 6th century BC, with many of France's regions dating their wine-making antiquity to Roman times. The wines produced today range from expensive high-end wines sold internationally, to more modest wines usually only seen within France.

Two concepts central to higher end French wines are the notion of "terroir", which links the style of the wines to the specific locations where the grapes are grown and the wine is made, and the Appellation d'Origine Contrôlée (AOC) system. Appellation rules closely define which grape varieties and winemaking practices are allowed in each of France's several hundred geographically defined appellations, which can cover entire regions, individual villages or even specific vineyards.

France is the source of many grape varieties that are now planted throughout the world, as well as several wine-making practices and styles of wine that are copied and imitated in other producing countries. Although some producers have benefited in recent years from rising prices and increased demand for some of the prestige wines from Burgundy and Bordeaux, the French wine industry as a whole has been influenced by a decline in domestic consumption as well as growing competition from both the New World and other European countries.

French wine originated in the 6th century BC, with the colonization of Southern Gaul by Greek settlers. Viticulture soon flourished with the founding of the Greek colony of Marseille. The Roman Empire licensed regions in the south to produce wines. St. Martin of Tours (316-397) was actively engaged in both spreading Christianity and planting vineyards. During the Middle Ages, monks maintained vineyards and, more importantly, conserved wine-making knowledge and skills during that often turbulent period. Monasteries had the resources, security, and motivation to produce a steady supply of wine both for celebrating mass and generating income. During this time, the best vineyards were owned by the monasteries and their wine was considered to be superior. Over time the nobility developed extensive vineyards. However, the French Revolution led to the confiscation of many of the vineyards owned by the Church and others.

The advance of the French wine industry stopped abruptly as first Mildew and then Phylloxera spread throughout the country, indeed across all of Europe, leaving vineyards desolate. Then came an economic downturn in Europe followed by two world wars, and the French wine industry didn't fully recover for decades. Meanwhile competition had arrived and threatened the treasured French "brands" such as Champagne and Bordeaux. This resulted in the establishment in 1935 of the Appellation d'Origine Contrôlée to protect French interests. Large investments, the economic upturn following World War 2 and a new generation of Vignerons yielded results in the 1970s and the following decades, creating the modern French wines we know today.

Quality Levels and Appellation System

In 1935 numerous laws were passed to control the quality of French wine. They established the Appellation d'Origine Contrôlée system, which is governed by a powerful oversight board. Consequently, France has one of the oldest systems for protected designation of origin for wine in the world, and strict laws concerning winemaking and production. Many other European systems are modelled after it. The word "appellation" has been put to use by other countries, sometimes in a much looser meaning. As European Union wine laws have been modelled after those of the French, this trend is likely to continue with further EU expansion.

French law divides wine into four categories, two falling under the European Union's Table Wine category and two falling under the EU's Quality Wine Produced in a Specific Region (QWPSR) designation. The categories and their shares of the total French production for the 2005 vintage, excluding wine destined for Cognac, Armagnac and other brandies, were:

Table wine:

- *Vin de Table (11.7 per cent)*: Carries with it only the producer and the designation that it is from France.
- *Vin de Pays (33.9 per cent)*: Carries with it a specific region within France and subject to less restrictive regulations than AOC wines. For instance, it allows producers to distinguish wines that are made using grape varieties or procedures other than those required by the AOC rules, without having to use the simple and commercially non-viable table wine classification. In order to maintain a distinction from Vin de Table, the producers have to submit the wine for analysis and tasting, and the wines have to be made from certain varieties or blends.

QWPSR:

- *Vin Délimité de Qualité Superieure (VDQS, 0.9 per cent)*: Less strict than AOC, usually used for smaller areas or as a "waiting room" for potential AOCs.
- *Appellation d'Origine Contrôlée (AOC, 53.4 per cent)*: Wine from a particular area with many other restrictions, including grape varieties and winemaking methods.

The total French production for the 2005 vintage was 43.9 million hl of which 28.3 per cent was white and 71.7 per cent was red or rosé. The proportion of white wine is slightly higher for the higher categories, with 34.3 per cent of the AOC wine being white. In years with less favourable vintage conditions than 2005, the proportion of AOC wine tends to be a little lower. The proportion of Vin de table has decreased considerably over the last decades, while the proportion of AOC has increased somewhat and Vin de Pays has increased considerably. In 2005 there were 472 different wine AOCs in France.

Wine Styles, Grape Varieties and Terroir

All common styles of wine-red, rosé, white, sparkling and fortified-are produced in France. In most of these styles, the French production ranges from cheap and simple versions to some of the world's most famous and expensive examples. An exception is French fortified wines, which tend to be relatively unknown outside France.

In many respects, French wines have more of a regional than a national identity, as evidenced by different grape varieties, production methods and different classification systems in the various regions. Quality levels and prices varies enormously, and some wines are made for immediate consumption while other are meant for long-time cellaring.

If there is one thing that most French wines have in common, it is that most styles have developed as wines meant to accompany food, be it a quick baguette, a simple bistro meal, or a full-fledged multi-course menu. Since the French tradition is to serve wine with food, wines have seldom been developed or styled as "bar wines" for drinking on their own, or to impress in tastings when young.

Grape Varieties

Numerous grape varieties are cultivated in France, including both internationally well-known and obscure local varieties. In fact, most of the so-called "international varieties" are of French origin, or became known and spread because of their cultivation in France. Since French appellation rules generally restrict wines from each region, district or appellation to a small number of allowed grape varieties, there are in principle no varieties that are commonly planted throughout all of France.

Most varieties of grape are primarily associated with a certain region, such as Cabernet Sauvignon in Bordeaux and Syrah in Rhône, although there are some varieties that are found in two or more regions, such as Chardonnay in Bourgogne and Champagne, and Sauvignon Blanc in Loire and Bordeaux. As an example of the rules, although climatic conditions would appear to be favorable, no Cabernet Sauvignon wines are produced in Rhône, Riesling wines in Loire, or Chardonnay wines in Bordeaux.

Traditionally, many French wines have been blended from several grape varieties. Varietal white wines have been, and are still, more common than varietal red wines.

At the 2007 harvest, the most common grape varieties were the following:

Table. Common Grape Varieties in France (2007 Situation, all Varieties over 1000 ha)

Variety	Colour	Area (per cent)	Area (hectares)
1. Merlot	red	13.6%	116 715
2. Grenache	red	11.3%	97 171
3. Ugni Blanc	white	9.7%	83 173
4. Syrah	red	8.1%	69 891
5. Carignan	red	6.9%	59 210
6. Cabernet Sauvignon	red	6.7%	57 913
7. Chardonnay	white	5.1%	43 887
8. Cabernet Franc	red	4.4%	37 508
9. Gamay	red	3.7%	31 771
10. Pinot Noir	red	3.4%	29 576
11. Sauvignon Blanc	white	3.0%	26 062
12. Cinsaut	red	2.6%	22 239
13. Melon de Bourgogne	white	1.4%	12 483
14. Sémillon	white	1.4%	11 864
15. Pinot Meunier	red	1.3%	11 335
16. Chenin Blanc	white	1.1%	9 756
17. Mourvèdre	red	1.1%	9 494
18. Colombard	white	0.9%	7 710
19. Muscat Blanc à Petits Grains	white	0.9%	7 634
20. Malbec	red	0.8%	6 291
21. Alicante Bouschet	red	0.7%	5 680
22. Grenache Blanc	white	0.6%	5 097
23. Viognier	white	0.5%	4 111
24. Muscat de Hambourg	red	0.4%	3 605
25. Riesling	white	0.4%	3 480
26. Vermentino	white	0.4%	3 453
27. Aramon	red	0.4%	3 304
28. Gewurztraminer	pink	0.4%	3 040
29. Tannat	red	0.3%	3 001
30. Gros Manseng	white	0.3%	2 877
31. Macabeu	white	0.3%	2 778
32. Muscat d'Alexandrie	white	0.3%	2 679
33. Pinot Gris	grey	0.3%	2 582
34. Clairette	white	0.3%	2 505
35. Caladoc	red	0.3%	2 449
36. Grolleau	red	0.3%	2 363
37. Auxerrois Blanc	white	0.3%	2 330
38. Marselan	red	0.3%	2 255

39. Mauzac	white	0.2%	2 077
40. Aligoté	white	0.2%	1 946
41. Folle Blanche	white	0.2%	1 848
42. Grenache Gris	grey	0.2%	1 756
43. Chasselas	white	0.2%	1 676
44. Nielluccio	red	0.2%	1 647
45. Fer	red	0.2%	1 634
46. Muscadelle	white	0.2%	1 618
47. Terret Blanc	white	0.2%	1 586
48. Sylvaner	white	0.2%	1 447
49. Piquepoul Blanc	white	0.2%	1 426
50. Villard Noir	red	0.2%	1 399
51. Marsanne	white	0.2%	1 326
52. Négrette	red	0.2%	1 319
53. Roussanne	white	0.2%	1 307
54. Pinot Blanc	white	0.2%	1 304
55. Plantet	white	0.1%	1 170
56. Jacquère	white	0.1%	1 052
All white varieties	30.1%	259 130	
All red, pink and grey varieties		69.9%	601 945
Grand total		100.0%	861 075

Terroir

The concept of Terroir, which refers to the unique combination of natural factors associated with any particular vineyard, is important to french vignerons. It includes such factors as soil, underlying rock, altitude, slope of hill or terrain, orientation towards the sun, and microclimate. Even in the same area, no two vineyards have exactly the same terroir, thus being the base of the Appellation d'origine contrôlée (AOC) system that has been model for appellation and wine laws across the globe. In other words: when the same grape variety is planted in different regions, it can produce wines that are significantly different from each other. In France the concept of terroir manifests itself most extremely in the Burgundy region. The amount of influence and the scope that falls under the description of terroir has been a controversial topic in the wine industry.

Labelling Practices

Many French wine labels contain a wealth of information for the knowledgeable reader. With the exception of wines from the Alsace region and their Germanic influence, France had no tradition of varietal labelling of wines. Varietal labelling was not allowed under appellation rules. Since New World wines made the varietal names "household names" on the export market, in the late 20th century, more French wineries started to use varietal labelling. In general, varietal labelling is most common for the Vin de Pays category. Some AOC wines in "simpler" categories are also allowed to display varietal names, but these wines are rather few. For most AOC wines, if varietal names are found, it will be in small print on a back label. An important bit of information is the place of bottling, as this can indicate on what "level" the wine is produced; that is, by a single producer, or more anonymously and in larger quantities:

- "Mis en bouteille..."
  - "... au château, au domaine, à la propriété": these have a similar meaning, and indicate the wine was "estate bottled", on the same property on which it was grown or at a cooperative of which that property is a member.
  - "... par..." the wine was bottled by the concern whose name follows. This may be the producing vineyard or it may not.
  - "... dans la région de production": the wine was not bottled at the vineyard but by a larger business at its warehouse; this warehouse was within the same winemaking region of France as the appellation, but not necessarily within the boundary of the appellation itself. If a chateau or domaine is named, it may well not exist as a real vineyard, and the wine may be an assemblage from the grapes or the wines of several producers.
  - "... dans nos chais, dans nos caves": the wine was bottled by the business named on the label.
- "Vigneron indépendant" is a special mark adopted by some independent wine-makers, to distinguish them from larger corporate winemaking operations and symbolize a return to the basics of the craft of wine-making. Bottles from these independent makers carry a special logo usually printed on the foil cap covering the cork.

If varietal names are displayed, common EU rules apply:

- If a single varietal name is used, the wine must be made from a minimum of 85% of this variety.
- If two or more varietal names are used, only the displayed varieties are allowed.
- If two or more varietal names are used, they must generally appear in descending order.

Wine Regions of France

The recognized wine producing areas in France are regulated by the Institut National des Appellations d'Origine-INAO in acronym. Every appellation in France is defined by INAO, in regards to the individual regions particular wine "character". If a wine fails to meet the INAO's strict criteria it is declassified into a lower appellation or even into Vin de Pays or Vin de Table.

Alsace

Alsace is primarily a white-wine region, though some red, rosé, sparkling and sweet wines are also produced. It is situated in eastern France on the river Rhine and borders Germany, a country with which it shares many grape varieties as well as a long tradition of varietal labeling. Grapes grown in Alsace include Riesling, Gewurztraminer, Pinot Gris, Pinot Blanc, Pinot Noir, and Muscat.

Bordeaux

Bordeaux is a large region on the Atlantic coast, which has a long antiquity of exporting its wines overseas. This is primarily a red wine region, famous for the wines Château Lafite-Rothschild, Château Latour, Château Mouton-Rothschild, Château Margaux and Château Haut-Brion from the Médoc sub-region; Château Cheval Blanc and Château Ausone in Saint-Émilion; and Château Pétrus and Château Le Pin in Pomerol. The red wines produced are usually blended, from Cabernet Sauvignon, Merlot and sometimes Cabernet Franc. Bordeaux also makes dry and sweet white wines, including some of the world's most famous sweet wines from the Sauternes appellation, such as Château d'Yquem.

Burgundy

Burgundy or Bourgogne in eastern France is a region where red and white wines are equally important. Probably more terroir-conscious than any other region, Burgundy is divided into the largest number of appellations of any French region. The top wines from Burgundy's heartland in Côte d'Or command high prices. The Burgundy region is divided in four main parts:

- The Cote de Nuits
- The Cote de Beaune
- The Cote Chalonnaise
- The Maconnais

Two parts of Burgundy that are sometimes considered as separate regions are:

- Beaujolais in the south, close to the Rhône Valley region, where mostly red wines are made in a fruity style that is usually consumed young. "Beaujolais Nouveau" is the only wine that can be legally consumed in the year of its production
- Chablis, halfway between Côte d'Or and Paris, where white wines are produced on chalky soil giving a more crisp and steely style than the rest of Burgundy.

There are two main grape varieties used in Burgundy-Chardonnay for white wines, and Pinot Noir for red. White wines are also sometimes made from Aligoté, and other grape varieties will also be found occasionally.

Champagne

Champagne, situated in eastern France, close to Belgium and Luxembourg, is the coldest of France's major wine regions and home to its major sparkling wine. Champagne wines can be both white and rosé. A small amount of still wine is produced in Champagne of which some can be red wine.

Corsica

Corsica is an island in the Mediterranean the wines of which are primarily consumed on the island itself. It has nine AOC regions and an island-wide vin de pays designation and is still developing its production methods as well as its regional style.

Jura

Jura, a small region in the mountains close to Switzerland where some unique wine styles, notably Vin Jaune and Vin de Paille, are produced. The region covers six appellations and is related to Burgundy through its extensive use of the burgundian grapes Chardonnay and Pinot Noir, though other varieties are used. It also shares cool climate with Burgundy.

Languedoc-Roussillon

Languedoc-Roussillon is the largest region in terms of vineyard surface, and the region in which much of France's cheap bulk wines have been produced. While still the source of much of France's and Europe's overproduction, the so-called "wine lake", Languedoc-Roussillon is also the home of some innovative producers who combine traditional French wine and international styles while using lessons from the New World. Much Languedoc-Roussillon wine is sold as Vin de Pays d'Oc.

Loire

Loire valley is a primarily white-wine region that stretches over a long distance along the Loire River in central and western France, and where grape varieties and wine styles vary along the river.

Four subregions are situated along the river:

- Upper Loire is known for its Sauvignon Blanc, producing wines such as Sancerre AOC, but also consisting of several VDQS areas;
- Touraine produces cold climate-styled white wines from Chenin Blanc in Vouvray AOC and red wines from Cabernet Franc in Bourgueil AOC and Chinon AOC;
- Anjou-Saumur is similar to the Tourain wines with respect to varieties, but the dry Savennières AOC and sweet Coteaux du Layon AOC are often more powerful than their upstream neighbours. Saumur AOC and Saumur-Champigny AOC provides reds; and
- Pays Nantais is situated closest to the Atlantic, and Muscadet AOC produces white wines from the Melon de Bourgogne grape.

Provence

Provence, in the southeast and close to the Mediterranean. It is perhaps the warmest wine region of France and produces mainly rosé and red wine. It covers eight major appellations led by the Provence flagship, Bandol. Some Provence wine can be compared with the Southern Rhône wines as they share both grapes and, to some degree, style and climate. Provence also has a classification of its most prestigious estates, much like Bordeaux.

Rhône

Rhone Valley, primarily a red-wine region in southeastern France, along the Rhône River. The styles and varietal composition of northern and southern Rhône differ, but both parts compete with Bordeaux as traditional producers of red wines.

Savoy

Savoy or Savoie, primarily a white-wine region in the Alps close to Switzerland, where many grapes unique to this region are cultivated.

South West France

South West France or Sud-Ouest, a somewhat heterogeneous collection of wine areas inland or south of Bordeaux. Some areas produce primarily red wines in a style reminiscent of red Bordeaux, while other produce dry or sweet white wines.

Areas within Sud-Ouest include among other:

- Bergerac and other areas of upstream Dordogne;
- Areas of upstream Garonne, including Cahors;
- Areas in Gascony, also home to the production of Armagnac, Madiran, Côtes de Gascogne, Côtes de Saint-Mont, Pacherenc du Vic-Bilh and Tursan;
- Béarn, such as Jurançon; and
- Basque Country areas, such as Irouléguy.

There are also several smaller production areas situated outside these major regions. Many of those are VDQS wines, and some, particularly those in more northern locations, are remnants of production areas that were once larger.

Trends

France has traditionally been the largest consumer of its own wines. However, wine consumption has been dropping in France for 40 years. During the decade of the 1990s, per capita consumption dropped by nearly 20 per cent. Therefore, French wine producers must rely increasingly on foreign markets. However, consumption has also been dropping in other potential markets such as Italy, Spain and Portugal.

The result has been a continuing wine glut, often called the wine lake. This has led to the distillation of wine into industrial alcohol as well as a government programme to pay farmers to pull up their grape vines through vine pull plans. A large part of this glut is caused by the re-emergence of Languedoc wine.

Immune from these problems has been the market for Champagne as well as the market for the expensive ranked or classified wines. However, these constitute only about five per cent of French production.

French regulations in 1979 created simple rules for the then-new category of Vin de pays. The Languedoc-Roussillon region has taken advantage of its ability to market varietal wines.

BUSINESS OF WINE IN GEORGIA

Georgia is the oldest wine producing region of the world. The fertile valleys of the South Caucasus, which Georgia straddles, are believed by many archaeologists to be the source of the world's first cultivated grapevines and neo-lithic wine production, over 7000 years ago. Due to the many millennia of wine in Georgian antiquity, the traditions of its viticulture are entwined and inseparable with the country's national identity.

Among the best-known regions of Georgia where wine is produced are Kakheti, Kartli, Imereti, Racha-Lechkhumi and Kvemo Svaneti, and Abkhazia.

It has been archaeologically proven that the roots of Georgian viticulture are between 7000 and 5000 BC, when peoples of South Caucasus discovered that wild grape juice turned into wine when it was left buried through the winter in a shallow pit. This knowledge was nourished by experience, and from 4000 BC Georgians were cultivating grapes and burying clay vessels, kvevri, in which to store their wine ready for serving at perfect ground temperature. When filled with the fermented juice of the harvest, the kvevris are topped with a wooden lid and then covered and sealed with earth. Some may remain entombed for up to 50 years.

This love affair with the grape was given further encouragement by the arrival of Saint Nino in the 4th century. Fleeing Roman persecution in Cappadocia, in what is now central Turkey, and bearing a cross made from vine wood and bound with her own hair. Saint Nino was swept up in the warm embrace of the Georgians, who became early converts to Christianity. Thus the cross and the vine became inextricably linked in the Georgian psyche, and the advent of the new faith served to sanction these ancient vinous practices. For centuries, Georgians drank, and in some areas still drink, their delicious wine from horns and skins specially treated for this purpose.

These drinking implements came from their herd animals, as no part of the valued and respected beasts went to waste. The horns were cleaned, boiled and polished, creating a unique, durable and quite stylish drinking vessel. These horns were prized by the merchants and warriors that travelled the fertile valleys of the Caucasus. Today they are still a prized symbol of the historic eras.

Wine vessels of every shape, size and design account for the bulk of earthenware artifacts unearthed by Georgian archaeologists. The Georgian craft of pottery is millennia old. Ancient artifacts attest to the high skill of Georgian craftsmen in whose hands water, clay and fire turned into an object of an exceptional beauty much admired by people. The most impressive of all archaeological finds are kvevri, giant clay vessels in which wine was fermented and stored up.

The old ones used to dig them into soil, just as we are doing now. Georgian museums have on display numerous clay vessels of all designations. Some were used to ferment grape juice and to store up wine, such as kvevri, chapi and satskhao, and others were used for drinking, such as khelada, doki, sura, chinchila, deda-khelada, dzhami and marani. For ages, artisans polished their skills to improve these vessels. The secrets of trade passed on from fathers to sons. Modern potters carefully study the ancient craft and decorative patterns and create their own pottery making extensive use of ancient national traditions and using the latest scientific and technological achievements to enrich ancient traditions.

Many of the unearthed silver, gold and bronze artifacts of the 3rd and 2nd millennia BC bear chased imprints of the vine, grape clusters and leaves. The State Museum of Georgia has on display a cup of high-carat gold set with gems, an ornamented silver pitcher and some other artifacts dated the 2nd millennium BC The museum of antiquity has a cameo depicting Bacchus. Numerous sarcophagi with wine pitchers and ornamented wine cups, found in ancient tombs, are a proof that wine was nothing unusual for Georgians at all times.

It is important to note, that while political tensions with Russia have contributed to the 2006 embargo of Georgian wine, wine produced within Georgia is also known for being counterfeit, which Russia states is the primary reasoning for the wine embargo. Counterfeiting problems stem from mislabeling by Georgian Producers and falsified "Georgian Wine" labels on wines produced outside of Georgia and imported into Russia under the auspices of being Georgian produced.

Winemakers in Georgia have also been known to import grapes and produce "falsified" Georgian Wine, leading then defence minister Irakli Okruashvili to note in 2006 that "several wineries that are still producing fake wine in [the eastern city of] Gori should be closed". However, these wines are currently being sold in the U.S. and the E.U. without any major difficulties noted in authenticity. Also, the shipment of counterfeit wine has been primarily channeled through Russian managed customs checkpoints in Abkhazia and South Ossetia, where little inspection and regulation has been done.

Viticulture in Georgia Today

Georgia ranks 2nd in grape production in the former Soviet Union behind Moldova, and Georgian wines have always been the most highly prized and sought after in the Soviet space. Presently, the wine is produced by thousands of small farmers as well as modern wineries, such as Teliani Valley, Telavis Marani, Tbilvino, Kindzmarauli Marani, Badagoni and Mukhrani.

Growing Conditions

When it comes to wine-making, Georgia is blessed. Extremes of weather are unusual: summers tend to be short-sleeve sunny, and winters mild and frost-free. Natural springs abound, and the Caucasian Mountain streams drain mineral-rich water into the valleys. Georgia's moderate climate and moist air, influenced by the Black Sea, provide the best conditions for vine cultivating.

Grape Varieties in Georgia

Traditional Georgian grape varieties are little known in the West. Now that the wines of Eastern and Central Europe are coming to international awareness, grapes from this region are becoming better known.

Although there are nearly 500 to choose from, only 38 varieties are officially grown for commercial viticulture in Georgia:

- Rkatsiteli (white) is a variety that is so widely grown in Eastern and Central Europe that it ranks third in the world in hectares grown. It is the most important grape varietiy used to make Georgian white wines. It is high in acidity and is capable of producing wines with fine character.
- Saperavi (red) produces substantial deep red wines that are suitable for extended aging, perhaps up to fifty years. Saperavi has the potential to produce high alcohol levels and is used extensively for blending with other lesser varieties. It is the most important grape variety used to make Georgian red wines.
- Mtsvani (white) is also important in Georgian wines, and is often blended with Rkatsiteli to which it adds a fruity, aromatic balance. In the Georgian language Mtsvane means green.
- Alexandrouli
- Alexandria
- Tsolikauri (white)
- Tetra (white)
- Mujuretuli (red)
- Ojaleshi (red) is cultivated on the mountain slopes overhanging the banks of the Tskhenis-Tskali river, particularly in the Orbeli village and Samegrelo district.
- Usakhelauri (red) is cultivated mostly in the Zubi-Okureshi district in Western Georgia.

- Izabela (red)
- Tavkveri (red)
- Asuretuli (red)
- Cabernet Sauvignon (red)
- Aladasturi (red)
- Tsitska (white)
- Tsolikouri (white)
- Khikhvi (white) is grown in Kardanakhi.
- Dzvelshava
- Krakhuna
- Chinuri (white)
- Gibrita (red)
- Manata (white)

Georgian Wine Varieties

Traditionally, Georgian wines carry the name of the source region, district, or village, much like French regional wines such as Bordeaux or Burgundy. As with these French wines, Georgian wines are usually a blend of two or more grapes. Georgian wines are classified as sweet, semi-sweet, semi-dry, dry, fortified and sparkling. The semi-sweet varieties are the most popular.

- *White*:
  - Pirosmani is a semi-sweet white wine made from a 40% Tsolikauri, 60% Tsitska blend. It has won 3 gold medals and one silver medal at international competitions.
  - Tsinandali is a blend of Rkatsiteli and Mtsvane grapes from the micro regions of Telavi and Kvareli in the Kakheti region.
  - Tvishi is a natural semi-sweet white wine made from Tsolikauri in the Lechkhumi region. It has won one gold medal, two silver medals and one bronze medal in international competitions.
  - Mtsvani is a dry white wine made from Mtsvani.
  - Alaznis Veli is white semi-sweet wine made from the Rkatsiteii, Tetra, Tsolikauri and other industrial grape varieties cultivated in Western and Eastern Georgia. The wine of straw colour has a characteristic aroma, a fine, fresh and a harmonious taste. It contains 9-11 per cent alcohol and has 6-7 per cent titrated acidity.
  - Anakopia is a white semi-dry table wine made from the Tsolikauri grape variety grown in the Sukhumi and Gudauta districts in Abkhazia. The colour range is from light to dark-straw. It has a specific aroma and a subtle fresh taste. The alcohol content in the ready wine is 9-11 per cent, sugar content 1-2 g/100 ml, titrated acidity 5-8 g/l. The wine has been produced since 1978.
  - Tbilisuri is pink semi-dry wine produced since 1984. It is made

from the Saperavi, Cabernet and Rkatsiteli grape varieties grown in East Georgia. The wine has a rich fruity taste. The alcohol content is 9-11.5 per cent, sugar content 1-2 per cent, titrated acidity 5-7 g/l.

- Khikkhvi is a vintage white dessert wine made from the Khikhvi grape variety grown in Kardanakhi. It has pleasant amber colour, a characteristic aroma and a delicate taste. Its strength is 15 vol. per cent, sugar content 18-20 per cent, titrated acidity 4-8 g/1. The wine has been produced since 1924. At international competitions it received 4 gold medals.
- Saamo is a vintage dessert white sweet wine is made from the Rkatsiteli grape variety cultivated in the Kardanakhi vineyards of the Gurjaani district in Kakheti. It takes the wine three years to mature. The golden-colour wine has an original fine bouquet, a pleasant taste with a harmonious honey fragrance. When ready for use, the wine contains 17 per cent alcohol, 13 per cent sugar and has 4-6 g/1 titrated acidity. It has been manufactured since 1980. At international exhibitions Saamo was awarded 4 gold and 1 silver medal.
- Gelati is a white dry ordinary wine made of the Tsolikauri, Tsitska and Krakhuna grape varieties cultivated in Western Georgia. The wine of straw colour has a characteristic savor with a fruity flavour and fresh harmonious taste. Its strength is 10.0-12.5 vol. per cent and titrated acidity 5-8 per cent.
- Kakheti is a white table wine made of the Rkatsiteli and Mtsvane grape varieties cultivated in Kakheti. The amber-colour wine has a fruity aroma with a vanillic flavour. It is characterized by an energetic, velvety and harmonious taste. Its strength is 10.5-13.0 vol. per cent and titrated acidity 4-6 per cent. At international wine competitions the Kakheti wine was awarded one silver and one bronze medal. It has been produced since 1948.
- Bodbe is made from the Rkatsiteli grape variety in the village of Bodbe in the Magaro microdistrict, one of the most beautiful places of Kakheti. The wine has a light-straw colour, a fine aroma of wild flowers and a pleasing tender taste which give the wine piquancy highly estimated by connoisseurs. The ready wine contains 10.5-11.5 per cent alcohol and has 5-7 per cent titrated acidity.
- Dimi is an Imeretian-type white ordinary wine. It is made from the Tsolikauri and Krakhuna grape varieties grown on small areas in Imereti by the old local technique consisting in fermenting the grapes pulp to which some quantity of grapes husks is added.

The dark-straw colour has a pleasant specific bouquet with a fruity flavour, a fresh harmonious taste and savory astringency. Its strength is 10.5-13.0 vol. per cent and titrated acidity 6.5-8.0 per cent. The wine has been produced since 1977.

- Gareji is a white dry ordinary wine made of the Rkatsiteli and Mtsvane grape varieties cultivated in Kakheti. The wine has a colour ranging from pale-straw to amber, a pleasing bouquet and a full harmonious taste. Its strength is 10.0-12.5 vol. per cent and titrated acidity 4-7 per cent.
- Ereti is a white dry ordinary wine made from the Rkatsiteli and Mtsvane grape varieties. It has a straw colour, a fine fruity bouquet and a full fresh and harmonious taste. Its strength is 10.0-12.5 vol. per cent and titrated acidity 5-8 per cent.
- Shuamta is a dry wine produced since 1984. It is made from the Rkatsiteli and Mtsvane grape varieties just as to the Kakhetian recipe. The wine is of amber or dark-amber colour and has a moderately astringent harmonious taste with a fruity aroma. The alcohol content is 10-12 per cent, titrated acidity 4-6 g/l, extractibility over 25 g/l.
- Alzani (white) is a mid-straw coloured semi-sweet wine made from 100 per cent Rkatsiteli. The name comes from one of the major river systems of Georgia that borders Georgia with Azerbaijan. The climate is slightly warmer than the rest of the Georgian Wine growing regions and gives rise to much sweeter grapes than those found elsewhere. It has won one silver and one gold metal in international competitions.

- Red:
  - Akhasheni is a naturally semi-sweet red wine made from the Saperavi grape variety grown in the Akhasheni vineyards of the Gurdzhaani district in Kakheti. The wine of dark-pomegranate colour has a harmonious velvety taste with a chocolate flavour. It contains 10.5-12.0 per cent alcohol, 3-5 per cent sugar and has 5-7 per cent titrated acidity. The wine has been manufactured since 1958. At international exhibitions it was awarded 6 gold and 5 silver medals.
  - Khvanchkara is a fine naturally semi-sweet red wine made from the Alexandria and Mudzhuretuli grape varieties cultivated in the Khvanchkara vineyards in Racha, Western Georgia. The wine has a strong specific bouquet and a harmonious velvety taste with a raspberry flavour. It is of dark-ruby colour. The Khvanchkara wine is one of the most popular Georgian semi-sweet wines. It contains 10.5-12.0 per cent alcohol, 3-5 per cent sugar and has 5.0-7.0 per

cent titrated acidity. The wine has been manufactured since 1907. For its excellent taste it was awarded 2 gold and 4 silver medals at international exhibitions.

- Kindzmarauli is a high quality naturally semi-sweet wine of dark-red colour. It is made from the Saperavi grape variety cultivated on the slopes of the Caucasian mountains in the Kvareli district of Kakheti. It has a strong characteristic bouquet and aroma, a gentle harmonious and velvety taste. The wonderful taste and curative properties have won Kindzmarauli general recognition. The wine contains 10.5-12.0 per cent alcohol, 3-5 per cent sugar and has 5.0-7.0 per cent titrated acidity. It has been manufactured since 1942. For its supreme qualities Kindzmarauli was 3 gold, 4 silver and 1 bronze medal at international wine competitions.
- Mukuzani is a dry red wine made from 100 per cent Saperavi in Mukuzani, Kakheti. The wine is sourced from the very best wines of the vintage that have been fermented at controlled temperatures and with selected yeast strains. The wines are then matured for 3 years in oak to give the wine-added complexity and flavour. Mukuzani is considered to be the best of the Georgian Dry Red wines made from Saperavi. It has won 9 gold medals, 2 silver medals and 3 bronze medals in international competitions.
- Napareuli
- Ojaleshi is one of the best red semi-sweet wines made from the grape variety of the same name cultivated on the mountain slopes overhanging the banks of the Tskhenis-Tskali river, particularly in the Orbeli village and Samegrelo district. Odzhaleshi has dark-ruby colour, a gentle bouquet and aroma, a harmonious rich taste with a fruity flavour. It contains 10-12 per cent alcohol, 3-5 per cent sugar and has a titrated acidity of 5-6 per cent.
- Pirosmani is a naturally semi-sweet red wine. It is made from the Saperavi grape variety cultivated in the Akhoebi vineyards of the Kardanakhi village in the Alazani Valley. The wine is fermented in clay jars buried in the ground, an ancient Kakhetian technology of wine-making. When ready for use, the wine contains 10.5-12 per cent alcohol, 1.5-2.5 per cent sugar and has 5-7 per cent titrated acidity.
- Saperavi is a red wine made from the Saperavi grape variety grown in some areas of Kakheti. It is an extractive wine with a characteristic bouquet, a harmonious taste and pleasant astringency. Its strength is 10.5-12.5 per cent and titrated acidity 5-7 per cent. At the international wine competitions this wine

received one gold and one silver medal. It has been produced since 1886.

- Usakhelauri is a naturally semi-sweet wine, which is superior to all other wines of this kind for its gentle and subtle qualities. It is produced from the excellent Usakhelauri grape variety cultivated mostly in the Zubi-Okureshi district in Western Georgia. Vineyards are arranged on the mountain slopes. The wine has attractive ruby colour, harmonious sweetness with a wild strawberry flavour. It is noted for a pleasant velvety taste, a delicate bouquet and inimitable piquancy. The wine contains up to 10.5-12.0 per cent alcohol, 3-5 per cent sugar and has 5-7 per cent titrated acidity. It has been manufactured since 1943. The word "Usakhelauri" means "nameless" in Georgia. The wine was so fine that it was hard to find an adequate name for it. At international exhibitions Usakhelauri was awarded 2 gold and 3 silver medals.
- Apsny is a naturally semi-sweet red wine made of red grape varieties cultivated in Abkhazia. The wine of pomegranate colour has a pleasant aroma, a full and harmonious taste with gentle sweetness. When ready for use, the wine contains 9-10 per cent alcohol, 3-5 per cent sugar and has 5-7 per cent titrated acidity. At an international exhibition the wine received one silver medal.
- Lykhny is a naturally semi-sweet pink wine made of the Izabela grape variety cultivated in Abkhazia. The wine has pink colour, a specific aroma and a fresh harmonious taste. When ready for use, the wine contains 8-9 per cent alcohol, 3-5 per cent sugar and has 5-7 per cent titrated acidity. At international exhibitions Lykhny was awarded one silver and one bronze medal.
- Mtatsminda is a pink table semi-dry wine produced since 1984. It is prepared by the original technology from the Saperavi, Tavkveri, Asuretuli, Rkatsiteli and other grape varieties grown in Tetritskaro, Kaspi, Gori and Khashuri districts. The wine is characterized by a harmonious taste with a fruity aroma and a beautiful colour. The alcohol content is 9-11.5 per cent, sugar content 1-2 per cent, titrated acidity 5-7 g/l.
- Aguna is a pink semi-dry wine produced since 1984. It is made from the Saperavi, Cabernet and Rkatsiteli grape varieties grown in East Georgia. The wine has a rich fruity taste. The alcohol content is 9-11.5 per cent, sugar content 1-2 per cent, titrated acidity 5-7 g/l.
- Sachino is a pink semi-dry wine produced since 1984. It is made by the original method from the Aleksandreuli, Aladasturi,

Odzhaleshi, Tsitska, Tsolikauri and other grape varieties cultivated in West Georgia. The wine is notable for a mild taste, a moderate extractibility, a pure aroma and a beautiful colour. The alcohol content is 9-11.5 per cent, sugar content 1-2 per cent, titrated acidity 5-7 g/l.

- Barakoni is a naturally semi-dry red wine made from the unique Alexandreuli and Mudzhuretuli grape varieties cultivated in Western Georgia on the steep slopes of the Rioni gorge in the Caucasian mountains. This top quality wine of light-ruby colour has a fine fragrance of violets, natural pleasant sweetness and a tender harmonious taste. When ready for use, Barakoni contains 10-12 per cent alcohol, 1.5-2.5 per cent sugar and has 5-7 per cent titrated acidity. The wine has been manufactured since 1981.
- Salkhino is a liqueur-type of dessert wine made from the Izabella grape variety with an addition of the Dzvelshava, Tsolikauri and other grape varieties cultivated in the Mayakovski district. It has characteristic ruby or pomegranate colour. The alcohol content is 15 per cent, sugar content 30 per cent, titrated acidity 3-7 g/l. At international competitions the wine received 6 gold medals. It has been produced since 1928
- Alaverdi (White and Red)
- Alazani (Red) is a light red, semi-sweet wine made from a 60 per cent Saperavi, 40 per cent Rkatsiteli blend. It has won 3 mold medals and 3 silver medals at international competitions. The name comes from one of the major river systems of Georgia that borders Georgia with Azerbaijan. The climate is slightly warmer than the rest of the Georgian Wine growing regions and gives rise to much sweeter grapes than those found elseware.
- Rkatsiteli Mtsvani
- Saperavi Dzelshavi

• *Fortified*:
  - Kardanakhi is a fortified vintage white wine of the type. It is made from the Rkatsiteli grape variety cultivated in the Kardanakhi vineyards of the Gurdzhaani district. The wine matures in oak barrels for three years. The amber colour wine has a pleasant specific bouquet with a typical port wine flavour and a fine honey fragrance. It contains 18 per cent alcohol, 10 per cent sugar and has 4-6 per cent titrated acidity. It was awarded 8 gold and one silver international medals.
  - Anaga is a madeira-type top-quality strong wine made from the Rkatsiteli, Khikhvi and Mtsvane grape varieties cultivated in the Gurjaani, Sighnaghi and Tsitel-Tskaro districts. The wine has

light-golden to dark-amber colour, a strong peculiar bouquet, an extractive harmonious taste with a clearly pronounced Madeira touch. The alcohol content is 19 per cent, sugar content 4 g/ml, titrated acidity 3 - 7 g/l. The Anaga wine was awarded 1 international silver medal.

- Sighnaghi is an ordinary strong wine of the port type made from the Rkatsiteli grape variety grown in the Sighnaghi district in Kakheti. The amber-colour wine has an extractive harmonious taste with a clearly pronounced fruity touch. The alcohol content 3 g/100 ml, titrated acidity 5 g/l.
- Veria is a fortified vintage white port made from the Rkatsiteli, Mtsvane, Chinuri and other commercial grape varieties grown in Eastern Georgia. The amber-colour wine has a peculiar aroma and harmonious taste. Its strength is 18 vol. per cent, sugar content 7 per cent, titrated acidity 3-7 g/1. At an international wine competition it received 1 gold medal. The wine has been produced since 1977.
- Lelo is a port-type wine made from the Tsitska and Tsolikauri grape varieties grown in Zestaphoni, Terjola, Baghdati and Vani districts. The wine has a rich harmonious taste with a fruity aroma and a beautiful golden colour. The alcohol content is 19 per cent, sugar content 5 per cent, titrated acidity 6 g/l.
- Marabda is a port-type wine made from the Rkatsiteli grape variety grown in Marneuli and Bolnisi districts. It has a full harmonious taste with a fruity aroma and light-golden colour. The alcohol content is 19 per cent, sugar content 5 per cent, titrated acidity 6 g/l.
- Kolkheti is a fortified vintage white port is made from Tsolikauri, Tsitska and other commercial white grape varieties grown in Western Georgia. The amber-colour wine has a specific bouquet and harmonious taste. Its strength is 18 vol. per cent, sugar content 7 per cent, titrated acidity 3-7 g/l. At an international competition the wine received one silver medal. It has been produced since 1977.
- Taribana is a port-type wine made from the Rkatsiteli grape variety cultivated in Kakheti. The wine has a mild oily taste, a low sugar content and a beautiful colour. The alcohol content is 19 per cent, sugar content 5 per cent, titrated acidity 5 g/l.

Wine Styles

- Lelo is a port-type wine made from the Tsitska and Tsolikauri grape varieties grown in Zestaponi, Terjola, Baghdati and Vani districts.

The wine has a rich harmonious taste with a fruity aroma and a beautiful golden colour. The alcohol content is 19 per cent, sugar content 5 per cent, titrated acidity 6 g/l.

- Akhasheni is a naturally semi-sweet red wine made from the Saperavi grape variety grown in the Akhasheni vineyards of the Gurdzhaani district in Kakheti, a province of Georgia. The wine of dark-pomegranate colour has a harmonious velvety taste with a chocolate flavour. It contains 10.5-12.0 per cent alcohol, 3-5 per cent sugar and has 5-7 per cent titrated acidity. The wine has been manufactured since 1958.
- Khvanchkara is a naturally semi-sweet red wine made from the Alexandrouli and Mudzhuretuli grape varieties cultivated in the Khvanchkara vineyards, near the town of Ambrolauri in Racha region of western Georgia. The Khvanchkara wine is one of the most popular Georgian semi-sweet wines. Along with Kindzmarauli, it was the favourite wine of the Soviet leader Joseph Stalin. It is of dark-ruby colour. It contains 10.5 - 12.0 per cent alcohol, 3 - 5 per cent sugar and has 5.0 - 7.0 per cent titrated acidity. The wine has been manufactured since 1907.

Wine-producing Regions of Georgia

There are five main regions of viniculture, the principal region being Kakheti, which produces seventy per cent of Georgia's grapes. Traditionally, Georgian wines carry the name of the source region, district, or village, much like French regional wines such as Bordeaux or Burgundy. As with these French wines, Georgian wines are usually a blend of two or more grapes. For instance, one of the best-known white wines, Tsinandali, is a blend of Rkatsiteli and Mtsvane grapes from the micro regions of Telavi and Kvareli in the Kakheti region.

- Kakheti, containing the micro-regions Telavi and Kvareli
- Kartli
- Imereti
- Racha-Lechkhumi and Kvemo Svaneti
- Ajara

BUSINESS OF WINE IN GERMAN

German wine is primarily produced in the southwest of Germany, along river Rhine and its tributaries, with the oldest plantations going back to the Roman era. Approximately 60 per cent of the German wine production is situated in the federal state of Rhineland-Palatinate, where 6 of the 13 regions for quality wine are situated. Germany has about 102,000 hectares of vineyard, which is around one tenth of the vineyard surface in Spain, France or Italy.

The total wine production is usually around 9 million hectoliters annually, corresponding to 1.2 billion bottles, which places Germany as the eighth largest wine-producing country in the world. White wine accounts for almost two thirds of the total production.

As a wine country, Germany has a mixed reputation internationally, with some consumers on the export markets associating Germany with the world's most elegant and aromatically pure white wines while other the country mainly as the source of cheap, mass-market semi-sweet wines such as Liebfraumilch. Among enthusiasts, Germany's reputation is primarily based on wines made from the Riesling grape variety, which at its best is used for aromatic, fruity and elegant white wines that range from very crisp and dry to well-balanced, sweet and of enormous aromatic concentration. While primarily a white wine country, red wine production surged in the 1990s and early 2000s, primarily fuelled by domestic demand, and the proportion of the German vineyards devoted to the cultivation of dark-skinned grape varieties has now stabilized at slightly more than a third of the total surface. For the red wines, Spätburgunder, the domestic name for Pinot Noir, is in the lead.

Wine Styles

Germany produces wines in many styles: dry, semi-sweet and sweet white wines, rosé wines, red wines and sparkling wines, called Sekt. Due to the northerly location of the German vineyards, the country has produced wines quite unlike any others in Europe, many of outstanding quality. Despite this it is still better known abroad for cheap, sweet or semi-sweet, low-quality mass-produced wines such as Liebfraumilch.

The wines have historically been predominantly white, and the finest made from Riesling. Many wines have been sweet and low in alcohol, light and unoaked. Historically many of the wines were probably dry, as techniques to stop fermentation did not exist. Recently much more German white wine is being made in the dry style again. Much of the wine sold in Germany is dry, especially in restaurants. However most exports are still of sweet wines, particularly to the traditional export markets such as Great Britain, which is the leading export market both in terms of volume and value. The United States and the Netherlands are two other important export markets for German wine.

Red wine has always been hard to produce in the German climate, and in the past was usually light coloured, closer to rosé or the red wines of Alsace. However recently there has been greatly increased demand and darker, richer red wines are produced from grapes such as Dornfelder and Spätburgunder, the German name for pinot noir.

Perhaps the most distinctive characteristic of German wines is the high level of acidity in them, caused both by the lesser ripeness in a northerly climate and by the selection of grapes such as Riesling which retain acidity even at high ripeness levels. Viticulture in present-day Germany dates back to Ancient Roman times, to sometime from the 1st to the 4th century AD. In those days, the western parts of today's Germany made up the outpost of the Roman empire against the Germanic tribes on the other side of Rhine. What is generally considered to be Germany's oldest city, Trier, was founded as a Roman garrison and is situated directly on the river Moselle in the eponymous wine region. The oldest archeological finds that may indicate early German viticulture are curved pruning knives found in the vicinity of Roman garrisons, dating from the 1st century AD. However, it is not absolutely certain that these knives were used for viticultural purposes. Emperor Probus, whose reign can be dated two centuries later than these knives, is generally considered the founder of German viticulture, but for solid documentation of winemaking on German soil, we must go to around 370 AD, when Ausonius of Bordeaux wrote Mosella, where he in enthusiastic terms described the steep vineyards on river Moselle.

The wild vine, the forerunner of the cultivated Vitis vinifera is known to have grown on upper Rhine back to historic time, and it is possible that Roman-era German viticulture was started using local varieties. Many viticultural practices were however taken from other parts of the Roman empire, as evidenced by Roman-style trellising systems surviving into the 18th century in some parts of Germany, such as the Kammerbau in the Palatinate.

Almost nothing is known of the style or quality of "German" wines that were produced in the Roman era, with the exception of the fact that the poet Venantius Fortunatus mentions red German wine around AD 570.

Before the era of Charlemagne, Germanic viticulture was practiced primarily, although not exclusively, on the western side of Rhine. Charlemagne is supposed to have brought viticulture to Rheingau. The eastward spread of viticulture coincided with the spread of Christianity, which was supported by Charlemagne.

Thus, in Medieval Germany, churches and monasteries played the most important role in viticulture, and especially in the production of quality wine. Two Rheingau examples emphasise this: archbishop Ruthard of Mainz founded a Benedictine abbey on slopes above Geisenheim, the ground of which later became Schloss Johannisberg. His successor Adalbert of Mainz donated land above Hattenheim in 1135 to Cistercians, sent out from Clairvaux in Champagne, who founded Kloster Eberbach.

Many grape varieties commonly associated with German wines have been documented back to the 14th or 15th century. Riesling has been documented from 1435 and Pinot Noir from 1318 on Lake Constance under the name Klebroth, from 1335 in Affenthal in Baden and from 1470 in Rheingau, where the monks kept a Clebroit-Wyngart in Hattenheim. The most grown variety in medieval Germany was however Elbling, with Silvaner also being common, and Muscat, Räuschling and Traminer also being recorded.

For several centuries of the Medieval era, the vineyards of Germany expanded, and is believed to have reached their greatest extent sometime around 1500, when perhaps as much as four times the present vineyard surface was planted. Basically, the wine regions were located in the same places as today, but more lands around the rivers, and land further upstream Rhine's tributaries, was cultivated. The subsequent decline can be attributed to locally produced beer becoming the everyday beverage in northern Germany in the 16th century, leading to a partial loss of market for wine, and to the Thirty Years' War ravaging Germany in the 17th century.

At one point the Church controlled most of the major vineyards in Germany. Quality instead of quantity become important and spread quickly down the river Rhine. The Development ended when Martin Luther's activities initiated revolts leading to the death of millions and affecting culture for centuries. In the 1800s Napoleon took control of all the vineyards from the Church, including the best, and divided and secularized them. Since then the Napoleonic inheritance laws in Germany broke up the parcels of vineyards further, leading to the establishment of many cooperatives. However, there are many notable and world-famous wineries in Germany, which have managed to acquire or hold enough land to produce wine not only for domestic consumption, but also for export.

An important event took place in 1775 at Schloss Johannisberg in Rheingau, when the courier delivering the harvest permission was delayed for two weeks, with the result that most of the grapes in Johannisberg's Riesling-only vineyard had been affected by noble rot before the harvest began. Unexpectedly, these "rotten grapes" gave a very good sweet wine, which was termed Spätlese, meaning late harvest. From this time, late harvest wines from grapes affected by noble rot have been produced intentionally. The subsequent differentiation of these late harvest wines into additional categories, starting with Auslese in 1787, laid the ground for the Prädikat system.

Most of the present German wine law was introduced in 1971, and definied the Prädikat designations as they have been since then.

Industry Structure

The German wine industry consists of many small vineyard owners. The 1999 viticultural survey counted 68 598 vineyard owners, down from 76 683 in Western Germany in 1989/90, for an average size of 1.5 ha. Most of the 40 625 operators of less than 0.5 ha should likely be classified as hobby winemakers. Many smaller vineyard owners do not pursue viticulture as a full-time occupation, but rather as a supplement to other agriculture or to hospitality. It is not uncommon for a visitor to a German wine region to find that a small family-owned Gasthaus has its own wine. Smaller grape-growers who do not wish or are able to commercialise their own wine have several options available: sell the grapes, deliver the grapes to a wine-making cooperative or sell the wine in bulk to winemaking firms which use them in "bulk brands" or as a base wine for Sekt. Those who own vineyards in truly good locations also have the option of renting them out to larger producers who will handle the entire operation of the vineyard.

5 892 vineyard owners owned more than 5 ha each in 1999, accounting for 57 per cent of Germany's total vineyard surface, and it is in this category that the full-time vintners and commercial operations are primarily found. However, truly large wineries, in terms of their own vineyard holdings, are rare in Germany. Hardly any German wineries reach the size of New World winemaking companies, and only a few are of the same size as a typical Bordeaux Grand Cru Classé château. Of the ten wineries considered as Germany's best by Gault Millau Weinguide in 2007, nine had 10,2-19 ha of vineyards, and one had 70 ha. This means that most of the high-ranking German wineries each only produces around 100,000 bottles of wine per year. That production is often distributed over, 10-25 different wines from different vineyards, of different Prädikat, sweetness and so on. The largest vineyard owner is the Hessian State Wineries, owned by the federal state of Hesse, with 200 ha vineyards, the produce of which is vinified in three separate wineries. The largest privately held winery is Dr. Bürklin-Wolf in the Palatinate with 85,5 ha.

BUSINESS OF WINE IN INDIA

Indian wine is wine made in the Asian country of India. Viticulture in India has a long antiquity dating back to the time of the Indus Valley civilization when grapevines were believed to have been introduced from Persia. Winemaking has existed throughout most of India's antiquity but was particularly encouraged during the time of the Portuguese and British colonization of the subcontinent. The end of the 19th century saw the phylloxera louse take its toll on the Indian wine industry followed by religious and public opinion moving towards the prohibition of alcohol. Following the country's independence from the British Empire, the Constitution of India declared that one of the government's aims was the total prohibition of alcohol. Several states went dry and the government encouraged vineyards to convert to table grape and raisin production. In the 1980s and 1990s, a revival in the Indian wine industry took place as international influences and the growing middle class increased started increasing demand for the beverage. By the turn of the 21st century, demand was increasing at a rate of 20-30 per cent a year.

Viticulture was believed to have been introduced to India by Persian traders sometime in the 4th millennia BC. Historians believe that these early plantings were used mostly for table grapes or grape juice rather than the production of an alcoholic beverage. During the Vedic period of the 2nd and 1st millennia, the Aryans tribes of the region were known for their indulgence of intoxicating drink and it seems probable that wine was a present beverage. The religious text of the Vedas mentions at least one alcoholic drink that may have been wine related-sura which seems to have been a type of rice wine that was fermented with honey. The first known mentioning of grape-based wines was in the late 4th century BC writings of Chanakya who was the chief minister of Emperor Chandragupta Maurya. In his writings, Chanakya condemns the use of alcohol while chronicling the emperor and his court's frequent indulgence of a style of grape wine known as Madhu.

In the centuries that would follow, wine became the privileged drink of the Kshatriya or noble class while the lower caste typically drank alcohol made from wheat, barley and millet. Under the rule of the Muslim Mughal Empire, alcohol was prohibited in accordance to Islamic dietary laws. However there are written reports about at least one Mughal ruler, Jahangir, who was fond of brandy wine. In the 16th century, Portuguese colonists at Goa introduced port-style wine and the production of fortified wines soon spread to other regions. Under British rule during the Victorian era, viticulture and winemaking was strongly encouraged as a domestic source for the British colonists. Vineyards were planted extensively through the Baramati, Kashmir and Surat regions. In 1883 at the Calcutta International Exhibition, Indian wines were showcased to a favorable reception. The Indian wine industry was reaching a peak by the time the phylloxera epidemic made its way to country and devastated its vineyards.

It was a long road for the Indian wine industry to recover from the devastation at the end of the 19th century. Unfavorable religious and public opinion on alcohol developed and culminated in the 1950s when many of India's states prohibited alcohol. Vineyards were either uprooted or encouraged to convert to table grape and raisin production. Some areas, like Goa, continued to produce wine but the product was normally very sweet and highly alcoholic. The turning part of the modern Indian wine industry occurred in early 1980s with the founding of Chateau Indage in the state of Maharashtra. With the assistance of French winemakers, Chateau Indage began to import Vitis vinifera grape varieties like Cabernet Sauvignon, Chardonnay, Pinot blanc, Pinot noir and Ugni blanc and started making still and sparkling wines. Other wineries soon followed as the emergence of India's growing middle class fueled the growth and development of the Indian wine industry.

Wine Regions

Vineyards in India range from the more temperate climate of the northwestern state of Punjab down to the southern state of Tamil Nadu. Some of India's larger wine producing areas are located in Maharashtra, Karnataka near Bangalore and Andhra Pradesh near Hyderabad. Within the Maharashtra region, vineyards are found on the Deccan Plateau and around Baramati, Nashik, Pune, Sangli and Solapur. The high heat and humidity of the far eastern half of the country limits viticultural activity.

Viticulture and Wine

The heat and humidity of India's wine region dictates many of the viticultural choices that are made in the vineyards. Vines are often trained on bamboo and wire in a pergola to increase canopy cover and to get the grapes off the ground where they would be more prone to fungal diseases. The canopy protects the grapes against sunburn and rows are spaced wide to help with aeration between the vines. Irrigation is essential in many of India's wine regions and since the 1980s, drip irrigation has been widely used. The tropical conditions often promote high yields which requires frequent pruning throughout the year. Harvest normally takes place in September and is usually done by hand. In the very warm wine regions of Tamil Nadu, Karnataka and Andhra Pradesh, grapevines can produce a crop twice a year.

India is home to several indigenous table grape varieties that can also be used in wine production with Anabeshahi, Arkavati and Arkashyam being the most common. Popular non-native grapes include the Bangalore Blue and Gulabi. The Turkish grape Sultana is the most widely planted grape in India, cover more than half of the 148,000 acres (60,000 ha) planted in the country. In addition to the imported French varieties that Chateau Indage planted, Sauvignon blanc, Zinfandel, Chenin blanc and Clairette have started to establish a presence in the Indian wine industry.

BUSINESS OF WINE IN ISRAELI

Israeli wine is produced by hundreds of wineries, ranging in size from small boutique enterprises to large companies producing over ten million bottles per year. Wine has been produced in the Land of Israel since biblical times. In 2009 Israel exports over $22 million worth of wine annually. Statistics show that Israeli wine exports in 2010 will be account to $30 million.

The modern Israeli wine industry was founded by Baron Edmond James de Rothschild, owner of the Bordeaux estate Château Lafite-Rothschild. Today, Israeli winemaking takes place in five vine-growing regions: Galil, the region most suited for viticulture due to its high elevation, cool breezes, marked day and night temperature changes and rich, well-drained soils; the Judean Hills, surrounding the city of Jerusalem; Shimshon, located between the Judean Hills and the Coastal Plain; the Negev, a semi-arid desert region, where drip irrigation has made grape growing possible; and the Sharon plain near the Mediterranean coast and just south of Haifa, surrounding the towns of Zichron Ya'akov and Binyamina, which is the largest grape growing area in Israel.

In 2007, recognized wine critic Robert Parker's The Wine Advocate awarded 14 Israeli wines its highest wine rating of "outstanding."

Viticulture has existed in the land of Israel since biblical times. The fruit of the vine was listed as one of the seven blessed species of fruit found in the land of Israel. The location of Israel along a historic wine trading route between

Mesopotamia and Egypt brought winemaking knowledge and influence to the area. Wine played a significant role in the religion of the early Israelites of grape growing, harvesting and winemaking often being used to emphasise religious ideals. In Roman times, wine from Israel was exported to Rome with the most sought after wines being vintage dated with the name of the winemaker inscribed on the amphora. In the 7th century AD, the Islamic conquest of the Middle East virtually wiped out the region's wine industry with wineries closing down and vineyards, planted with now lost indigenous grape varieties, pulled out. During the Crusades, Christian Crusaders and entourages temporarily revived winemaking between 1100 to 1300 AD but the return of Islamic rule and the subsequent Jewish Diaspora extinguished the industry once again.

In 1848, a rabbi in Jerusalem founded the first documented winery in modern times but its establishment was short lived. In 1870, the first Jewish agricultural college, Mikveh Israel, was founded and featured a course on viticulture. The root of the modern Israeli wine industry can be traced to the late 19th century when the French Baron Edmond de Rothschild, owner of the Bordeaux estate Château Lafite-Rothschild, began importing French grape varieties and technical know how to the region. In 1882, he help establish Carmel Winery with vineyards and wine production facilities in Rishon LeZion and Zikhron Ya'akov near Haifa. Still in operation today, Carmel is the largest producer of Israeli wine and has been at the forefront of many technical and historical advances in both winemaking and Israeli antiquity. One of the first telephones in Israel was installed at Carmel and the country's first Prime Minister, David Ben-Gurion, worked in Carmel's cellars in his youth.

For most of its antiquity in the modern era, the Israeli wine industry was based predominately on the production of Kosher wines which was exported worldwide to Jewish communities. The quality of these wines were varied with many being produced from high yielding vineyards that valued quantity over quality. Many of these wines were also some what sweet. In the late 1960s, Carmel Winery the first Israeli winery to make a dry table wine. It wouldn't be till the 1980s when the industry as a whole saw a revival in quality winemaking when an influx of winemaking talent from Australia, California and France brought modern technology and technical know how to the growing Israeli wine industry. In 1989, the first boutique winery in Israel, Margalit Winery, was founded. By the 1990s, Israeli estates such as Golan Heights Winery and Domaine du Castel were winning awards at international wine competitions. The 1990s saw a subsequent "boom" in the opening of boutique wineries. By 2000 there 70 wineries in Israel and by 2005 that numbered jumped to 140.

Today, less than 15 per cent of Israeli wine is produced for sacremental purposes. The three largest producers-Carmel Winery, Barkan Wine Cellars and Golan Heights Winery account for more than 80 per cent of the domestic market. The United States is the largest export destination. Even though it contains only around a quarter of the planted acreage as Lebanon, Israel has emerged as a driving force for winemaking in the Eastern Mediterranean due to its willingness to adopt new technology and its large export market. The country has also seen the emergence of a modern wine culture with up-scale restaurants featuring international wines dedicated to an ever increasing wine-conscious clientele.

Wine Regions

Israeli wine is produced in five regions: Galilee; the Judean Hills, surrounding the city of Jerusalem; the Samson region, located between the Judean Hills and the Coastal Plain; the Negev desert region; and the Shomron region, which includes the Sharon plain located near the Mediterranean coast and just south of Haifa. More than 80 per cent of the vineyards planted in Israel are located in the Shomron, Samson and Galilee regions. As of 2005, there were 14,820 acres (6,000 hectares) under vine.

The Golan contains some of the highest elevated vineyards in Israeli-controlled territory, with vineyard planted upwards of 4,000 feet (1,200 meters) from the Sea of Galilee towards Mount Hermon. There are seven Israeli wineries in the Golan Heights that cultivate a total of 1,600 acres (648 hectares). These include four boutiques, and Chateau Golan, Bazelet Hagolan, and the Golan Heights Winery whose Yarden, Gamla, and Golan labels enjoy international renown..

The Golan Heights, occupied by Israel since the Six-Day War in 1967, are located northeast of Israel proper, though Israel considers it a sub-region of the Galilee. The political status of the Golan Heights has resulted in controversy on the export market. In one example, following domestic demand for kosher wine, a number of Golan Heights wines were marketed by Systembolaget, Sweden's state-owned monopoly alcohol retailer, as "Made in Israel" on shelves and in the sales catalogue. Following customer complaints and consultation with Sweden's foreign ministry, Systembolaget changed the shelf labelling to read, "Made in Israeli-occupied Syrian territories." However this prompted further complaints, from some customers and a Member of Parliament. Systembolaget's solution was to simply remove all reference to the product's country of origin on shelves and in catalogues, classifying the wine as of "other origins." The actual bottles remained unchanged throughout the controversy, and carried the producer's English-language labels.

Grape Varieties

During centuries of Islamic rule, alcohol production was banned as part of the Islamic dietary laws. Ancient Israeli vineyards were pulled out along with any indigenous grape varieties. Today, the wine industry produces primarily French grape varieties imported during the late 19th century. The most widely planted varieties include Cabernet Sauvignon, Chardonnay, Merlot and Sauvignon blanc. Emerging varieties that have recently been increasing in popularity include Cabernet Franc, Gewurztraminer, Muscat Canelli, Riesling and Syrah. Other varieties planted to some significant degree include Emerald Riesling, Muscat of Alexandria and the crossing Argaman.

A primary concern in Israeli wine production is maintaining acid levels to balance the naturally high sugars that this warm climate region produces. Vineyards at higher elevations, as opposed to the lower coastal plains, have more consistently produced wines wines with the necessary acid balance. Cabernet Sauvignon has shown the most potential to age and develop. The smooth texture and ripe tannins of Israeli Merlot has increased that wine's popularity in the market. Chardonnay grown in Israeli has shown itself to be highly reflective of terroir and reflective of the particularly characteristics of vineyard soils. It is also the primary grape used in Israeli sparkling wine production made just as to the methode champenoise.

Production

As of 2008, the Israeli wine industry produced an average of 30 million bottles of wine annually in a variety of styles ranging from red, white, rosé, still, sparkling and dessert wines. Large wineries and co-operatives still dominate the industry but there is an emerging culture of small production boutique wineries. The 8 largest wineries in Israel, in terms of production volume, are Carmel, Barkan, Golan Heights, Efrat Wine Cellars, Binyamina Wine Cellar, Tishbi Winery, Segal Winery and Dalton Winery.

Wine Tourism

It was announced in early 2008 that a 150-acre (0.61 km2) wine park would be created on the slopes between Zichron Ya'akov and Binyamina in order to promote tourism in the area and wine tourism in Israel in general.

BUSINESS OF WINE IN ITALY

Italian wine is wine produced in Italy, a country which is home to some of the oldest wine-producing regions in the world. Etruscans and Greek settlers produced wine in the country long before the Romans started developing their own vineyards in the 2nd century BC. Roman grape-growing and winemaking was prolific and well-organized, pioneering large-scale production and storage techniques like barrel-making and bottling.

Two thousand years later, Italy is one of the world's foremost producers, responsible for approximately one-fifth of world wine production in 2005. In 2008, Italy bested France for the title of world's biggest producer for the first time in a decade, at nearly six billion liters. Wine is extremely popular in Italy. Italians lead the world in wine consumption by volume, 59 liters per capita.

(Compare this to the United States, at 7.7 liters per capita.) Grapes are grown in almost every region of the country. More than 1 million vineyards are under cultivation.

Although wines had been elaborated from the wild Vitis vinifera grape for millennia, it wasn't until the Greek colonization that wine-making flourished. Viticulture was introduced into Sicily and southern Italy by the Mycenaean Greeks, and was well established when the extensive Greek colonization transpired around 800 BC. It was during the Roman defeat of the Carthaginians in the second century BC that Italian wine production began to further flourish. Large-scale, slave-run plantations sprang up in many coastal areas and spread to such an extent that, in AD92, emperor Domitian was forced to destroy a great number of vineyards in order to free up fertile land for food production.

During this time, viticulture outside of Italy was prohibited under Roman law. Exports to the provinces were reciprocated in exchange for more slaves, especially from Gaul where trade was intense, just as to Pliny, due to the inhabitants being besotted with Italian wine, drinking it unmixed and without restraint. It was customary to mix wine with a good proportion of water which may otherwise have been unpalatable, making wine drinking a fundamental part of early Italian life.

As the laws on provincial viticulture were relaxed, vast vineyards began to flourish in the rest of Europe, especially Gaul and Hispania. This coincided with the cultivation of new vines, like biturica. These vineyards became hugely successful, to the point that Italy ultimately became an import centre for provincial wines.

Depending on the vintage, modern Italy is the world's largest or second largest wine producer. In 2005, production was about 20 per cent of the global total, second only to France, which produced 26 per cent. In the same year, Italy's share in dollar value of table wine imports into the U.S. was 32 per cent, Australia's was 24 per cent, and France's was 20 per cent. Along with Australia, Italy's market share has rapidly increased in recent years.

Italian Appellation System

Italy's classification system has four classes of wine, with two falling under the EU category Quality Wine Produced in a Specific Region (QWPSR) and two falling under the category of 'table wine'. The four classes are:

Table Wine:

- Vino da Tavola (VDT)-Denotes simply that the wine is made in Italy. The label usually indicates a basic wine, made for local consumption.
- Indicazione Geografica Tipica (IGT)-Denotes wine from a more specific region within Italy. This appellation was created in 1992 for wines that were considered to be of higher quality than simple table wines, but which did not conform to the strict wine laws for their

region. Before the IGT was created, "Super Tuscan" wines such as Tignanello and Sassicaia were labeled Vino da Tavola.

QWPSR:

- Denominazione di Origine Controllata (DOC).
- Denominazione di Origine Controllata e Garantita (DOCG).

Both DOC and DOCG wines refer to zones which are more specific than an IGT, and the permitted grapes are also more specifically defined. The DOC system began in 1963, seeking to establish a method of both recognizing quality product and maintaining the international and national reputation of that product. The main difference between a DOC and a DOCG is that the latter must pass a blind taste test for quality in addition to conforming to the strict legal requirements to be designated as a wine from the area in question. After the sweeping wine laws of 1992, transparent rules were made regarding requirements for DOCG entry, imposing new limits regarding the production of grapes per hectare and minimum natural alcohol levels, among others.

The overall goal of the system is to encourage producers to focus on quality wine making.

BUSINESS OF WINE IN MEXICO

Mexican wine and wine making began with the Spanish, who brought vines here from Europe. They found that grapevines did very well in the colony of New Spain and by the 17th century wine exports from Spain to the New World fell. In 1699, Charles II of Spain prohibited wine making in Mexico, with the exception of wine for Church purposes. From then until Mexico's Independence, wine was produced here only on a small scale.

After Independence, wine making for normal purposes was no longer prohibited and production rose, especially in the last 19th and early 20th century. However, the Mexican Revolution set back wine production, especially in the north of the country. Wine production here has been rising in both quantity and quality since the 1980s although competition from foreign wines and 40 per cent tax on the product makes competing difficult within Mexico.

Mexico is not traditionally a wine-drinking country, but rather prefers beer and tequila. Interest in wine, especially in the major cities and tourists areas has grown, along with Mexican wines' reputation. Various wine producers from Mexico have won international awards for their products.

There are three major wine producing areas in Mexico, with the Baja California area producing 90 per cent of Mexico's wine. This area is promoted heavily for wine tourism with the "Ruta del Vino", which connects over fifty wineries with the port of Ensenada and the border and the annual Vendimia harvest festival.

Hernán Cortés and his soldiers quickly depleted the wine they brought with them from Spain celebrating the conquest of the Aztec Empire in 1521.

Because of this, one of Cortés' first acts as governor was to order the planting of grapevines throughout New Spain.

In the early colonial era, ships arriving to Mexico and Spain's other colonies carried grapevines. In certain areas Coahuila, Spainards found a native type of grapevine, but it did not lend itself well to winemaking. However, vines from Europe grew very well here, and they were planted in monasteries and haciendas in the states of Puebla, Coahuila, Zacatecas and others. In 1597, Casa Madero was founded by Lorenzo Garcia in the town of Santa María de las Parras as the oldest winery in the Americas. This area of Coahuila soon became a major wine producer due to its climate and good supplies of water. The vines that were established here were later exported to the Napa Valley in California and South America.

Vineyards in the Americas, especially New Spain were successful enough that wine exports from Spain to America plummeted. Because of this, Charles II decided to prohibit the production of wine in Spain's colonies, especially Mexico, except for the making of wine for the Church in 1699. That prohibition stayed in force until Mexico's Independence. However, many missionaries refused to abide by the edict and continued to produce wine for normal consumption on a small scale. One of these was Jesuit priest Juan Ugarte, who planted the first vines in Baja California when he arrived at the Loreto mission in 1701.

From the end of the 18th century to the middle of the 19th, most wine production was done by clergy. The Santo Tomás Mission, founded in Baja California by Jesuit priests in 1791, reactivated larger scale production of wine in Mexico. In 1843, Dominican priests began growing grapes at the nearby Nuestra Señora de Guadalupe del Norte mission, located in what is now called the Valley of Guadalupe. This valley is one of the few in the world, along with others such as the Napa Valley and the Rhone Valley, in which premium wine grapes can be grown.

In the 1850s, as part of Mexico's Reform War, many of the Church's land holdings were taken by the state. Most of the small wineries tended by missionaries were eventually abandoned. In 1888, the former lands of the Santo Tomás Mission were sold to a private group, which established the first large-scale commercial winery and the earliest winery in continuous operation, called Bodegas Santo Tomás. Initially, the wine made by the group was sweet and of low quality.

During the period of Mexican antiquity known as the Porfirato (1880-1910), wine production in Mexico increased and spread to other regions of the country. In the Baja California area in 1904, Russian immigrants known as Molokans, a pacifist religious group fleeing service in the Czar's army, purchased 100 acres of land and began producing wine grapes. They encouraged others to do the same, helping the area acquire a reputation for making good wine. However, winemaking was set back by the Mexican Revolution as many lands were abandoned by their owners or destroyed by the rebels.

Wine making in Mexico began to experience a comeback in the 1980s, with wine production peaking at four million cases a year in the latter part of the decade. However, the 1980s also opened Mexico's small wine market to foreign competition, which hurt it. Baja California, which produces 90 per cent of Mexico's wine, only sells about 1.5 million cases a year today, but the quality of this wine is generally higher.

Since the 1980s, wine production, especially in Baja California, has been steadily improving with better tending of vineyards and incorporating modern advancements in winemaking. Most wineries here are young, established only since the 1980s and 1990s, but some enthusiasts are calling the Valley of Guadalupe area the "next Napa Valley." The wine industry is growing rapidly and the quality of the wine is improving. Mexican wine can be found in 38 countries in the world and many vintages have won international awards.

Wine Consumption in Mexico Today

Despite Mexico's Spanish heritage, it is not a wine-drinking country, but rather a beer and tequila country. Average wine consumption per capita is only two glasses a year. The Mexican government imposes taxes of 40 per cent per bottle, making it hard to compete with beer and tequila. However, consumption of wine in Mexico is growing, with imports of wine in 2005 being nearly four times higher than ten years before. Most wine is consumed in major cities such as Mexico City, Monterrey, Guadalajara and Puebla, and is also commonly found in the tourist areas, such as Cancun and Cabo San Lucas.

Most of the wine consumed in Mexico is imported from places like Europe, Chile, Australia and New Zealand, with about forty per cent coming from domestic wineries. However, wine consumption continues to grow with one factor being increased interest in it by the middle classes, especially in Mexico City. As the reputation of Mexican wines increases, preference for native wines is also increasing in Mexico. At one time, no sophisticated restaurant in Mexico City would serve Mexican wine. Today, newer restaurants always include selections from Mexico on their wine lists.. While wine drinking is not widespread in Mexico, the consumption of brandy, or distilled wine is. Brandy, especially the sherry variety, is the most widespread distilled liquor in Mexico. It is even more popular than rum or tequila. Mexico is the fourth largest consumer of brandy in the world behind the Philippines, Germany and Equatorial Guinea. The last of Mexico's tariffs on imported brandy were lifted in the 2000s, with sales and consumption expected to rise.

Wine Producing Greas and Vintages in Mexico

Nearly 6,200 acres are planted to grapes in Mexico. Principal white wine grapes include chenin blanc, chardonnay, sauvignon blanc and viognier, and reds include all five Bordeaux varietals plus Grenache, tempranillo, dolcetto, syrah and petite sirah.

There are three areas in Mexico where wine grapes are grown. The North area includes Baja California and Sonora; the La Laguna area is in Coahuila and Durango and the Center area consists of Zacatecas, Aguascalientes and Querétaro. Most of these areas have fairly warm climate, which tend to make Mexican wines spicy, full-bodied and ripe; however, Northern Baja's humid winders, dry warm summers and sea breezes allows for most of the same varietals produced in California. The La Laguna region is the oldest wine-making area of Mexico, and straddles the states of Coahuila and Durango, with grapes thriving in the Parras Valley. This valley is a microclimate in the desert area of these states at an altitude of 1,500 meters. The valley has warm days, cool nights and low humidity with inhibits insect and fungus damage to the vines. Mountain springs provide sufficient water in this arid part of Mexico. The temperature difference of 12C between day and night is also beneficial to the grapes. The valley primarily produces reds based on Bordeaux such as cabernet sauvignon, Shiraz, merlot and Tempranillo. Some whites are produced as well. More than 400 families arrive to the Parras Valley in August and September for the annual grape harvest called "la vendimia."

The most important winery here is Casa Madero, the oldest winery in the New World, when it was founded in 1597 as Hacienda San Lorenzo. This label includes a range of varietals, with its chardonnay, chenin blanc and Syrah winning awards. Its brandies are considered among the best in Mexico. Another important winery here is Bodegas Ferrino, founded by a 19th century Italian immigrant near the town of Cuatro Ciénegas.

Another interesting winery is located in Tarahumara country at the edge of the Copper Canyon in Coahuila, in a small valley named Cerocahui. In 1680, Father Juan María de Salvaterra arrived here to establish a mission. Later Jesuits brought cuttings of French and Spanish vines. When the Jesuits were forced out of Mexico in the 1700s, the Cerocahui vineyards where destroyed except for a few cuttings secretly kept and grown by the Jose María Sanchez family. These vines were cared for by the family until the late 20th century, when the last of the family died without heirs. The gardener for the family saved cuttings from the vines and with the Misión Hotel and planted them at what was the Girls Boarding School. Since then the town has had over 4,000 vines under cultivation and a winery has been established at the hotel.

The Center region consists of areas in Querétaro, Zacatecas and Aguascalientes. Most vineyards are found at an altitude of 6,500 feet, and most of the wine produced here is of the sparkling variety. However, other types such as Sauvignon blanc, St. Emilion, cabernet sauvignon and pinot noir can be found as well. The best-known vintor here is the Mexican operation of Spain's

Freixenet winery. This label is known for dry sparkling wines called "vinos espumosos", which come in satiny black bottles and based on Dom Perignon's champagne fermentation methods. Some still red wines are also produced. Another major producer is Compania Vinicola Los Eucaliptos in the town of Ezequiel Montes. A locally known label is Vinos Hidalgo La Madrilena in the San Juan del Río region. Los Azteca Hacienda Mexicana dates back to the 1700s which recently became a winery. Another vintor called La Ronda specializes in growing grapes to make Kosher wine sold in certain markets in Mexico City.

Most of vineyards in Zacatecas are in the municipalities of Ojo Caliente and Valle de la Macarena. This area has very cool winters and fairly cool summers, which combined with its moisture-holding clay soils is best for fast-maturing grapes with a high sugar content. A number of European red varieties such as cabernet sauvignon and merlot are grown here as well as American varieties such as zinfandel, Black Spanish and Lenoir. Some white grapes also do well here. Wineries here are smaller operations then in other parts of the country, with the best known local label being Casa Cachola just outside of Valle de las Arisnas.

The North zone, produces ninety per cent of Mexico's wines today, with almost all of that coming from three regions near the port city of Ensenada: the San Antonio de las Minas, which includes the Valley of Guadalupe, the San Vicente Valley and the Santo Tomás Valley. This area is noted for its deep granite soils, warm sunny days nights cool due to breezes from the nearby Pacific Ocean. The area is ideal for both red and white wines, and one of the few in the world that can grow grapes for world-class wines. Grapes for Baja California wines are also grown in areas in neighbouring Sonora state. The varieties of red wine produced in the Baja California region are Cabernet Sauvignon, Ruby Cabernet, Zinfandel Grenache and Mission. The white wines are Chenin Blanc, Palomino, Riesling, Sauvignon Blanc, Sémillon, Saint Emilion and Malaga. There are three major wine producers in this area, Viños L.A.Cetto in the Calafia Valley, Viños Pedro Domecq and Bodegas de Santo Tomás in the Santo Tomás Valley. All have had wines that won international competitions including two medals won by Santo Tomás at a recent VinoChallenge International in Atlanta. Many of these wines are now exported to Europe, the U.S. and Canada, and most wineries offers tours and wine tasting.

Most of Mexico's wine innovation occurs in the Ensenada area, in the form of the so-called "boutique" producers such as Casa de Piedra, whose first vintage was produced in 1997. This operation only produces one white, called Piedra del Sol and a red called Viño del Sol. Another small producers is Viña de Liceaga, which produces reds. Don Miller owns a ranch and winery called Casa Adobe Guadalupe with a wine school here to help small producers make a profits and draw tourists. There is even one organic wine producer by the name of Doña Lupe.

Wine Tourism and Festivals in Mexico

Wine tourism in Mexico is centered on the Norte region, although wine festivals exist in the other wine-producing regions. The "Ruta del Vino" connects the wine producing areas of the municipality of Ensenada, such as the Valley of Guadalupe, the Valley of Llano Colorado, Valley of Santo Tomás and the Valley of San Vicente with the port city of Ensenada and the border cities of Tijuana and Tecate. The Route connects over fifty wineries, along with upscale restaurants, hotels, museums and other attractions of this part of Baja California state. The route is marked by "Ruta del Vino" signs on the roads and highways to promote the area for wine tourism, especially from the U.S. border.

Another major tourism draw is the Fiesta de la Vendimia, which takes place in Ensenada and the Valley of Guadalupe every year in August. The festivals include wine tasting and contests, winery tours, fishing tournaments, cook-offs, gourmet food and concerts. These events are sponsored and/or organized by the area's wineries. Since the event occurs in the summer, temperatures can hover around 100F. Some of the events include "Noche de Cofradia en Ensenada", which features wine and food tasting from about thirty wineries and restaurants, matching local wines with local culinary specialties. The annual Malagon Family Celebration is held on a 500 acre ranch, vineyard with winery and bed and breakfast. This event includes a horse show, live music, food and wine. The Concurso Internacional Ensenada Tierra del Vino wine competition is also held in the city. Perhaps the most unusual event is at Bibayoff Winery with Russian music, dancers, food and wines.

However the drug war, which mostly takes place in border cities like Tijuana, has hurt this tourism to the area significantly as many U.S. tourists do not want to pass the border towns to get to the relatively calm wine valleys of Baja California. The Parras Valley in Coahuila has held its Feria de la Uva y el Vino since 1945, centered on the town of Parras de la Fuente. The event showcases the area's wines as well as other local products such as handcrafts, candies, denim clothing and food. This event is generally held in June.

In the Center area, Tequisquiapan, Querétaro sponsors an annual cheese and wine festival called the Feria Nacional del Queso y de Vino in the month of June. This event draws local, national and international participants to compete for prizes and provide samples to visitors. This part of Querétaro is not only in wine country, but very near the center of where most Mexican cheeses were developed. Wines featured at this event are sparkling wines, but chardonnays, sauvignon blanc, merlots, pinot noirs and cabernets are also available for tasting. Wines from other parts of Mexico and the world also appear here. A more local celebration in the same area is Querétaro's version of the Vendimia first harvest festival which occurs at various wineries in the state in July. The most notable events occur at the Viñedos La Redonda Winery near Tequisquiapan with music, wine tasting and competitions, gourmet food and a handcrafts exposition.

BUSINESS OF WINE IN MOLDOVA

Moldova has a well established wine industry. It has a vineyard area of 147,000 hectares (360,000 acres), of which 1,025 km2 (396 sq mi) are used for commercial production. Most of the country's wine production is for export. Many families have their own recipes and strands of grapes that have been passed down through the generations.

Fossils of Vitis teutonica vine leaves near the Naslavcia village in the north of Moldova indicate that grapes grew here approximately 6 to 25 million years ago. The size of grape seed imprints found near the Varvarovca village, which date back to 2800 BC, prove that at that time the grapes were already being cultivated. The grapegrowing and winemaking in the area between the Nistru and Prut rivers, which began 4000-5000 years ago, had periods of rises and falls but has survived through all the changing social and economic conditions.

By the end of the 3rd century BC, trading links were established between the local population and the Greeks and from 107 AD with the Romans, a fact which strongly influenced the intense development of the grapegrowing and winemaking.

After the formation of the Moldovan feudal state in the 14th century, grapegrowing began to develop and flourished in the 15th century during the kingdom of Stephen the Great, who promoted the import of high quality varieties and the improvement of the quality of wine, which was one of the chief exports of Moldova throughout the medieval period, especially to Poland, Ukraine and Russia.

During the 300 years of Ottoman rule, Moldova saw a big decline in grapegrowing, as winemaking was forbidden by law. After the Treaty of Bucharest in 1812, when the region became a province of the Russian Empire, the wine industry flourished again. The main varieties were the traditional ones: Rara Neagr?, Plavai, Galbena, Zghiharda, Batuta Neagr?, Feteasc? Alb?, Feteasc? Neagr?, T?mâioasa, Cabasia and many other local, Hungarian, Bulgarian, Greek, and Turkish varieties. In this period, the grape growers gained governmental support and by 1837 the vineyard area in Bessarabia reached 14,000 hectares, and the wine production reached 12 million litres.

The second half of the 19th century saw an intensive planting of newly introduced French varieties, such as Pinot Blanc, Pinot Noir, Pinot Gris, Aligote, Cabernet Sauvignon, Sauvignon Blanc, Gamay, Muscat Blanc. It was at this time that wines like Negru de Purcari and Romanesti, which have made Moldova famous as a fine wine producer, began to be produced.

After the phylloxera damage at the end of the 19th century, it was only in 1906 that the vineyards began to recover with grafted planting material. By 1914 Bessarabia had the biggest vineyard area in the Russian Empire.

Both World Wars damaged the Moldovan vineyards and the wine industry considerably. The re-establishment of Moldovan vineyards began during Soviet years, in the 1950's. Over 150,000 hectares were planted in 10 years, and by 1960 the total vineyard area had reached 220,000 hectares.

In 2006, a diplomatic conflict with Russia resulted in the 2006 Russian ban of Moldovan and Georgian wines, damaging the wine industry of Moldova considerably, as Russia remains the largest importer of Moldovan wines by far.

Wine Industry

The Moldova Wine Guild is a non-profit association established in August 2007 by several of Moldova's leading private wineries, *i.e.* Acorex Wine Holding, Vinaria Bostavan, Chateau Vartely, DK-Intertrade, Dionysos-Mereni, Lion-Gri, and Vinaria Purcari.

Together, the wineries export more than one third of all Moldovan wine. The member wineries are united by their desire to raise Moldova's profile as a major European wine producing country. To accomplish this goal, the members work together to promote their wines on the international market through joint marketing initiatives and to educate the international wine trade and press about Moldova.

BUSINESS OF NEW ZEALAND WINE

New Zealand wine is largely produced in ten major wine growing regions spanning latitudes 36° to 45° South and extending 1,600 km (1,000 miles). They are, from north to south Northland, Auckland, Waikato/Bay of Plenty, Gisborne, Hawke's Bay, Wellington, Nelson, Marlborough, Canterbury/Waipara and Central Otago.

Backdrop

Wine making and vine growing go back to colonial times in New Zealand. British Resident and keen oenologist James Busby was, as early as 1836, attempting to produce wine at his land in Waitangi. In 1851 New Zealand's oldest existing vineyard was established by the Roman Catholic church on land in Hawke's Bay. Due to economic (the importance of the protein export industry), legislative and cultural factors wine was a marginal activity. Dalmatian immigrants at the end of the nineteenth and beginning of the twentieth century brought with them viticultural knowledge and set up the nascent NZ wine industry in West and North Auckland. Typically their vineyards produced sherry and port for the palates of New Zealanders of the time, and table wine for their own community.

The three factors that held back the development of the industry simultaneously underwent subtle but historic changes in the late 1960s and early 1970s. In 1973 Britain entered the European Economic Community, which required the ending of historic trade terms for New Zealand meat and dairy products. This led ultimately to a dramatic restructuring of the agricultural economy. Before this restructuring was fully implemented, diversification away from traditional protein products to products with potentially higher economic returns was explored. Vines, which produce best in low moisture and low soil fertility environments, were seen as suitable for areas that had already been marginal pasture. The end of the 1960s saw the end of the New Zealand institution of the "six o'clock swill", where pubs were open for only an hour after the end of the working day and closed all Sunday. The same legislative reform saw the introduction of BYO licences for restaurants. This had a profound and unexpected effect on New Zealanders' cultural approach to wine.

Finally the late 1960s and early 1970s noted the rise of the OE, where young New Zealanders travelled and lived and worked overseas, predominantly in Europe. The OE as a cultural phenomenon goes back before this time, but by the 1960s a distinctly Kiwi identity had developed and the passenger jet made the OE experience possible for a large amount of New Zealanders who experienced first-hand the decidedly different wine-drinking cultures of Europe.

First Steps

In the 1970s, Montana in Marlborough started producing wines which were labelled by year of production and grape variety. The first production of a Sauvignon Blanc of great note appears to have occurred in 1977. Also produced in that year were superior quality wines of Muller Thurgau, Riesling and Pinotage.

The excitement created from these successes and from the early results of Cabernet Sauvignon from Auckland and Hawkes Bay launched the industry with ever increasing investment, leading to more hectares planted, rising land prices and greater local interest and pride. Such was the boom that over-planting occurred, particularly in the "wrong" varietals that fell out of fashion in the early 1980s.

In 1984 the then Labour Government paid growers to pull up vines to address a glut that was damaging the industry. Ironically many growers used the Government grant not to restrict planting, but to swap from less economic varieties to more fashionable varieties, using the old root stock. The glut was only temporary in any case, as boom times returned swiftly.

Sauvignon Blanc Breakthrough

New Zealand is home to what many wine critics consider the world's best Sauvignon Blanc. Oz Clarke, a well known British wine critic wrote in the 1990s that New Zealand Sauvignon Blanc was "arguably the best in the world". Historically, Sauvignon Blanc has been used in many French regions in both AOC and Vin de Pays wine. The most famous had been France's Sancerre. It is also the grape used to make Pouilly Fumé.

Following Robert Mondavi's lead in renaming Californian Sauvignon Blanc Fumé Blanc there was a trend for oaked Sauvignon Blanc in New Zealand during the late 1980s. Later the fashion for strong oaky overtones and also the name waned.

In the 1980s, wineries in New Zealand, especially in the Marlborough region, began producing outstanding, some critics said unforgettable, Sauvignon Blanc. "New Zealand Sauvignon Blanc is like a child who inherits the best of both parents-exotic aromas found in certain Sauvignon Blancs from the New World and the pungency and limy acidity of an Old World Sauvignon Blanc like Sancerre from the Loire Valley". One critic said that drinking one's first New Zealand Sauvignon Blanc was like having sex for the first time. "No other region in the world can match Marlborough, the northeastern corner of New Zealand's South Island, which seems to be the best place in the world to grow Sauvignon Blanc grapes".

Industry Structure and Production Methods

There are a diversity of methods of production of New Zealand wine. The traditional concept of a vineyard, whereby grapes are grown on the land surrounding a central simply-owned or family-owned estate with its own discrete viticultural and wine making equipment and storage is only one model. While the European cooperative model is uncommon, contract growing of fruit for wine-makers has been a feature of the NZ industry since the start of the wine making boom in the 1970s.

Indeed a number of well known quality wine producers started out as contract growers. Alternately, many fledgling producers started out using solely contract fruit as their own vines matured into production. Some producers use contract fruit to supplement the range of varieties they market, even using fruit from other geographical regions. It is common, for example, an Auckland producer market a "Marlborough Sauvignon Blanc", or a Marlborough producer market a "Gisborne Chardonnay".

Contract growing is an example of the use of indigenous agri-industrial methods that pre-date the NZ wine industry. Another example of the adaptation of NZ methods towards the new industry was the universal use of stainless steel in wine making adapted from the norms and standards of the New Zealand dairy industry. There was an existing small scale industrial infrastructure ready for wine makers to economically employ. It should be remembered that while current wine making technology is almost universally sterile and hygenic world-wide, the natural antibiotic properties of alcohol production were more heavily relied upon in the 1970s when the NZ wine industry started.

This pervasive use of stainless steel almost certainly had a distinctive effect on both New Zealand wines styles and the domestic palate. The early wines which made a stir internationally were lauded for the intensity and purity of the fruit in the wine. Indeed the strength of flavour in the wine favoured bone dry styles despite intense acidity. While stainless steel did not produce the intensity of fruit, it allowed for its exploitation. Even today, NZ white wine tends towards drier end of the spectrum.

Varieties, Styles and Directions

Red Blends and Bordeaux Varieties

New Zealand Reds are typically made from either a blend of varietals or Pinot Noir. Recently, in Hawkes Bay there have been wines made from Syrah, either solely or blends, and even Tempranillo, Montepulciano and Sangiovese.

Early success in Hawkes Bay in the 1960s by McWilliams, and in the 1980s by Te Mata Estate, lead to red wine planting and production concentrating on Cabernet Sauvignon by Corbans, McWilliams and Mission Estate among others. As viticulture improved with experience of New Zealand's maritime climate, more Merlot and other blending wines were employed, with quality and quantity increasing. This trend continues and can be seen in the NZ Wine Institute statistics where plantings of Cabernet Sauvignon, Merlot, Cabernet Franc, Malbec and Syrah now account for 2,496 hectares.

Typically "bordeaux blends" come from regions and sub-regions that are relatively hot and dry for New Zealand. 86 per cent of production is centred in Hawke's Bay with Waiheke Island also producing some notable wines. Wines that have made a name for Waiheke Island include Stonyridge Larose and Goldwater Estate. Wines that typify the best of Hawkes Bay include Te Mata Estate's Coleraine and Awatea, Craggy Range's Sophia, Esk Valley's The Terraces and Villa Maria's Reserve Merlot/Cabernets. In Marlborough there are also a small number of producers of bordeaux varietal wines.

However, examples of bordeaux blends can be found as far south as Waipara, in Canterbury where Pegasus Bay's Maestro has demonstrated a drift away from Cabernet Sauvignon predominant blends to Merlot predominant with the addition of Malbec.

In general New Zealand red wine tends to be forward and early maturing, fruit-driven and with restrained oak. No definitive regional characteristics have developed in New Zealand, the principal differences between wines being determined by the vintage, vineyard and wine-maker's philosophy. However, some preliminary trends are worth commenting on. Central Otago particularly Bannockburn pinot noir can have distinct earthy, mineral and wild thyme notes. Hawkes Bay bordeaux blends have greater body than other New Zealand reds. Marlborough Pinot Noirs are notable for their ripeness and fruitiness.

Pinot Noir

Pinot Noir is a grape variety whose importance in New Zealand is greater than the weight of planting. Early in the modern wine industry, the comparatively low annual sunshine hours to be found in NZ discouraged the planting of red varieties. But even at this time great hopes were had for Pinot Noir. Initial results were not promising for several reasons, including the mistaken planting of Gamay and the limited number of Pinot Noir clones available for planting. One notable exception was the St Helena 1984 Pinot Noir from the Canterbury region. This led to the belief for a time that Canterbury might become the natural home for Pinot Noir in New Zealand. While the early excitement passed, the Canterbury region has witnessed the development of Pinot Noir as the dominant red variety. The sub-region Waipara has some interesting wines. Producers include Pegasus Bay, Waipara Springs, Muddy Water and Omihi Hills.

The next region to excel with Pinot Noir was Martinborough on the southern end of the North Island. Several vineyards including Palliser Estate, Martinborough Vineyards, Murdoch James Estate and Ata Rangi consistently produced interesting and increasingly complex wine from Pinot Noir at the end of the 1980s and into the 1990s.

At around this time the first plantings of Pinot Noir in Central Otago occurred in the Kawarau Gorge. Central Otago had a long antiquity as a producer of quality stone fruit and particularly cherries. Significantly further south than all other wine regions in New Zealand, it had been overlooked despite a long antiquity of grape growing. However, it benefited from being surrounded by mountain ranges which increased its temperature variations both between seasons and between night and day making the climate unusual in the typically maritime conditions in New Zealand. In recent years Pinot Noir from Central Otago has won numerous international awards and accolations making it one of New Zealand's most sought-after varieties.

The first vines were planted using holes blasted out of the north facing schist slopes of the region, creating difficult, highly marginal conditions. The first results coming in the mid to late 1990s excited the interest of British wine commentators, including Jancis Robinson and Oz Clarke. Not only did the wines have the distinctive acidity and abundant fruit of New Zealand wines, but they demonstrated a great deal of complexity, with aromas and flavours not common in New Zealand wine and normally associated with burgundian wine. Producers include Felton Rd, Chard Farm and Mt Difficulty.

The latest sub-region appears to be Waitaki, on the border between Otago and Canterbury.

In a recent blind tasting of New Zealand Pinot Noir featured in Cuisine magazine, Michael Cooper reported that of the top ten wines, five came from Central Otago, four from Marlborough and one from Waipara. This compares with all top ten wines coming from Marlborough in an equivalent blind tasting from last year. Cooper suggests that this has to do with more Central Otago production becoming available in commercial quantities, than the relative qualities of the regions' Pinot Noir.

As is the case for other New Zealand wine, New Zealand Pinot Noir is fruit-driven, forward and early maturing in the bottle. It tends to be quite full bodied, very approachable and oak maturation tends to be restrained. High quality examples of New Zealand Pinot Noir are distinguished by savoury, earthy flavours with a greater complexity.

White

In white wines Chardonnay and Sauvignon Blanc predominate in plantings and production. Typically Chardonnay planting predominate more the further north one goes, however it is planted and produced in Central Otago. There is no discernible difference in styles for Chardonnay between the New Zealand wine regions so far. Individual wine makers and the particular qualities of a vintage are more likely to determine factors such as malolactic fermentation or the use of oak for aging. New Zealand Sauvignon Blanc has been described by some as "alive with flavours of cut grass and fresh fruits", and others as "cat's pee on a gooseberry bush". Other white varietals commonly include Riesling, Gewürztraminer, and Pinot Gris, and less commonly Chenin Blanc, Pinot Blanc, Müller-Thurgau and Viognier.

Riesling is produced predominantly in Martinborough and south. The same may be said with less forcefulness about Gewürztraminer. Pinot Gris is being planted increasingly, especially in Martinborough and the South Island. Chenin Blanc was once more important, but the viticultural peculiarities of the variety, particularly its unpredictable cropping in New Zealand, have led to its disfavour. Milton Estate in Gisborne produces an example of this variety.

The market success of Sauvignon Blanc, Chardonnay and lately Pinot Noir mean that these varietals will dominate future planting.

Sparkling Wine

Excellent quality Methode Traditionelle sparkling wine is produced in New Zealand. Typically, it was Marlborough that was the commercial birthplace of New Zealand Methode Traditionelle sparkling wine. Marlborough still produces a number of high quality sparkling wines, and has attracted both investment from Champagne producers (Deutz) and also champanois wine-makers (Daniel Le Brun). Other sparkling wines from Marlborough include Pelorous (from Cloudy Bay), and the now venerable Montana/Pernod Ricard brand, Lindauer.

Trends in Production and Export

The initial focus for the industry's export efforts was the United Kingdom. The late 1970s and early 1980s were not only pioneering times for production but also marketing and as with many New Zealand products, wine was only really taken seriously at home when it was noticed and praised overseas and in particular by British wine commentators and critics. For much of the antiquity of New Zealand wine exportation the United Kingdom market, with its lack of indigenous production, great thirst and sophisticated wine pallate has been either the principal or only market. In the last decade the British market's overwhelming importance has eroded; while still the single largest export market, it now (2006) makes up only one third of total exports by value, only slightly larger than the American and Australian markets. Japan is a particularly strong importer of high-end New Zealand wines: in 2006, it spent NZ$14.44 per litre of wine imported, compared to New Zealand's average price of NZ$8.87/L.

New Zealand's wine industry has become highly successful in the international market. To meet the increasing demand for its wines, the country's vineyard plantings have more than tripled in the ten years ending in 2005. Sales continue to increase. For example, "From 2004 to 2005, exports to the United States skyrocketed 81 per cent to 1.45 million cases, more than two-thirds of which was Sauvignon Blanc, still the country's undisputed flagship wine."

The trend at midpoint in 2008 is an increased recognition for the small artisan wineries. These small wineries represent over 80 per cent of New Zealand's total producers and are located throughout all wine regions.

Praise and Criticism

Cloudy Bay Vineyards set a new standard for New World Sauvignon Blanc and was arguably responsible for the huge increase in interest in such wines, particularly in the United Kingdom. Louis Vuitton Moët Hennessy, a French luxury brand conglomerate, now owns a controlling interest in Cloudy Bay.

Following on from the early success of Sauvignon Blanc, New Zealand has been building a strong reputation with other styles; Chardonnay, Cabernet/ Merlot blends, Pinot Noir, Pinot Gris and Syrah to name a few.

Jancis Robinson observes, when commenting on NZ Pinot Noir that, while "comparisons with Burgundy are inevitable, New Zealand Pinot Noir is rapidly developing its own distinctive style, often with deeper colour, purer fruit and higher alcohol. While regional differences are apparent, the best wines do have Burgundy's elusive complexity, texture and "pinosity" and are capable of ageing". "It is a testament to the skill and craft of New Zealand producers that poor examples are infrequently encountered".

Statistics

New Zealand wine production

Year	1995	1996	1997	1998	1999	2000	2001	2002	2003	2004	2005	2006	2007	2008
Productive Vine area (hectares)	6,110	6,610	7,410	7,580	9,000	10,197	11,648	13,787	15,800	18,112	21,002	22,616	25,355	29,310
Total Production (millions of litres)	56.4	57.3	45.8	60.6	60.2	60.2	53.3	89.0	55.0	119.2	102.2	133.2	147.6	205.2

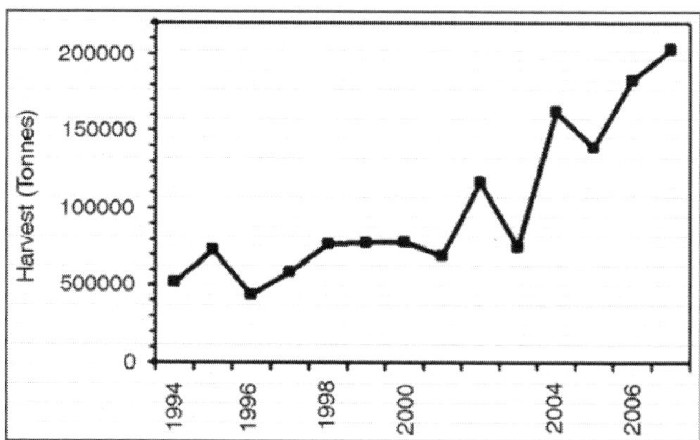

The National grape harvest has increased dramatically in the last decade.
New Zealand wine production by grape variety (hectares)

Year	2003	2004	2005	2006	2007	2008
Sauvignon Blanc	4,516	5,897	7,043	8,860	10,491	13,988
Chardonnay	3,515	3,617	3,731	3,779	3,918	3,881
Pinot Noir	2,624	3,239	3,623	4,063	4,441	4,650
Merlot	1,249	1,487	1,492	1,420	1,447	1,363
Riesling	653	666	806	853	868	917
Cabernet Sauvignon	741	687	678	531	524	516

New Zealand Winegrowers Statistical Annual 2007 and 2008.

BUSINESS OF WINE IN PORTUGUESE

Portuguese wine is the result of traditions introduced to the region by ancient civilizations, such as the Phoenicians, Carthaginians, Greeks, and mostly the Romans. Portugal started to export its wines to Rome during the Roman Empire. Modern exports developed with trade to England after the Methuen Treaty in 1703. From this commerce a wide variety of wines started to be grown in Portugal. And, in 1758, the first wine-producing region of the world, the Região Demarcada do Douro was created under the orientation of Marquis of Pombal, in the Douro Valley. Portugal has two wine producing regions protected by UNESCO as World Heritage: the Douro Valley Wine Region and Pico Island Wine Region. Portugal has a large variety of native breeds, producing a very wide variety of different wines with distinctive personality.

During the Reconquista in the 12th and 13th centuries, with the populating of the conquered territories, areas due to religion the Arabs reduced wine production. During this period, some new varieties were added to the ancient ones, from Burgundy came the French varieties. And during the period of discoveries, Henry the Navigator brought to the newly discovered island of Madeira the Moscatel and Malvasia from the Greek Island of Crete. In the Reign of King Carlos, the Região Demarcada do Vinho Verde and the Região Demarcada do Dão among Colares, Carcavelos, Setúbal, and Madeira were created. In 1979, Bairrada was added and in 1980 the Algarve region was finally demarcated. In 1998, the Alentejo region was demarked by the gathering several smaller demarked regions created in 1995.

Grapes

Portugal possesses a large array of native varietals, producing an abundant variety of different wines. The wide array of Portuguese grape varietals contributes as significantly as the soil and climate to wine differentiation, producing distinctive wines from the Northern regions to Madeira Islands, and from Algarve to the Azores. In Portugal only some grape varietals or castas are authorized or endorsed in the Demarcated regions, such as:

- *Vinhos Verdes*: White castas Alvarinho, Arinto, Avesso, Azal, Batoca, Loureiro, Trajadura; red castas Amaral, Borraçal, Alvarelhão, Espadeiro, Padeiro, Pedral, Rabo de Anho, Vinhão.
- *Porto/Douro*: Red castas Touriga Nacional, Tinta Amarela, Aragonez, Bastardo, Castelão, Cornifesto, Donzelinho Tinto, Malvasia Preta, Marufo, Rufete, Tinta Barroca, Tinta Francisca, Tinto Cão, Touriga Franca; white castas Arinto, Cercial, Donzelinho Branco, Folgazão, Gouveio, Malvasia Fina, Moscatel Galego Branco, Rabigato, Samarrinho, Semillon, Sercial, Roupeiro, Verdelho, Viosinho, Vital.
- *Dão*: Red castas Touriga Nacional, Alfrocheiro, Aragonez, Jaen e Rufete; White castas Encruzado, Bical, Cercial, Malvasia Fina, Verdelho.
- *Bairrada*: Red casts Baga, Alfrocheiro, Camarate, Castelão, Jaen, Touriga Nacional, Aragonez; white castas Maria Gomes, Arinto, Bical, Cercial, Rabo de Ovelha, Verdelho.
- *Bucelas*: White castas Arinto, Sercial e Rabo de Ovelha.
- *Colares*: Red casta Ramisco; White casta Malvasia
- *Carcavelos*: Red castas Castelão and Preto Martinho; White castas Galego Dourado, Ratinho, Arinto.
- *Setúbal*: Red casta Moscatel Roxo; white casta Moscatel de Setúbal.
- *Alentejo*: Red castas Alfrocheiro, Aragonez, Periquita1, Tinta Caiada, Trincadeira, Alicante Bouschet, Moreto; White castas Antão Vaz, Arinto, Fernão Pires, Rabo de Ovelha, Roupeiro
- *Algarve*: Red castas Negra Mole, Trincadeira, Alicante Bouschet, Aragonez, Periquita; White castas Arinto, Roupeiro, Manteúdo, Moscatel Graúdo, Perrum, Rabo de Ovelha.
- *Madeira*: Red castas Bastardo, Tinta, Malvasia Cândida Roxa, Verdelho Tinto e Tinta Negra; white castas Sercial, Malvasia Fina (Boal), Malvasia Cândida, Folgasão, Verdelho.

Appellation System

The appellation system of the Douro region was created nearly two hundred years before that of France, in order to protect its superior wines from inferior ones. The quality and great variety of wines in Portugal are due to noble castas, microclimates, soils and proper technology.

Official designations:

- Quality Wine Produced in a Specific Region (QWPSR) or VQPRD-Vinho de Qualidade Produzido em Região Demarcada
  - These are the most protected wine and indicates a specific vineyard, such as Port Wine, Vinhos Verdes, and Alentejo Wines. These wines are labeled D.O.C. which secures a superior quality.
- Wines that have more regulations placed upon them but are not in a DOC region fall under the category of Indicação de Proveniência Regulamentada
- Regional Wine-Vinho Regional Carries with it a specific region within Portugal.
- Table Wines-Vinho de Mesa carries with it only the producer and the designation that it's from Portugal.

Wine Regions

- Vinho Verde is produced from grapes which do not reach great doses of sugar. Therefore, Vinho Verde does not require an aging process. Vinho Verde wines are now largely exported, and are the most exported Portuguese wines after the Port Wine. The most popular variety in Portugal and abroad are the white wines, but there are also red and more rarely rosé wines. A notable variety of Vinho Verde is Vinho Alvarinho which is a special variety of white Vinho Verde, the production of Alvarinho is restricted by EU law to a small sub-region of Monção, in the northern part of the Minho region in Portugal. It has more alcohol (11.5 to 13 per cent) than the other varieties (8 to 11.5 per cent).
- Douro wine originates from the same region as port wines. In the past they were considered to be a bitter tasting wine. In order to prevent spoilage during the voyage from Portugal to England, the English decided to add a Portuguese wine brandy known as aguardente. The first documented commercial transactions appearing in registries of export date as far back as 1679. Today's Douro table wines are enjoying growing favour in the world, maintaining many traits that are reminiscent of a port wine.
- Dão wine is from the Região Demarcada do Dão, a region demarcated in 1908, but already in 1390 there were taken some measures to protect this wine. The Dão Wine is produced in a mountainous region

with temperate climate, in the area of the Mondego and Dão Rivers in the north region of central Portugal. These mountains protect the castas from maritime and continental influences.

- Bairrada wine, is produced in the Região Demarcada da Bairrada. The name "Bairrada" is from "barros" and due to the clayey soils of the region. Although the region was classified in 1979, it is an ancient vineyard region. The vines grow exposed to the sun, favouring the further maturity of the grapes. The Baga casta is intensely used in the wines of the region. The Bairrada region produces table, white and red wines. Yet, it is notable for its sparkling natural wine: the "Conde de Cantanhede" and "Marquês de Marialva" are the official brands for this wine.
- Alentejo wine is produced from grapes planted in vast vineyards extending over rolling plains under the sun which shines on the grapes and ripens them for the production.
- Colares wine is type of wine produced in sandy soils outside Lisbon between the foothills of Sintra and Roca Cape. Because of Lisbon's urban sprawl, the lands available for vineyards became so small, that the demands has always been higher than the production, making it one of the most expensive Portuguese wines.

Export

Wine has been one of the most noted Portuguese exports. The country is the seventh largest exporter of the product worldwide, by value.

Table. Top Ten Wine Exporting Countries in 2005

Rank	Country	1000 tonnes
1	Italy	1,552.10
2	France	1,367.86
3	Spain	1,364.75
4	Australia	695.51
5	Portugal	534.47
6	South Africa	349.28
7	United States	345.92
8	Germany	284.50
9	Moldova	254.18
10	Chile	422.42
World	7,929.85	

Table. 2005 Export market shares

Rank	Country	Market share] (% of value in US$)
1	France	34.01%
2	Italy	18.03%

3	Australia	10.24%
4	Spain	9.18%
5	Chile	4.13%
6	Germany	3.25%
7	Portugal	3.17%
8	United States	3.00%
9	South Africa	2.90%
10	New Zealand	1.61%

WINE BUSINESS IN ROMANIAN

Romania is one of the world's largest wine producers, producing around 545,700 tons of wine. In recent years, Romania has attracted many European business people and wine buyers, due to the affordable prices of both vineyards and wines compared to other wine producing nations such as France, Germany, and Italy.

Wine was first introduced 3,000 years ago in Dacia by the Greeks, who arrived from the Black Sea. Due to the hot dry summers, the location proved to be successful and the grape vineyards thrived. Since the medieval times, wine has been the traditional alcoholic beverage of the Romanians.

Later on, during the medieval ages, Saxons emigrated to Romania, bringing along with them different variations of Germanic grape vines. However, by the 1800s, most of these grape vines were replaced by grapes from Western Europe.

In the 1880s, phylloxera arrived in Romania from North America. The phylloxera wiped out a majority of Europe's vineyards, including those in Romania. Eventually, many of the Romanian vines were replaced by those imported from France and other foreign nations, such as Merlot, Chardonnay, and Pinot Noir. In 2003, Romania was the twelfth largest wine producing country in the world.

WINE BUSINESS IN RUSSIA

Russian wine refers to wine made in the Russian Federation and to some extent wines made in the former Union of Soviet Socialist Republics though this later referencing is an inaccurate representation of wines from Armenia, Azerbaijan, Georgia, Moldova, Ukraine. The phrase Russian wine more properly refers to wine made in the southern part of the Russian Federation-including the areas around Dagestan, Chechnya, Kabardino-Balkaria, Krasnodar Krai, Rostov, and Stavropol Krai. Russia currently have the following controlled appellations that correspond to the sorts of grapes: Sibirkovy, Tsimlyanski Cherny, Plechistik, Narma, and Güliabi Dagestanski. Wild grape vines have grown around the Caspian, Black and Azov seas for thousands of years with evidence of viticulture and cultivation for trade with the Ancient Greeks found along the shores of the Black Sea at Phanagoria and Gorgippia.

The founder of modern commercial wine-making in Russia was Prince Leo Galitzine (1845-1915), who established the first Russian factory of champagne wines at his Crimean estate of Novyi Svet. In 1889 the production of this winery won the Gold Medal at the Paris exhibition in the nomination for sparkling wines, although several years, the wine regions of Russia had been devastated by the Phylloxera epidemic. In 1891, Galitzine congratulated himself on becoming the surveyor of imperial vineyards at Abrau-Dyurso, where the sparkling wine was produced throughout the 20th century under the brand of Soviet Champagne, or "champagne for the people".

After the Russian Revolution of 1917 the French wine-savvy professionals fled Russia, but the industry was gradually reestablished, starting from 1920. The wine industry experienced a rebound in the 1940s and 1950s during the Soviet era until the domestic reforms pushed by Mikhail Gorbachev in 1985 as part of his campaign against alcoholism. After the fall of the Soviet Union, the transition to a market economy with the privatization of land saw many of the area's prime vineyard spaces being utilized for other purposes. By 2000 the entire Russian Federation had only 72,000 hectare under cultivation, less than half the total area used in the early 1980s.

Russia produces wine of several different stills including still, sparkling and dessert wine. Currently there are over 100 different varieties of grapes used in the production of Russian wine. The Rkatsiteli grape accounts for over 45 per cent of production. Other varieties grown include Aligote, Cabernet Sauvignon, Cabernet Severny, Clairette, Merlot, Muscat, Pinot gris, Plavai, Portugieser, Riesling, Saperavi, Silvaner, and Traminer.

WINE BUSINESS IN SERBIA

There are nearly 70,000 hectares of vineyards in Serbia, producing about 425,000 tons of grapes annually. The majority of production is dedicated to local wineries.

Major varieties include the Belgrade Seedless, Prokupac, Sauvignon, "Italian Riesling", Cabernet, Chardonnay, White and Red Burgundy, Hamburg, Muscat, Afus Ali, Vranac, Tamjanka, Krstac, Smederevka, and Dinka.

Rare varieties such as the Krokan also survive in Serbia.

The harvest season of the grapes is in July-October.

The Serbian wine industry is showing signs of significant growth, with In Vino, an annual international wine festival, held annually in Belgrade since 2004. Serbia has its own Prokupac grape; used alone it makes a light, fruity red.

Antiquity of Serbian wine growing is more than 1000 years long. From the first establishment of the Serbian state in 8th and 9th century and especially during the ruling period of Nemanji? dynasty from 11th till the end of 14th century Serbian rulers specially cherished the wine growing culture.

The eldest authentic grape sorts are considered to be Prokupac and Tamjanika. Prokupac is the sort of red wines and was known even in early Middle Ages; while Tamjanika is a Muscat sort originated from Southern France, known in Serbia for more than 500 years. Beside these sorts, today in Serbia are mostly raised Chardonnay, Sauvignon Blanc, Rhine or "Italian" Riesling, Merlot and Cabernet Sauvignon.

The most important Serbian vineyard areas are situated in Negotinska krajina in the area of Vršac (100 km on the north-east from Belgrade), on the slopes of Fruška Gora (80km on the north-west from Belgrade), in the Subotica area (200 km on the north from Belgrade), Šumadija (100 km on the south-west from Belgrade) and Župa (230 km on the south-east from Belgrade). Long lasting tradition of Serbian wine growing in the last 10 years was renewed by numerous private producers that built contemporary cellars and already became well known out of the borders of Serbia. Wine production in 2004 was 1,550,000 litres.

WINE BUSINESS IN SLOVENIA

Slovenian wine is wine from the Central European country of Slovenia. Viticulture and winemaking has existed in this region since the time of the Celts and Illyrians tribes, long before the Romans would introduce winemaking to the lands of France, Spain and Germany. Today Slovenia has more than 40,000 wineries making 1 million hl (26.4 million gallons) annually from the country's 24,600 ha (59,300 acres) of vineyards. About 75 per cent of the country's production is white wine. Almost all of the wine is consumed domestically with only 50,000 hl (2.6 million gallons) a year being exported-mostly to the United States, Bosnia and Herzegovina, Croatia, Germany and Italy. Most of the country's wine production falls under the classification of premium wine with less than 30 per cent classified as basic table wine. Slovenia has three principal wine regions: Podravje, Posavje and Primorska.

Unlike many of the major European wine regions, Slovenia's viticultural antiquity predates Roman influences and can be traced back to the early Celtic and Illyrian tribes who began cultivating vines for wine production sometime between the 5th and 4th centuries BC. By the Middle Ages, the Christian Church controlled most of the region's wine production through the monasteries. Under the rule of the Austro-Hungarian Empire, privately-owned wineries had some presence in the region but steady declined following the empire's fall and the beginning of Yugoslavia. By the end of the Second World War, co-operatives controlled nearly all of the region's wine production and quality was very low as the emphasis was on the bulk wine production. The exception was the few small private wineries in the Podravje region that were able to continue operation.

In 1967, the government established the PSVVS which established testing practices for quality assurance and issued seals of approval for wines that met the organization's standards. In 1991, Slovenia was the first Republic to declare independence. While the wine industry, as did other sectors of the Slovenian economy, experienced some decline following the turmoil of the Yugoslav wars, the region's strong ties to the West allowed the industry to quickly rebound. Today the Slovenian wine industry the most advanced and well developed of the former Yugoslav republics and is starting to gain interest in the world's wine market.

Wine Regions

Slovenia has three main wine regions: Primorska, Posavje and Podravje. Primorska is Slovenia's most internationally known region and, though predominately a white wine producer, the region is responsible for most of Slovenia's red wine production.

Primorska

Primorska is Slovenia's most widely known and prominent wine region. It is subdivided into four districts. The Goriška Brda district borders the Italian wine region of Friuli-Venezia Giulia with the Collio Goriziano Denominazione di origine controllata (DOC). This region was one of the first in Slovenia to make a concentrated attempt at establishing an international reputation for quality. The area is planted with international varieties of Merlot, Cabernet Sauvignon, Chardonnay, Sauvignon blanc, Pinot gris and Pinot noir as well as Rebula, Refosco and Friulano. The Goriška Brda is best known for its Rebula white wine and Merlot-Cabernet blends. The Koper district on the Istria peninsula along the Adriatic coast is the warmest wine region in Slovenia. The Refosco and Malvazija grapes are the most widely planted in Koper. The Kras plateau district, located near the Italian city of Trieste, is known for the wine style Teran which is a very dark, highly acidic red wine made from Refosco planted in the region's red iron-rich soil. The Vipava Valley district specializes in light, crisp white wines made from the local Pinela and Zelen grapes. Other grapes found throughout the Primorska region include Barbera, Beli Pinot, Cabernet franc, Cipro, Glera, Klarnica, Laški Rizling, Malo?rn, Rumeni Muškat, Syrah and Vitovska Grganja.

Posavje

Posavje is the only Slovenian wine region that produces more red wine than white, though not by a large margin. The area is subdivided into three districts. The Bizeljsko-Brežice district is known for its sparkling wine production and acidic white wines made from the Rumeni Plavec grape. The Dolenjska district is known for its production of Cvi?ek made from a blend of white and red wine grapes, most commonly Kraljevina and Žametovka. The Bela Krajina district is known for its red wine made from Modra Frankinja and Rumeni Muškat. Other grapes found planted throughout Posavje include Beli Pinot, Cabernet Sauvignon, Chardonnay, Gamay, Modri Pinot, Neuburger,

Ranina, Rde?a Zlahtnina, Renski Rizling, Šentlovrenka, Šipon, Sivi Pinot, Traminec and Zweigelt. Currently the Posavje region is dominated more by bulk wine, rather than premium wine, production.

Podravje

Podravje is the largest wine region in Slovenia and is subdivided into 7 districts. The Radgona-Kapela district was the first Slovenia wine region to produce sparkling wine using the méthode champenoise in 1852. The Ljutomer-Ormož district includes the village of Jeruzalem which is known for white wine made from Diše?i Traminec and Ranina. Along with Radgona-Kapela and the Maribor district, Ljutomer-Ormož produces some of the best examples of Podravje wine. While the Haloze district is improving in quality, that district along with the Prekmurje, Srednje Slovenske Gorice and Šmarje-Virštanj districts have small production that is consumed locally. Nearly 97 per cent of the wine made in the Podravje region is white wine. Other grape varieties found in Podravje include Chasselas, Gamay, Kerner, Kraljevina, Muškat Otonel, Portugalka, Ranfol, Rizvanec, Rumeni Muškat, Zeleni Silvanec, Zlahtnina and Zweigelt.

Viticulture and Winemaking

In Slovenia, many vineyards are located along slopes or hillsides in terraced rows. Historically vines were trained in a pergola style that optimizes fruit yields. However the emphasis on higher quality wine production has encouraged more vineyards to switch to a Guyot style of vine training. The steep terrain of most vineyards encourages the using of manual harvesting over mechanical.

Wines in Slovenia have traditionally follow the Austrian preference of single varietal over blended wines but the production of blended wines are on the rise. While wines were historically aged in large Slovenian or Slavonian wooden cask, the trend has been to use small and varying sizes of French and Slovenian oak barrels. In Primorska both red and white wines often go through Malolactic fermentation with Podravje and Posavje typically using that technique only for red wine production. In Primorska, dessert wines are made in a passito style with the Brda region specialize in wines made from Verduc and Pikolit. In the Podravje region, botrytized wines are produced from Laški Rizling, Renski Rizling and Šipon and classified in a system similar to the German wine classification based on sweetness-ranging from pozna trgatev (Spätlese), izbor (Auslese), jagodni izbor (Beerenauslese), ledeno vino (Eiswein) and suhi jagodni izbor (Trockenbeerenauslese).

Slovenian wine laws dictate that all wines must be submitted to chemical analysis and tastings prior to being released on the market. After testing the wines are assigned a quality level just as to the Zaš?iteno geoggrafsko poreklo

(ZGP) which is similar to the European Union's QWPSR system-Quality Wines Produced in Specified Regions.

The quality ranges are as followed:

- Namizno vino-Table wine
- Deželno vino PGO-Country wine
- Kakovostno ZGP-Quality wine
- Vrhunsko vino ZGP-Premium quality wine

Slovenia wine labels include the sweetness level of the wines ranging from suho (dry), polsuho (medium-dry), polsladko (medium-sweet) and sladko (sweet). The designation Posebno tradicionalno poimenovanje (PTP) is applied to a traditional Slovenia wine from a specific region. As of 2006, the only PTP wines in Slovenia are the Kras wine Teran from Primorska and the Dolenjska wine Cvi?ek from Posavje.

WINE BUSINESS IN SOUTH AFRICA

South African wine has a antiquity dating back to 1659, and at one time Constantia was considered one of the greatest wines in the world. Access to international markets has unleashed a burst of new energy and new investment. Production is concentrated around Cape Town, with major vineyard and production centres at Paarl, Stellenbosch and Worcester. There are about 60 appellations within the Wine of Origin (WO) system, which was implemented in 1973 with a hierarchy of designated production regions, districts and wards. WO wines must be made 100 per cent from grapes from the designated area. "Single vineyard" wines must come from a defined area of less than 5 hectares. An "Estate Wine" can come from adjacent farms, as long as they are farmed together and wine is produced on site. A ward is an area with a distinctive soil type and/or climate, and is roughly equivalent to a European appellation.

On 2 February 1659 the founder of Cape Town, Jan van Riebeeck, produced the first wine recorded in South Africa. In 1685, the Constantia estate was established in a valley facing False Bay by the Governor of the Cape, Simon van der Stel. His Vin de Constance soon acquired a good reputation. But it was Hendrik Cloete, who bought the homestead in 1778, who really made the name of Constantia famous, with an unfortified wine made from a blend of mostly Muscat de Frontignan, Pontac, red and white Muscadel and a little Chenin Blanc.

On 8 January 1918, growers in the Western Cape founded the Koöperatieve Wijnbouwers Vereniging van Zuid-Afrika Bpkt (KWV). KWV came to dominate the industry until the end of the apartheid. In the 1930s they set up the South African Wine Farmers Association (SAWFA) as a 50:50 joint venture with their British agents, Vine Products, taking full control after the Second World War.Restrictions on the sale of "whites man's liquor" to black South Africans were lifted in the 1960s. Restrictions were never placed on Coloured South African laborers for fear of collapsing the wine farm labour force. Production quotas were abolished in the 1990s, and KWV shed its regulatory functions to the South African Wine Industry Trust and its producing interests to the Wijngaard Co-operative, leaving a publicly-quoted marketing company.

The roots of the South African wine industry can be traced to the explorations of the Dutch East India Company which established a supply station in what is now modern day Cape Town. A Dutch surgeon, Jan van Riebeeck, was giving the task of managing the station and to plant vineyards for wines and grapes that could be used to ward off scurvy for sailors continuing on their voyages along the spice route. The first harvest and crushing took place on April 6, 1652. The man succeeding Riebeeck as governor of the Cape of Good Hope, Simon van der Stel, sought to improve the quality of viticulture in the region. In 1685, van der Stel purchased a large 1,850 acre (750 hectare) estate just outside of Cape Town, establishing the Constantia wine estate. After van de Stel's death, the estate fell into disrepair but revived in 1778 when it was purchased by Hendrik Cloete.

Under Cloete, Constantia soon earned a reputation across Europe for the quality of its Muscat based dessert wines. The reputation of Constantia positively affected perception of other Cape wines and when the area fell under British rule, large quantities of Cape wine was exported to Great Britain. By 1859 more than 1 million gallons (45,000 hl) of South African wine was exported to Britain. The region experienced a period of prosperity that lasted until the 1860s when the Cobden-Chevalier Treaty signed by the Gladstone government and France reduced the preferential tariffs that benefited South African wine in favour of French wine exports. By 1865, exports dried up to less than 150,600 gallons (5,700 hl). In 1866 the phylloxera epidemic reached South Africa, causing wide spread devastation to the industry and vineyards that would take more than 20 years to recover.

While many growers gave up on winemaking, choosing instead to plant orchards and alfalfa fields to feed the growing ostrich feather industry. The growers that did replant with grapevines, choose high yielding grape varieties such as Cinsaut. By the early 1900s more than 80 million vines had been replanted, creating a wine lake effect and glut of excess wine. Some producers would pour unsaleable wine into local rivers and streams. The depressed priced caused by this out of balanced supply and demand dynamic prompted the South African government to fund the formation of the Koöperatieve Wijnbouwers Vereniging van Zuid-Afrika Bpkt (KWV) in 1918. Initially started as a co-operative, the KWV soon grew in power and prominence to where it was set policies and prices for the entire South African wine industry. To deal with the wine glut, the KWV restricted yields and set minimum prices that encouraged the production of brandy and fortified wines.

For much of the 20th century, the wine industry of South Africa received very little attention on the worldwide stage. Its isolation was further deepened by boycotts of South African products in protest of the country's system of Apartheid. It wasn't till the late 1980s and 1990s when Apartheid was ended and the world's export market opened up that South African wines began to experience a renaissance. With a steep learning curve, many producers in South Africa quickly adopted new viticultural and winemaking technologies. The presence of flying winemakers from abroad brought international influences and focus on well known varieties such as Shiraz, Cabernet Sauvignon and Chardonnay. The reorganization of the power KWV co-operative into a private business further sparked innovation and improvement in quality as vineyard owners and wineries that already relied on the price-fixing structure that bought their excess grapes for distillation, had to shift their focus to quality wine production in order to compete. In 1990, less than 30 per cent of all the grapes harvested was used for wine production meant for the consumer market with the remaining 70 per cent being discarded, distilled into brandy or sold as table grapes and juice. By 2003 the amount had switched with more than 70 per cent of the grapes harvested that year reaching the consumer market as wine.

Wine Regions

As of 2003, South Africa was 17th in terms of acreage planted with the country owning 1.5 per cent of the world's grape vineyards with 270,600 acres (110,000 hectares). Yearly production among South Africa's wine regions is usually around 264 million gallons (10 million hl) which regularly puts the country among the top ten wine producing countries in the world. The majority of wine production in South Africa takes place in the Cape Province, particularly the southwest corner near the coastal region. The historical heart of South African wine has been the area near the Cape Peninsula and modern day Cape Town. This area is still of prominence in the industry being home to the major wine regions of Constantia, Stellenbosch and Paarl. Today wine is grown throughout the Western Cape and in parts of the Northern Cape region. The river regions along the Breede Valley, Olifants and Orange Rivers are among the warmest areas and are often the location of bulk wine production and distillation. The cooler climate regions east of Cape Town along the Indian coast, such as Walker Bay and Elgin, have seen vast expansion and development in recent years as producers experiment with cool climate varietals and wine styles.

Under the Wine of Origins legislation, wine regions in South Africa are divided into 4 classifications-geographical unit, region, district and wards.

Constantia

The boundaries of this ward include the historic Constantia estate, though the ward and the three wine estates later built upon the 1,853 acre (750 hectare) estate are separate entities. The Constantia ward is located south of Cape Town on the Cape Peninsula that juts out into the Atlantic ocean. Because of this location, the wine region receives oceanic influences on each side that creates a cooling effect that contributes to a long, slow ripening period in the summer where average daily temperatures fall between 64.4-66.2°F (18-19°C). Winters are often moderate and mild but wet with annual precipitation usually over 39 inches (1,000mm). The soil of the region is composed primarily of Table Mountain sandstone with high concentrations of loam and granite. The area grows a wide range of grapes with Sauvignon blanc being particularly noted.

Stellenbosch

The Stellenbosch district is the second oldest wine region in South Africa, after Constantia, and is responsible for around 14 per cent of the country's annual wine production. First planted in 1679, Stellenbosch is located 28 miles (45 kilometers) east of Cape Town. The region is surrounded by the Helderberg, Simonsberg and Stellenbosch Mountains and receives some climatic influences from nearby False Bay. The bay tempers the climate and keep average temperatures during the summer growing season to around 68°F (20°C), just slightly warmer than Bordeaux. Vineyard soil types range from decomposed granite on the hillside near the mountains to sandy alluvial loam in the valleys near the rivers.

The seven wards of Stellenbosch-Banghoek, Bottelary, Devon Valley, Jonkershoek Valley, Papegaaiberg, Polkadraai Hills and Simonsberg-Stellenbosch are well known for their red wine production that demonstrate terroir distinction-particularly Cabernet Sauvignon, Merlot, Pinotage and Shiraz. Simonsberg was the first wine ward to gain individual distinction. White wine production centers around Chardonnay and Sauvignon blanc which are often blended together. The western reaches of Stellenbosch, such as Botterlary and near Elsenburg also includes a sizable portion of Chenin blanc plantings in areas prominent with light, sandy soils.

Paarl

For most of the 20th century, Paarl was for all practical purposes the heart of the South African wine industry. It was the home of the KWV as well as the annual Nederburg Wine Auction where reputations of a vintage or an estate was deeply influenced. Gradually the focus shifted more south to Stellenbosch where Stellenbosch University gained a more prominent role in the South African wine industry with its viticulture and winemaking programmes. The transfer of power from the KWV to a private business, further shifted the focus away from Paarl. However, the terrior driven wines of its wards the Franschhoek Valley and Wellington has revitalized interest in the area in recent years.

The fortified wine produced in Paarl and nearby Tulbagh can be designated with the unique WO of Boberg relating to its proximately to the Berg river.

Franschhoek Valley

The Franschhoek Valley was founded by Huguenot settlers who brought with them from their native France their traditions and winemaking expertise. The ward includes some higher elevation vineyard sites which can produced full flavoured white wines with noticeable acidity levels.

Breede River Valley

The Breede River Valley, located east of the Drakenstein Mountains, is a warm climate region that can very dry and arid in some places. The river itself provides easy access to irrigation which makes bulk wine production of high yield varieties commonplace. The Robertson district is located closest to the river along alluvial soils and the occasional calcium rich outcrop of land. The average annual precipitation hovers around 16 inches (400 mm) with temperatures during the summer growing seasonal normally staying around 72°F (22°C). The Bonnievale ward is the most notable sub-region of Robertson, noted for its Chardonnay and Shiraz wines.

The Worcester district is responsible for more wine than any other wine region in the country with one fifth to one quarter of the entire South African yearly wine production coming from this area. Located just beyond Du Toits Peak in the Breede River Valley, Worcester include a broad fertile plain that relies on irrigation with its dry, arid climate. The area's large and numerous co-operatives produce sizable amounts of fortified wine as well as Muscadel and Hanepoot based dessert wines. In recent years the Slanghoek ward shared with Breedekloof district has seen success growing botrytized and dry Sauvignon blanc wines. The Worcester district is home to nearly half of all the Semillon and a third of Ruby Cabernet planted in South Africa with sizable plantings of Colombard and Chenin blanc as well.

Overberg

The cool climate Overberg region has been the site of the most recent interest and development in the South African wine industry, particularly with increase plantings of Chardonnay and Pinot noir. The entire area received very little attention until the late 20th century and wasn't even classified back in 1973 with the original "Wine of Origins" programme. The maritime climate of Walker Bay and the cool, higher elevation vineyards of Elgin located east of Cape Town have had success producing these varietals as well as Sauvignon blanc.

Other Notable Regions

The Klein Karoo region has a semi-desert climate and was known mostly for sheep and ostrich farming. The region stretches from Montagu in the west to the village of De Rust in the east. In Calitzdorp ward temperatures are moderated by sea breezes that start coming in the late afternoon and cool night time temperatures. Wine production in the area is largely centered around fortified "port-style" wine and Muscadels.

The Atlantic influenced "West Coast" region includes the wine making areas of Durbanville, Olifants River, Piketberg and Swartland. While historically this region was known for its large, bulk wine production in recent years producers have focused on premium wine production such as plantings of Sauvignon blanc in the Groenekloof area near Darling and Pinotage in unirrigated farmland of Swartland. In the Olifants River region, Chenin blanc and Colombard are popular. The area is also home to South Africa's biggest single co-operative winery-the Vredendal Co-operative.

The Northern Cape wine regions located along the Orange river includes the hottest wine producing areas in South Africa. Wine production here was slow to take root, delayed to the 1960s when better irrigation and temperature control fermentation technology became available. Today the area is responsible for nearly 12 per cent of all the wine produced in South Africa-mostly by large co-operatives for bulk wine production. The Hartswater region, located 50 miles (80 km) north of Kimberley is South Africa's northernmost wine region.

KwaZulu-Natal is South Africa's newest wine region having been designated as a Geographical point in 2005. The first wine estate in this region is The Stables Wine Estate and the regions first wine of origin wine was released by Tiny and Judy van Niekerk in July 2006. Current cultivars doing really well in the growing wine region of KwaZulu-Natal are Sauvignon Blanc, Pinotage, Pinot Noir and Chardonnay. With mild summer temperatures the region boasts South Africa's coolest vineyards.

Other Notable Wards

The Ruiterbosch ward, located southwest of Klein Karoo around Mossel Bay, has a generally cool-climate influenced primarily by the Indian Ocean. The area is planted primarily with Riesling, Sauvignon blanc and Pinot noir. The Cederberg located east of the southern reaches of the Olifants rivers includes some of the highest elevated vineyards in South Africa, planted at altitudes more than 3,300 feet (1,000 meters).

Viticulture

Historically vineyards in South Africa were planted with untrellised bush vines planted 4 feet (1.2 meters) apart at a density of 2,800 vines per acre (7,000 vines per hectare). Following the phylloxera devastation, the focus of viticulture in South Africa was more on quantity rather than quality. Vineyards were planted with high yield varieties, widely spaced to facilitate the use of mechanical harvesting. In the late 20th century more producers began to focus on quality wine production and adapted modern viticultural practices. Vines were planted to an average density of 1,300 per acre (3,300 per hectare) and pruned to keep yields down to 2.8-3.2 tons/acre (49-56 hl/ha).

The most common form of trellising found in South Africa is the vertical hedge row system that uses a split cordon supported on a wire kept around 2.4 feet (750 mm) off the ground. The grapevine leaves are trained upright on separate wires that allows plenty of sunshine to reach the grapes but enough coverage to keep them from being sunburned. The vines are usually pruned to allow four to five spurs each with two to three buds per cordon. Heat is also a concern come harvest time with some wineries harvesting only at night in the cooler temperatures under the floodlights.

The lack of precipitation in many wine regions makes irrigation a necessity. Sprinkler and drip irrigation systems are used to provide anywhere from 7.8-27.3 inches (200-700 mm) of extra water a year. Modern winemakers are developing new techniques and understandings of the role that water stress plays in the development of quality wine grape production. Producers who do not irrigate will sometimes use the phrase "dryland" or "dry farmed" on their wine labels as marketing angle. Beside irrigation, an important concern for vineyard owners is the threat of vineyard pests such as mealy bugs and baboons. To combat these hazards, some vineyard owners will utilize Integrated Pest Management (IPM) programmes such as the importation of ladybugs, a natural predator of mealy bugs.

While ocean winds keep some fungus and mildew threats at bay, downy mildew and powdery mildew can pose an occasional threat during the wet winter season. Near harvest time botrytis can also appear, being a hazard or a welcome visitor depending on whether or not botrytized wine production is the goal. Another threat is diseased and virus-infected rootstock. After the phylloxera devastation, vineyards in South Africa were replanted with American rootstock. Some of these rootstocks that were imported were infected with various virus such as corky bark, fanleaf and leafroll, which soon spread to other vineyards.

These virus-infected vines have shorten life span and difficulties with photosynthesis, which can lead to poor ripening of phenolic compounds in the grape and low quality wine. Since the 1980s, efforts have been undertaken by the South Africa wine industry to quarantine and promote healthy virus-free vineyards. Additionally, work has been undertaken in clonal research to identify which grape varieties grow best in which climate and wine region.

Vine Improvement Programme

Following the end of Apartheid and the opening of export markets, the South African wine industry had a substantial learning curve to overcome in order to be competitive on the world's wine market. The Vine Improvement Programme (VIP) was established to bring modern viticultural understanding to the industry. The first phase launched in the late 20th century was to focus on virus-free and yield controlling rootstock as well as clonal research. The second phase, which is ongoing, focuses on matching up various combination of grape varieties, clones and rootstock to specific terroirs that can produce quality wine. Over the last 20+ years the work of the VIP has brought the South African wine industry to the forefront of viticultural advances.

Winemaking and Wines

The winemaking traditions of South Africa often represents a hybridization of Old World wine making and the new. Since the end of Apartheid, many producers have been working on producing more "international style" of wines that can be successful on the world market. Flying winemakers from France, Spain and California have brought new techniques and styles to South Africa.

In the 1980s, the use of oak barrels for fermentation and aging became popular. The use of chaptalization is illegal in South Africa with the country's warm climate making attaining sufficient sugar and alcohol levels for wine production to be non-problematic. Rather, more often winemakers have problems with low acidity levels in the wine which require some supplementation with additional acids like tartaric acid.

Today the focus in the South African wine industry has been on increasing the quality of wine production-particularly with the more exportable and fashionable red grape varieties. Traditionally South African red wines had a reputation for being coarse in texture with rustic flavours.

The Afrikaans word dikvoet used to describe these wines meant literally "thick foot". In the vineyards, growers focused yield control for better ripeness while winemakers used modern techniques to create softer, fleshier wines. Temperature control fermentation as well as controlled malolactic fermentation were more widely used as well as less dependency on filtration as a means of stabilization.

Cape Port-style Wine

The South African wine industry has a long antiquity of fortified wine production produces wines known colloquially as "Cape port". These wines are made from a variety of grapes, such as Shiraz and Pinotage, as well as Portuguese varieties like Tinta Barroca, Touriga Nacional, Souzão and Fernão Pires. The minimum alcohol level for these wines must be between 16.5-22 per cent. The many styles of "Cape port" parallel closely their Portuguese counterparts and include:

- Cape White port-Can be made from any white grape varieties except for Muscats. Required to be aged in wood barrels for at least six months.
- Cape Ruby port-Usually a blend of several fruity, full bodied wines that have at least been aged six months in wood for each wine and at least a year total for the entire blend.

- Cape Tawny port-A blend that has been aged in wood long enough to acquire a tawny colour with a smooth, slightly nutty flavour. Blending Ruby and White ports to create Tawny to create Tawny port is prohibited.
- Cape Late Bottled Vintage (LBV) port-A wine composed of grapes harvested in a single vintage that is aged at least two years in oak and three to six years total before being bottled. South Africa wine laws require that the term "Late Bottled Vintage" or "LBV" appear on the wine label along with the vintage and bottling year.
- Cape Vintage port-A wine composed of grapes harvested in a single vintage, aged in wood and released with the words "Vintage port" and the vintage year on the label.
- Cape Vintage Reserve port-A wine produced in a vintage year recognized by the South African wine industry and/or trade publications as being of exceptional quality. The wine must be aged for at least one year in oak and sold exclusively in glass wine bottles. The words "Vintage Reserve port" and vintage date must appear on the wine label.

Other Fortified and Dessert Wines

In addition to port-style wine, South African wine makers also produce "sherry-style" wines produced in a solera system and a unique vin de liqueur made from Muscat known as Jerepigo. With Jerepigo the brandy is added to the must prior to fermentation which leaves the wine with a residual sugar (RS) level of at least 160 grams per litre.

South Africa's long antiquity of late harvest dessert wines include the modern day Edel Laat-oes wines infected with noble rot and containing at least 50 grams of residual sugar per litre. Wine labeled simply as Laat-oes are from grapes harvested late but not infected with botrytis. These wines must have an alcohol content of at least 10 per cent and residual sugar levels between 10-30 grams per litre. Wines above 30 grams RS maybe called Spesiale Laat-oes or "special late harvest" which may imply that some grapes infected with botrytis were used.

Sparkling Wines

Sparkling wines in South Africa are produced with both the Charmat and the traditional "Champagne Method". To distinquish South African sparkling wines, wines made in this traditional bottled fermented method are labeled as Cap Classique. These wines have been traditionally made using Sauvignon blanc and Chenin blanc but in recent years have seen more of the traditional "Champagne grapes" of Chardonnay and Pinot noir being used. Red sparkling wine made from Pinotage can also be found.

Labeling Laws

South African labeling law focus largely on geographical origins, falling under the purview of the "Wine of Origin" legislation. Single vineyard designated wine can be produced, provided that the vineyard is registered with the government and all the grapes used in the production of the wine was grown in that vineyard. While the term "estate" no longer qualifies as a designation of geographic origins, wineries can still label "estate wines" provided that all the grapes were grown and the wine vinified and bottled on the same property. The South African Wine and Spirit Board operates a voluntary programme that allows South African wines to be "certified" for quality and accuracy in labeling. Under this certification process, vintage dated wine must be composed of at least 85 per cent grapes that were harvested that vintage year. Varietal wines must also be composed of at least 85 per cent of the listed varietal. Blends, such as a Cabernet Sauvignon and Pinotage blend, can have both varietals listed on the label provided that the two wines were vinified separately. A wine that has been "co-fermented", with both grapes crushed and vinified together such as a Shiraz-Viognier, can not list both varietals. As of 2006, about 35 per cent of Cape wineries participated in this voluntary programme.

Grape Varieties

Grape varieties in South Africa are known as cultivar, with many common international varieties developing local synonyms that still have a strong tradition of use. These include Chenin blanc, Riesling, Crouchen, Palomino, Trebbiano, Sémillon and Muscat of Alexandria. However, wines that are often exported overseas will usually have the more internationally recognized name appear on the wine label. In 2006, SAWIS (South African Wine Information and Systems) reported that the country had 100,146 hectares of vineyards, with about 55 per cent planted to white varieties. Chenin blanc has long been the most widely planted variety, still accounting for at least one-fifth of all grape varieties planted in South Africa as of 2004 though that number is decreasing. In the 1980s and 1990s, interest in international varieties saw increase in plantings of Chardonnay and Sauvignon blanc. Other white grape varieties with significant plantings include Colombard, Cape Riesling, Gewürztraminer, Hanepoot, Muscat Blanc à Petits Grains, Riesling and Sémillon. Both red and white mutants of Muscat Blanc à Petits Grains as well as Chenel and Weldra, two Chenin blanc-Ugni blanc crossings, are used for brandy distillation and fortified wine production.

Since the 1990s, interest and plantings of red grape varieties have been steadily on the rise. In the late 1990s, less than 18 per cent of all the grapes grown in South Africa were red. By 2003 that number has risen to 40 per cent and was still trending upwards. For most of the 21st century, the high yielding Cinsaut was the most widely planted red grape variety but the shift in focus to quality wine production has saw plantings of the grape steadily decline to where it represented just 3 per cent of all South Africa vineyards in 2004. In its place Cabernet Sauvignon, Shiraz and Pinotage have risen to prominence with Cabernet Sauvignon being the most widely red grape variety covering 13 per cent of all plantings in 2006. Other red grape varieties found in South Africa include Carignan, Gamay, Grenache, Pontac, Ruby Cabernet, Tinta Barroca and Zinfandel

There is a wide range of lesser known groups that are used to feed the country's still robust distilled spirits and fortified wine industry. These grapes usually produce bland, neutral wine that lends itself well to blending and distillation but is rarely seen as varietal bottlings. These include Belies, False Pedro, Kanaän, Raisin blanc, Sultana and Servan.

Important Organizations

The South African wine industry has been led by many powerful organizations in both the private sector and through governmental agencies. Unlike other New World wine regions, the South African wine industry is largely influenced by several large co-operatives. The Koöperatieve Wijnbouwers Vereniging van Zuid-Afrika Bpkt (KWV) was a co-operative first created through the funding and encouragement of the South African government as a force that can stabilize and grow the South African wine industry. As the KWV is now a privately owned winemaking co-operative some of its regulatory responsibilities has fallen to other organizations such as the South African Wine and Spirit Board. The Wine and Spirit Board runs the voluntary certification programme that allows South African wines to be "certified" for quality and accuracy in labeling. In addition to submitted to various labeling guidelines, wines are blind tasted by a panel of experts for quality and are put through an analytical test for faults. Like the vintage and varietal labeling guidelines, these test are voluntary but wines that do not submit for testing are liable for random testing for health requirements.

The Wine and Spirits board also operates the South African Wine Industry Trust which serves as funding for the marketing and development of the South African Wine Industry Trust (SAWIT). Established in 1999 by a joint agreement between the South African government and the KWV, which put forth 369 million rands ($46 million USD), SAWIT works to promote the export market of South African wines abroad and the development of new technologies and education. Additionally SAWIT works with the Black Economic Empowerment (BEE) programme to promote the black community's involvement in the South African wine industry-including ownership opportunities for vineyards and wineries.

WINE BUSINESS IN SPAIN

Spanish wines are wines produced in the southwestern European country of Spain. Located on the Iberian Peninsula, Spain has over 2.9 million acres (over 1.17 million hectares) planted-making it the most widely planted wine producing nation but it is only the third largest producer of wine in the world, the largest being Italy and France. This is due, in part, to the very low yields and wide spacing of the old vines planted on the dry, infertile soil found in many Spanish wine regions. The country is ninth in worldwide consumptions with Spaniards drinking, on average, 10.06 gallons (38 liters) a year. The country has an abundance of native grape varieties, with over 600 varieties planted throughout Spain though 80 per cent of the country's wine production is from only 20 grapes-including Tempranillo, Albariño, Garnacha, Palomino, Airen, Macabeo, Parellada, Xarel·lo, Cariñena and Monastrell. Major Spanish wine regions include the Rioja and Ribera del Duero which is known for their Tempranillo production; Jerez, the home of the fortified wine Sherry; Rías Baixas in the northwest region of Galicia that is known for its white wines made from Albariño and Catalonia which includes the Cava and still wine producing regions of the Penedès as well the Priorat region.

Backdrop

The abundance of native grape varieties fostered an early start to viticulture with evidence of grape pips dating back to the Tertiary period. Archaeologists believe that these grapes were first cultivated sometime between 4000 and 3000 BC, long before the wine-growing culture of the Phoenicians founded the trading post of Cádiz around 1100 BC. Following the Phoenicians, the Carthaginians introduced new advances to the region-including the teachings of the early viticulturist Mago. Carthage would wage a series of wars with the emerging Roman Republic that would lead to the Roman conquest of the Spanish mainland, known as Hispania.

From Roman Rule to the Reconquista

Under Roman rule, Spanish wine was widely exported and traded throughout the Roman empire. The two largest wine producing regions at the time were Terraconensis in the north and Baetica in the south. During this period more Spanish wine was exported into Gaul than Italian wine, with amphorae being found in ruins of Roman settlements in Normandy, the Loire Valley, Brittany, Provence and Bordeaux. Spanish wine was also provided to Roman soldiers guarding border settlements in Britain and the Limes Germanicus in Germania. The quality of Spanish wine during Roman times was varied, with Pliny the Elder and Martial noting the high quality associated with some wines from Terraconensis while Ovid notes that one popular Spanish wine sold in Rome.

Following the decline of the Roman Empire, Spain was invaded by various barbaric tribes-including the Suebi and the Visigoths. Little is known about progress of viticulture and winemaking during this period but there is evidence that some viable form of wine industry was present when the Moors conquered the land during the early 8th century AD. While the Moors were Muslim and subjected to Islamic dietary laws that forbid the use of alcohol, the Moorish rulers held an ambiguous stance on wine and winemaking during their rule. Several caliphs and emirs owned vineyards and drank wine. While there were laws written that outlawed the sale of wine, it was included on lists of items that were subject to taxation in Moorish territories.

The Spanish Reconquista reopened the possibility of exporting Spanish wine. Bilbao emerged as a large trading port; introducing Spanish wines to the English wine markets in Bristol, London and Southampton. The quality of some of these exported Spanish wines appears to have been high. In 1364, the court of Edward III established the maximum price of wine sold in England with the Spanish wines being priced at the same level as wines from Gascony and higher than those from La Rochelle. The full bodied and high alcohol in most Spanish wines made them favoured blending partners for the "weaker" wines from the cooler climate regions of France and Germany though there were laws that explicitly outlawed this practice.

Colonization of the New World

Following the completion of the Spanish Reconquista in 1492, Christopher Columbus discovered the New World under the sponsorship of the Spanish crown. This opened up a new export market as well as new opportunity for wine production. Spanish missionaries and conquistadors brought European grape vines with them as they colonized the new lands. During this period Spanish exports to England began to wane as Spanish-English relations steadily deteriorated following the divorce of Henry VIII of England from his Spanish wife Catherine of Aragon.

English merchants from the Sherry producing regions of Jerez and Sanlúcar de Barrameda as well as Málaga fled the area due to the fear of persecution by the Spanish Inquisition.

The defeat of the Spanish Armada by Elizabeth I of England greatly reduced the strength of the Spanish navy and contributed to the country's debt incurred during the reign of Philip II. Spain became more dependent on the income from its Spanish colonies, including the exportation of Spanish wine to the Americas. The emergence of growing wine industries in Mexico, Peru, Chile and Argentina were a threat to this income with Philip III and successive monarch issuing decrees and declarations ordering the uprooting of New World vineyards and halting the production of wine by the colonies. In some countries, like Chile, these orders were largely ignored but in other regions, like Argentina, they served to stunt growth and development till they gained independence from Spanish rule.

From Phylloxera to Modern-day

The 17th and 18th centuries saw periods of popularity for various Spanish wines-namely Sherry, Malaga and Rioja wine but the Spanish wine industry was falling behind other European countries which were embracing the developments of the early Industrial Age. A major turning point occurred in the mid 19th century when the phylloxera epidemic ravaged European vineyards-most notably those of France. With the sudden shortage of French wine, many countries turned to Spain, with French winemakers crossing the Pyrenees to Rioja, Navarre and Catalonia-bringing with them their expertise and winemaking methods.

One of these developments was the introduction of the 59 gallon (225 litre) oak barrica. Phylloxera eventually reached Spain, devastating regions like Malaga in 1878 and reaching Rioja in 1901. Its slow progress was due in part to the wide tracts of land, including the Meseta Central, that separated the major Spanish wine regions from each other. By the time the Spanish wine industry felt the full force of phylloxera, the remedy of grafting American rootstock to the European vines had already been discovered and widely utilized.

The end of the 19th century also saw the emergences of Spain's sparkling wine industry with the development of Cava in Catalonia. As the 20th century progressed, the production of Cava would rival the Champagne region in worldwide production. Civil and political upheaval would mark most of the 20th century, including a military dictatorship under General Miguel Primo de Rivera. One of the measures instituted by Primo de Rivera was the early groundwork of the Denominación de Origen (DO) appellation system first developed in Rioja in 1926. The Spanish Civil War saw vineyards neglected and wineries destroyed throughout Spain with regions like Catalonia and Valencia being particularly hard hit. The Second World War closed off European markets to Spanish exports and further damaged the Spanish economy.

It wasn't till the 1950s that domestic stability helped to usher in a period of revival for the Spanish wine industry. Several large co-operative wineries were founded during this period and an international market was created for generic bulk wines that were sold under names like Spanish sauternes and Spanish chablis. In the 1960s, Sherry was rediscovered by the international wine market and soon Rioja wine was in demand. The death of Francisco Franco in 1975 and the Spanish transition to democracy allowed more economic freedom for winemakers and created an emerging market with the growing middle class of Spain. The late 1970s and 1980s saw periods of modernization and renewed emphasis on quality wine production. The 1986 acceptance of Spain into the European Union brought economic aid to the rural wine industries of Galicia and La Mancha. The 1990s saw the influence of flying winemakers from abroad and broader acceptance of the use of international grape varieties like Cabernet Sauvignon and Chardonnay.

In 1996, the restrictions on irrigation were lifted which gave winemakers greater control over yields and what areas could be planted. Soon the quality and production volume of premium wines began to overtake the presence of generic Spanish bulk wines on the market and Spain's reputation entering the 21st century was that of a serious wine producing country that could compete with other producers in the world wine market.

Classification

Spanish wine laws created the Denominación de Origen (DO) system in 1932 and were later revised in 1970. The system shares many similarities with the hierarchical Appellation d'origine contrôlée (AOC) system of France and Italy's Denominazione di origine controllata (DOC) system. As of 2009, there were 77 Quality Wine areas across Spain. In addition there is Denominación de Origen Calificada (DOCa or DOQ in Catalan) status for DOs that have a consistent track record for quality. There are currently two DOCa/DOQ regions: Rioja and Priorat. Each DO has a Consejo Regulador, which acts as a governing control body that enforces the DO regulations and standards involving viticultural and winemaking practices.

These regulations govern everything from the types of grapes that are permitted to be planted, the maximum yields that can be harvested, the minimum length of time that the wine must be aged and what type of information is required to appear on the wine label. Wineries that are seeking to have their wine sold under DO or DOC status must submit their wines to the Consejo Regulador laboratory and tasting panel for testing and evaluation. Wines that have been granted DO/DOC status will feature the regional stamp of the Consejo Regulador on the label.

Following Spain's acceptance into the European Union, Spanish wine laws were brought in line to be more consistent with other European systems. One development was a five-tier classification system that is administered by each autonomous region. Non-autonomous areas or wine regions whose boundaries overlap with other autonomous communities are administered by the Instituto Nacional de Denominaciones de Origen (INDO) based in Madrid. The five-tier classifications, starting from the bottom, include:

- Vino de Mesa (VdM)-These are wines that are the equivalent of most country's table wines and are made from unclassified vineyards or grapes that have been declassified through "illegal" blending. Similar to the Italian Super Tuscans from the late 20th century, some Spanish winemakers will intentionally declassify their wines so that they have greater flexibility in blending and winemaking methods.
- Vinos de la Tierra (VdlT)-This level is similar to France's vin de pays system, normally corresponding to the larger comunidad autonóma geographical regions and will appear on the label with these

broader geographical designations like Andalucia, Castilla La Mancha and Levante.

- Vino de Calidad Producido en Región Determinada (VCPRD)-This level is similar to France's Vin Délimité de Qualité Supérieure (VDQS) system and is considered a stepping stone towards DO status.
- Denominación de Origen (Denominació d'Origen in Catalan-DO)- This level is for the mainstream quality-wine regions which are regulated by the Consejo Regulador who is also responsible for marketing the wines of that DO. In 2005, nearly two thirds of the total vineyard area in Spain was within the boundaries a DO region.
- Denominación de Origen Calificada (DOCa/DOQ-Denominació d'Origen Qualificada in Catalan)- This designation, which is similar to Italy's Denominazione di Origine Controllata e Garantita (DOCG) designation, is for regions with a track record of consistent quality and is meant to be a step above DO level. Rioja was the first region afforded this designation in 1991 and was followed by Priorat in 2003, and Ribera del Duero in 2008.

Additionally there is the Denominación de Pago (DO de Pago) designation for individual single-estates with an international reputation. As of 2009, there were 9 estates with this status.

Spanish Labeling Laws

Spanish wines are often labeled just as to the amount of ageing the wine has received. When the label vino joven ("young wine") or sin crianza, the wines will have undergone very little, if any, wood ageing. Depending on the producer, some of these wines will be meant to be consumed very young-often within a year of their release. Others will benefit from some time ageing in the bottle. For the vintage year (vendimia or cosecha) to appear on the label, a minimum of 85 per cent of the grapes must be from that year's harvest. The three most common ageing designations on Spanish wine labels are Crianza, Reserva and Gran Reserva.

- Crianza red wines are aged for 2 years with at least 6 months in oak. Crianza whites and rosés must be aged for at least 1 year with at least 6 months in oak.
- Reserva red wines are aged for at least 3 years with at least 1 year in oak. Reserva whites and rosés must be aged for at least 2 years with at least 6 months in oak.
- Gran Reserva wines typically appear in above average vintages with the red wines requiring at least 5 years ageing, 18 months of which in oak. Gran Reserva whites and rosés must be aged for at least 4 years with at least 6 months in oak.

Wine Regions

Spain has a relatively large number of distinct wine-producing regions, more than half having the classification Denominación de Origen (DO) with the majority of the remainder classified as Vinos de la Tierra (VdlT). There are two regions nominated as Denominación de Origen Calificada (DOCa)-Rioja and Priorato-the flagship regions of Spanish winemaking. While most make both red and white wine, some wine regions are more dominated by one style than the other.

Viticulture

Viticulture in Spain has developed in adaptation to the varied and extreme climate of the region. The dry weather in many parts of Spain reduces the threat of common viticultural hazards like downy mildew and powdery mildew as well as the development of Botrytis cinerea. In these parts, the threat of drought and the poor fertility of the land has encouraged Spanish vineyard owners to plant their vines with widely spaced so that there is less competition between vines for resources. One widely adopted system is known as marco real and involves having 8 feet (2.5 m) of space between vines in all directions. These areas, mostly in the south and central regions, have some of the lowest vine density in the world-often ranging between 375-650 vines per acre (900-1600 vines per hectare). This is less than 1/8th of the vine density commonly found in other wine regions such as Bordeaux and Burgundy. Many Spanish vineyards are several decades old, with the old vines producing even lower yields of fruit. In the Jumilla region of Castile-La Mancha, for example, yields are often less than 1.1 ton and acre (20 hl/ha).

In the 1990s, the use of irrigation became more popular after droughts in 1994 and 1995 severely reduced the harvest in those years. In 1996, the practice of using irrigation in all Spanish wine regions was legalized with many regions quickly adopting the practice. In the Toledo province, Australian flying winemakers helped to popularize the use of underground drip irrigation to minimize the effects of evaporation. The widespread use of irrigation has encouraged higher density of vine plantings and has contributed to higher yields in some parts of Spain.

While traditionally Spanish vineyards would harvest their grapes by hand, the modernization of the Spanish wine industry has seen increased use of mechanical harvesting. In years past, most harvesting had to be done in the early morning with wineries often refusing grapes after mid-day due to their prolonged exposure to the blistering heat. In recent years, aided in part by the wider spread of the use of mechanical harvesting, more harvests are now being done in the cooler temperatures at night.

Grape Varieties

Some records estimate that over 600 grape varieties are planted throughout Spain but 80 per cent of the country's wine production is focused on only 20 grape varieties. The most widely planted grape is the white wine grape Airén, prized for its hardiness and resistance to drop. It is found throughout central Spain and for many years served as the base for Spanish brandy. Wines made from this grape can be very alcoholic and prone to oxidation. The red wine grape Tempranillo is the second most widely planted grape variety, recently eclipsing Garnacha in plantings in 2004. It is known throughout Spain under a variety of synonyms that may appear on Spanish wine labels-including Cencibel, Tinto Fino and Ull de Llebre. Both Tempranillo and Garnacha are used to make the full-bodied red wines associated with the Rioja, Ribera del Duero and Penedès with Garnacha being the main grape of the Priorat region. In the Levante region, Monastrell and Bobal have significant plantings, being used for both dark red wines and dry rosé.

In the northwest, the white wine varieties of Albariño and Verdejo are popular plantings in the Rías Baixas and Rueda respectively. In the Cava producing regions of Catalonia and elsewhere in Spain, the principal grapes of Macabeo, Parellada and Xarel·lo are used for sparkling wine production as well as still white wines. In the southern Sherry and Malaga producing regions of Andalucia, the principal grapes are Palomino and Pedro Ximénez. As the Spanish wine industry becomes more modern, there has been a larger presence of international grape varieties appearing in both blends and varietal forms-most notably Cabernet Sauvignon, Chardonnay, Syrah, Merlot and Sauvignon blanc. Other Spanish grape varieties that have significant plantings include Cariñena, Godello, Graciano, Mencia, Loureira, and Treixadura.

Winemaking

In Spain, winemakers often use the Spanish word elaborar rather than fabricar when describing the Spanish winemaking philosophy. This relates to the view that the winemaker acts as more of a nurturer of the grapes and wine rather than as a producer. For many years, Spanish winemaking was very rustic and steeped in tradition. This included the judicious use of oak with some wines, even whites, spending as much as two decades ageing in the barrel. This created distinctly identifiable flavours that were internationally associated with the wines from regions such as the Rioja. In the 19th century, wine writers held negative views about Spanish winemaking.

Richard Ford noted in 1846 that the Spanish made wine in an "unscientific and careless manner" while Cyrus Redding noted in his work the Antiquity and Description of Modern wines that Spanish gave "rude treatment" to the grapes. Some of these criticisms were rooted in the traditional manners of winemaking that the were employed in Spain. Crushing and fermentation would take place in earthenware jars known as tinajas. Afterwards the wine was stored in wooden barrels or pig skin bags lined with resin known as cueros. In the warmer climate and regions of lower elevation, the red wines tilted towards being too high in alcohol and too low in acidity. The standard technique to rectify those wines was the addition of white wine grapes which balanced the acidity but diluted some of the fruit flavours of the red grapes.

The advent of temperature control stainless steel fermentation tanks radically changed the wine industry in warm climate regions like Andalucia, La Mancha and the Levante, allowing winemakers to make fresher and fruitier styles of wine-particularly whites. While many producers focused on these crisp, fresh styles in the early 1990s there was a resurgence in more active use of barrel fermenting whites as a throwback to the traditional, more oxidized styles of the 19th century.

The use of oak has a long tradition in Spanish winemaking, dating back even centuries before the French introduced the small 59 gallon (225 litre) barrica style barrels. Gradually Spanish winemakers in the late 19th and early 20th century started to develop a preference for the cheaper, and more stronger flavoured, American oak. Winemakers in regions like the Rioja found that the Tempranillo grape, in particular, responded well to new American oak.

In the 1990s, more winemakers started to rediscover the use of French oak and some wineries will use a combination of both as a blend. Most DOs require some minimum period of barrel ageing which will be stipulated on the wine label by the designations-Crianza, Reserva and Gran Reserva depending on how long it spends in the barrel. The tradition of long barrel and bottle ageing has meant that most Spanish wines are ready to drink once they hit the market. A new generation of winemakers have started to produce more vino joven (young wines) that are released with very little ageing.

Sherry

Sherry is a fortified wine produced in southern Spain around the towns of Jerez, Sanlúcar de Barrameda, and El Puerto de Santa María. In the 1990s, the European Union restricted the use of name "Sherry" to the wine made from this region. It mostly made from the Palomino grape, accounting for nearly 95 per cent of the region's plantings, but Moscatel and Pedro Ximenez can also be used. While the wine is ageing in the barrel, a naturally occurring yeast native to the region, known as flor, will develop and distinguish certain styles of Sherry. The flor needs fresh wine in order to survive and is added by the use of a solera system that also gradually blends the wines of different vintages together. Palomino wine, by itself, typically ferments to an alcohol level of around 12 per cent with Sherry producers adding brandy to the wine in order to increase the alcohol level or kill the flor yeast which will not thrive in alcohol levels above 16 per cent.

Sherry has many categories:

- Fino Sherry is a very light and delicate Sherry. These wines are characterized by flor. It often contains 15 to 18 per cent of alcohol.
- Manzanilla Sherry comes from the Sanlucar district along the sea

coast. The sea air leads the Sherry to develop a salty taste. These wines also have flor. This wine is produced using exactly the same process than Fino, but as weather conditions are very different in Sanlucar district it develops into a slightly different kind of wine. It often contains 15 to 19 per cent of alcohol.

- Amontillado Sherry is similar to Fino. However, it does not have as much flor development.It is deeper in colour and drier than Fino and is left in the barrel longer. It often contains 16 to 22 per cent of alcohol.
- Oloroso Sherry is deeper/darker in colour and has more residual sugar. It is more fortified, and often contains 17 to 22 per cent of alcohol.
- Cream Sherry is very rich and can be a good dessert-style wine. It often contains 15.5 to 22 per cent of alcohol.
- Pedro Ximénez Sherry is very rich and is a popular dessert-style wine. It's made from raisins of Pedro Ximenez grapes dried in the sun. It often contains around 18 per cent of alcohol.
- Palo Cortado Sherry is very rare, as it is an Oloroso wine that ages in a different, natural way not achievable by human intervention. It often contains 17 to 22 per cent of alcohol.

Cava

Cava is a Spanish sparkling wine made in the traditional method of the French sparkling wine Champagne. It originated in the Catalonia region at the Codorníu Winery in the late 19th century. The wine was originally known as Champaña until Spanish producers officially adopted the term "Cava" in 1970 in reference to the underground cellars in which the wines ferment and age in the bottle.

The early Cava industry was nurtured by the phylloxera epidemic of the late 19th that caused the destruction and uprooting of vineyards planted with red grape varieties. Inspired by the success of Champagne, Codorníu and others encouraged vineyard owners to replant with white grape varieties like Macabeo, Parellada and Xarel·lo to use for sparkling wine production. These grapes are still the primary grapes of Cava today though some producers are experimenting with the use of the Champagne wine grapes of Chardonnay and Pinot noir.

For most of existence, the production of Cava was not regulated to a particular region of DO but rather to the grapes and method of production. Upon Spain's acceptance into the European Union in 1986, efforts were undertaken to designate specific areas for Cava production. Today use of the term "Cava" is restricted to production around select municipalities in Catalonia, Aragon, Castile and León, Valencia, Extremadura, Navarra, Basque Country and Rioja.

Around 95 per cent of Spain's total Cava production is from Catalonia with the village of Sant Sadurní d'Anoia being home to many of Spain's largest production houses.

WINE BUSINESS IN SWEDEN

Swedish wine, in terms of wine produced commercially from grapes grown in Sweden, is a very marginal but growing phenomenon which saw its first beginnings in the late 1990s.

In less strict usage, the term "Swedish wine" has also been applied to fruit wine from Sweden, which has a very long tradition, and wine produced in Sweden from imported grape juice, which goes back longer than actual viticulture in Sweden.

Sweden is well north of the area where the European vine, Vitis vinifera, occurs naturally, and there is no tradition of wine production from grapes in the country. Some sources claim that some monasterial vineyards were established when the Roman Catholic church established monasteries in Sweden in Medieval times, but traces of this supposed viticulture is much less evident than the corresponding activities in England, for example.

Small-scale growing of grapes in Swedish orangeries and other greenhouses have occurred for a long time, but the purpose of such plantations were either to provide fruit or for decoration or exhibition purposes, and not to provide grapes for wine production.

Towards the end of the 20th century, commercial viticulture slowly crept north, into areas than the well-established wine regions, as evidenced by Canadian wine, English wine and Danish wine. This trend was partially made possible by the use of new hybrid grape varieties, and partially by new viticultural techniques.

The idea of commercial freeland viticulture in Sweden appeared in the 1990s. Some pioneers, especially in Scania, took their inspiration from nearby Denmark, where viticulture started earlier than in Sweden, while others took their inspiration from experiences in other winemaking countries.

Perhaps surprisingly, the first two wineries of some size were not established in the far south of Sweden, but in Södermanland County close to Flen and on the island of Gotland, which has the largest number of sunshine hours in Sweden. Later expansions have mostly taken place in Scania, though.

There are also small-scale viticulturalists who grow their grapes in greenhouses rather than in the open.

Small quantities of a few commercial wines made their way into the market via Systembolaget from the early 2000s.

Only a handful of Swedish producers can be considered to be commercial operations, rather than hobby wine makers. In 2006, the Swedish Board of Agriculture counted four Swedish companies that commercialised wine produced from their own vineyards. The total production was 5 617 liters, of which 3 632 liters were red and 1 985 litre white, and this amount was produced from around 10 hectares (25 acres) of vineyards.

The Association of Swedish winegrowers estimates 30-40 vinegrowing establishments in Scania, but this number includes hobby growers with a fraction of a hectare of vineyards.

WINE BUSINESS IN SWITZERLAND

The Swiss wine region has nearly 15 000 hectares of vineyards, and the wines are mainly produced in the west and in the south of Switzerland, in the cantons of Geneva, Neuchâtel, Ticino, Valais and Vaud.

Just as to data from the Swiss Federal Office of Agriculture, the Swiss wine production in 2005 was about 1 million hectoliters, divided into 479 000 hl of white wine and 522 000 hl of red wine. Nearly all the national production is drunk within the national boundaries; less than 2 per cent of the wine is exported.

The tradition of wine and viticulture in Switzerland is very old, at minimum from the Roman era. Some archaeological evidence seems to prove that the grapes were planted in Valais earlier than the Roman era. In an archaeological excavation near Gamsen, some old grape seed was found, and they date to the Iron Age. Also in Ticino some pollen was found in a palynology excavation. But this evidence does not really prove that the grapes were cultivated, as opposed to spontaneous grapes.

The first bottle, made in ceramic, was found near Sembrancher, in a Celtic tomb of a lady of 2nd century BC. These bottles are named vases a trottola, and they are produced in some Celtic farms in northern Italy. From an inscription on the bottle, we know that it contained wine. Around the 150s BC, in the Celtic era, the people in Valais offered wine to the dead, and probably they also drank the same wine. After a century, the Roman amphorae also appeared.

WINE BUSINESS IN TURKEY

Turkish wine is wine made in the transcontinental Eurasian country of Turkey. The Caucasus region, where the countries of Georgia, Armenia and Turkey are located today, played a pivotal role in the early antiquity of wine and is likely have been one of the earliest wine-producing regions of the world.

Ampelographers estimate that Turkey is home to between 600-1200 indigenous varieties of Vitis vinifera, though less than 60 of these are grown commercially. With over 1,500,000 acres (6,100 km2) planted under vine, Turkey is the world's fourth-leading producer of grapes.

Mustafa Kemal Atatürk, Turkey's first president, established the country's first commercial winery in 1925. Just as to the OIV, the total wine production in 2005 was 287,000 hl. In the first half of 2009, wine consumption in Turkey reached 20,906,762 litres.

Grapes and Wine

With between 600 to 1200 indigenous grape varieties, there are numerous options that Turkish winemakers can pursue to make wine. Currently only 60 varieties are commercially cultivated. Some of the native Turkish varieties include the Yap?ncak and Papazkaras? grown in Thrace; the Sultaniye of the Aegean coast; the Öküzgözü and Bo?azkere of Eastern Anatolia; the Çalkaras? of the Denizli Province in Western Anatolia, and the Kalecik Karas?, Narince and Emir of Central Anatolia. In recent years, some of the international grape varieties have increased their presence, including Sémillon, Riesling, Muscat, Gamay, Cinsault, Grenache, Carignan, Cabernet Sauvignon and Merlot.

Table. Grape Varieties of Turkey

Region	White grapes	Red grapes
Marmara(Thracian) Region	Clairette Chardonnay Riesling Sémillon Beylerce Yapıncak Vasilaki	Pinot Noir Adakarası Papazkarası Sémillon Kuntra Gamay Karalahna Cinsault
Aegean Region	Sémillon Bornova Misketi	Carignan Çal Karası Merlot Cabernet Sauvignon Alicante Bouschet Shiraz Kalecik Karası Sauvignon Blanc Chardonnay
Black Sea Region	Narince	Öküzgözü Boğazkere
Central Anatolia Region	Emir Hasandede	Kalecik Karası Papazkarası Dimrit
Mediterranean Region	Kabarcık Dökülgen	Sergi Karası Burdur Dimriti
Eastern Anatolia Region	Narince Kabarcık	Öküzgözü Boğazkere
Southeastern Anatolia Region	Dökülgen Kabarcık Rumi	Horoz Karası Öküzgözü Boğazkere Sergi Karası

Wineries

As of 2008, the largest winery of Turkey is operated by Tekel, which started as a state-owned monopoly. Other notable wineries include Sarafin on the Gallipoli peninsula in Thrace, which was Turkey's first privately-owned "boutique winery", Doluca of Thrace and Kavakl?dere of Anatolia.

Buzba? is a full flavoured red wine made from Bo?azkere grapes grown in the Anatolia region of Turkey. The wine is a red wine with high tannic levels. It is sometimes produced in an ice wine fashion with the grapes allowed to hang on the vine till the first frost and then crushed while the grapes are still frozen. Historically, the area where Buzba? is produced is considered a possible birthplace of wine. The biblical accounts of Noah after the flood has him planting a vineyard near the area where the ark landed. This area is presumed to be Mt. Ararat were Buzba? is still being produced today by the state run vineyards of Tekel near the town of Elaz?? by the Euphrates river.

Bibliography

Ahana Chakraborty and B K Chakravarti: *Global Tourism*, APH Publication, Delhi, 2007.

Alek Clark: *Food Tourism*, Discovery Publishing, Delhi, 2011.

Alek Clark: *Wine Tourism*, Discovery Publishing, Delhi, 2011.

Amit Gaur: *Food and Wine Tourism*, Sonali Publication, Delhi, 2011.

Amitabh Mishra: *Heritage Tourism in Central India : Resource Interpretation and Sustainable Development Planning*, Kanishka Publication, Delhi, 2007.

Anand Ballabh: *Fundamentals of Travel and Tourism*, Akansha Publication, Delhi, 2005.

Ashim Gupta: *Hotel Tourism and Catering Management*, Centrum Press, Delhi, 2011.

B S Badan and Harish Bhatt: *Global Tourism*, Commonwealth Publication, Delhi, 2007.

Chaman Lal Raina and Abhinav K Raina: *Fundamentals of Tourism and Indian Religion : Principles and Practices*, Kanishka Publication, Delhi, 2005.

Jack Randall: *Heritage Tourism*, Discovery Publishing House, Delhi, 2011.

Jagmohan Negi: *Foundations for Tourism Development (Developing and Underdeveloped Regions)*, Galgotia Publication, Delhi, 2002.

Jagmohan Negi: *Grading and Classification of Hotels, Tourism Resorts and Restaurants : Principles and Practices*, Kanishka Publication, Delhi, 2003.

M. Sarngadharan and V.S. Sunanda: *Health Tourism in India*, New Century Publications, Delhi, 2009.

M.P. Bezbaruah: *Frontiers of New Tourism*, Gyan Publication, Delhi, 2002.

Meenakshi Thakur: *Global Tourism : Challenge and Development*, Omega Publication, Delhi, 2008.

N.K. Verma: *Future Directions of Tourism*, Prateeksha Publications, Delhi, 2011.

N.K. Verma: *HRM in Tourism Industry*, Prateeksha Publications, Delhi, 2011.

Nikunj Tarun: *Fundamentals of Travel and Tourism*, Alfa Publication, Delhi, 2006.

O.P. Kandari and Ashish Chandra: *Hotel, Tourism and Catering Management*, Shree Publication, Delhi, 2004.

P.C. Sinha: *Global Tourism Policies, Laws and Action Plans : Select Case Studies and Model Approaches*, SBS Publication, Delhi, 2006.

P.C. Sinha: *Global Tourism, Sustainable Tourism and Eco-Tourism : Code of Ethics, Charter, Guidelines, Resolutions*, SBS Publication, Delhi, 2006.

Percy K Singh: *HRM in Hotel and Tourism Industry : Existing Trends and Practices*, Kanishka Publication, Delhi, 2008.

Poonam Chaudhary: *Heritage and Cultural Routes: An Anthology : Global Cultural Routes: Tourism and Socio-Economic Viability*, Shubhi Publications, Delhi, 2012.

Prabhas Chandra: *Global Ecotourism : Codes Protocols and Charters*, Kanishka Publication, Delhi, 2011.

R. Thompson: *Health Tourism*, Discovery Publishing House, Delhi, 2011.

Rajesh Kumar: *Global Trends in Health and Medical Tourism*, SBS Publication, Delhi, 2009.

Rajesh Singh: *HRM in Travel and Tourism Industry*, Sonali Publications, Delhi, 2011.

Ravee Chauhan: *Heritage and Cultural Tourism*, Vista International, Delhi, 2006.

Robinet Jacob: *Health Tourism and Ayurveda*, Abhijeet Publication, Delhi, 2008.

Vandana Yadav and Upasana Sharma: *Global Tourism : Explorations of Key Issues*, Shree Publication, Delhi, 2008.

Index

M

O

R

S

W